THE TIMES

LIVES
~ REMEMBERED ~

OBITUARIES FROM
1993

FOREWORD BY
~ ROY HATTERSLEY ~

EDITED BY
ANTHONY HOWARD AND DAVID HEATON

BLEWBURY

Published by The Blewbury Press
Pound House, Church Road, Blewbury,
Oxon OX11 9PY

Jacket design by Gary Cook

© The Blewbury Press 1993
ISBN 0 9518282 3 1 Hardback
ISBN 0 9518282 4 X Paperback

Typeset by Avocet Typesetters, Bicester, Oxon
Printed in Great Britain by Biddles Ltd,
Guildford, Surrey

1003650620

Foreword by
ROY HATTERSLEY

These days, I look first at the date of birth. According to the legends, Harold Macmillan did the same. But he greeted the death of a contemporary as a victory for his own longevity which deserved to be celebrated as a personal triumph. I react differently. I greet news of the premature departures of men or women who were born in the Forties or Fifties with genuine, but detached, regret. But, as John Donne almost said, reading the obituary of anyone who was born in the Thirties diminishes me. The message of the sub-text, which never varies, is that time is sharpening its abhorred shears.

I think that I developed my views about death – terror only slightly mitigated by amusement – during a childhood spent in a house with a churchyard at the bottom of the garden. For several summers I played in the long grass which half hid the weeping angels, broken columns and draped urns. Sometimes I sat on the heaps of soil that Fred Guest, the verger, had dug from the graves in which he was preparing for a second burial. We always talked about the war. Sometime between Dunkirk and the invasion of Normandy, I started to read the inscriptions on the gravestones.

Often the messages were what, in this age and generation, would be called "inspirational". The dear departed was described as living "in the certainty of everlasting life" and dying "confident in God's lasting mercy". To suggest that I was in any way envious of the human remains which lay beneath the marble and granite slabs would be a gross misrepresentation of my feelings. But I did wish that, like them, I awaited resurrection day with absolute confidence. I wish it still. But all the intimations are of mortality.

An obituary in *The Times* is a sort of immortality in itself and, if there is anything more enduring than that, it is achieved by what began as ephemeral newsprint being bound between hard covers. It is proof that Walter Raleigh – right about so much – was wrong about death. We are not all covered with the two narrow words, *hic jacet*.

The hierarchy of death is complicated. Even those who qualify for inclusion in the pantheon are graded, according to importance, and allocated appropriate space and position on the page. Hannibal's view that no more than his name was needed on his memorial is not an opinion that *The Times* is likely to endorse. The great Carthaginian would have qualified for a large picture and several thousand words. For weeks after his death, friends would have written letters which (having begun with congratulations on the obituary's quality) would then have gone on to describe some aspects of the deceased's life and character which had been overlooked.

I suppose that the irresistible temptation to be flippant about death is what psychologists call a defence mechanism. I try to laugh at the thought of time's winged chariot running me down, because the only alternative is to cry. In my more rational moments, I realise that the serious obituary – as the tabloids used to write − is an essential contribution to history. Whatever the theory of progress and change − man charting his own course on the human race tossed about on the sea of fate − the description of individual lives is an invaluable account of the great events in which they took part. *The Times* obituary page is best seen not as a mark of respect, recognition of achievement or proof of distinction, but as contemporary (if not quite living) history.

On the afternoon, many years ago, when my friend Christopher Rowland died, I was telephoned by Harold Evans, then managing editor of the *Sunday Times*. He too liked and admired Rowland and believed that an obituary ought to be published on the next day. He had checked with *The Times* and there was nothing in the files − not surprisingly since Rowland was a thirty-five-year-old backbench MP who, until the previous week, had appeared to be in perfect health. Could I write six hundred appropriate words in the next couple of hours?

It was not a task which I had the slightest wish to perform. I wanted to huddle for warmth amongst my friends and family and concentrate all my energy on being sad. At that moment, the world's opinion seemed supremely unimportant and I did not believe that either the widow or her young children should be confronted by my inadequate *Nunc Dimittis*. Twenty five years on, I am profoundly glad that I forced myself to sit down and write.

The pleasure which I feel at the publication of that brief tribute has nothing to do with Chris Rowland receiving the accolade which he deserved. I am comforted by the thought that, long after the world has forgotten the details of what happened in our time, all sorts of men and women who want to know about parliament in the 1960s − PhD students from mid-Western universities, biographers of politicians who lived longer and therefore did more, amateurs who are just interested in the past − will stumble across the name of Christopher Rowland and, if I did my job half-adequately, realise that he might have played a greater part in British history.

Inevitably, most of the men and women who received a *Times* threnody have lived long, full lives and leave behind them a great body of work or a record of substantial national achievement. But recently there has been a welcome change at least of emphasis. By their nature, the mute inglorious Miltons and the village Hampdens never appear. But merit and distinction which only a few years ago would have been regarded as too limited for recognition are now acknowledged. If obituaries are to be regarded as real history they have to tell the stories of all sorts of contributions to the nation's life.

And they have to tell the truth. There is, among most decent people, a natural disinclination to speak ill of the dead − particularly when they have been protected from libel in life and the reporters' notebooks have been locked away in anticipation of the happy day when injunctions and damages are no longer a threat. But the obituary that paints only the attractive part of the picture is a fraud. It is neither worth reading nor writing and, paradoxically, diminishes the memory of its subject. Of course, the hard truth does nothing to help anyone who reads the obituaries for therapy — either seeking proof that hundreds of men live to be ninety or attempting to reconcile themselves to the fact that some barely make sixty. But they are past help when they read the obituary page of *The Times*. It is (as Gerard Manley Hopkins almost said) themselves they look for.

ACKNOWLEDGEMENTS

The publishers would like to thank the relatives, friends and organisations for their kind permission to reproduce the following photographs in the book:

Columbia Pictures Corporation (p 4), Via Com (p 6), Channel Four (p 10), Associated Press (pp 19, 38, 82, 103, 120, 193, 270), Barratts (p 26), Francis Sitwell (p 36), Air Ministry (p 43), Lou-Lou Rendell (p 46), Elliott & Fry (p 48), Brodie family (p 52), Bufton family (p 54), Reuters (p 59, p 61), Ministry of Defence (p 62), Imperial War Museum (p 65), Gretton family (p 69), Minski family (p 77), Planet News (pp 74, 206), Hulton Deutsch (pp 77, 282), Packard family (p 86), The Duke of Valderano (p 90), Freeman Penrose (p 92), Newsteam (p 96), Camera Press (pp 100, 208, 211), Gamma (p 114), EPA (pp 118, 149), Australian Minister for External Affairs (p 124), Universal (pp 128, 160, 177), Press Association (pp 130, 186), US Government (p 132), *The Spectator* (p 137), Aston Martin Lagonda Ltd (p 141), *Financial Times* (p 147), Inchcape PLC (p 153), Rover Co Ltd (p 154), John Harris (p 165), Hodder & Stoughton (p 168), Robert Hale (p 172), *Belfast Telegraph* (p 184), Granada Television (p 188), Knopf (p 194), Syndication International (p 198), BIPPA (p 216), Desmond O'Neill (p 218), Keystone (pp 234, 240), Fiona Holmes (p 236), Pym family (p 248) Billett Potter (p 256), *Country Life* (p 260), Thos Agnew & Sons Ltd (p 268), Charterhouse (p 298), Edinburgh University (p 300)

THE CONTRIBUTORS

The publishers wish to acknowledge their gratitude for the co-operation and guidance of *The Times* team of obituaries writers Peter Davies, Michael Knipe and Lois Rathbone.

EDITORS' NOTE

The obituaries reproduced in this book were chosen from those published in *The Times* between 3 November 1992 and 7 October 1993.

CONTENTS

Contents

Originals

Painters and the Visual Arts

Reprobates

Sports

University and Academics

BERNARD BRADEN

Bernard Braden, Canadian-born actor and broadcaster, and husband of Barbara Kelly.

LISTING his occupations in *Who's Who* as "freelance performer and dabbler", Bernard Braden for many years successfully combined several careers, including West End actor, radio comedian and television personality, and brought to them all a friendly personality, warm voice and relaxed style.

He will be best remembered for pioneering a new type of television programme which mixed light-hearted comments on the week's events with consumer items poking fun at bureaucracy and exposing injustices and frauds. He introduced the formula on the ITV series, *On the Braden Beat*, and later took it to the BBC as *Braden's Week* where it launched the television career of Esther Rantzen, who started on the show as a researcher. She used similar ingredients for her own immensely successful and long-running series, *That's Life*.

By contrast, Braden's own career languished. From being one of the best-known faces on television he virtually disappeared from view. There were attempts at a comeback: on radio, television and the odd excursion on the stage. But none of these in any sense re-established his career. He and his glamorous Canadian wife, Barbara Kelly – herself one of the most popular personalities on British television in her day – were left, in their latter years, to experience the painful neglect of those audiences (and television executives) who had once idolised them.

The son of a clergyman father and a mother who sang and taught music, Braden grew up in Vancouver. He trained as a singer, making his mark as a boy soprano and later as a baritone. He successfully auditioned for the Metropolitan Opera in New York but hopes of a singing career were dashed by a long spell of tuberculosis and the realisation that he was not quite good enough.

When he recovered from the illness, he went into radio. He started as an engineer and announcer. Later he wrote and performed plays.

He first came to Britain in 1947, to make a series of radio documentaries for the Canadian Broadcasting Corporation and write a book about the British people. He returned in 1949 and stayed for good.

Though he had never acted on the stage, he soon secured the part of Mitch in Laurence Olivier's West End production of *A Streetcar Named Desire*. He appeared in several other West End plays during the 1950s and 1960s, usually in comedy roles, as well as a sprinkling of films. In 1950 he launched his own comedy series, *Breakfast with Braden*, on BBC radio. It went out on Saturday mornings, with Pearl Carr, Benny Lee and Nat Temple. The writers included Frank Muir and Denis Norden.

The sequel, *Bedtime with Braden*, featured the same cast as well as Braden's wife, Barbara Kelly, who went on to a successful broadcasting career of her own. Slick and irreverent, the shows made a distinctive contribution to a rich period of radio comedy. By now Braden was emerging as a versatile all-round broadcaster. He was in the radio commentary team for the 1953 Coronation, while on television he presented the first schools broadcast, a documentary on Canada, and was chairman of *The Brains Trust*.

His surprise appointment to chair *The Brains Trust* in 1957 led to the resignation of the programme's best-known panellist, Dr Jacob Bronowski, who said that Braden would attract the wrong kind of audience for a serious discussion. *On the Braden Beat* (which ran for six years during the 1960s) and *Braden's Week* (which enjoyed a four-year run) confirmed their host and creator as one of Britain's most polished television performers. But when *Braden's Week* ended in 1972 he found that he was no longer in demand.

The next few years were ones of virtual obscurity for him. In 1976 he tried to make a comeback with a quiz programme, *The Sweepstake Game*, but it was dropped after only 13 episodes. Plans for a new late-night show for Thames Television failed to progress beyond the pilot. Amid these disappointments, Braden turned his energies to his company, Adanac (his native Canada spelt backwards) Productions, which ran courses for company executives in public speaking and television technique.

Eventually he returned to radio, presenting *Feedback*, the listeners' letters programme, and in 1986 he was seen on the West End stage in Shaw's *The Apple Cart* with Peter O'Toole. In the following year he was at last back on television, presenting Granada TV's series about the events of 25 years ago, *All Our Yesterdays*. But other performers had established the programme and his participation never became a more than marginal affair.

Braden married Barbara Kelly in 1942. They had a son, Christopher, a television director, and two daughters, Kelly and Kim. As a child actress, Kim played the lead in a television production of *Anne of Green Gables*.

b 16.5.16   d 2.2.93   aged 76

The Bradens at the opening of the Ritz Casino (1978)

BERNARD BRESSLAW

Bernard Bresslaw, comic actor.

PLAYING a naturally prognathous, pop-eyed look for all it was worth, Bernard Bresslaw shot to fame in the 1950s as an oversized oaf of a private soldier in the BBC television series *The Army Game*. In later years Private Popplewell may have become something of a millstone round the neck of an actor who always, at bottom, yearned to do something substantial in the straight theatre (for example, in 1970 at short notice he was able to take over the lead role in Somerset Maugham's *Home and Beauty* from Laurence Olivier when the latter fell ill). But in 1957 the character with its unchanging response to life's perplexities ("I only arsked . . .") propelled an indigent actor into the well-heeled ranks of television stars at a then substantial salary of £750 a week.

Having got hold of him, comedy would not let him go. *The Army Game*, which was to run for five years until 1962, almost immediately spawned a film, *I*

Only *Arsked* (1957). Thereafter the stereotype of the giant, shambling incompetent was a difficult one to shake off for a man who not only had a gift for this type of comedy, but whose 6ft 7in frame effortlessly lent itself to simply "getting in the way" on set. From that point onwards he was a natural whenever the *Carry On* production team were casting round to spice up their next film.

Bernard Bresslaw was born in the East End of London, the son of a Jewish immigrant tailor of Polish ancestry. A 10lb 4oz giant at birth, he was wearing size nine shoes before he was into his teens, a fact which scotched his mother's desire to make a tap dancer of him. He was educated at Coopers School, Mile End, from where he won a scholarship to RADA. There he won a part in the academy's performance of Christopher Fry's *Venus Observed* at the Phoenix Theatre and did well enough in the role to be commended by the playwright himself. At RADA he was known as a conscientious and increasingly knowledgeable student of the theatre who slogged for two years to master Stanislavsky's Method system of acting. He was ever afterwards proud of his classical actor's training and often reminded press interviewers of it when they came to "write him up" yet again as being merely the moronic man-mountain of low comedy.

From RADA he went into a particularly gruelling form of rep, playing RAF and Army camps, Borstals and mental institutions. He was later to say that he found the discipline of playing to all-male audiences – and, at that, male audiences with a notoriously low micky-taking threshold – an invaluable one. He often likened this experience to that of playing hostile fast bowling.

After that, Bresslaw had a variety of work on stage and in films. He played a dumb Irish wrestler in a stage comedy. He was a dim-witted sheriff's man in the film *Men of Sherwood Forest*, in which his sole *raison d'être* was to be bashed over the head every time Robin Hood's men ambushed the Nottingham party. He applied for the part of the monster in *The Curse of Frankenstein*, but always claimed he was turned down because he was "*too* 'orrible".

From such humiliations Private Popeye Popplewell rescued him forever. National Service as a driver-clerk in the Royal Army Service Corps had given him some insight into the character of the downtrodden squaddie and he used it to great effect. There were musical spin-offs from the series. The record of the show's signature tune, featuring Bresslaw and other members of the cast, made number 5 in the hit parade in May 1958, while his own rendering of "Mad, Passionate Love" also made the Top Ten that autumn.

For the next five years Bresslaw was one of the best-known names in British television, but with the inevitable typecasting that went with such success. Indeed, Bresslaw was always inclined to see Popeye as malign *Doppelgänger* rather than jovial alter ego and was wary of the role's tendency to take over his life

even while gratefully accepting its financial rewards.

Although the *Carry On* films continued *The Army Game*'s vein of low comedy, they at least enabled Bresslaw to desert the Popeye character, allowing him to don outrageous disguises: bearded sheikhs, Hindu warriors, even, on one occasion, a lover. Latterly, in tandem with such well-paid frolics, Bresslaw pursued a career on the straight stage as earnestly as opportunity would admit. He was filming *Up Pompeii!* when Laurence Olivier was ordered to take a rest from *Home and Beauty* in the West End and the opportunity this presented involved him in the daily metamorphosis from Roman muscleman at Elstree studios by day to Maugham's starchy lawyer at the Old Vic by night.

Bresslaw kept in touch with Shakespeare, enjoying minor comic roles: Launce in *Two Gentlemen of Verona*; Dogberry in *Much Ado About Nothing*; and Peter Quince in *A Midsummer Night's Dream*. At the time of his collapse he was waiting to go on stage as Grumio in the New Shakespeare Company's production of *The Taming Of The Shrew*.

In the 1980s deteriorating sight had threatened prematurely to end his career. At one point he was virtually blind for five months. But in 1990 new surgical techniques at Moorfields Eye Hospital restored his vision. After an operation he was able to see without spectacles for the first time in many years. Bresslaw always drove himself hard and had collapsed at a showbusiness dinner last year, suffering from exhaustion.

In his spare time Bresslaw was an avid reader and collector of books. Visitors to his home might well find him immersed in Racine, a biography of Milton, the Old Testament, Rupert Brooke, Chaldean history, or a Napoleonic wars pamphlet. In earlier life he had also been a keen footballer, turning out to represent the Television All-Stars XI.

He leaves his widow Elizabeth and three sons.

b 25.2.34 d 11.6.93 aged 59

RAYMOND BURR

Raymond Burr, television actor.

THE name of Raymond Burr is synonymous with two of the most successful television detective series, *Perry Mason* and *Ironside*. Strictly speaking, the first of these was not a detective series at all but a courtroom drama featuring Burr as the defence counsel supreme. But in the course of the nine years over which it ran, Mason, aided by his assistant Paul Drake, managed to pack in more investigating than Lieutenant Columbo, James Rockford and the entire cast of *Miami Vice* put together.

The programme went on air in 1957 just as large numbers of the American public were buying television sets for the first time and immediately became required Saturday night viewing. Its success was in no way hindered by the predictability of the plot which barely changed from week to week. The murdered victim was normally widely-hated, but still things would look hopeless

for the accused − usually a young woman − when, at the last minute, Paul Drake would walk into court holding some vital piece of information. In a dramatic finale, the true culprit would then break down under the relentless fire of Mason's cross-examination.

Mason's performance in court bordered on the god-like. Over the course of 271 episodes, he lost only three cases, those few provoking a storm of outraged letters from viewers. To many fans Perry Mason and Raymond Burr were one and the same person. At the height of his fame, Burr was receiving several thousand letters a week asking for legal advice and was frequently being called upon to address legal gatherings.

Success had come to him almost by accident. After ten years of playing small-time villains and mobsters in Hollywood, he learnt, in 1956, that casting was in progress for a new court-room drama series and was invited to audition for the part of the long-suffering District Attorney Hamilton "Ham" Burger. He agreed to do so only on the condition that he could try out at the same time, with 200 other hopefuls, for the part of Perry Mason.

The writer, Erle Stanley Gardner, had watched with growing horror as some of his previous Perry Mason books received the Hollywood treatment. Determined to be more involved in the television series, he viewed the screen tests. The moment he saw Burr's avuncular features fill the screen, he leapt to his feet, shouting: "That's him! That's Perry!"

Raymond William Stacey Burr was born in Canada, the eldest son of a hardware merchant. When he was one the family moved to China, returning five years later. His parents divorced soon afterwards (they remarried 30 years later).

Their separation had an unhappy effect on the young Raymond who turned to food for comfort. He moved to California where his grandfather ran a small hotel and attended the San Rafael Military School in San Francisco (from which he hoped to qualify for the Indianapolis Naval Academy). Burr was

12 when the Depression hit America. He was forced to leave school and took a succession of odd jobs on sheep and cattle ranches.

He had always been happiest on stage, though at this point his experience was limited to Sunday School productions. At the age of 19 a chance meeting with the film director Anatole Litvak persuaded him to take up acting professionally. After appearing in regional theatres in Britain and Australia, Burr became director of the Pasadena Community Playhouse in California.

During the second world war he served in the Navy but was invalided out when a piece of shrapnel lodged against a nerve in his spine. Having spent a year recuperating in a wheelchair, he arrived in Hollywood where his build (by now he weighed 24 stone) made him a natural screen "heavy". For the next decade he made a steady living, specialising in burglars, gangsters and psychopaths.

Among around fifty largely forgettable films, Burr played the prosecutor of Montgomery Clift in *A Place in the Sun* (1951) and the stalker of the young Natalie Wood in *A Cry in the Night* (1956). (Studio bosses put a stop to their off-screen romance which was thought damaging to Wood's wholesome image.) He was also the suspicious neighbour of James Stewart in Hitchcock's *Rear Window* (1954) and his low, rumbling voice brought him regular radio work in the *Dragnet* and *Fort Laramie* series.

Burr's sudden fame as Perry Mason was hence both unexpected and welcome, but the nine gruelling years of filming took their toll of his health. After the last series, in 1966, Burr retired to his own 4,000-acre tropical island near Fiji, and threw himself into local community projects. But he found it difficult to adapt to the slower pace and 18 months later agreed to a role that would mean his spending the best part of the next eight years in a wheelchair.

Ironside had not been a planned move. Burr had originally agreed to star in a one-off television drama, playing the part of Robert T. Ironside, chief of detectives

in the San Francisco police and had taken the part specifically on the condition that it would not develop into a series. But the film was a runaway success, and Burr, by now bored with his island, returned to California. The series, released under the title *A Man Called Ironside* in Britain, proved almost as popular as *Perry Mason*.

In it he played the part of a senior policeman who is shot by a would-be assassin, and finds himself paralysed from the waist down. Burr's convincing portrayal of a paraplegic led to his becoming something of a spokesman for the disabled. But in real life his health, always fragile from the constant battle with obesity – he topped 27-stone at times – was declining rapidly and in 1974 he suffered a major heart attack. The last series of *Ironside* was filmed that year and, from that point on, Burr's acting career began to wind down.

But his status as Perry Mason remained as strong as ever and in 1986 he was persuaded to return for a series of two-hour TV Perry Mason films (shown in Britain from 1990). Paunchier, grey-haired, bearded, and relying on a walking stick, Mason was now promoted to the rank of Appeal Court judge, while his faithful secretary Della Street, played by Barbara Hale, was a top executive secretary to one of the richest men in the world.

In 1983 Burr sold his island and moved to California, where he herded sheep, grew orchids and made wine. A millionaire many times over, he devoted much of his wealth to charity, "adopting" 25 underprivileged children scattered throughout the world from Italy to Southeast Asia.

Burr lost his first wife in an air crash off Portugal in 1943 (in which the actor Leslie Howard also died). Shortly afterwards, their young son died of leukaemia. After Burr's second marriage had ended in divorce, he married again in 1950, but his third wife died the following year of cancer.

b 21.5.17   d 12.9.93   aged 76

LES DAWSON

Les Dawson, comedian.

THE comic persona of Les Dawson was that of the eternal loser, the pessimist who had every reason for fearing the worst. "Failure doesn't bother me," he would declare, "I was a failure during the boom." He transmitted his melancholy through a precise Northern voice and a pudgy, rumpled face that spoke volumes.

Fashioned by his harsh upbringing in the Manchester slums, Dawson's humour enabled audiences who had shared his experiences to laugh at them; but he touched on wider human emotions and his appeal was universal. His frequent butts were the mother-in-law ("she's got a face like a bag of nails") and domestic disharmony: "My wife's gone off with the man next door", he would exclaim, tears welling in his eyes, "Oh, I do miss him".

Interspersed with the one-line gags were longer, more elaborate jokes in which he would soar into the flights of picaresque fantasy and come abruptly back to earth with a terse, devastating punchline. He wrote much of his own material, showing a relish for language that set him apart from most fellow practitioners. Indeed, behind the deadpan face lay the mind of an author, as he was to prove later in his career, and an actor yearning for a serious part.

In his misogyny (which did not extend into his private life: he was an affectionate husband and father) and in his prickly demeanour he resembled the American comedian, W. C. Fields. But Dawson, who greatly admired Fields, was a true original, a naturally funny comedian with a style that was uniquely his own.

Dawson was born in Collyhurst, a poor suburb of Manchester, the only child of a bricklayer who was often out of work. The formative years of struggle and want left their mark and he retained precise memories of them long after he had become rich and famous. Meanwhile, he went through the gamut of jobs available to a boy leaving school early with no qualifications: he was a bricklayer's navvy, a hotel porter, a vacuum cleaner salesman and apprentice electrician. He spent much of his National Service in Korea and after leaving the Army went, Hemingway-style, to live in Paris with the ambition of becoming established as a writer. When he failed to earn a living by the pen, he turned to playing the piano, initially in the bar of a brothel, and this, eventually, gave him an entry into showbusiness when he returned to England.

But it was a long apprenticeship, spent mostly in the hard world of the Northern working men's clubs where audiences were disinclined to tolerate the second best. Dawson dated the turning-point in his fortunes to an engagement at the Trawlerman's Club in Hull, where he won over a hostile audience by abandoning his usual act and trading insults. "The audience had come straight from the sea, stinking of Icelandic cod, with about £160 in their pockets to spend on booze," he later recalled. "I died every night from Monday to Thursday and then, finally, struck with blinding disenchantment and bravado from too many lemon shandies, I got up from the piano and told them just how bloody life really was. That did it. I knew I could be a comedian and gave up the piano."

He made his first television appearance in 1965 and in the following year emerged as a star of the talent show *Opportunity Knocks*. By the end of the decade he had his own series, *Sez Les*, where he would insult his fellow artists as cheerfully as he had the fishermen of Hull. The programme ran for eight years and by the time it ended and Dawson switched channels to the BBC he was a household name.

Dawson was essentially a stand-up comic of the traditional school. He was at his best as himself, in direct relationship with his audience; and, unlike some other comedians, he did not translate happily to plays or situation comedies. He needed to give his personality full rein.

He was successful on radio, where the loss of his physical presence was balanced by his facility with words; and he appeared regularly in summer season shows and pantomime; he was a superb dame – sublimely hideous in rusty ringlets and outsize corsets.

In 1984 he succeeded Terry Wogan as the host of the game show, *Blankety Blank*, gloriously transcending an inane format with his subversive humour. He regarded the celebrity guests as fair game for the sharp edge of his tongue.

Dawson was always seeking new career challenges. In the mid-1970s he starred in a BBC series of three Alan Plater plays called *The Loner*. In 1989 the Royal Shakespeare Company asked him to play Falstaff in *Henry IV*. Although he turned down the offer he always retained a desire to broaden his career by doing more serious acting. Two years ago he moved a little nearer his goal by playing a greedy 100-year-old Argentinian matriarch in the BBC2 play *Nona*; but further opportunities eluded him.

Starting with *A Card For the Clubs* in 1974, he was the author of a dozen books which showed considerable inventiveness, literary talent and wide reading. *Well Fared My Lovely*, for example, was a clever pastiche of Raymond Chandler.

His first wife, Meg, whom he married in 1960 and with whom he had two daughters and a son, died in 1987. Two years later he married his second wife, Tracy, with whom he had a daughter Charlotte. The couple's romance and marriage enjoyed substantial tabloid newspaper publicity which they both relished. They wore identical diamond rings with the initials "PL" for their fond nicknames for each other "Lump" (Dawson) and "Poo". In the middle of his romance with his second wife, the comedian suffered a mild heart attack following which, with her support, he gave up his 50-cigarettes-a-day smoking habit and stopped drinking whisky which he said he had been consuming at more than a bottle a day.

Dawson's most recent work on radio was a series called *Come Back With the Wind* for Radio 2, in which he recited from his novel of the same name. He was working on a new series which was to have been launched during Radio 2's comedy season next spring.

b 2.2.33   d 10.6.93   aged 60

LILLIAN GISH

Lillian Gish, silent screen actress who made her first film with D. W. Griffith in 1912.

LILLIAN GISH was the finest actress produced by the silent cinema. Her career developed in tandem with that of the great pioneer director, D. W. Griffith, and together they helped to fashion the development of film art during the formative years of the new medium. Griffith's contribution was to give the film its grammar and to demonstrate its narrative power, while Lillian Gish mastered more successfully than anyone the challenge of acting before a camera without the prop of words.

Much silent screen acting looks unacceptably exaggerated today and really works only in the area of slapstick comedy. Lillian Gish's approach — an instinctive one, for she had no formal training — was more subtle. She realised the possibilities of underplaying a scene, of conveying emotion not through frenzied gestures but with the curve of the mouth or the flicker of an eyelid.

Many of the films she made with Griffith were frankly sentimental and melodramatic; he was a director who never escaped his Victorian roots. For Lillian Gish's playing, however, few allowances have to be made. She was acclaimed at the time as the cinema's equivalent of Bernhardt and Duse and her acting could still move an audience 60 years later.

She was a small, frail-looking woman of delicate beauty whose career as an actress spanned more than 80 years. Surprisingly, she made only spasmodic appearances in sound films but she played with distinction in the theatre, which became her main outlet, and later in television.

Lillian Gish was the older sister of Dorothy Gish, who also had a distinguished career in silent films. The family was abandoned by their father and to help make ends meet their mother decided to put the girls on the stage, Lillian making her debut at the age of five. As "Baby Lillian" she toured in stock companies and in one of these made the acquaintance of a young actress, Gladys Smith, later Mary Pickford.

It was Pickford who got Lillian and Dorothy their chance in films, introducing them to D. W. Griffith at his Biograph studios, where they were put under contract. They made their first film, *An Unseen Enemy*, in 1912, and went on to gain experience in a succession of one and two-reelers. As Griffith moved to more ambitious projects, so the Gish sisters, and particularly Lillian, became indispensable assets. In Griffith's first feature-length picture, *Judith of Bethulia*, (1914), Lillian played the young mother; and she had important parts in his celebrated epics, *The Birth of a Nation* and *Intolerance*.

In the second she was the cradle rocker who holds together the four stories illustrating man's intolerance from ancient Babylon to the present day.

She went on to appear in *Hearts of the World*, Griffith's wartime propaganda piece, and *Broken Blossoms*, in which she was a young Limehouse waif living in terror of her brutal father; her depiction of the girl's descent into madness still has remarkable power. In lighter vein was *True Heart Susie*, one of several excursions by Griffith into rural romance, and in 1920 she turned director with *Remodelling Her Husband* which starred her sister Dorothy.

It was followed by *Way Down East*, the archetypal Griffith melodrama and his most popular film after *The Birth of a Nation*. She played an orphan girl who has an unwanted baby and when, later, this ghastly secret is revealed, she is turned out into a wintry blizzard and has to be rescued from an ice floe. It says much for her acting that she managed to make such a piece credible.

Orphans of the Storm (1922), a story from the French Revolution, marked her break with Griffith after an association that had lasted ten years. The film went over budget and he could no longer afford her salary; so they parted. She moved to another company, making *The White Sister*, with Ronald Colman, and *Romola*, from George Eliot's novel, both in Italy; and then signed a six-picture contract with MGM that was worth $800,000 and gave her script approval.

Artistically the deal proved a considerable success. She played Mimi opposite John Gilbert in *La Bohème* and gave two of her finest performances in films directed by the Swede, Victor Sjostrom: *The Scarlet Letter*, and *The Wind*, in which she was the girl from Virginia driven into a loveless marriage and eventually to murder.

Despite their critical success, however, the films failed at the box office. As a means of reviving her popularity MGM suggested to Lillian Gish that they should manufacture a scandal for her; she declined and the contract was ended with one picture to go. Other actresses, notably Garbo, were coming to the fore and MGM decided that Gish was expendable. Suddenly, she was no longer wanted.

She did make a couple of talking pictures, *One Romantic Night* and *His Double Life* and then disappeared from the screen for nearly two years. She turned instead to the stage, playing in *Uncle Vanya* and *Camille* on Broadway and in 1936 she was Ophelia to John Gielgud's *Hamlet*. During the 1940s she started making occasional films again and in 1946 gained her only Oscar nomination as Lionel Barrymore's consumptive wife in the Western *Duel in the Sun*.

Of her later pictures the most effective was Charles Laughton's *The Night of the Hunter* in which she was the old lady protecting two children from a deranged preacher. In 1957 she made her first film in Britain, *Orders to Kill*; she was in John Huston's 1960 Western, *The Unforgiven*; partially redeemed a poor version of Graham Greene's *The Comedians*; and after a long gap played the bride's grandmother in Robert Altman's satirical comedy, *A Wedding* (1978).

But her main work was elsewhere. On television she played genteel spinsters in *Ladies in Retirement* and *Arsenic and Old Lace*, while her stage plays included *The Chalk Garden* and *I Never Sang for My Father*. To her subsequent regret she turned down the chance to play Blanche Dubois in the first version of *A Streetcar Named Desire*, which Tennessee Williams wrote especially for her.

In 1983 she attended the London Film Festival for a revival of her silent classics, *Broken Blossoms* and *The Wind*, and demonstrated her resilience at the age of 87 with a punishing round of television and newspaper interviews. In the same year she completed another film, *Hambone and Hillie*.

Lillian Gish, who never married, published two volumes of memoirs: *Life and Lillian Gish* (1932) and *The Movies, Mr Griffith and Me*, in 1969.

b 14.10.93   d 27.2.93   aged 99

STEWART GRANGER

Stewart Granger, actor.

SMOULDERING good looks, a 6ft 2in physique and a nimble athleticism brought Stewart Granger film stardom playing swashbuckling romantic or villainous leads in a clutch of costume dramas in the postwar years. His starring roles in *The Man in Grey*, *Fanny By Gaslight*, *King Solomon's Mines*, *Scaramouche* and *The Prisoner of Zenda* led to him being dubbed "the English Douglas Fairbanks".

For a while − along with Michael Wilding, James Mason and David Niven − he was one of the most sought-after British film actors and one of the top ten money-spinners in the film business. Over a quarter of a century from 1943 he made at least one, usually two, occasionally three − and once four − films a year. But many of the productions in which he starred were mediocre and, later, Granger was the first to admit that, although he

made more than 50 films, he never realised his full potential as an actor.

He was a rumbustious and abrasive individual, thrice married and divorced and given to a devil-may-care outspokeness which never endeared him to either fellow-actors, directors or studio bosses. But he was also extremely self-depreciating about his career and blamed his failure to make more of his opportunities mostly on his own inept decisions. "I've seldom, if ever, made a film I have really liked or been proud of," he told one interviewer in 1968. "To spend a life making even reasonable films is bad enough, but to spend one, as I have, making terrible ones tends to be a little dispiriting."

He would probably have won critical acclaim if he had not been persuaded, first in Britain and then in the United States, to sign long-term contracts that forced him to appear in too many mediocre films. Blessed as he was with a debonair handsomeness, a commanding presence and a manner that could be supremely suave or sardonic, Granger exuded old-style Hollywood stardom.

Stewart Granger was the son of an army officer, and brought up in Polperro, Cornwall. His real name was James Lablache Stewart, which he was obliged to change to avoid being confused with the Hollywood actor James Stewart, but he remained Jimmy to his friends. Following school at Epsom College, his first ambition was to forge a career in medicine but this was thwarted when a change in the family's financial circumstances led him to abandon his studies and to look for other outlets. After a spell as a salesman for a bell-punch company he decided to try for work as a film extra.

That gave him a taste for acting and he trained at the Webber-Douglas drama school. His first professional job was in repertory at Hull; he later moved to Birmingham Rep and, in 1936, to the Malvern Festival. His first London stage appearance was as Captain Hamilton in *The Sun Never Sets* at the Drury Lane Theatre in 1938 and the following year he joined the Old Vic Company under Tyrone Guthrie. He played alongside Robert Donat, as Anderson to Donat's Dick Dudgeon in *The Devil's Disciple* and as Tybalt to his Romeo. He also had small parts in films but his film career did not take off until he was invalided out of the Black Watch in the middle of the second world war.

Robert Donat recommended Granger to Gainsborough Pictures, who gave him a part in a 1943 costume melodrama *The Man in Grey*. Set in Regency times, the film — which also featured James Mason, Margaret Lockwood and Phyllis Calvert — caught the imagination of the war-weary public and thrust Granger into the limelight. Against the advice of Donat, Granger signed a seven-year contract with Gainsborough which was later absorbed by the Rank Organisation.

He soon became second only to James Mason as the British cinema's biggest box-office draw. Of his films of the period, *Waterloo Road* (1944) was a rare but effective venture into contemporary drama and he supported Vivien Leigh and Claude Rains in the disastrously extravagant *Caesar and Cleopatra* (1945) from the play by G. B. Shaw. But he was more characteristically cast in such pictures as *Fanny By Gaslight* (1943), *Love Story* (1944), *Captain Boycott* (1947) and *Saraband for Dead Lovers* (1948).

Granger's relations with the press were never easy and they reached their nadir when the gossip columnists made hay of his friendship with an actress 15 years his junior, Jean Simmons. (His first marriage, to the actress Elspeth March, had ended in divorce in 1949.) After losing most of their money producing a Russian play, *The Power of Darkness*, in an unsuccessful theatre venture in London, Granger and Simmons took off for Hollywood and were married at Tucson, Arizona, in December 1950. Fairly desperate for work, Granger agreed to star in *King Solomon's Mines*, a 1950 version of the Rider Haggard novel co-starring Deborah Kerr, and on the strength of its success signed another seven-year contract with its producers MGM. The studio provided a ready stream of vehicles to exploit his talent for sword-play and riding, even if most of them were inferior re-makes of previous films. They included *Scaramouche* (1952) — a French revolutionary tale featuring Granger in a swordfight which, at six-and-a-half minutes, is credited with being the longest in cinema history — *The Prisoner of Zenda* (1952) (as Rassendyll), and *Beau Brummel* (1954).

Fritz Lang's version of the smuggling story, *Moonfleet* (1955), was a far better, if less popular, picture and Granger also appeared to good effect in *Bhowani Junction* (1956), set in imperial India, *The Last Hunt* (1956), a Western with Robert Taylor, and in 1960 a roistering gold rush adventure, *North to Alaska*, opposite John Wayne.

In 1956 he had become a US citizen but after six years he reverted to British nationality. His marriage to Jean

Simmons was dissolved in 1960 and by this time his career was on the wane. Granger had gained a reputation for declining to laugh at the bad jokes of producers and for putting up none-too-gracefully with directors he regarded as ill-skilled.

He spent the early 1960s filming on the Continent: there was a Biblical epic, *Sodom and Gomorrah* (1962), and a surprisingly successful series of German "Westerns" made in Yugoslavia and based on Karl May stories. But other continental ventures came to little and Granger virtually abandoned the cinema for American television where he joined the nine-year-old Western series, *The Virginian*, (re-titled *The Men from Shiloh*) and played Sherlock Holmes in *The Hound of the Baskervilles*.

His third marriage in 1964 to a 22-year-old Belgian beauty queen, Caroline Lecerf, ended in 1969 and he devoted his professional energies to playing the property market in Arizona and Spain.

Granger's business acumen was no better in real estate than it was in films however and he was forced, for financial reasons, to continue acting in such television series as *Loveboat*, even taking a modest role playing Prince Philip in one of the more excruciating American television "faction" productions, *The Royal Romance of Charles and Diana*.

He returned to the cinema screen after a ten-year gap in 1978, supporting Richard Burton and Richard Harris in a story about mercenaries called *The Wild Geese*. Granger, by this time a silver-haired 65, played a suavely corrupt merchant banker.

After this his health, if not his looks, was in decline. He had part of a lung removed in 1981 and in the same year published his autobiography *Sparks Fly Upwards*.

It had always been a matter of regret to Granger that he had not made more of his stage career and in 1990 he returned to the boards after a 40-year absence, appearing on Broadway with fellow veterans Rex Harrison and Glynis Johns in the Somerset Maugham play, *The Circle*. Later the same year, following the death of Rex Harrison, he toured Britain with the play alongside Ian Carmichael and Rosemary Harris.

Stewart Granger is survived by three daughters and a son.

b 6.5.13   d 16.8.93   aged 80

With Jean Simmons 1955

AUDREY HEPBURN

Audrey Hepburn, actress.

WHEN she burst on an unsuspecting world in *Roman Holiday* in 1953, Audrey Hepburn seemed, and was, a totally original creation. It was just the time that the whole film world seemed to be swarming, understandably, in the direction of Marilyn Monroe, the other late flower of the Hollywood system. Monroe inspired dozens of imitators, but one could hardly imagine Hepburn inspiring any. Monroe was the busty blonde in excelsis, easy to ape superficially, if impossible to equal;

Hepburn was tall, dark, gawky, strange-looking, a star who had, perforce, to create her own style. And so, indeed, she did.

Her figure was a dress-designer's dream (she had been briefly a fashion model) and she worked out for herself that the ideal designer for her was Givenchy, with his uncompromising simplicity. She was a lady, in a cinema which was emphatically reacting against any such notion of womanhood. She was elfin, ethereal, with a touching, almost waif-like quality about her which fitted her particularly for the romantic fairy story. And above all, she had charm and a sparkling sense of humour which made the whole world fall in love with her at first sight.

Well, not, perhaps, quite at first sight. Before she was picked by William Wyler to play the errant princess in *Roman Holiday*, she had made brief appearances in several European-made films. She was a cigarette girl in the opening scene of *The Lavender Hill Mob* in 1951 and played a substantial role in Thorold Dickinson's serous but flawed *The Secret People*, before being spotted by Colette in a hotel lobby while making a film called *Nous Irons à Monte Carlo*. At Colette's suggestion she was auditioned by Gilbert Miller for the title role in a Broadway adaptation of Colette's novel *Gigi*. She got the role, and achieved a great personal success in it, but Paramount were still tentative enough about her screen possibilities to sign her up for only one film in the first instance.

So she was not quite an overnight sensation, though it looked very much like it when she went on to win the New York Critics' Award and the Best Actress Oscar for *Roman Holiday*. Paramount wanted, too late, to put her on an exclusive long-term contract, but discovered that instead they had to hire her services from Associated British, which had already signed her as a starlet during her brief period in British films.

She was the daughter of an English banker working in Brussels, Joseph Anthony Hepburn-Ruston, and his wife, the Dutch Baroness Ella van Heemstra. Audrey (originally Edda) was the only child of this marriage, though she had two half-brothers from one of her mother's prevous marriages. She seems to have been a solitary and withdrawn child, brought up bilingual and, after the break-up of her parents' marriage in 1935, commuting awkwardly between their respective homes in England and Holland. She was also, amazingly for those who remember her spare elegance as an adult, inclined to be plump and considered rather plain.

When war broke out her mother brought her back quickly from England, thinking that Holland would be safer. She was in Arnhem when the Germans invaded, already studying the dance with the hope of becoming a ballerina. On several occasions during the occupation she and her family were close to starvation, but she survived, took up her dance studies again, and in 1947 emigrated with her mother to London, where chances seemed to be better for making dancing her profession. She returned briefly to Holland for a small part in an obscure film, but did not take the possibility of becoming an actress seriously. She continued her dance studies with the Ballet Rambert, and danced in the chorus of *High Button Shoes* and in the revues *Sauce Tartare* and *Sauce Piquante* in the West End before playing a bit in the film *Laughter in Paradise*. This led to the Associated British contract and further small parts before the encounter with Colette.

Once she was launched in America she was unstoppable: major film-makers fell over themselves to give her major roles. If *Roman Holiday* was a Cinderella story in reverse, Billy Wilder's *Sabrina* was the classic article, and for the first time on screen she was allowed to become glamorous and sophisticated. Back on Broadway she played in Giraudoux's *Ondine*, co-starring with Mel Ferrer, whom she subsequently married and appeared with in King Vidor's version of *War and Peace*, in which she was a dazzling Natasha. Throughout the 1950s she went from triumph to triumph, singing and dancing with Fred Astaire in *Funny Face*, having another May/December affair with Gary Cooper in *Love in the Afternoon*, and rounding out the decade with the enormous success of Fred Zinneman's *The Nun's Story*.

Her first real failure was Mel Ferrer's unconvincing version of W. H. Hudson's *Green Mansions*, a fantasy about a girl who lives with the birds. Memory of this was soon wiped out by another of her classic roles, as Holly Golightly in *Breakfast at Tiffany's*, a film the original author Truman Capote heartily disliked, but everyone else adored. Wyler's second version of Lillian Hellman's *The Children's Hour* (called *The Loudest Whisper* in Britain), with Hepburn and Shirley MacLaine as the teachers whose lives are ruined by scandal, was less successful, but her teaming with Cary Grant in Stanley Donen's decorative comedy-thriller *Charade* worked perfectly. Another peak in her career came in 1964 with her casting as Eliza Doolittle in George Cukor's version of *My Fair Lady* − inspired casting, which yet caused some resentment in that it involved passing over the claims of Julie Andrews, who had played the role on Broadway. It also required the dubbing of Hepburn's singing voice (by Marni Nixon).

This phase of her career continued with two more big successes. Stanley Donen's *Two for the Road*, in which she was coupled with Albert Finney in an intricately structured anatomy of a marriage, and an all-out thriller, *Wait Until Dark*, in which she could pull out all the stops as a threatened blind girl.

By this time the external circumstances of her life had changed. In 1968 her marriage to Mel Ferrer broke up, and soon after she married an Italian psychologist called Andrea Dotti. Living with him and her son by her first marriage, Sean, in Rome, she did not feel particularly drawn to movie-making, and she had had another son, Luca, before she returned to the screen in 1976 with Sean Connery in Richard Lester's bitter-sweet Sherwood Forest tale *Robin and Marian*. People were pleased that she was back, though the film was only a moderate success. And from there her films were few and far between. At least she played a full-blooded leading role (rather than a mature star's cameo) in *Bloodline*, a thriller of considerable foolishness, but one made close to home. On the other hand, her next film, Peter Bogdanovich's *They All Laughed*, took her back to America and signalled her separation from Dotti, though not, for several years, their divorce.

At various times in the 1980s she was announced for films she did not make, and certainly was offered many roles that she refused. She was rich, she was living with a rich man, Robert Wolders, widower of Merle Oberon, and she did not need to work unless she wanted to.

Instead she devoted herself to working for Unicef on behalf of starving and endangered children, focusing public attention on their plight by her visits to areas of devastation and famine. She was spurred on in this activity by her memories of her own childhood in Nazi-occupied Holland. In 1990, however, she suddenly reappeared on screen, looking as gorgeous as ever, playing the custodian of the fantasy heaven in Stephen Spielberg's *Always*.

Last September, after a visit to Somalia, she appeared before the press and television cameras in London to recall, vividly, the horrific conditions she had witnessed.

Two months later she underwent treatment for cancer of the colon and was too ill to visit Los Angeles, three weeks ago, to receive the Screen Actors Guild award for lifetime achievement.

b 4.5.29   d 20.1.93   aged 63

In How to Steal a Million (1966)

RUBY KEELER

Ruby Keeler with Dick Powell in Shipmates Forever *(1935)*

Ruby Keeler, dancer and actress and former wife of Al Jolson.

IT WAS her marriage to Al Jolson in 1928 that propelled Ruby Keeler to movie stardom, but her dancing talent was her own. Her name became synonymous with the extravagant Hollywood musicals of the 1930s.

Virtually without formal training, her fancy footwork had been honed and sharpened in the Prohibition speakeasies of New York City where, as a teenager, she tap-danced her way through the almost mythical world of F. Scott Fitzgerald and Michael Arlen, gangsters and Broadway producers. One of those producers, Charles Dillingham, spotted the young dancer in a smoke-filled saloon and gave her a job in the chorus of the 1927 Broadway musical *Bye Bye Bonnie*, which was soon followed by a featured role in *The Sidewalks of New York* later that year. The critics took notice. So did Florenz Ziegfeld, who signed Keeler up

as chief tap dancer for *Whoopee!*, a 1928 musical starring Eddie Cantor and Ruth Etting. But Keeler never made the New York opening of that show.

In the summer, while waiting to go into rehearsal, she travelled to the West Coast where she met Al Jolson. Jolson, at the height of his popularity, had already married and divorced three times. On September 21, 1928, Ruby Keeler became Mrs Jolson No 4, and an instant celebrity. At Jolson's insistence she left the cast of *Whoopee!* after the out-of-town tryouts, and returned with him to California.

It was to be a recurring pattern. There was only room for one star in the Jolson family, and when Ruby returned to Broadway in 1929 to take up a large part in Ziegfeld's musical *Show Girl*, getting excellent notices, she was swiftly whisked back to Hollywood and her role as Mrs Jolson.

For four years she lived in relative obscurity. Then, in 1933, a screen test she had done for a Jolson film was seen by

Darryl F. Zanuck. He signed her for the ingénue role in *42nd Street*, playing opposite Dick Powell, with dance numbers arranged by the legendary Busby Berkeley. The critics were ecstatic, with *The New York Herald Tribune* calling her "one of the best of all possible tap dancers". "The surprise among the players," added the *Los Angeles Times*, "is Ruby Keeler, whose hesitant clear speech and demurely fresh appearance make her a far more effective and appealing personality in her screen début than her husband, Al Jolson."

This did not go down too well at home, but Keeler and Powell were now unstoppable. In rapid succession they starred together in *Gold Diggers of 1933, Dames, Footlight Parade, Flirtation Walk, Shipmates Forever* and *Coleen*, mostly under the direction of Busby Berkeley with spectacular visual effects. Keeler made only one film with her husband: *Go Into Your Dance*, in 1935, which was well reviewed but not wildly successful. The era of the lavish musical was coming to an end. As she herself recalled in 1950, "In my day, musicals didn't get better – they just got bigger."

Her marriage was ending, too. It was not just the conflict between their careers, but the difference in their personalities that drove Keeler and Jolson apart. She was essentially shy; he was an extrovert who loved parties and crowds. The 25-year age gap between them, and the fact that she was a Roman Catholic and he a Jew, didn't help either. They finally separated in 1939 and were divorced the following year.

There was one last film, *Sweetheart of the Campus*, in 1941, and then Keeler married John Lowe, a California real estate broker, and left show business to settle down and raise a family. Little more was heard of her for 30 years, apart from a few television appearances, and then,

in 1970, following the death of her husband, she was offered a leading role in a Broadway revival of the 1925 musical *No, No, Nanette.*

At first, Keeler thought it was a joke. She was, after all, 60 years old. But she took the part on hearing that Busby Berkeley had been hired as production supervisor, and got rave reviews when the show opened in January 1971. Still slim and athletic, she seemed to have no trouble holding her own with the Berkeley girls. "Ruby Keeler," wrote the critic for the *New York Post*, "can still do a tap dance or a soft shoe number that is a joy."

No, No, Nanette ran for 871 performances, with wide agreement that it was her performance that made the show work. When it finally closed, Ruby Keeler hung up her dancing shoes for the last time.

She is survived by one son and three daughters from her second marriage, and an adopted son from her first.

b 25.8.10   d 28.2.93   aged 82

RUDOLF NUREYEV

Rudolf Nureyev, ballet dancer.

WITH his grace and athletic prowess, Rudolf Nureyev was one of 20th-century ballet's most extraordinary and charismatic figures. He dominated the world of ballet, by a force of personality and an eagerness, a greed even, to perform that has been rivalled only by Anna Pavlova in her great pilgrimage of dance around the world. Like Pavlova, Nureyev could and did dance unceasingly, more indeed than any dancer except Pavlova in this century. And like Pavlova's, his name became synonymous for the general public – far removed from the closed world of the theatre – with the art he served with such passion.

Rudolf Hametovich Nureyev was a Tartar, born on a train travelling round Lake Baikal near Irkutsk. A difficult childhood spent in the town of Ufa during and just after the war was enlightened by his scholastic ability and then by a first sight of professional dancing which determined him that this must be his career. By the age of 11 he had the good fortune to be taken under the wing of a former member of the Diaghilev corps de ballet, Anna Udeltsova: she it was who confirmed that the boy should become a dancer. Despite family opposition, the young Nureyev persisted in seeking training, basic though it was, and even then his determination was finally to bring him – after setbacks and battles into which his temperament led him – to his ultimate goal, the Vaganova School in Leningrad. Here, in the cradle of Russian ballet, he had the immense good fortune to enter the class directed by a master pedagogue, Aleksandr Pushkin, who saw than in this raw, difficult, gifted 17-year-old, there was the potential for greatness.

In his student years with Pushkin, Nureyev's talent was shaped, his temperament focused upon work, his insatiable need for information slaked by the opportunities to learn repertory. On graduation into the Kirov Ballet – a fact that had seemed wholly unlikely to his contemporaries when he joined the school – Nureyev was given the extraordinary accolade of appearing with Natalya Dudinskaya, the reigning prima ballerina of the company, as his first professional engagement. In the next three years he danced principal roles in much of the repertory with a series of leading ballerinas, his performances in Leningrad already surrounded with a theatrical magic that his every interpretation would generate thereafter. But the young man was already a stormy petrel. He queried official decisions, sought extra occasions to dance. During the Kirov Ballet's first major visit to the West in 1961, Nureyev's performances in Paris had been greatly admired; his nonconformist behaviour off-stage – meeting and moving freely with French friends – had excited official disapproval. As the Kirov Ballet prepared to leave for its first Covent Garden season, Nureyev was told that he would have to return to the Soviet Union to dance at a Kremlin gala. The message seemed clear to Nureyev: he would return to Russia, never to leave again. His decision was brave and immediate. He sought and was granted asylum in France, and thereby opted to leave all the security of the Soviet state ballet system behind him, and rely upon his talent.

The international fuss attendant upon this decision projected Nureyev into a limelight which was not thereafter to desert him. Never seeking publicity, Nureyev nonetheless attracted it at every turn throughout his career. He became the first male super-star in ballet since Nijinsky, his features recognised world-wide, his every least action chronicled, the larger dramas of his career charted and discussed interminably in the press.

He found his first role in the West in an over-decorated staging of *The Sleeping Beauty* presented by the de Cuevas Ballet, in which he was at least to dance with an outstanding ballerina, Nina Vyrubova. He was also soon to meet the great Danish danseur Erik Bruhn, whose Apollonian style he admired without qualification,

and who was to become a close friend. And he was to make his London début at a gala in aid of the Royal Academy of Dancing whose president was Margot Fonteyn. On this occasion, Frederick Ashton was to compose a brief, ardent solo – *Poème Tragique* to Scriabin music – which seemed to typify the fire and passion of Nureyev as he launched himself upon the Western world. A consequence of this performance was an invitation to appear as Albrecht to Fonteyn's Giselle with the Royal Ballet at Covent Garden, the initiation of a partnership which was to enrapture audiences wherever the couple danced during the next decade.

The partnership between the classically elegant Fonteyn, whose every dance quality seemed to celebrate the virtues of lyricism and dramatic sensitivity, and the flaring romanticism of Nureyev, was unlikely. Aged 24, Nureyev was 19 years Fonteyn's junior, and temperament, as well as artistic background, seemed to separate them. But as their first appearance together in *Giselle* got underway, the Covent Garden audience was to be profoundly moved by the emotional power, the intuitive responsiveness, of their interpretation. Thereafter, their joint appearances generated a massive public response in everything they performed in every theatre.

From this performance onwards, Nureyev was to have a profound influence upon British ballet – as he was, indeed, to have with many other companies worldwide. His reassertion of the importance of the male dancer; the bravura and intensity of his dancing and his interpretations – far less conventional than had been known previously in British ballet – all led to a sense of controversy as well as stellar glamour about his appearances. There also became current at this time reports of bad temper, bad manners, intolerance of inadequacy from associates. Certainly Nureyev's hair-trigger temperament led to explosions of anger when, as a highly concentrated and highly conscientious worker, he found that other people did not respond to his own sense of urgency in getting work as perfect as was humanly possible. Arrogant he might also seem, but it was an arrogance based upon his own awareness of his value, of his achievement and of his dedication to an art he served with extreme intelligence as well as passion.

The career in the West, thus launched in the 1960s, was to seem insatiable for new experience, new roles, new challenges. For a decade the partnership with Fonteyn − immortalised in the portraits of each performer drawn by Frederick Ashton in *Marguerite and Armand* − held every audience enthralled, and gave the Royal Ballet exceptional cachet. Nureyev also began producing and staging for the company − notably the Kingdom of Shades scene from *La Bayadère* − and set about reviving and revising works from his Russian inheritance for ballet companies throughout the world. His versions of *The Sleeping Beauty*, *Raymonda*, *The Nutcracker*, *Don Quixote*, and *Swan Lake* were to enter the repertories of many troupes, with Nureyev's presence as director and star a galvanic influence upon the company, and the box-office.

Films of these stagings ensued, and inevitably were followed by others featuring Nureyev (*I am a Dancer*, *Valentino* among them) which further helped promote his image. There seemed no company with whom Nureyev was not prepared to appear if new repertory, new incentives to his artistry, were available. He was the ultimate "bankable" name for impresarios.

Seasons took place in London, New York and on international tours, in which ballet companies were engaged as backing for his stellar figure, the posters announcing that "Rudolf Nureyev will dance at every performance". And not just once during the evening: he thought it right that his public should see him in three contrasted roles during a programme of short ballets. A prodigious routine of performance, a tireless immolation of himself in front of a public

every night, seemed the ideal for which Nureyev strove year after year. He could and did accept every challenge even, as the years progressed, the challenge of his own younger self.

Where once the jumps had seemed tigerish, broadly soaring, the inevitable depredations of the years brought a sad diminution of physical powers. Nevertheless, Nureyev still strode the stage as ballet's youthful princes and heroes, still excited his public to ardent applause, still offered what was becoming almost a caricature of his old manner.

He choreographed ballets, without lasting success, sought further new roles and fresh areas to conquer − he appeared with modern dance troupes, dancing with Martha Graham's company, with Paul Taylor − and in 1983 was appointed as director of the Ballet at the Paris Opera.

With the departure of Serge Lifar in 1958 as director of the Opera Ballet, which he had dominated and revivified during nearly 30 years, France's national troupe had seemed ungovernable. A series of directors had been little more than caretakers of a technically superb but unfocused organisation. Nureyev, possessed of an identity as commanding and demanding of respect as Lifar's, took charge and revitalised the company, providing a fascinating repertory made up of his own stagings and imaginative acquisitions and commissions.

He dominated the Byzantine organisation of the Palais Garnier, promoting young dancers, restoring to the ensemble a sense of international significance that it had long lacked, and dividing critical opinion, as always throughout his career.

For six years, sharing his time between the demands of the Opera and his own urgent need to continue performing worldwide, Nureyev brought back to the company a lustre it had not known for many years. But changes in the organisation of the Paris lyric theatres – the creation of the Bastille opera house – and the decisions of Pierre Bergé as *supremo* for both opera houses, brought a conflict of ideas. Nureyev did not renew his contract, and what had been one of the most stimulating periods for the Paris Opera Ballet came to an end.

Nureyev, meanwhile, had found a new theatrical vehicle in an extended North American tour of the musical *The King and I*, in which he played the role of the King of Siam. He also made his return to Russia in 1989 as a dancer (he had two years previously been allowed a brief visit to see his grievously ill mother). Arriving back in Leningrad in November 1989, he was to dance the role of James in *Les Sylphides* at the Kirov, his home theatre, for two performances (characteristically, he insisted upon dancing even though he was suffering from an injury). And among the audience was the centenarian Anna Udeltsova, who had been his first teacher 40 years before. On his return to Europe, Nureyev once again embarked upon a series of tours, as punishing in their demands as any he had undertaken as a younger man. The saddening fact for his long-time admirers was that Nureyev's indomitable will to perform was now being eroded by his declining physical powers, and by illness. But nothing –

neither the limitations of his health, nor adverse comment – could deflect him from his mission to dance. The circumstances of his last tour in Britain, when he chose two roles that suited his powers – the insane teacher in Flemming Flindt's *The Lesson* and Othello in José Limon's *The Moor's Pavane* – were less than happy as he drove himself through performances under conditions that were far from flattering or worthy of his name.

It was at this time that Nureyev made a move as bold as any in his career, by deciding to train as an orchestral conductor. With the intelligence and intense application that marked all his work, he set about learning conducting technique in Vienna, and within months he had made his début directing the Vienna Residenz Orchestra in works by Haydn, Mozart, Stravinsky and Tchaikovsky.

Further conducting engagements, and a last sad tour of Australia as a dancer, were constrained by ill health, but in April 1992 he was in New York to conduct *Romeo and Juliet* for American Ballet Theatre. His final contact with the ballet was to come in October, when he realised a long held ambition to stage *La Bayadère* at the Paris Opera. His ill health was now causing great concern but he made a last appearance upon the stage, on which he had first set foot during the visit of the Kirov Ballet to Paris in 1960. He looked exhausted, and stood supported by the principal dancers to whom he had made this last and splendid gift. The audience rose, cheering, and Nureyev seemed to take strength from their adulation – as he had done throughout his professional life. It was a heartbreaking farewell.

Writing about Nureyev in the 1970s, the critic "Alexander Bland" (the husband and wife team of Nigel Gosling and Maude Lloyd) assessed his character as "burning with curiosity, energy and adventure, in which an almost academic professionalism (he is a much valued coach) is always imbued with passion. He has been self-propelled and self-sufficient all his life, a lone-ranger of the dance. A constellation rather than a star, he has excelled in many fields. To each he brings the whole of himself, and it is that self which has made him a legend." This view was acutely true at that time, and remained so throughout Nureyev's career.

Nureyev dominated the consciousness of the ballet world from the moment he leapt to freedom in Paris. His devotion to the art of ballet was total, and used his every gift. Few performers have so bravely spoken of dedication to their art in every aspect of their lives. To stellar presence, Nureyev added a brilliant intelligence. He understood the art he served, and why he served it, and his performances touched and excited his public because they responded to his own passion for dancing.

b 17.3.38   d 6.1.93   aged 54

Rudolph Nureyev in Romeo and Juliet

CARDEW ROBINSON

Cardew Robinson, the actor and comedian.

BEST known for the schoolboy character Cardew the Cad that he created in the 1940s, Cardew Robinson was a thin, gangling fellow who always managed to retain his popularity with the public. The Cad was a mixture of the "sons" of Harry Tate in an old fashioned music hall sketch entitled *Motoring* and the pupils of Will Hay in the immortal *Fourth Form at St Michael's*.

It gained fame for its creator first on the radio and variety stage. Later it became a strip cartoon character in children's newspapers both in England and abroad. It was from this strip cartoon that a film, *Fun at St Fanny's*, was made and brought Robinson new success.

Perhaps the reason for Robinson's continuing prosperity when music hall, variety and radio comedy began to leave us was the fact that he was versatile enough to make the switch to other branches of entertainment with little difficulty.

He tackled all types of roles in the West End and was perhaps most widely acclaimed as the comedy lead King Pellenore in *Camelot* at the Theatre Royal, Drury Lane, during every one of its 650 performances. He also appeared in films and nightclub spots at the same time that his soppy king was raising laughs in the theatre. This was the time when he began to write comic material, not only for himself but for contemporaries including Peter Sellers and Dick Emery.

Away from his most famous character he found time to go straight, making guest appearances on television in *Call my Bluff, Celebrity Squares, Who Dunnit?, Looks Familiar, The Small World of Samuel Tweet, Quick Draw, Three Two One* and *The End of the Pier Show.* He was a good interviewer, but when he was interviewed he left the comic interrogations (as he did several times with Wogan), to his host.

The long-running Radio 2 show *You've got to be Joking* was his own creation and was highly popular during its run of five series. He also found time to make several films including *Pirates* for Roman Polanski, *Shirley Valentine* and *A Connecticut Yankee at the Court of King Arthur.* An accomplished after-dinner speaker he also wrote catchy songs with Roger Whittaker, including *The First Hello, the Last Goodbye.*

Robinson was a quiet studious man, whose private face belied his public appearance. His hobbies were golf (he was a past captain of the Vaudeville Golfing Society), listening to classical music and studying the ways and history of the North American Indians.

Robinson was married for 25 years to Eileen Kay, a former dancer who now lives in Miami. They had two daughters who also now live in Florida.

b 14.8.17 d 27.12.92 aged 75

BEN WARRISS

Ben Warriss (right) with Jimmy Jewel

Ben Warriss, comedian and actor.

BEN Warriss was often more like an aggressive gangster than a comedian. Yet his outrageous antics in bullying, cajoling or cheerfully tormenting his cousin and stage partner Jimmy Jewel, helped keep them at the top as a double act in the demanding world of comedy for 33 years. Forceful, nattily dressed, he had eyes that popped and bulged while he bellowed his disdain. Even his prominent ears seemed to dominate the gentle-hearted Jewel who patiently suffered all manner of humiliation.

Warriss was nevertheless the straight man who built the gag or comic situation. Jewel would pause, then dryly deliver the "put down" or simply win the laugh with his disbelieving "get away screamer" catchphrase. The inspired lunacy of Jewel and Warriss could make even the Goons seem logical; indeed, the pair were among the forerunners of crazy cross-talk, their partnership having been formed as early as 1934 when, in those prewar years, they

were playing most of the nation's then thriving music halls.

Typical of their material was the sketch in which they would dress up as a pair of lumberjacks and sing a song called "Timber" in which the first line was: "Timber, can't you hear us calling for timber?" A vast heap of firewood packed in boxes would then fall on their heads from the flies. The first time they tried this one, in Nottingham, the theatre manager was upset because he had just had a new maple floor laid.

The reason for their often intensely physical comedy was because they were playing in large theatres and they wanted a guaranteed visual impact. They were more production comics, employing props and assistance, rather than simply front cloth funnymen. However even when they went on in the war and postwar years to achieve enormous success on radio and later television, the simulated but unmistakable aggression continued unabated. In the five years that their popular radio series *Up the Pole* was running Ben Warriss received bundles of letters from listeners demanding that he curb his bullying of Jewel.

Warriss, older than his partner, was born literally in the same bed as his cousin – their mothers were sisters – in a large house in Sheffield shared for a time by the two families. His father was a bookmaker but showbusiness seemed the destined career for the cousins. As boys they assisted Jewel's father, also Jimmy Jewel, a theatrical promoter famous in the north of England for his successful touring reviews and variety companies.

At first the two went their separate ways to learn their stagecraft. Ben Warriss played in panto as young as 11 when he was in the 1920 production of *Babes in the Wood* on Brighton's Palace Pier. He went on to develop an act in which he blacked up and did impressions.

Both he and Jewel were experienced performers by the time they decided to team up in 1934 going on, eventually, to top the bill at the London Palladium and play seven Royal Command performances as well as successful summer seasons and regular panto. Radio spots were offered. Among them such wartime shows as *Happydrome*, *Musical Hall*, and *BBC Playtime*. In 1946 they starred in the *Jewel and Warriss Showboat of the Air* which was a postwar variation of the popular variety show *Navy Mixture*. In 1947 they landed what was to be their most successful radio series, *Up the Pole*, which ran until 1952. It was originally set in the frozen north although later a thaw set in when the ice gags ran out. The supporting cast included a youthful Jon Pertwee as Mr Burp.

Warris and his partner's radio popularity remained durable for years and in 1950 they took their first tentative steps into legitimate acting with *Jimmy and Ben*, a series of comedy thrillers written by Ronnie Hanbury. In 1957 they landed yet another comedy series *The Jewel and Warriss Show*. The scripts were by Sid Green and Dick Hills who went on to write for another famous double act, Morecambe and Wise.

In spite of initial reservations that television might cramp their manic style, Jewel and Warriss crossed over successfully with their own BBC series *Turn it Up*, which topped the ratings, and later to ITV with the show *Startime*. However, by 1967 the craze for satire had taken over from the declining music hall style of comedy and Ben Warriss decided to call it a day. Jimmy Jewel agreed and, while he went on to make a new career as a straight actor, Warriss retired from showbusiness and ran a successful restaurant near Bath. Later, he found he couldn't resist the whiff of the greasepaint and made a comeback.

He chaired a *Good Old Days* variety show in Blackpool and honed his own hour-long solo routine. Like Jewel he "went legit" and continued for many years to appear in plays ranging from the Jewish caretaker in Jean-Claude Grumberg's *Dreyfus* to the lead in John Osborne's *The Entertainer*. He was still working steadily until his 82nd year when he was taken ill in his digs while appearing as the Sheriff of Nottingham in a panto at Whitchurch. He was taken to Brinsworth House, run by the Entertainment Artists' Benevolent Fund. This was fitting because Ben Warriss was a stout worker for charity. He was a prominent member of the showbusiness charity, the Grand Order of Water Rats, and was its president, or King Rat, for the years 1953, 1961 and 62.

In the beginning he and Jewel were very close but inevitably because of their different lifestyles – Jewel preferred the simpler life, Warriss who married three times, liked his luxuries – they drifted apart although remaining friends.

Only recently Ben Warriss, the dark hair swept back, ever brilliantined, now grey but the voice still booming, was recalling the old days, the peak years when the duo were the lead strip cartoon in the *Radio Fun* comic, and when they were each picking up £1,500 a week touring the clubs and halls. Still bellowing, he confirmed: "We had a wonderful life."

b 29.5.09   d 14.1.93   aged 83

MARGARET DUCHESS OF ARGYLL

Margaret Duchess of Argyll.

MARGARET Duchess of Argyll was one of the outstanding British beauties of the century. For more than 30 years, she was among the most popular and celebrated figures in London society, until her position was undermined by the scandal resulting from the sensational divorce action brought against her and won by her second husband, the 11th Duke of Argyll.

A full-blooded Scot by both birth and ancestry, Ethel Margaret Whigham was the only child of George Hay Whigham, chairman and founder of the £32 million British Celanese fibre corporation, and his beautiful first wife, Helen Hannay. She was born at The Broom, Newton Mearns, the Renfrewshire estate of her maternal grandfather, Douglas Hannay, the Scottish cotton magnate. For the first 14 years of her life, she lived in New York, and attended Manhattan's most exclusive school, Miss Hewitt's Classes, where her closest friend was the Woolworth heiress, Barbara Hutton.

In 1926 the Whighams returned to live in London, and Margaret — she rejected the name, Ethel — briefly attended Heathfield as a day pupil, and later completed her education at the Ozanne School in Paris.

Prior to her coming-out ball, held at 6 Audley Square, Mayfair, on May 1, 1930, Margaret was virtually unknown to the British public. But such was the impact of her flawless alabaster skin, haunting green eyes and dark, dramatic beauty, that within weeks she had become the most photographed woman in Britain, and columnists began calling her "The Whigham".

She was presented at Buckingham Palace, where her uncle, General Sir Robert Whigham, was ADC to King George V, and became Debutante of the Year. She was supposed to lack a sense of humour, and one elderly peer, who sat next to her at dinner, complained, "She don't make many jokes, do she?". But a fascinated press copiously chronicled her romances with Prince Aly Khan and the young Max Aitken, the breaking off of her engagement to the 7th Earl of Warwick in 1932, and the hysterical crowds that jammed the streets and gatecrashed Brompton Oratory to watch her wedding, on February 21, 1933, to the handsome American stockbroker and amateur golfer, Charles Sweeny. She had converted to Roman Catholicism, her new husband's religion.

A year later, when eight months pregnant, she contracted double pneumonia, was given the last rites, and newspaper placards appeared all over London in purple letters, as if for a royal death. She recovered, but her child, a girl, was stillborn.

Voted one of the ten best-dressed women in the world, her fame became international, and Cole Porter included the beautiful Mrs Sweeny in the lyrics of his hit song, "You're the Top", sandwiched between Mussolini and Camembert cheese.

A daughter, Frances, was born to the Sweenys in 1937, and a son, Brian, in 1940. Pressure was exerted on Margaret by the American ambassador, Joseph P. Kennedy, to leave Britain on the outbreak of war, because of her husband's nationality. She rebuked the ambassador publicly, moved into the Dorchester Hotel, and remained in London throughout the blitz, helping her husband with his formation of the Eagle Squadron of American pilots to fight alongside the Royal Air Force. She also worked long hours as a waitress for Commonwealth troops at the Beaver Club and did valuable work as entertainments officer of the American Red Cross.

She divorced Charles Sweeny in 1947, by which time she had taken over her father's Queen Anne house in Mayfair, 48 Upper Grosvenor Street, where her dinner guests included Anthony Eden, Noël Coward, Paul Getty, Elsa Maxwell, Stavros Niarchos, Bob Hope and members of the royal family.

On March 22, 1951 Margaret Sweeny married, as his third wife, Ian Douglas Campbell, the 11th Duke of Argyll, a man of great charm and intelligence, but deep-rooted indolence, whose life had been marred by compulsive gambling and chronic alcoholism. It was largely through the new Duchess's wealth and determination that the Duke's ancestral Scottish home, Inveraray Castle, was restored and opened to the public. She was also responsible for reviving the Inveraray Games, and did valuable work for the Highland Fund and the Royal College of Midwives.

In 1958 her daughter, Frances Sweeny, married Charles Manners, the 10th Duke of Rutland, and the seeds of future discord were sown when Margaret Argyll insisted to the staunchly Protestant Manners family that all children of the union should be brought up as Roman Catholics.

On August 14, 1959, the Argyll marriage, always turbulent, reached a terminal crisis when the Duchess submitted to a High Court injunction undertaking never again to "utter forgeries" impugning the legitimacy of the Duke's two sons by his second marriage. A month later the Duke obtained a Scottish High Court interdict, barring her from entering Inveraray Castle, and charging her with forgery and "multiple adultery".

In December 1959 the Duke's second wife, Louise Clews Timpson, applied for an order to commit the Duchess to prison for alleged breaches of the injunction regarding the forgeries. The application, heard in private, was denied.

In May 1960 the Duke gave evidence against his wife in a case brought against her for libel and slander by her former social secretary, Yvonne MacPherson. The plaintiff's counsel, Gilbert Beyfus, described the Duchess as "a dazzling figure, high in rank, the possessor of great wealth and famous beauty". It was, he said, as if all the good fairies had assembled at her christening and showered their gifts upon her. But a bad fairy had come uninvited. The Duchess, he said, had become "a poisonous liar". She lost the case and had to pay £7,000 in damages.

Further litigation followed regarding the ownership of the Argyll heirlooms and the Duchess's diaries, before the Argyll divorce action finally reached the Court of Session in Edinburgh in 1963. The Duke cited four men: a German diplomat, Baron Sigismund von Braun; an American advertising executive, John Cohane; a former Savoy Hotel press officer, Peter Combe, and an unnamed man who appeared naked with the Duchess in two polaroid photographs, and who was later to be immortalised by Lord Denning, in the Denning Report, as "the Man without a Head (the Conservative cabinet minister, Duncan Sandys, was cleared of being the figure in the photograph).

On May 8, 1963, the judge, Lord Wheatley, in a 65,000-word judgment of unprecedented severity, awarded a decree to the Duke and savagely condemned the Duchess's character, describing her attitude to marriage as "wholly immoral" and herself as "vindictive" and "a highly sexed woman who had ceased to be satisfied with normal sexual relations and had started to indulge in disgusting sexual

activities to gratify a debased sexual appetite".

Following this crushing defeat, the Duchess's social life narrowed dramatically, and several close friends of long standing severed their relationships with her. Added to these, ultimately, were her son-in-law and daughter, the Duke and Duchess of Rutland, and their children, who were estranged from her after 1970, when it was announced, amid further controversy, that she had privately adopted two "underprivileged" brothers, Richard and Jamie Gardner, aged nine and seven respectively, from Dormston in Worcestershire.

She appeared undaunted, and played a prominent part in the 1968 campaign to save the Argyll and Sutherland Highlanders from disbandment. She also single-handedly rescued Bleakholt Animal Sanctuary in Lancashire from closure.

In 1972 she made a notable social comeback when she hosted a glittering eightieth birthday party for her friend, J. Paul Getty, at the Dorchester, and in the following year, she was hostess to Prince Michael of Kent, the first member of the royal family to attend one of her parties since her divorce.

There were signs, however, that her wealth was ebbing away. In 1975, she published her autobiography, *Forget Not*, a distinctly muted version of the Argyll divorce, and opened her Mayfair house to £7.50-a-head guided tours. In 1978 the house was sold, her staff disbanded, and her possessions reduced to fit into an eighth-floor penthouse suite in the Grosvenor House Hotel.

A surprising success as a society columnist for *Tatler* came to an abrupt end when she fell and broke her hip in 1981. This was the prelude to a long series of falls and other injuries which rendered her increasingly frail. Estranged from her family, in worsening financial circumstances, and often alone, save for her beloved black French poodle, Louis, she continued to attract headline coverage all over the world. Her beauty remained astonishing, even in old age, and throughout all the battles of her long life, she showed remarkable courage, as well as a charm and wit that delighted her many admirers.

In February 1990 she was evicted from her penthouse suite in Grosvenor House Hotel for non-payment of £33,000 in back rent. She moved to a small service flat off Sloane Square and was sued by Barclays Bank for non-payment of a £26,000 overdraft. Bankruptcy proceedings were averted through the chivalrous intervention of her first husband, Charles Sweeny, who settled the debt.

He and their two children subsequently made her a voluntary allowance of £12,000 a year, but her health rapidly declined through a series of strokes, and in October 1990, accompanied by her dog, Louis, she entered St George's Nursing Home in Pimlico, where she startled visitors by insisting that she would shortly be moving to the Dorchester.

Although it was more than 30 years since she had left the Argyll ancestral stronghold, her affection for it remained undiminished. The last clause in her final will, which was drawn up in 1987, directed that she should be buried "in a churchyard close to Inveraray Castle".

The 11th Duke of Argyll, whom she had seen only once since their divorce, died in 1973. She is survived by her daughter, Frances, the Duchess of Rutland, and her son Brian Sweeny, an investment consultant. Charles Sweeny died in March 1993, but she was prevented from attending his funeral, despite a strong desire to do so, because of her poor health.

b 1.12.12   d 25.7.93   aged 80

Arriving at Caxton Hall with the Duke of Argyll

CHARLES SWEENY

Sweeny and his daughter on her marriage to the 10th Duke of Rutland (1958).

Charles Sweeny, American financier, amateur golfer, and founder of the wartime RAF Eagle Squadrons.

WITH his Irish-American Kennedy-style good looks, dazzling prowess on the golf course, and financial wizardry in many a spectacular City coup, Charles Sweeny was what his first wife, Margaret Duchess of Argyll, described as "the epitome of male glamour". His popularity in London society assumed heroic proportions during the second world war, when he banded together 244 American fighter pilots resident in Britain and formed the three RAF Eagle Squadrons, providing crucial support to Britain's air power long before the United States officially entered the war.

Born in Scranton, Pennsylvania, Charles Francis Sweeny was the elder son of a wealthy Wisconsin lawyer, Robert Sweeny, a leading figure in the Republican party, and of his wife, Teresa Hanaway. His godmother was Millicent Hearst, wife of the American newspaper magnate, William Randolph Hearst.

Sweeny was educated at Loyola School, New York, then at Canterbury School in New Milford, Connecticut. He passed the entrance examination for Yale, but decided in favour of Oxford, becoming an undergraduate at Wadham College, where he was joined by his younger brother Robert, who was two years his junior.

The Sweenys, already skilful golfers, joined the Oxford team and both became amateur champions. Bobby, the more accomplished of the two, went on to win the British Amateur Open Championship, while Charlie's looks and charm conquered not only Mayfair but also Hollywood, where Louis B. Mayer, head of MGM, offered him $30,000 to appear in three films, which he turned down.

On leaving Oxford, Sweeny became a City banker with the Charterhouse Investment Trust and was escorting the young and still unknown Merle Oberon when he met the beautiful Margaret Whigham, Britain's debutante of the year, and heiress to the £32 million British Celanese fibre fortune. She was to marry the 7th Earl of Warwick, but the engagement was broken off with dramatic suddenness and on February 21, 1933, she married Sweeny at Brompton Oratory, while huge, excited crowds jammed the streets outside, and more than a thousand uninvited guests gatecrashed the ceremony. Edward, Prince of Wales, whom Sweeny had introduced to golf, sent monogrammed gold cuff-links as a wedding present. A daughter, Frances, was born in 1937, and a son, Brian, in 1940.

On the outbreak of war Sweeny and his wife firmly ignored the advice of the American ambassador, Joseph Kennedy, to leave Britain. The legacy of an operation for a perforated appendix made Sweeny ineligible for active service, but in May 1940 he proposed the formation of the Eagle Squadrons, manned by American pilots, the first of which, No 71 Squadron, was activated in June and joined the Royal Air Force as a fighting unit in September 1940. During one spell in 1941, when it was employed on fighter sweeps over France, it had the highest score of enemy aircraft shot down of any RAF squadron on operations. Two further squadrons of aircraft flown by Americans were added, and the success and fame of Sweeny's inspirational plan was celebrated in the 1942 Hollywood film, *Eagle Squadron*.

Sweeny also personally supervised the importation from America of sub-machine guns, automatic rifles and armoured cars to equip the 1st American Motorised Squadron, manned entirely by American citizens, which became a unit of the British Home Guard. After the United States entered the war Sweeny overcame concerns regarding his health and was commissioned as a major in the G4 supply section of the Service Command of the US 8th Air Force, stationed at Warton, Lancashire.

Margaret Whigham's marriage to Sweeny was dissolved in 1947 and four years later she became the third wife of the 11th Duke of Argyll. This marriage ended in 1963 in a sensational and bitterly-contested divorce action, but Sweeny remained on good terms with his former wife and showed exemplary loyalty to her throughout and after her divorce. It was Sweeny's influence, as a member of White's, that was instrumental in the Duke's resignation from the club after he had published newspaper articles about the Duchess.

In 1957 Sweeny married the New York model Arden Sneed. The marriage ended nine years later in divorce and in 1958 Sweeny and his former wife, Margaret Argyll, were together at the marriage of their daughter Frances to the 10th Duke of Rutland.

Maintaining his Mayfair home in Chesterfield House, South Audley Street, Sweeny showed continued flair in a series of adroit deals with City associates such as Lord Hanson, Sir Isaac Wolfson, Sir Charles Clore and "Tiny" Rowland. He also became one of London's most noted clubmen, playing backgammon daily at first the St James's, then the Cleremont and finally Aspinall's.

In 1986, in the presence of Sweeny and of Princess Alexandra and Prince Bernhard of The Netherlands, the prime minister, Margaret Thatcher, unveiled a memorial to the Eagle Squadrons in the form of an obelisk in Grosvenor Square Gardens, bearing the words, "Founded by Charles F. Sweeny, June 1940". In 1987, Sweeny received the Medal of Honour, awarded by the Veterans of Foreign Wars of the United States.

He published his autobiography, *Sweeny*, in 1990.

Asked once what sort of death he would prefer, he replied: "Like Caesar's, an unexpected one." It came, as he wished, sitting beside a swimming pool in his favourite American resort, Bal Harbor.

He is survived by his daughter the Duchess of Rutland, and by his son.

b 3.10.09   d 11.3.93   aged 83

VISCOUNT MASSEREENE AND FERRARD

Viscount Massereene and Ferrard, landowner, sportsman and devoted member of the House of Lords.

THE 13th Viscount Massereene and 6th Viscount Ferrard, Baron of Loughneagh and Baron Oriel, lived at Chilham Castle in Kent but it would be easy to imagine him living in P. G. Wodehouse's Blandings Castle. In the House of Lords he stood out as an eccentric in a chamber never short of unusual characters. Few novelists would have dared to invent him.

He was born John Clotworthy Talbot Foster Whyte-Melville Skeffington and his life was as complicated as his name. He went to Eton, served in the Black Watch and joined the Carlton, the Turf, Pratt's and the Royal Yacht Squadron. He farmed, raced, shot and was Master

of the Ashford Valley Foxhounds and Commodore of the House of Lords Yacht Club. But there the orthodoxy ended.

There were, above all, his speeches. As president of the Monday Club they could well have been predictable. In fact they were far from being hardline right-wing. Indeed, they were among the most bizarre heard in the Lords in recent times. He was one of the few peers who could be relied on to electrify the chamber. One of his Conservative colleagues said that listening to him was like being the driver in the lorry laden with explosives in the French film *The Wages of Fear*. One never knew when there was going to be some shattering comment, but his listeners, unlike some cinema goers, always left their seats feeling they had had their money's worth.

His seemingly odd suggestions often proved, on examination, to have some common sense at their centre. His speeches were spiced with persona anecdotes and the extraordinary experiences wsith which he illustrate his views. The looser rules in the Upper House allowed him to range far beyond what would have been allowed in the Commons. They also gave him the opportunity to display his great quality: charm. Despite his varied life he retained a residual innocence in many matters.

But his activities in the Lords were only part of his career. He once produced the operetta *Princess Maritza* at the Palace Theatre in London. He helped to pioneer the commercial development of Cape Canaveral in Florida. In his twenties, he crowned his motor-racing career by driving the leading British car at Le Mans in 1937.

His political views were summed up in a preface to *The Lords*, his book on the Upper House: "I have witnessed the swift disintegration of everything the word 'British' once stood for and I have seen the world, in consequence, become a poorer place." In his speeches, often self-deprecating, invariably idiosyncratic, striving to conquer his stammer, he would argue for an older morality and way of life which to him, if not to all his listeners, seemed desirable and still achievable.

He spoke on many more subjects than most peers but he was concerned primarily with the countryside and field sports. During the debates on the Wildlife and Countryside Bill in 1981 he spoke on nearly 80 occasions. He introduced the Deer Act into the Lords in 1963, the two Riding Establishment Acts in 1964 and 1970 and the Export of Animals for Research Bill in 1968. His attempts to regain the right of Irish peers to sit in the Lords — he was the holder of four Irish peerages as well as his United Kingdom one — were unsuccessful.

He will be remembered for his highly personalised views. Unemployment, he maintained, was not as bad as it seemed. He knew this from his own experience when he had been unable to obtain an under-gardener for Chilham Castle. On another occasion he offered to solve the problems of over-crowded prisons and unemployment in one simple way: build more prisons. That would produce jobs and provide more prison space at the same time. And always there were his special observations ranging from curlews ("filthy to eat") to the Channel tunnel ("I hope that the ventilation arrangements will not stick up a long way above the sea because that would obviously interfere with ships").

He was married in 1939 to Annabelle Lewis. He is succeeded by his son, the Hon John David Clotworthy Whyte-Melville Foster Skeffington.

b 23.10.14   d 27.12.92   aged 78

GERTRUDE STEVENSON

Gertrude Stevenson, housekeeper, friend and confidante to the Sitwell family over more than sixty years.

GERTRUDE COOPER, as she was then known, was the seventh child of a mining family at Ridgeway in Derbyshire near the Sitwell family seat, Renishaw Hall, and liked to claim that her family had lived in the area for as long as the Sitwells had.

Her parents both died in the influenza epidemic of 1919 and she was brought up by her elder sister, Mary, who gave up her post in service at Kedleston Hall to mother the family. Her close connection with Sacheverell Sitwell and his wife Georgia began in 1928 when she left Derbyshire to become Georgia's lady's maid at Weston Hall, their Northampton-shire home. Soon after her arrival, Georgia wrote in her diary: "Decided to sack Gertrude. Sad but inevitable." Gertrude, however, remained in the Sitwells' service until after the deaths first of Georgia in 1980 and then finally of her beloved "Mr Sachie" in 1988.

By then she had become an honorary member of the Sitwell family and was certainly the greatest repository of knowledge about her employers' lives. As Georgia's maid she accompanied them on their travels, first to Romania in 1937 when Sachie was researching for his book *Roumanian Journey*.

Staying at Princess Anne-Marie Callmachi's magnificent house in Bucharest, she was shocked by the squalid conditions in which the hordes of family servants lived. She herself was served in a room apart — by a butler who lavished on her caviar which she hated and persuaded him to pocket instead.

In Berlin on the way home she saw Hitler and Goering arrive to call on Mussolini who was staying next door, and in 1939 she embarked with the Sitwells and "Baba" Metcalfe on a long tour of the southern Sahara and Libya, a trip described by Sachie in *Mauretania*.

Back home in the Thirties she had sustained Sachie and Georgia through all their vicissitudes both financial and amorous, somehow making ends meet as they struggled to keep up with their much richer friends, and acting as lady's maid on grand weekends at places like Longleat and Wilton. During one particularly sticky patch when the Sitwells abandoned Weston to share Faringdon House with their friend Lord Berners, Gertrude encountered Bernard Stevenson, then a footman at Faringdon whom she married in 1933.

Bernard later joined the Sitwell household as chauffeur/butler/valet. After he was called up by the Army in May 1940 Gertrude stepped in as cook-housekeeper and general prop and stay, a role in which she continued almost to the day of Sachie's death.

Gertrude's relationship with her employers was a curious one, very much in the Sitwell tradition. When Evelyn Waugh visited Renishaw in 1930 he was shocked by the "terms of feudal familiarity" on which they lived with their "very curious servants".

Sir George's comedy double act with his valet/butler, Henry Moat, has been vividly described by Osbert in his autobiography: "My Father always referred to Henry, as 'The Great Man' and Henry for his part, mixed with feelings of the utmost disrespect, cherished towards him as well, sentiments approaching veneration." Moat remained with Sir George for some 42 years including periods of absence when he would resign in outrage at one of the baronet's more eccentric ideas.

Gertrude enjoyed a somewhat similar relationship with Georgia, often on the point of resigning or being sacked but always remaining. As Georgia's son Francis remarked, they were more like sisters, than employee and employer, with frequent rows and reconciliations.

Gertrude's greatest loyalty, however, was to "Mr Sachie" whom she hero-worshipped and cherished to the end. Their Derbyshire roots were a common bond. She would cook him Bakewell tarts and talk to him about Renishaw and the bluebells of the Eckington woods which featured in his poems. She would organise his social life, telephoning old friends like Peter Quennell or Patrick Leigh-Fermor to come down and entertain him.

Gertrude's knowledge of the Sitwell family and their circle was an invaluable source of information for the recent biography of Sacheverell. Having known the famous literary trio of Osbert, Edith and Sacheverell for so many years and at close quarters she, perhaps alone, knew what they really thought and felt about each other and about other people.

Equally, she was well informed about the lives of their friends about whom she had strong opinions. Peter Quennell, the handsome, dashing poet, was a favourite, Evelyn Waugh and Cyril Connolly, both of whom she found ugly and disagreeable, were not.

Sachie's relationship with Gertrude was indeed a feudal one, despite its intimacy; on one occasion he was heard loftily declaring that his family and Gertrude's had lived on feudal terms for five hundred years.

It would, however, be a mistake to depict Gertrude as either humble or subservient. She was pretty, strong-minded, intelligent and had great natural dignity. She was well-read and became an expert on the social milieu in which the Sitwells moved. She was also a shrewd observer of the *comédie humaine* of which the Sitwells provided so rich an example. Gertrude's diary, had it existed, would have been as interesting a document as anything the Sitwells themselves have written.

She is survived by her husband, Bernard, and their daughter, Sybil.

b 21.8.08   d 17.8.93   aged 84

CORNELIUS VANDERBILT WHITNEY

Cornelius Vanderbilt Whitney, founder of Pan American Airways, philanthropist, financier, and horse-racing enthusiast.

CORNELIUS Whitney may have been born with a silver spoon in his mouth — in his case the metal was probably gold — but it served as no impediment to a life of considerable achievement. And yet, for all his wealth and social standing, and his colossal diversity of interests, he remained largely unknown to the outside world.

In the public mind he was often confused with his younger cousin, John Hay (Jock) Whitney, who was publisher of the *New York Herald Tribune* and ambassador to the Court of St James.

In 1941, at the peak of his many careers, *The New Yorker* magazine said of him: "Cornelius Vanderbilt Whitney is living proof that a man can inherit $20 million, bear two of the most socially and financially prominent names in the country, become chairman of the board of two of America's giant business enterprises, run for Congress, own a racing stable, build and operate a large commercial aquarium, and at the same time preserve a personality so self-effacing that the public does not know exactly who he is."

Whitney, known to his friends as Sonny, was fabulously well-connected from the day of his birth. His paternal grandfather, William C. Whitney, had made several fortunes in oil, tobacco and New York City streetcars, and had served as Secretary of the Navy under President Grover Cleveland.

His mother, Gertrude Vanderbilt, was the daughter of Cornelius Vanderbilt II, one of the legendary railroad barons of the late 19th century. And his great-uncle, Oliver C. Payne, was treasurer of the Standard Oil Company.

As a boy Whitney saw little of his parents, who were often away on long trips abroad. He was packed off to the exclusive Groton School at the age of 12, but refused to go straight to college when he graduated in 1917.

Instead, Whitney, volunteered for pilot training in the aviation section of the US Army, was commissioned the following year, and became a flying instructor at Carruthers Field in Texas.

With the end of the first world war he left the Army and enrolled at Yale, where his achievements were less academic than sporting. He rowed for the university's crew, was captain of the squash team and gained something of a reputation as a playboy before graduating in 1922. Backed by his family's enormous wealth, Whitney promptly embarked on a variety of business enterprises. Together with Juan Trippe, a friend from his days at Yale, he founded Pan American Airways in 1927 and served as chairman of the board during the airline's enormous expansion between 1931 and 1941, when it became a symbol of America's technological prowess.

His other ventures included the acquisition of the Hudson Bay Mining and Smelting Company in 1931 (he remained its chairman until 1964) and the opening of the Marine Studios in St Augustine, Florida, which later became the underwater attraction of Marineland. An unsuccessful run for Congress as a Democrat in 1932 apparently satisfied Whitney's appetite for politics.

He bought his father's 1,000-acre horse farm and racing stable in Kentucky, breeding a string of successful racehorses that were to enter the winner's circle at tracks around the world over the next half-century and gain him most of the sport's highest honours.

He also went into movie-making, joining with David O. Selznick to finance and produce such Hollywood epics as *Gone With the Wind, A Star is Born* and *Rebecca*.

With the entry of America into the second world war in 1941, Whitney promptly returned to active duty in the Air Corps. He served as a staff officer in the Pacific, India and the Middle East, rising to the rank of colonel and receiving the Legion of Merit and the Distinguished Service Medal, among other decorations.

In 1947 he joined the Truman administration first as assistant secretary of the United States Air Force, and two years later was named under secretary of commerce. He also served as a presidential envoy to Britain, Italy, Spain and Luxembourg in 1950.

In his personal life, Whitney was somewhat less fortunate. He was married four times in all: to Marie Norton from 1923 to 1929; to Gladys Hopkins from 1931 to 1941; to Eleanor Searle from 1941 to 1958; and since then to the former actress Marylou Hosford.

With his last marrige Whitney became established as a leader of high society, philanthropist to a myriad of causes, and a patron of the arts. His beneficiaries included the Whitney Museum of American Art, which was founded by his mother, and the financially-troubled 1980 Winter Olympics at Lake Placid, New York.

Cornelius Whitney is survived by his wife, by three of his five children, and by four step-children.

b 20.2.99   d 13.12.92   aged 93

MARY DUCHESS OF BUCCLEUCH

At her wedding to the then Earl of Dalkeith in 1921

Mary Duchess of Buccleuch, widow of the 8th Duke of Buccleuch.

ONE of the last links with the glamorous 1920s world of the Bright Young Things has snapped with the death of Mary ("Mollie") Duchess of Buccleuch. Married to the then Earl of Dalkeith at St Margaret's, Westminster, in the spring of 1921, she was one of the legendary social figures of the interwar years.

There was, though, nothing of the *grande dame* about Mollie Buccleuch herself. She drew her friends from all walks of life and had a consuming, passionate interest in people. In a relative sense, her own was something of a rags-

to-riches story. Born a Lascelles, both her parents died when she was young. She and her sister were brought up by a step-aunt, Lady Richard Cavendish, at Holker in North Lancashire. It was clear from the outset that she would have to make her own way in the world – and this she triumphantly did (at least in the eyes of her somewhat patronising relations) when at the age of 20 she married the heir to one of the largest estates and biggest fortunes in the United Kingdom.

Her marriage to Walter Montagu Douglas Scott, the 8th Duke of Buccleuch and the 10th Duke of Queensberry, moved the centre of gravity in her life to the Scottish borders, which she grew to love, and where so many of her next 72 years were spent.

She and Walter lived at Eildon until he succeeded to the dukedom in 1935. Situated on the southern slope of the Eildon Hills, looking towards the Borders, in rolling agricultural and pastoral land with its pink soil and the River Tweed nearby, it was just the setting for her to come to know her husband's home country. She certainly grew to appreciate just why the Scotts of Buccleuch so loved the Borders.

Walter became member of Parliament for Roxburgh and Selkirk in 1923. Mollie's encyclopaedic knowledge of the Borders, its geography and its people stemmed from those early political campaigns in which she was an energetic and effective canvasser. Her support of a rather shy candidate, her husband, must have made all the difference to his success. Years later she talked about the friendliness and warmth of the people in the mill towns and villages, despite the poverty and unemployment. "We were only booed once and that was by the Duke of Roxburghe's tenants. I expect Bobo put them up to it".

The 8th Duke died in 1935, which meant, for Walter, an end to his life in the House of Commons and, for them both, the move from Eildon. To assume the responsibility for three major houses, Drumlanrig, Bowhill and Boughton, must have seemed a daunting prospect. All three were in considerable need of modernisation, particularly of the heating and plumbing. During the first winter at Bowhill, the cold was so intense that coats, hats and gloves were worn day and night and dinner was served in the dining room fireplace.

With her accustomed energy and attention to detail, Mollie gradually transformed her three palaces − Dalkeith, built for Monmouth and his wife Anne Buccleuch, had been abandoned some years before − so that over the years they became not only the most delightful places in which to stay, but also very characteristic of her. The photograph albums and the visitors'

books are a fascinating record of an interesting and varied period of British history.

Before the war, Mollie welcomed to Boughton many political figures, mainly Conservative, but by no means all sharing the same political views. Churchill, Chamberlain, Eden and Duff Cooper all stayed at Boughton within two years of the start of the war. Another notable visitor, at the request of the Foreign Office during the negotiation of the Anglo-Egyptian Treat, was King Farouk. The visit was made even more memorable by a last minute switch of bedrooms. Mollie decided to put Farouk's mother, Queen Nasil, into her own bedroom, while she slept in the bedroom originally assigned to the queen. Her sleep and that of the other guests was interrupted by the Controller of the Royal Household, trying to find Queen Nasil, his lover. Mollie described the night as being "full of soft padding of feet in the passage, with doors opening and shutting, followed by 'so sorry' ''.

Shortly before the war, the Buccleuchs moved to Drumlanrig and this was their main home until the death of the Duke in 1973. Built of pink sandstone, overlooking the Nith and surrounded by the Lowther Hills, it is part castle, part Renaissance palace. Its beauty and the splendour of the surrounding countryside make it one of the most distinguished houses in Britain. Mollie grew quickly to love it and knew the history of every picture and piece of furniture in it. Her guided tours of the house for those lucky enough to stay there were a fascinating canter through the history of Scotland and England, both artistic and political, not, one might say, totally accurate as to fact, but definitely colourful.

Drumlanrig's visitors' book contained an amazing mixture of distinguished people of their time. Sir Stafford Cripps, Sir John Anderson, Lord Woolton, Lady Reading (in her role as head of the WVS), Joyce Grenfell (who was also a relation), Noël Coward, Malcolm Sargent, King Olaf of Norway and many others stayed there during the war. After the war came most members of the royal family, many politicians, Douglas Fairbanks, the Menuhins and a multitude of artists who were in Scotland for the Edinburgh Festival. One year with the Menuhins and others staying for the Festival, the staff were taken ill. Mollie persuaded a distinguished Italian conductor, Vittorio Gui, to do the cooking and a well-known opera singer, Paolo Silveri, acted as butler.

Wartime at Drumlanrig was in its way a rewarding time with the family in the house and many people to stay. Rationing was strictly applied but game was in abundance and the household, to a considerable extent, lived off the land. Walter has been considered, with little justification, to have admired Hitler and to have been a friend of Ribbentrop's. His name is frequently bracketed with people who undoubtedly were more sympathetic to Germany's cause. Yet many who stayed at Drumlanrig during the war will remember Walter's story of his one meeting with Hitler when he told him in no uncertain terms that Britain would fight if pushed to it. They will also remember his jokes about Pommery champagne, the last good year of which was 1920, "the year before Ribbentrop became Sales Manager". Fortunately, there was a plentiful supply of Pommery 1920. Mollie was never to be drawn on the nature of Walter's political views. She brushed aside questions about appeasement by saying she took no real interest in political issues at that time.

This may well have been right. Her real interest was in people rather than issues. She saw good and bad in them, and counted as friends as wide a range of people as can be imagined. She was the least "toffee-nosed" person imaginable. People who didn't know her were frequently surprised by her friendships. For instance, she admired and got on well with David Kirkwood, the left-wing Clydeside MP. Another unexpected friend was Will Y. Darling, the draper who was Provost of Edinburgh. They all worked together for the benefit of the Scottish war effort.

Mollie's influence turned the minds of many of the younger generation of her family towards appreciation of the arts, of literature and of music. But you needed to have your wits about you. When, as a child, you were asked what you were thinking about, it was no good replying "food" or even "my pony". Something like "Mary, Queen of Scots" was a much more acceptable reply.

Mollie knew everyone around Drumlanrig, their names, their children's names, even the names of their canaries or dogs. Everyone enjoyed her visits and appreciated her qualities. The same is true of the people around Boughton – the immaculate restoration of which was very much her personal achievement. She was very proud of the peal of bells rung by the church in Kettering to celebrate her 80th birthday and was touched that they wanted to give her this mark of appreciation.

In old age, Mollie's brain remained alert as ever. She maintained a keen interest in what was going on in the world. She was regularly to be seen at her daughter Lady Caroline Gilmour's June garden parties – and, indeed, was there last summer with the young, as usual, sitting at her feet.

She was not without her faults. She held strong and provocative opinions, some of which were unashamedly biased. But she combined her prejudices with wisdom – and it was usually the wisdom that prevailed. Yet, above all, she had style. That, too, remained with her till the end.

She is survived by her son, the 9th Duke of Buccleuch, her elder daughter, now Elizabeth Duchess of Northumberland and her younger daughter who is married to the former Conservative cabinet minister, Lord Gilmour of Craigmillar.

b 17.9.00   d 9.2.93   aged 92

MARSHAL OF THE RAF SIR DERMOT BOYLE

Marshal of the Royal Air Force Sir Dermot Boyle, GCB, KCVO, KBE, AFC, Chief of the Air Staff from 1956 to 1959.

DERMOT BOYLE came to the head of the Royal Air Force at its most critical time since it had fought for its independent existence after the first world war. The future of Fighter Command was spoken of as being under threat. The land-based Thor missile, to be bought from the Americans, seemed poised to supersede the indigenous V-bomber force as Britain's contribution to strategic deterrence. An arid future, leading into an era of automatism, seemed to many to face the RAF.

This prospect had a highly disturbing effect not only on the younger officers but on many in the upper reaches of the service. Boyle's task was to sustain a belief in the manned aircraft at a time when the advocates of a push-button solution to Britain's defence problems appeared to have won the day. He exerted all his energy and Irish persuasiveness to try to preserve the integrity of air power and his service's belief in itself and its mission.

It was Lord Trenchard who had told cadets at Cranwell that the RAF would not come into its own until one of them became Chief of the Air Staff. He did not live to see his wish fulfilled and it was Dermot Boyle who brought Trenchard's vision to reality.

Dermot Alexander Boyle was not only the first Cranwell cadet to become CAS, he was also the first Irishman. Born at Abbeyleix, Queen's County, he was educated at St Columba's College, Dublin, from where he entered Cranwell in 1922. He soon became known as one of the best fliers in the RAF. Skill and precision were allied to dash and daring. He served in Iraq with both 1 and 6 Squadrons and his flying prowess against keen competition was confirmed when he was appointed to the Central Flying School in 1927. He flew in the school's aerobatic team in the following two years when he returned to Cranwell as an instructor.

He took part in the 1928 and 1929 RAF pageants at Hendon. Training for the pageants always tested both aircraft and pilot to the limits. Aerobatics were performed as close to the ground as possible and frequently led to horrific crashes of the type which later cost Douglas Bader both his legs. On one occasion Boyle, like Bader, was rolling his aircraft at low level when a wingtip hit the ground and the plane disintegrated. Unlike Bader he was fortunate enough to walk unscathed from the wreckage.

Boyle got his first command in 1936. It was of No 83 Squadron which was equipped with the 150 mph Hawker Hind biplane, then regarded as the latest in British day bombers. Such a judgment speaks volumes for the perilous obsolescence of the RAF, when compared to a *Luftwaffe* which already had the Heinkel He 111 and the Dornier Do 17 in service – both 100 mph faster than the Hind and carrying three or four times the bomb-load. After six months with the squadron Boyle returned to Cranwell as chief flying instructor and received the AFC in 1939.

Soon after war broke out he went out to France on the staff of the Advanced Air Striking Force which was then engaged on the pointless task of dropping leaflets on Germany – and losing aircraft and crews unnecessarily while doing so. The AASF's baptism of fire was to come with the opening of the Blitzkrieg on May 10, 1940. But Boyle was not there to witness its catastrophic losses, since he

had been brought back to Bomber Command Headquarters.

But he was soon put in charge of No 83 Squadron again, commanding it until early in 1941. It was by now equipped with Handley Page Hampden bombers. This could scarcely help being an improvement on the Hind but was, again, an utterly inadequate design for carrying out the tasks the squadron had to undertake. Losses were heavy in attacks on German shipping being assembled in Channel ports for invasion, but Boyle was mentioned in dispatches.

Throughout the rest of the war Boyle held a succession of operational commands and senior staff posts, most notably as a group commander of the 2nd Tactical Air Force, which was formed to support Allied armies fighting the Germans in northwest Europe. In July 1945 he was given command of the famous 11 Group, and had responsibility for converting it from piston-engined aircraft to jets.

In the postwar years his rise to the top of his service was even swifter than his admirers could have predicted. En route he was AOC of No 1 (Bomber) Group from 1951 to 1953, during which period he led a Canberra force on a goodwill visit to South America and the Caribbean. On this 24,000-mile tour, in several of the countries visited the force had to put down on airfields which had never before taken jet aircraft.

From 1953 to 1955 Boyle was AOC-in-C, Fighter Command. It was a period which embraced the Coronation Review of the RAF, held at Odiham in June 1953. Boyle's personal drive and interest ensured that this, the last assembly of aircraft on such a scale in the RAF's history, was an impeccable display. This earned him his second knighthood, this time in the Victorian Order, his KBE having already been conferred on him.

When, on January 1, 1956, he became Chief of the Air Staff he came to office without the usual prerequisite of earlier membership of the Air Council. Certainly, he could have done with that sort of negotiating experience to withstand the violent effects on the future that Duncan Sandys's white paper of 1957 seemed to portend.

In April 1958 Boyle's thinking on the future of the RAF became apparent when he staged a conference, aptly dubbed "Prospect". In the presence of 300 representative figures from national life he made it clear that the Air Staff saw the manned aircraft, rather than the missile as proposed by Sandys, as the ultimate means of defence. He clearly did not foresee the political uproar that this apparent confrontation of RAF thinking and government policy would cause. In some quarters he was branded a rebel and the prime minister, Harold Macmillan, was forced to insist to the Commons that the head of the RAF had not really said what had been reported. But the rumpus did not quickly die down and for the rest of his term of office Boyle trod warily in the public arena.

Nevertheless by continuing to keep his officers, both senior and junior, informed about the progress of developments, in a series of tours to bases throughout the world, he ensured, when he relinquished office at the end of 1959, that he handed over to his successor a service that had,

again, a belief in itself and confidence in its future.

In 1961 he joined the board of the British Aircraft Corporation, becoming vice-chairman in 1962. This gave him the opportunity to press on with the development the Air Staff had, perhaps prematurely, disclosed during the 1958 "Prospect" conference – the TSR2 tactical reconnaissance bomber. This project helped ameliorate the bitterness he felt at the abandonment of the air-launched Skybolt ballistic missile at the Nassau meeting between Harold Macmillan and President Kennedy in December 1962. Alas, this sense of consolation was to prove short-lived – TSR2 itself being cancelled in April 1965. The failure of his successors to fight this decision only increased his feeling that the Chiefs of Staff Committee had become, as he wrote at the time of the abandonment of Skybolt, "less effective militarily and more involved politically, both highly undesirable tendencies from the country's point of view".

In 1931 Boyle married Una Carey. She and two sons and a daughter survive him.

b 2.10.04   d 5.5.93   aged 88

At the Cranwell Passing Out Parade 1956

MONIQUE AGAZARIAN

Monique Agazarian, pioneer woman wartime ferry pilot with the Air Transport Auxiliary.

MONIQUE "Aggie" Agazarian was a member of that relatively small band of women who were recruited by the Air Transport Auxiliary (ATA) during the war, to help deliver aircraft from the factories to the squadrons. It was a job requiring versatility since the ATA pilots were required to fly everything from light trainers, through high performance interceptor fighters to four-engined strategic bombers. But Monique Agazarian came of a family which had aviation in its veins. As a child, her favourite "toy" had been a first world

war Sopwith Pup fighter, which her mother had bought at an auction for £5 and installed at the bottom of the garden. It was a favourite plaything for Monique and her four brothers, one of whom became a second world war fighter ace.

Monique was the daughter of a French mother and an Armenian father who had met in London in 1911. She went to the Convent of the Sacred Heart, Roehampton, and a finishing school in Paris, followed by a stint at the Royal Academy of Dramatic Art.

Soon after the start of the second world war she became a nurse at RAF Uxbridge. But flying was becoming an obsession. When the ATA was formed specifically to ferry new aircraft from the factories to the squadrons, thereby to relieve the pressure on service and factory pilots, some of the volunteers for it were women who already had civil licences. Among them was the famed Amy Johnson who parachuted to her death in ice-cold water when the aircraft she was delivering ran out of fuel over the Thames estuary in January 1941.

Monique Agazarian was not a qualified pilot but, after pestering the ATA for almost a year, she was accepted for pilot training during September 1943. After being taught to fly she was very soon being entrusted with high performance aircraft such as the Spitfire (always her favourite), the Mustang and the formidable Hawker Typhoon ground attack fighter which weighed almost six tons. Agazarian made her last wartime flight in a Seafire (naval Spitfire), swooping low over Knightsbridge where her mother had a flat.

Her brothers, too, had played their part in the war in different ways. Jack joined the Special Operations Executive and undertook a number of missions in France. After some narrow escapes he was captured by the Gestapo and, though horribly tortured, maintained a heroic silence to the end about the considerable store of knowledge he possessed. He was shot by the Gestapo at Flossenbürg, Bavaria, six weeks before the end of the war. His is one of SOE's unsung stories of heroism. Noel had fought throughout the Battle of Britain as a Spitfire pilot with 609 Squadron, shooting down six enemy aircraft. He then went to North Africa with a Hurricane squadron, No 274, and had a total of 7½ kills confirmed and three aircraft damaged by the time he was himself shot down and killed on May 16, 1941. Another brother, too, flew with the RAF.

After the war "Aggy" gained a professional pilot's licence and joined the newly-formed Island Air Services, flying boxes of flowers from the Isles of Scilly to the mainland. Then the company obtained a contract to fly people on joyrides from the public enclosure at Heathrow airport. With Captain Ray Rendall she eventually took over the company. For a number of years they were married but Monique always used her maiden name in aviation. The company expanded its activities, flying passengers to Deauville in eight-seat de Havilland Rapide aircraft and giving joyrides at air displays up and down the country. It was not uncommon for them to fly more than 800 joyride passengers in a single day. However, the growth in airline traffic at Heathrow made it impossible to integrate joyriding activities with scheduled flights and at the end of 1957 the company ceased operations.

For the next seven years she lived in Lebanon where her husband was an airline captain with Middle East Airlines. On her return to England, Monique resumed flying on charter operations and in 1973 she joined the late Graeme Percival who ran an instrument flying school. Together they pioneered an interesting pilot training concept. An instrument flying simulator was installed in a bedroom leased at the Grosvenor Hotel, Victoria. It was surrounded by a circular wall, painted on the inside to represent a horizon, blue sky, a few clouds and various ground features. Student pilots were given tuition in the simulator which was "flown" visually, using the painted wall as a reference. After ten or so hours the trainees went to Biggin Hill airport where, for the first time, they were strapped into a light aircraft and told to take off, climb, level out at prescribed height, turn left and right, then descend towards the airfield. The experiments indicated that considerable cost-savings could be achieved by conducting early training in a simulator, something the major airlines have more recently come to recognise.

Monique Agazarian continued giving flying and instrument training until last October. She is survived by her three daughters.

b 17.7.20   d 3.3.93   aged 72

AIR CHIEF MARSHAL SIR DENIS BARNETT

Air Chief Marshal Sir Denis Barnett, GCB, CBE, DFC, who as Commander Allied Air Task Force, Near East, was in overall command of the British and French air forces during the Suez campaign of 1956.

AMID the general atmosphere of débâcle which surrounded the Anglo-French attempt to crush Egypt in the autumn of 1956 Denis Barnett's handling of the air component of the attack stands out in pleasant contrast. A bomber man all his life, he was accustomed to organising and handling large forces. And the political misjudgments which inspired the operation cannot detract from the fact that he executed his aim of neutralising

Egyptian air power with a minimum of civilian casualties, in a highly economical manner.

He was lucky in having effective instruments at his disposal in the Canberra and Valiant jet bombers. The Canberra in particular, Britain's first jet bomber and one of the best designs ever to fly with the Royal Air Force, was ideal for both high and low level attacks (so good was the airframe that an adapted version saw prolonged service as a USAF spy plane).

It had not always been Barnett's fortune to operate with such up to date equipment. He had had grim experiences of flying hopelessly inadequate aircraft in the early days of the second world war and in the counter-insurgency operations over Malaya in the 1950s.

A New Zealander, he had come to Britain to take a degree at Cambridge in the 1920s. He learnt to fly with the university air squadron and was commissioned into the RAF reserve of officers. In his early days he had periods as an instructor and had some experience of what was then the fledgling art of army co-operation. But from the latter 1930s onwards he was committed to bombers and in 1937 got his first command – of a squadron of antiquated biplane Vickers Vincents in Iraq.

Bomber Command entered the second world war, still with an inventory of perilously obsolete aircraft, many of which were merely death traps for their crews and had little chance of inflicting much damage on the enemy. After the fall of France, Barnett was given command of No 40 squadron of Blenheims and ordered to attack German shipping in the Channel ports, where amphibious forces were being assembled for an invasion of Britain. Less publicised than the more glamorous sorties of Fighter Command, these raids nevertheless called for just as much skill and courage. Lacking any real punch in terms of bomb load, lightly armed and with a low top speed that made it an easy prey for fighters, the Blenheim and its crews were faced with a difficult as well as dangerous task. Nevertheless Barnett and his crews stuck to it in a series of raids whose nuisance value – even if material destruction was not great – was enough to make life uncomfortable for the assembling enemy. His leadership in these operations earned Barnett the DFC.

Later in the war Barnett went on to command bomber stations and a bomber group, subsequently occupying posts in the higher directorate of bomber operations. After periods in India and Pakistan in the latter 1940s, he was confronted, as director of operations at the Air Ministry, with the Malayan emergency of the early 1950s. Once again he found himself having to organise bombing operations with an aircraft

(personified in this case by the piston-engined Avro Lincoln) which would have been more at home in the previous aviation era. Certainly the lumbering four-engined bomber was not able to make much impact against guerrillas hiding in thick jungle.

Yet only a few years on, the Suez crisis presented a very different picture. Barnett now had an all-jet bomber force at his disposal and was able to deploy it rapidly in Cyrpus and Malta. When the Anglo-French offensive opened on October 31, 1956, Valiants and Canberras, together with the Navy's carrier-borne aircraft struck at the Egyptian air force on the ground, virtually annihilating it within 48 hours. This paved the way for the invasion which went ahead mercifully untroubled by air attack. Having, as they felt, done so well, Barnett and his airmen were naturally disappointed to be called off when American pressure brought the Anglo-French action to an end on November 6. Still, the result, in terms of the use of air power, was a tribute to Barnett's ability to organise, and to his profound appreciation, garnered from long experience of the precise capabilities of the aircraft types at his disposal.

Thereafter his career flourished. He commanded the RAF staff college at Bracknell, 1956; was AOC-in-C Transport Command, 1959–62; and OAC-in-C Near East, 1962–64. In this, his last RAF job, he was responsible for British forces in Cyprus and the administration of the Sovereign Base Areas. In retirement he was, from 1965 to 1972, member for Weapons Research and Development, Atomic Energy Commission.

Barnett was a quiet, modest man, whose leadership was of a thoughtful rather than fiery nature. But his modesty concealed great personal bravery and a capacity for the type of tactical analysis which tends to save lives at the "sharp" end of operations.

He leaves his widow, Pamela, and a son and two daughters.

b 11.2.06   d 31.12.92   aged 86

HANS BAUR

Hans Baur, Hitler's personal pilot from 1932 until the Führer's death.

HANS BAUR was probably the final survivor of those who saw Hitler in his last days. He was also a key witness after the war — insisting, at a time of widespread confusion, that both Hitler and Eva Braun killed themselves in the burning ruins of the Berlin chancellery, although he himself did not see their bodies. He said Hitler had told him as he took his leave that he intended to commit suicide because the situation was hopeless.

Hans Baur was a loyal and highly-decorated servant of the Führer. He had been a fighter ace in the first world war and shot down nine allied aircraft before becoming a pilot for the first German post office air mail service. In 1926, he became a flight captain for the civil airline, Lufthansa, and regularly flew the Munich-Milan-Rome route. In 1921 he joined the fledgling Nazi party and was one of Hitler's earliest supporters as he rose to the leadership of the NSDAP (National Socialist German Workers Party).

In 1932, a year before the Nazi seizure of power, Baur became Hitler's personal pilot, flying him to party meetings and rallies all over the country in a special version of that indefatigable Luftwaffe workhorse, the three-engined Junkers Ju52 transport aircraft. Later, after Hitler had become chancellor, the aircraft Baur piloted became more splendid, as befitted his boss's enhanced status. Eventually Baur graduated to the four-engined, long-range reconnaissance bomber, the Focke-Wulf Fw200 Kondor; besides being the bane of Atlantic convoys it was much prized by Hitler as an impressive example of German aircraft technology which he could brandish before his opposite number, Mussolini, on his visit to the Duce in Italy in 1943. Baur's privileged position carried with it the rank of general.

In the final days of the war Baur was with the Nazi hierarchy in Berlin as the Russians closed in, and flew a number of difficult missions out of the city, taking out papers and bringing in some of the last people to see Hitler alive. His last order was to take Martin Bormann to safety, but with the Russians then virtually in full control of the city he was unable to take off. He always maintained that Bormann was killed in his attempt to flee from the bunker, and consistently refuted assertions that the Reichsminister had escaped to safety in South America.

Captured by the advancing Russians, Baur spent ten years as a Soviet prisoner-of-war. He had been severely wounded in the final days of fighting and later had to have part of one leg amputated by the Russians. He was to have been brought back to Berlin under armed guard by the Russians for a week in 1946 to testify to the death of Hitler but, before he set out, the order was countermanded, and he found himself sentenced to 25 years' hard labour.

The ten years he actually spent in the Soviet Union were punctuated by regular and brutal interviews with the MGB (predecessor of the KGB) whose officers, perhaps understandably, simply could not believe that such a close associate of the Führer could have so little knowledge of the workings of the party and government

machines of the Third Reich. Throughout this gruelling experience Baur stuck to his story that he had been nothing more than Hitler's aerial chauffeur.

Baur finally returned to Germany in October 1955, settling in Herrsching am Ammersee in upper Bavaria, where he lived until his death.

In his autobiography, *Hitler's Pilot*, published in English in 1958, he asserted afresh that his job had been merely to ferry Hitler and that he knew nothing of the atrocities of his master's regime. The book gave insights into Hitler's character in other respects: his fascination for women, his sentimentality about animals, his ability to bend the wills of others to his own. However, on total revelation it fell short. Given Baur's disciplined, Teutonic manner it had clearly never occurred to him to gossip with Hitler and thereby garner a store of potentially marketable information.

During the investigations into the forged Hitler diaries in April 1983 considerable attention focused again on Baur, as the forgers insisted that he knew that a number of key documents had been flown out of the chancellery in the final days. However, although he claimed he remembered Hitler's distress at hearing of the crash of a plane which had taken his personal papers out of Berlin, his testimony (by then he was 86) was clearly flawed and threw doubt on some of his other wartime recollections.

Baur was a holder of many awards including the Bavarian medal of courage; he remained a defender of Hitler and the Nazi party until his death. His family did not announce it immediately, inserting a notice in the *Süddeutsche Zeitung* after the private family funeral had already taken place. The notice said that Baur had been "called to his last take-off".

His wife predeceased him; he leaves four children.

b 6.97 d 17.2.93 aged 95

MAJOR-GENERAL THOMAS BRODIE

Major-General Thomas Brodie, CB, CBE, DSO, who commanded Britain's 29 Infantry Brigade in the Korean war.

TOM BRODIE won his DSO on the Imjin River, that battle of the Korean War in which the "Glorious Glosters" won their sobriquet. No single confrontation since Rorke's Drift so seized the imagination of the British public, as that which raged along the swiftly flowing Imjin during the Chinese spring offensive in April 1951. Perhaps no battle in the history of the British Army has seen British troops inflict such grievous losses on a numerically superior enemy as 29 Brigade's stand at Imjin did.

True, there was a price for the brigade. To enable the rest of its battalions to withdraw in the face of odds of 20−1 Colonel Carne and his 1st Gloucesters had to fight to the bitter end and the survivors passed into captivity in conditions of the utmost rigour which they endured for 19 months. But it is estimated that of the 60,000 Chinese who attacked the brigade's positions, 10,000 were left dead on the battlefield. As a result the Chinese spring offensive was brought to a halt. The communist leadership's hopes of spending May Day

in the South Korean capital were utterly dashed.

Brodie's most bitter decision during the battle was the wireless message he had to send to Carne, telling him that the Gloucesters were expendable and that the other elements of his force − the Royal Ulster Rifles, the Northumberland Fusiliers, the 8th Hussars and the Belgian battalion − would have to withdraw to safety from their support positions on the flank. Carne understood. Between him and Brodie subsisted an absolute respect.

The citation to Brodie's DSO paid tribute to his "conspicuous courage and tenacious leadership" and said he was "an inspiration to his officers and enlisted men" as he strode among his troops during critical periods of the fighting. The Americans were equally generous in their comments in awarding him their Silver Star for gallantry, a medal which roughly equates to the MC, and in appointing him to the US Legion of Merit.

Brodie was a character who knew how to establish his presence in the brigade and sensed how best to contribute to morale. This capacity to cheer the troops was sometimes involuntary, as when, visiting the Royal Ulster Rifles unannounced, he and his helicopter nearly demolished the officers' latrines, to the great delight of the enlisted men. When the troopships carrying 29 Brigade had sailed for Korea late in 1950 it seemed that the war would soon be over. Brodie made sure he had his polo sticks with him and drew up plans for acquiring the necessary ponies on arrival. He was also once quoted by the press as wryly complaining that the fighting had forced him to cancel a planned tiger shoot.

However, he was no Colonel Blimp. These minor eccentricities were underpinned by a shrewd tactical brain. As soon as 29 Brigade disembarked in Korea it was clear that the whole character of the war had changed. The Chinese were massing for a major offensive. Polo and other sporting frolics were off the agenda. One of Brodie's first and wisest actions was to issue orders abolishing executions in his area, thus ending the practice indulged in by vengeful South Koreans of summarily shooting those suspected of collaborating with the North.

He had served with General Orde Wingate, commanding 14th Infantry Brigade with the Chindits in Burma in 1944, where again he attracted attention by riding around on horseback.

In Palestine in 1947–48, commanding 51 Lorried Infantry Brigade, he was first mentioned in dispatches, then appointed a CBE. The citation praised his "resourcefulness and firmness in dealing with difficult situations" which did much to raise British prestige.

Yet Brodie had not set out to join the Army. A farmer's son from Northumberland, he had read history at Durham University with no apparent military ambitions. While an undergraduate, however, he joined the OTC and became hooked.

He followed a friend into the Cheshire Regiment, joining the 2nd Battalion at Tidworth in 1926. He became its adjutant in 1934 when the CO was a Lieutenant-Colonel Arthur Percival, later to find himself commanding the Singapore garrison when the island surrendered to the Japanese.

Meanwhile Brodie made a reputation as a sportsman, running in the regiment's athletics team which went on to win the Army championships in 1937–39. He helped make its Rugby XV one of the best in the Army in the late 1920s, and played polo for the Cheshires in Malta in the early 1930s when it beat every side whom it played – including Lord Louis Mountbatten's naval team.

In 1936, however, Brodie narrowly escaped with his life when an aircraft in which he was a passenger crashed in the Western Desert. One of only three survivors, he spent many months in hospital, losing most of one ear and some fingers through severe burns.

He spent the next few years as an instructor, first at the Royal Military Academy Sandhurst, then at the staff college and finally at the senior officers' school – before being giving command of the 2nd Battalion the Manchester Regiment in 1942 and taking it to India. He served briefly as a staff officer with the 70th Division before being sent to join the second Wingate campaign in 1944. He commanded the 1st Cheshires in Germany after the war.

On his return from Korea in 1952, Brodie was promoted major-general and given command of the 1st Infantry Division in the Canal Zone, returning in the year before Suez.

He was then scheduled to take over as C-in-C Austria. But the Austrian State Treaty of 1955 saw the restoration of Austria as an independent country and the withdrawal of occupying forces. His job taken away from him, Brodie briefly commanded on Salisbury Plain and went on a lecture tour before retiring from the Army in 1957.

In the same year he joined the Economic League, an allegedly non-political organisation which nevertheless saw its task as fighting left-wing subversion in British industry and keeping secret files on those it regarded as industrial saboteurs. He became its regional director in the Midlands, ultimately joining its central council and retiring at the age of 80. He was honorary colonel of the Cheshires from 1955 to 1961.

Tom Brodie was essentially a fighting soldier and had little sophistication about politics. Probably the most striking characteristic of his career was the way in which he contrived to steer clear of Whitehall. A modest man, he seldom spoke of his war service. His family, then living in Colchester in married quarters, first heard of his exploits in Korea through a letter from his batman.

He married his wife Jane in 1938 and five generals, all ex-Cheshires, were on parade at their golden-wedding party five years ago. She died last year. Tom Brodie himself lived just long enough to be aware of his old regiment's achievements in Bosnia with the United Nations.

He is survived by three sons and a daughter.

b 20.10.03   d 1.9.93   aged 89

AIR VICE-MARSHAL S. O. BUFTON

Air Vice-Marshal Sydney Osborne Bufton, CB, DFC, the man behind the Pathfinder force in the second world war.

WINSTON Churchill called him "the little air commodore" and offered him regular audiences at Downing Street in 1944 to protect him from the political flak in Whitehall. "Buf" Bufton politely declined and continued to fight his battles on his own, inspired by his deeply-held convictions on air warfare. But Churchill's approach reflected the prime minister's respect for his integrity.

Bufton, a close friend of Barnes Wallis and Frank Whittle, inventors of the dambuster bomb and Britain's jet engine, made his own mark on history in 1942. Already a decorated bomber pilot, with

experience of commanding a squadron and air station, he had recently been appointed to the Air Ministry as deputy director of bombing operations. A gifted electrical engineer, he had himself developed, while flying, a number of aids to help night-time operations, including more accurate, barometrically-fused flares to illuminate precise targets on the ground. But as bombs continued to be dropped wide of their mark, exemplified by wasteful raids on Essen and Mannheim, he realised that something else had to be done.

In a series of letters to Air Chief Marshal Sir Arthur Harris, who had just been appointed to lead Bomber Command, Bufton argued the case for an élite force of "pathfinders" who would find and illuminate the targets for the bombers. He won the ear of Sir Wilfred Freeman, vice-chief of the air staff and of Henry Tizard, the RAF's chief scientific adviser, and then the support of Charles Portal, chief of the air staff.

But it was only after a thinly-veiled threat from Portal that "Bomber" Harris finally gave way. The Pathfinders (they were christened by Harris) were established in August 1942 under the command of Air Commodore Donald Bennett – who was also to become Bufton's lifelong friend. But the Pathfinders' champions have always maintained that "Bomber" Harris stubbornly avoided giving Bennett's crews the equipment that they needed to secure early results.

Bufton, then a temporary 34-year-old group-captain, was promoted in the following year and made director of bomber operations for the rest of the war. In this post he still fearlessly continued to engage the senior air staff in pressing his own views on attack strategy. He was not only vigorously opposed to area bombing but criticised the Tedder-Zuckerman policy of interdicting enemy communications in 1944. He determinedly pressed the case, instead, for concentrating on destroying German oil refineries, pointing out in later years that by September 1944 the supply of fuel to the Luftwaffe was down to less than 10 per cent of their needs. Had that been achieved six months earlier, he argued, the second world war might have been shortened.

In 1945 Bufton was made air officer commanding (AOC) in Egypt. He was later deputy chief of staff (operations/ plans) Air Forces Western Europe, 1948–51; director of weapons at the Air Ministry, 1951–52; air officer administration at Bomber Command, 1952–53; AOC British Forces Aden, 1953–55; senior air staff officer (SASO) Bomber Command, 1955–58; and finally assistant chief of the air staff (intelligence), 1958–61, when he retired. It was widely believed that Bufton, a quiet, unostentatious man, might have

climbed higher, but for his refusal to compromise his beliefs.

He had been born, the second of three brothers (all of whom had distinguished RAF careers in the war), at Llandrindod Wells in mid-Wales. His father was a successful estate agent and the family were prominent in the town. "Buf" who went to Dean Close School, Cheltenham, showed an early aptitude for radio and made some of the first crystal sets in Wales. (With a shrewd respect for authority – something he did not always display in later years – he immediately presented two of the sets he had made to the town mayor and the local police chief.)

This aptitude was to give him a second career. After fitting a home-made transistor into a Perspex sandwich box which his elder daughter could smuggle into her strict boarding school, he started marketing a radio construction kit called Radionic. On leaving the RAF he began his own Radionic company and ran it at Crawley for eight years before he was bought out by Phillips.

In 1967 his old county honoured him and his family by appointing him high sheriff of Radnorshire and three years later he was made a fellow of the Royal Aeronautical Society (Frank Whittle and Barnes Wallis were his proposers). His wartime decorations included his being made a commander both of the US Legion of Merit and of the Dutch Order of Orange Nassau (with swords).

He was a notable sportsman in his youth. He played hockey for Wales, the RAF and the Combined Services, won championship medals for boxing and diving and had a golfing handicap of five. He also painted in oils and had started to compile his autobiography.

In 1943 he married Sue, a Wren who modelled for WRNS advertising during the war and whom he met at a Grosvenor House tea dance for young officers. They celebrated their golden wedding last New Year's Day and he is survived by her and their two daughters.

b 12.1.08   d 29.3.93   aged 85

AXEL VON DEM BUSSCHE

Axel von dem Bussche, one of the last surviving members of the group of Wehrmacht officers who made repeated attempts on Hitler's life in 1943–44.

AXEL von dem Bussche was one of that high-minded band of Wehrmacht officers led by Claus von Stauffenberg, which set itself against the Hitler evil and organised the famous, but failed July plot of 1944. But he deserves honour in his own right as the volunteer for quite the most ingenious of the Hitler assassination attempts — one which, had it been successful, would have involved the sacrifice of his own life.

"Operation Overcoat", as it was styled, was scheduled for November 1943. The opportunity was presented by Hitler's finicking interest in the mundanest details of military equipment. It was announced that a new uniform greatcoat was to be introduced into the Wehrmacht. Hitler wanted to judge for himself the aesthetic qualities of the new apparel before it was officially adopted. It was arranged that the greatcoat should be exhibited for his inspection at his headquarters at Rastenburg in East Prussia.

An aristocratic young battalion commander in the 9th Infantry Regiment, Freiherr Axel von dem Bussche volunteered to model the new coat before his Führer. In the bulky pockets Bussche was to secrete one, possibly two *Eihandgranaten*, egg-shaped grenades whose four-second time fuses he would trigger as Hitler stood before him. He would then grapple the Führer, clinging to him until the grenades exploded, killing them both.

The plan had simplicity as well as self-sacrificial bravery on its side. At Hitler's normal public appearances his personal bodyguard, the fanatical and lynx-eyed SS *Leibstandarte*, were on watch for any hostile movement in the crowd. Such a suicide plot was one that seemed capable of thwarting even their famed watchfulness.

However, Hitler's legendary sixth sense of impending danger made the ensuing days nerve-wracking ones for Bussche. Time after time the Führer cancelled the demonstration. But at last a day was fixed upon and Bussche made his final preparations.

It was not to be. On the allotted day a sudden Allied air raid threw the arrangements for the military fashion show into total disarray. Worse, bombs wrecked the train which was bringing the display of coats to the inspection, and it was postponed.

There was not to be another chance for Bussche. He had to rejoin his regiment on the eastern front. Shortly after that he was severely wounded and had a leg amputated. He was under constant suspicion from the Nazi hospital staff (he even had to get rid of the bombs, which he still had in his kit). But the long hospitalisation which followed – isolating him from his fellow conspirators – undoubtedly saved his life. The Stauffenberg plot of July 1944 failed disastrously. Stauffenberg and most of the other members of the German resistance, including von dem Bussche's closest friend, Fritz von der Schulenburg, were all executed.

Bussche was born into an old Saxon family, although his mother was Danish. It was his mother's side which, ironically, gave him the blond, blue-eyed good looks which later enabled him to pass as the "typical" German type beloved of the Führer. It was natural for him to join the army as a career, but, as he was later to recall, it was an army with very little enthusiasm for Nazism. In Bussche's unit,

the 9th Infantry Regiment, based at Potsdam, professional soldiering was the talk of the mess and the crudities of Nazi propaganda were held in almost open contempt. When war came, the main aim of the 9th was to acquit themselves as had the generation of 1914–18.

On the first day of the war, one of von dem Bussche's comrades to be killed – a few yards from him – was the brother of today's president of Germany, Richard von Weizsäcker, who was to remain a close friend. The invasion of Poland in 1939 gave him his first glimpses of Nazi vileness as he saw Jews being brutally herded from villages into waiting trains.

However, the following May, with scores to settle against the French, for 21-year-old von dem Bussche the fast-moving Blitzkreig seemed like a "jolly picnic", with his foot-sore men wheeling their weapons along through the Ardennes in commandeered prams. For his role in the French campaign he was awarded the *Ritterkreuz* (Knight's Cross) – equivalent of the British VC – which was to give him his special access to the Führer.

In June 1941 his regiment was in the vanguard for the attack on Leningrad, but it was while resting in the Ukraine the following year that he had first-hand experience of what *Die Endlösung* – the "final solution" – really meant. On an unused airfield, his regiment was ordered to take part in a "special operation". With some intuition of what was afoot, the CO refused and a renegade unit of Ukrainians was employed instead. Many years later von dem Bussche recalled "there in the beautiful autumn sunshine was a queue about a mile long of old men, women, children, babies – all naked. Large trucks were driving away with their clothes. It was the Jewish population. They were waiting to lie down in these enormous holes – graves which they had themselves been forced to dig – and be shot by the SS."

Von dem Bussche urged his commanding officer to do something. The other officers were left in a state of shock. It was the moment when he resolved to assassinate Hitler — whatever the cost. He was put in touch with the "underground" opposition to Hitler early in 1943 by Fritz von der Schulenburg. Schulenburg had been deputy president of the police in Berlin and then had a senior post in Breslau and had early experience of the dark side of the Third Reich. He introduced Bussche to von Stauffenberg who elucidated "Operation Overcoat" and asked him if he would undertake it. Bussche unhesitatingly volunteered. In the atmosphere of evil which had overspread the German spirit he felt no sense of heroics. Indeed he always deprecated a later generation's interest in the cloak and dagger nature of the assassination attempt. For him the *raison d'être* of the operatoin was simply the hideous nature of Hitler's crimes.

After the war, badly handicapped from his wounds (he had also lost a thumb at the crossing of the Meuse in 1940), he married a daughter of an Irish earl, Camilla Stauffenberg, herself widow of the chief conspirator's cousin. With his unblemished credentials he was the natural choice to become one of the leaders of the newly-formed Bundeswehr. But in 1952, and over a matter of principle — he feared that some of the old evils of Prussianism were creeping back — he resigned. It seemed that he over-reacted; nevertheless the huge publicity both inside Germany and in the world press undoubtedly helped assure that the democratic reformers won the day at this crucial moment in German history.

He became head of the famous Salem School but had to give that up after a heart attack. For a period he lived in Switzerland working for the World Council of Churches. But he was probably at his happiest in America. It was only in the States, he sometimes used to say, that he felt relieved of the intolerable burden of the European past.

He played a prominent role in the early days of the Königswinter Anglo-German Association. In 1985 he spent a year, with Camilla (who pre-deceased him), at St Antony's College, Oxford, endeavouring to write his memoirs. But it was marred by a total blockage; the bad dreams of the past would not allow him to get it all down on paper.

Nobody who met this 6ft 5in giant, with a single crutch and piercing blue eyes, ever forgot his quite extraordinary presence. As well as being a man of high seriousness, he was also a great humanist and possessed of a unique sense of humour.

In his last years he finally moved back to Germany, to Bonn. To his many friends across the world he stood for more than just the conscience of Germany.

b 1919   d 26.1.93   aged 73

SIR EDWARD DUNLOP

Sir Edward "Weary" Dunlop, AC, CMG, OBE, Australian surgeon and war hero who cared for prisoners of war on the notorious Burma railway.

EDWARD DUNLOP was by any standards a distinguished surgeon and rose high in his profession. But his name has a place of honour in Australia for his untiring struggle to alleviate the sufferings of prisoners of war who were compelled by their Japanese captors to work on the construction of the Burma-Siam railway.

A prisoner himself after being captured in Java in 1942, Dunlop was often beaten and tortured for standing up for the rights of his men and for the superhuman efforts he devoted to their care. On one occasion he was threatened with execution by disembowelment, and made to stand manacled to a tree with four bayonets jabbing into his belly while a Japanese officer impassively counted out the thirty seconds "grace" in which he might compose himself for death. At the last second he was reprieved, but during this terrible ordeal, as he recalled: "I pined for a cyanide pill."

Such mental and physical torment continued almost daily, but Dunlop refused to be cowed. Treating wounds often with the most primitive of surgical instruments, which he improvised from whatever came to hand, he was, throughout those years of appalling privation on the infamous railway, an inspiration to thousands of men who might otherwise have abandoned all hope.

His efforts belied his nickname which he bore through life and by which he was universally known. It naturally had nothing to do with the deportment of this energetic man. In fact it arose through one of the more bathetic puns ever to have inflicted a sobriquet on an individual. In youth, his surname apparently gave rise to thoughts of a certain brand of tyre in the minds of his fellows. Tyre, in its turn, metamorphosed into tired . . . and thus the most inappropriate of nicknames was born — and stuck fast.

Ernest Edward Dunlop was the son of a farmer and grew up at Sheepwash Creek, in the northeast corner of Victoria. He was educated at Benalla High school and Victoria College of Pharmacy, Melbourne, before continuing his medical education at Melbourne University and St Bartholomew's Hospital, London.

After house appointments at the Royal Melbourne Hospital and a year at the Royal Children's Hospital, Melbourne, he came to London to the postgraduate medical school at Hammersmith in 1938. In 1939 he was appointed specialist surgeon to the emergency medical services at St Mary's Hospital, Paddington.

Before the war he had been a member of Australia's part-time militia, and when war broke out he took a commission in the Royal Australian Army Medical Corps where he was to spend the next six years, rising to the rank of colonel. In 1941 Dunlop served in Greece, Crete and North Africa. Then, in 1942, he was sent to Java as part of a hastily-organised unit thrown into the Dutch East Indies to try to prevent them from falling into the hands of the Japanese. As the Japanese advanced it was open to Dunlop to be evacuated, but he refused, saying that it was his duty to stay with the wounded in his hospital.

Taken prisoner, he was transported for forced labour in Burma and Siam. There, as leader of the PoWs in a camp on the Burma-Siam border, for the next three years he became the inspiration and instrument of physical and spiritual survival to the thousands of captives toiling in atrocious conditions on the railway designed to link the two countries. In the words of a fellow PoW: "When despair and death reached for us, Weary Dunlop stood fast, a lighthouse of sanity in a universe of madness and suffering." Through his bearing in the face of shared privation, and by the ingenuity with which he improvised medical care for them, Dunlop helped his fellow prisoners to endure the unendurable. Finally, on August 16, 1945, gaunt and emaciated as they were, the prisoners learnt that the Japanese had surrendered and that their sufferings were to have an end.

After the war Dunlop stayed in Thailand for some time, playing a major role in helping repatriate PoWs. Then, back in Australia, he continued his medical career and in 1967 he became consultant surgeon to the Royal Melbourne Hospital. He was a particular expert on cancer and his book *Carcinoma of the Oesophagus: Reflections upon Surgical Treatment* was published in 1960. He was also concerned with alcoholism and drug addiction and chaired a number of committees dealing with the problem in his home state as well as being patron of the Australian Foundation on Alcoholism and Drug Dependency.

He was active in the international community, particularly among the developing nations of the Far East. After the Colombo Plan for economic and social development in Asia and the Pacific was established in 1950 he served as its adviser for Thailand and Ceylon, 1956, and for India, 1960–64. He was also instrumental in the launching of the Dunlop/Boon Pong Medical Exchange Foundation between Thailand and Australia, established in 1986 in honour of those who had worked on the Burma-Siam railway. This was one among many contributions he made to the health and welfare of populations across Asia and he was an honorary fellow of a number of national colleges of surgeons throughout the region in recognition of his work.

When Australia committed troops to the Vietnam war in the latter 1960s Dunlop donned uniform again. In 1969 he went to South Vietnam as leader of the Australian surgical team there.

One of his principal interests was the effects of their war experiences on the soldiers he had tended in Burma. He worked hard to better the plight of returning PoWs, many of whom needed support and counselling for long after they had returned home. Among the many state and national organisations through which he carried out this work was the Prime Minister's PoW Relief Fund, of which he was chairman. In 1986 the government of Australia announced that a Melbourne research foundation to study war veterans' needs was to be named after him.

Dunlop was a fine sportsman. He was a university Blue in both boxing and Rugby football and was capped at Rugby for Australia twice against New Zealand, in 1932 and 1934. While working as a surgeon in London he played for the Barbarians in 1939.

In 1986 he published *The War Diaries of Weary Dunlop*. These consisted of notes which he had made in Burma at the time of his captivity and, remarkably, had managed to conceal from the Japanese. They amounted to a unique contemporaneous record of conditions on the railway there.

Appointed OBE for his war work in 1947, he was created CMG in 1965 and knighted for his services to medicine in 1969. He was appointed a Companion of the Order of Australia (AC) in 1987.

Dunlop was a robust individual who seemed to epitomise much that is characteristic of the Australian mentality. He could be relied on as a stalwart "mate" when the going got tough. To the end he remained devoted to the corner of Victoria where he had been born and remained closely involved in the affairs of his state. Throughout his life he was sustained by a simple but strong Christian faith. He never bore a grudge against his captors for the suffering they had inflicted.

Dunlop married, in 1945, Helen Ferguson. She died in 1990 and their two sons survive him.

b 12.7.07   d 2.7.93   aged 85

At the Hellfire Pass dedication service 1987

LORD ELWORTHY

Marshal of the Royal Air Force Lord Elworthy, KG, GCB, CBE, DSO, LVO, DFC, AFC, Chief of Defence Staff.

AT THE point at which he took over command of the RAF in 1963, the career of Charles Elworthy had been one of almost unalloyed brilliance. He was commanding a bomber squadron in 1940 within four years of being granted a permanent commission. In a single year of operations he won three medals, the DSO, DFC and AFC. In the early postwar period he established himself as one of the persuasive influences on the development of bomber tactics. As Commander-in-Chief in the Middle East for three years from 1960 he enabled Britain to be a stabilising force in a highly volatile region – and in 1961 foiled an

Iraqi attempt to seize Kuwait. A lawyer by education, he combined in abundant measure intellectual capacity with an ability to sway the minds of his fellow men and bend them to his opinion.

Many thus felt it sad that, when he reached the top of his service, it was largely as the instrument of a government policy of swingeing defence cuts which hit the RAF particularly badly. When he became Chief of Defence Staff four years later it was, as he himself said, virtually to discharge the duties of an undertaker on all three forces. He felt these humiliations keenly. His senior colleagues found it ironic that the RAF should have to suffer so badly under one of its youngest and most able commanders. Some looked for his resignation as a point of honour – as they did those of the other service chiefs. Elworthy felt he ought to stay in place, if only to try to minimise damage through repeated warnings of the consequences of defence cuts. It was not his fault that those warnings were totally ignored.

Sam Elworthy, as he was known throughout his service career, was born in New Zealand, the son of a wealthy farmer. He was sent to Britain to be educated at Marlborough and Trinity College, Cambridge. There he read law and was a keen oarsman, rowing for the First Trinity Boat Club and twice reaching the semi-final of the Ladies Plate at Henley Regatta. At Cambridge he learnt to fly and subsequently joined 600 (City of London) Squadron, Auxiliary Air Force, a bomber unit.

He graduated in law in 1933 and was called to the Bar in 1935. But after less than a year at Lincoln's Inn, he joined the RAF and was given a permanent commission. After a year with No 15 Squadron he was appointed personal assistant to the AOC-in-C Bomber Command. For one so junior this was an acknowledgement of the powers of analysis and organisation that were later to take him to the top.

Soon after the outbreak of war, he was sent to an operational training unit to prepare young bomber pilots and navigators for operational flying. Although important, this job did not recommend itself to a man who was itching to get to grips with the enemy. Elworthy restlessly agitated for a transfer to an operational unit and in December 1940 was given command of No 82 Squadron, equipped with Blenheims. To a man less totally dedicated this might have seemed something of a poisoned chalice. The Blenheim, wretchedly inadequate for its task, with a maximum bomb load of 1,000lb, was a poor cousin of the vastly superior Wellington. Indeed No 82 had been so savaged during the Battle of France that it had been deemed no longer to exist after one raid in which it had lost 11 out of 12 aircraft. Only the vigorous exertions of its then leader, Wing Commander the Earl of Bandon,

had saved it from extinction as a fighting unit.

Now, based in Norfolk, it had the thankless task of trying to inflict damage on Axis shipping and on targets in occupied territories. Elworthy rose above the technical shortcomings of his equipment and through sheer force of personality and flying skills welded it into a remarkably effective force. By the end of the year he had not only managed to avoid getting killed – a considerably more than 50-50 chance for a bomber squadron commander over 12 months of operations in those days – but he had been awarded the AFC, DFC and DSO.

Rested from operations, he next had staff appointments at No 2 Group and at Bomber Command headquarters where his experience and success as a squadron commander were useful in the planning of future bomber tactics. For a year from the spring of 1942 he commanded RAF Waddington, Lincolnshire, before being transferred back to Bomber Command HQ and then to No 5 Group where he ended the war as senior staff officer. His reputation as both operational commander and staff officer was, by then, a matter of discussion in the senior echelons of the RAF.

From 1945 to 1947 he commanded the Central Bomber Establishment and led its first overseas liaison mission to the Far East, Australia and New Zealand. His appointment as CBE in 1946 recognised his contribution to the development of bomber tactics and the testing of new equipment.

Among subsequent postings were secondments to the new Indian and Pakistani air forces and in 1953 he was selected to command the RAF station Odiham where the Queen's Coronation Review was held in June of that year. The success of this RAF occasion earned him appointment as MVO (fourth class) subsequently translated to LVO. From command of the RAF Staff College, Bracknell, he became Deputy Chief of the Air Staff in 1959. But in the following year this appointment was cut short when he was sent to Aden as Commander-in-

Chief Middle East. It was a testing time. The region was politically unstable and trouble was never far below the surface. The increasing tempo of Arab nationalism was beginning to concentrate its attentions on the British presence in Aden.

Among Britain's tasks were protection of her oil interests, defence of the nascent Federation of Sheikhdoms against Yemen and support for the Sultan of Muscat and Oman against rebellious elements. But the most pressing danger was the long-standing claim on Kuwait by President Kassim of Iraq.

As soon as he arrived in Aden, Elworthy moved fast to complete a reorganisation of the Aden headquarters to enable the command to be reinforced by balanced forces in strength and at speed. Training was pressed forward relentlessly in temperatures which often reached 125F (46C). Within six months the new headquarters had become a symbol of Britain's will and capacity to intervene anywhere in the Middle East in defence of her own or her allies' interests.

This contingency planning was not completed a moment too soon. On June 25, 1961, Kassim suddenly and vociferously renewed his claim that Kuwait was part of Iraq. Soon afterwards British intelligence reported that a large Iraqi armoured force was massing close to the Kuwaiti frontier. The British government immediately ordered Elworthy to reinforce Kuwait. Commandos from the aircraft carrier *Bulwark*, en route from the Far East, were ashore by July 1. In a few hours they had secured the airport, allowing a squadron of Hunter jet fighters to be flown in. More commandos were brought in from Aden while elements of the Coldstream Guards arrived from Bahrain. Two troops of Centurion tanks were disembarked from the landing ship *Striker*. Thus by nightfall small but effective infantry forces with armour and air support were in position to counter an Iraqi threat. Over the following days more armour and infantry with the most modern anti-tank missiles arrived to build the defenders up to a full-strength brigade. Faced with this armed resolve, the Iraqi tanks stayed where they were. It was a lesson in deterrence, which stands in marked contrast to the indecision which necessitated the dispatch of a huge and costly multinational expeditionary force to perform the same task in 1991.

In September 1963 Elworthy returned to the United Kingdom to become Chief of the Air Staff. He brought to the Air Ministry a wealth of experience and a fund of good will. Outwardly the RAF appeared to be a happy and efficient service with a great future ahead of it. But the new Chief of Air Staff was destined to preside over some of the heaviest cuts ever administered to the services. After an unhappy four years the situation had not in any way changed when, in August 1967, he became Chief of Defence Staff.

Many of his greatest admirers regretted that such a brilliant career in the RAF should have ended coincidentally with the introduction of a redundancy scheme for the services which became operative almost on the day he handed over as Chief of the Air Staff. Many officers and men left the service disappointed and disillusioned.

Nevertheless, Sam Elworthy will be remembered for his many personal qualities. His unhappy time at the top of his profession does not detract from his qualities as a strategic thinker of the highest calibre and as a leader able to translate theory into concrete activity.

From 1971 to 1978 he was Constable and Governor of Windsor Castle and from 1973 to 1978 Lord Lieutenant of Greater London. In 1972 he was made a life peer. He retired to live in New Zealand in 1978.

He married, in 1936, Audrey Hutchinson, who died in 1986. They had three sons and one daughter.

b 23.3.11   d 4.4.93   aged 82

RICHARD BURTON, VC

Richard Henry Burton, VC, former Army private.

RICHARD BURTON was company runner in the 1st Battalion the Duke of Wellington's Regiment in Italy in October 1944 when he won his VC. The battalion was then part of 1st Division, which had the task of breaking through the Northern Apennines towards Imola in the Po Valley. The route was barred by the experienced 71st German Division, holding the 2,000 ft Monte Ceco.

The six-day battle for the mountain was fought in pouring rain. Three attacks by other battalions failed to clear the summit. The Duke's made the fourth attempt during the early afternoon of October 8 when the Germans seemed least alert. They stormed the crest in a silent attack using only their own weapons and, despite heavy casualties including the death of their CO, they seized and held the feature largely through the extraordinary bravery of Burton. His citation ran:

"The assaulting troops made good progress to within 20 yards of the crest, when they came under withering fire from Spandaus on the crest . . . Private Burton rushed forward and, engaging the first Spandau with his tommy gun, killed the crew of three. When the assault was again held up by murderous fire from two more machineguns, Private Burton, again showing complete disregard for his own safety, dashed toward the first gun, using his tommy gun until his ammunition was exhausted. He then picked up a Bren gun and, firing from the hip, killed or wounded the crews of the two machineguns. Thanks to his outstanding courage, the company was then able to consolidate the forward slope of the feature.

"The enemy immediately counterattacked, but Private Burton, in spite of most of his comrades being either dead or wounded, once again dashed forward and directed such accurate fire with his Bren gun that the enemy retired, leaving the feature firmly in our hands. The enemy later counter-attacked again on the adjoining platoon position and Private Burton, who had placed himself on the flank, brought such accurate fire to bear that this counter-attack also failed.

"Private Burton's magnificent gallantry and total disregard for his own safety in many hours of fierce fighting in mud and continuous rain were an inspiration to all his comrades."

Burton's VC was the 124th of the war and the 44th won by the Army.

Richard Henry Burton was born in the small market town of Melton Mowbray. Leaving the town's Boys Modern School in 1938 at the age of 15, he started an apprenticeship in the building and construction industry. He was 6ft 3ins tall, powerfully built and a bricklayer like his father and grandfather.

Early in 1942 he joined the Northamptonshire Regiment, but was transferred to the Duke of Wellington's and sailed with them to French North Africa in the spring of 1943, taking part in the battles for Tunis and the invasion of Pantellaria in 1943, and the Anzio landings and the advance northwards through Italy to Monte Ceco in 1944.

He is survived by his wife, their daughter and two of their three sons.

b 29.1.23   d 11.7.93   aged 70

MAJOR-GENERAL J. D. FROST

Making the film A Bridge Too Far *with Anthony Hopkins*

Major-General J. D. Frost, CB, DSO and Bar, MC, the commander of the 2nd Parachute Battalion, who held the bridge at Arnhem.

"JOHNNIE" FROST carved his name in the annals of Anglo-American military history by reaching and holding the bridge at Arnhem until his ammunition ran out in September 1944, although surrounded by SS Panzers. His name was later illuminated by Cornelius Ryan's book and Richard Attenborough's film, *A Bridge Too Far* in which he was portrayed by Anthony Hopkins. Frost's epic fight at Arnhem, where his sterling qualities were tested to the full, was but the climax of his wartime service with the 2nd Parachute Battalion. He was a founder member of "2 Para", and his indomitable leadership as adjutant, company commander and then commanding officer, established its fighting traditions, which were so evident 40 years later in the battle for Goose Green during the Falklands war.

John Dutton Frost was born in Poona, the son of Brigadier F. D. Frost. He was educated at Wellington College, Monkton Combe School and Sandhurst before being commissioned into the Cameronians (The Scottish Rifles) in 1932. His early service was in Palestine, and in 1938 he was seconded to the Iraq Levies with whom he served until 1941. Feeling that the war was passing him by, he engineered his return to England. Before he left Iraq he was presented with a hunting horn by the Royal Exodus Hunt of which he had been master. That horn was to be heard at critical phases of his future battles as he rallied his men. Once home, he volunteered for the Special Air Service and was posted as Adjutant of the 2nd Parachute Battalion, which was just forming. Completing five instead of the recognised seven jumps in three days, he was given his wings and command of C Company.

Frost's first task as a paratroop commander was to lead the raid on the German radar station at Bruneval on the French coast 12 miles east of Le Havre on the night of February 27/28, 1942. British scientists needed the cacinotron from the heart of one of the latest

German radars in order to devise counter-measures. Frost's C Company was to drop on Bruneval and protect the radar specialist, Flight Sergeant E. W. F. Cox, and his Sapper team while they dismantled the radar and carried it back to waiting Royal Naval landing craft.

The Bruneval raid was one of the few entirely successful second world war parachute operations, thanks to Frost's meticulous planning, training and inspiring leadership. His hunting horn was heard, for the first time in battle, as the Bruneval garrison was over-run and captured or killed while the radar was being dismantled. His force escaped in the nick of time with the precious cacinotron stowed safely on board the landing craft as German tanks reached the cliffs above the beach. The MC was his reward.

When the battalion sailed for the Allied invasion of French North Africa in November that year as part of the 1st Parachute Brigade of the 1st Airborne Division, the commanding officer fell ill and Frost was promoted to command. In the chaos of the initial race for Tunis, which the Allies lost, Frost's battalion was dropped near Pont Du Fahs with the task of destroying Axis aircraft on its airfield and on Depienne and Oudna as well, the last being only 15 miles due south of Tunis where Axis forces were landing in strength. He was then to link up with British forces advancing on the city from the west.

Frost was faced almost at once with a double disaster: there were no aircraft to destroy on the airfields, and the British advance was checked at Medjez el Bab, 30 miles west of Oudna. Frost had to fight his way to them while the Germans made repeated attempts to encircle and destroy his battalion. By sheer dogged determination and tactical skill, he succeeded in a three-day running battle, but it cost the battalion almost half its fighting strength. Frost was understandably bitter about the waste of his battalion on this ill-conceived mission. It was little consolation to be told that his wild-goose chase had diverted considerable German strength at a critical juncture in the first Allied attempt to take Tunis.

In the subsequent fighting in Tunisia, the battalion took part in the fighting around Djebel Mansour in February, and in checking the German *Ochsenkopf* offensive through Sedjennane along the north coast in March, Frost's battalion repelled three successive attacks at Tamera by the German paratroopers of Battle Group Witzig: the first quite easily, the second with difficulty and the third after a desperate struggle in which they narrowly missed capturing the much decorated Colonel Witzig. In the fighting to re-take Sedjennane, Frost, sounding his hunting horn, led the decisive bayonet charge which obliterated the remnants of the Witzig Group. He received his first DSO for his battalion's part in the Tunisian Campaign.

During the early phases of the invasion of Sicily in July 1943, Frost's battalion was dropped by night with the rest of 1st Parachute Brigade on the Primasole bridge just north of Syracuse. Frost's task was to hold the high ground to the south. Again little went right: many of the American pilots lost their way; the parachute aircraft were shot at by Allied warships as they crossed the coast; and less than a fifth of the brigade landed anywhere near the bridge. By dawn Frost had as few as a hundred men to fend off counter-attacks by paratroopers of the Schmalz Group. The battle lasted until the 8th Army's advance guard reached the bridge as dusk fell that evening.

Many plans were made for using 1st Airborne Division in France and Belgium during the summer of 1944, but nothing came of any of them until the Arnhem operation, which began on September 17.

The plan, code-named Market Garden, was to take advantage of the chaotic and headlong German retreat in the west by concentrating the Allied attack in a narrow surprise thrust to capture the Ruhr and race on east to Berlin before the Russians. Montgomery, the operation's principal architect and advocate, planned to drop a "carpet of airborne forces" behind the German lines along a 60-mile corridor from the Belgian border to Arnhem on the far side of the Rhine. The paratroopers were to seize and hold five vital bridges across rivers and canals over which the ground forces of the British Second Army would sweep into Germany.

Frost's 2nd Parachute Battalion was given the task of advancing as rapidly as possible along the north bank of the Lower Rhine to capture and hold the railway and road bridges in Arnhem some eight miles away from its dropping zone. There were said to be only lightly armed training and reserve units in the area. So confident was Frost of success that he ordered his batman to load his golf clubs and shot gun in his follow-up baggage.

Again little went right: the 9th and 10th SS Panzer Divisions were refitting in the area, and, although taken by surprise, were soon opposing the British advance into Arnhem. Opposition grew in intensity and the Germans succeeded in blowing the railway bridge just as Frost's men were approaching it. It then took until dusk for the battalion to fight its way to the northern end of the road bridge, but all attempts to cross it were driven back. For the next three nights and two days Frost held the buildings around the north end of the bridge against a succession of determined German tanks and infantry attacks while the rest of the division tried to reach him. During the third night he was badly wounded by a mortar bomb. Soon afterwards, the Germans managed to set on fire the upper floors of the building in the cellars of which the severely wounded were being sheltered. Fearing that they would be engulfed in the flames, he finally agreed to surrender. The Bar to his DSO recognised his and his men's stoical endurance; and the Dutch later named the re-built bridge after him.

In the years after the battle Frost maintained that, despite the outcome and the shortcomings in the planning of the operation, the effort at Arnhem had been worthwhile, saying that if it had been successful it would have ended the war in 1944.

After the war Frost's career was unexceptional; commanding the re-formed 2nd Parachute Battalion in Palestine in 1946; student at the Staff College in 1947; staff officer in Lowland District, 1948–49, at the Senior Officers School, 1949–52, and in 17th Gurkha Division's Headquarters in Malaya during the anti-terrorist campaign, 1952–55; Commandant of Netheravon, 1955–57; commander of the 44th Parachute Brigade (TA), 1958–61 and of Lowland District, 1961–64; and finally General Officer Commanding British Troops, Malta and Libya, 1964–66.

In 1984, 40 years after the Arnhem battle, Frost returned to the re-built bridge across the Rhine which now bears his name to meet his German adversary in the battle, Brigadier-General Heinz Harmel, the commander of the 10th Waffen-SS Panzer Division. Without bitterness, the two old soldiers shook hands under the bridge and chatted about their experiences.

Johnnie Frost will be remembered as a great leader of parachute troops, who had deep reserves of courage and willpower. He inspired his officers and men, who had implicit faith in his personal integrity and confidence in his military judgement. He was surprisingly modest and discreet for a man with his strength of character; indeed, he was quite shy. Like all true Scots, he liked his "Wee Dram", and as he grew older tended towards irascibility. He crossed swords with his colleagues of the Diplomatic Service in the Mediterranean, which was perhaps why he was not given further military employment. He retired in 1967 and became a successful farmer in Hampshire.

In his retirement he wrote three books: *A Drop Too Many* about Arnhem; *Two Para – Falklands*, recounting his old battalion's feats in the South Atlantic Campaign of 1982; and *Nearly There*, his own autobiography.

He married Jean MacGregor Lyle in 1947. They had a son and a daughter. His family survive him.

b 31.12.12   d 21.5.93   aged 80

VICE-ADMIRAL SIR PETER GRETTON

Vice-Admiral Sir Peter Gretton, KCB, DSO and two Bars, OBE, DSC, was a leading wartime convoy escort commander who subsequently rose to become a Lord Commissioner of the Admiralty, Deputy Chief of Naval Staff and Fifth Sea Lord, 1962–1963. In retirement he was domestic bursar, University College, Oxford, 1965–71, and senior research fellow, 1971–79.

ALONG with his great contemporary, Captain F. J. Walker (who died tragically of a heart attack in 1944) Peter Gretton is one of the imperishable names among the dedicated band of convoy escort commanders who defeated the U-boat packs and won the Battle of the Atlantic in the second world war. It was Gretton who, as commander of B7 escort group, conducted the critical seven-day battle around the outward convoy ONS5 in April–May 1943 when it was beset by four enemy groups, totalling some 50 U-boats, between Iceland and Greenland. The weather was atrocious; icebergs and pack ice were a constant hazard; storm succeeded storm as the convoy groped its way eastwards into the dreaded Greenland "air gap", where no air cover could be expected. Visibility was down to almost zero, making it extremely difficult for the escort group to find the merchantmen.

In these less than ideal conditions for submarine operations Admiral Doenitz had managed to position over 30 of his U-boats right in the path of the convoy while another dozen lay in wait further ahead. A slaughter, harking back to the dark days of the ill-starred Arctic convoy PQ17 the summer before, might well have been in prospect, but for B7. Gretton's group, which comprised two destroyers, one frigate, four corvettes and two rescue trawlers was, thanks to his rigorous training, one of the best prepared in the Atlantic. As the enemy closed in, 13 of ONS5's 390 merchant ships were sunk, but this was only achieved at a cost in U-boat casualties that Doenitz could not sustain. Attack and counter-attack followed in relentless succession and though shortage of fuel caused Gretton's own ship, HMS *Duncan*, to leave the battle at its height, his lieutenants continued to execute his painstaking game-plan of search and destroy with deadly effect.

With the help of two other groups sent out from St John's, Newfoundland, eight U-boats were sunk and many others seriously damaged. During the passage of the next eastward convoy escorted by Gretton's group none of the 38 merchant ships was lost and five U-boats were sunk. On May 22 Doenitz finally called off the campaign, having suffered the loss of 31 U-boats since the beginning of the month. The crisis had been surmounted and the U-boats were never again to threaten Britain's vital supply lines. That this was so was due to men like Gretton, their understanding and acceptance of centimetric radar and co-operation with aircraft (not a common thing in the hidebound service that the Royal Navy was at that time) and the quantum leap in standards of training which Gretton's group had achieved since the grim days of 1941 and 1942. Gretton was a tough – even ruthless – commander, who did not hesitate to replace those subordinates who did not measure up to his own standards. But he also early understood – as so many did not – that even courage and endurance were no substitute for the intelligent use of modern technology.

Peter William Gretton was educated at the Dartmouth and Greenwich Royal Naval colleges. In the examinations for the rank of lieutenant he gained first-class certificates in all five subjects. However, most unusually at a time when specialisation was regarded as the golden road to promotion, he chose to remain a "salt horse" – i.e. non-specialist seaman – officer.

In the years leading up to the outbreak of war his career was a mixture of the colourful and – for him – the tedious. He had exciting moments during the Arab rebellion in Palestine in 1936 when he led a mixed party of sailors and stokers ashore at Haifa to help the police keep order in the *souk* there. This earned him the DSC. But a less exciting appointment followed, that of sports and seamanship officer of the boys' training establishment

at Devonport, HMS *Impregnable*. He next had a spell on the training staff at Dartmouth.

His one nod in the direction of specialisation, however, was to be decisive. In the spring of 1939 he took a week's course in anti-submarine warfare at HMS *Osprey* at Portsmouth. Slender though this introduction to the painstaking art of A/S tactics was, it was to stand him in good stead in what followed.

His apprenticeship in convoy work began on the east coast soon after the outbreak of war. In April 1940 he was appointed First Lieutenant of Captain Philip Vian's famous destroyer *Cossack*. In this ship he took part in the second battle of Narvik when all the survivors of the ten large German destroyers which had reached the port in the first invasion moves against Norway were sunk by the battleship *Warspite* and her destroyer escort. Gretton was mentioned in dispatches for his part in the action.

Early in 1941 Gretton got his first command – the destroyer *Sabre* – and from then until 1944 he was deeply involved in the Atlantic battle. He also had an active interlude escorting the famous Malta convoy of August 1942. While commanding the destroyer *Wolverine*, he spotted an Italian submarine on the surface recharging its batteries, rammed it and sank it. For this he was was awarded the first of his three DSOs. In the autumn of that year Gretton graduated to command of his own group – just in time to join in the decisive battles in the Atlantic.

Gretton was promoted captain in 1948 at the early age of 36. After various seagoing commands (including command of the naval task group for the Christmas Island atomic bomb tests) and shore appointments, he served as senior naval member of the directing staff at the Imperial Defence College, 1958–60, and was in command of the Sea Training Squadron, based on Portland, in 1960–61. He next joined the Board of Admiralty as Deputy Chief of Naval Staff and Fifth Sea Lord. But the strain of his arduous and prolonged war service had taken its toll of his health and in 1963 he retired from the navy.

After a restful year, 1964, Gretton was appointed domestic bursar of University College, Oxford, where he quickly adapted himself to the academic world and soon became well-known and well-liked. However, his health was still not robust and in 1971 he resigned the bursarship and was elected into a research fellowship at the same college.

Gretton wrote several books including an account of his war service, *Convoy Escort Commander* (1964); a review of British defence problems in the twentieth century, *Maritime Strategy* (1965); and a study of Churchill as First Lord of the Admiralty, *Former Naval Person* (1969). He also wrote in the journal of the Royal United Services Institution.

In particular, as a man who had operated the close escort system at first hand, Gretton deplored what appeared to be a shift of interest in naval staff thinking away from the convoy and towards the theory of "defended lanes". In a letter to *The Times* in July 1981 he reminded the then defence secretary, John Nott, that the abandonment of convoys and the espousal of just such a "defended lane" system by John Jellicoe in the first world war had been within a whisker of bringing Britain to her knees in 1917. Gretton challenged the defence minister to make clear what would be Nato policy for the supply and reinforcement of Britain in the event of another war. This sparked off a lively debate during which it became clear that what had been thought of as a novel idea was, in fact, a harking back to practices which had been totally discredited 64 years ealier.

In 1943 Gretton married Nancy, daughter of James du Vivier of Belgium. She survives him with their three sons and one daughter.

b 27.8.12   d 11.11.92   aged 80

Convoy escort (1939)

MAJOR JOSEF MINSKI

Major Josef Minski, a senior member of Britain's Polish community who fought with Polish units during the struggle for Monte Cassino in 1944.

JOSEF Minski had the unusual distinction of serving in the armies of four different nations in three separate wars. In the last of these, while attached to the British 8th Army in Italy he was credited with the key wireless intercept which enabled the Polish Second Corps to take Monte Cassino Abbey.

Minski was brought up bilingual in

Polish and German and spoke fluent Russian. During the first world war he served with the Austro-Hungarian Army as a lancer in Count Esterhazy's regiment. Shot out of the saddle during a cavalry charge in 1916, he was taken prisoner by the Russians and put in a PoW camp in Moscow.

In 1917, in the turmoil of the Russian Revolution, the camp guards simply walked away one morning and Minski escaped and made his way to the home of family friends in the Moscow Polish community. They obtained fake identity papers for him and a job as a Russian factory worker. He then waited to attempt to reach France where a Polish division was being formed.

In 1918, he was evacuated from the Crimea to France, where he served with the French Army on the Western Front.

Returning to Crakow (by then in Poland) in 1919, he fought with the new Polish Army in the Russo-Polish War. In a cavalry battle in 1920, he was again shot from the saddle. At a field hospital a surgeon gave him only two hours to live. Seventy years later, he would recount with gusto how his anger with the surgeon for dismissing his life so casually gave him the will to survive. The hospital was captured by the Red Army and he spent two more years as a PoW.

Repatriated at the end of the Russo-Polish War, he played a significant role in the establishment of the Polish National Radio Service and by 1939 he was chief engineer for the Lwow station and a reserve captain in an artillery regiment. Ordered to remain at his post with the transmitter, he took no part in the campaign of September 1939 during which Poland was invaded first by Germany from the west and then occupied by the Soviet Union from the east. The military agreed to surrender the city to the Red Army in return for transport to join Polish forces in France. After the surrender the Red Army ignored its agreement and imprisoned all the Lwow defenders; Minski became an internee in the Ukraine.

When the Germans invaded in 1941 Minski and his fellow prisoners were forced to go on the infamous Ukraine Death March in which guards marched the sick and famished Polish prisoners for several hundred miles. Those who fell behind were summarily executed. Minski's shoes eventually fell to pieces and he tore his feet to shreds walking the stony tracks in bare feet. Too ill to continue, he resigned himself to being shot. But two officers from his regiment refused to let him fall out, carrying him on their backs for two days until a railhead was reached.

After a period in hospital in Siberia, he was evacuated to Iraq where he joined the British Army. The Royal Signals were anxious to recruit bilingual German speakers to man interception units and he was given a commission.

His unit was attached to Polish II Corps, led by General Anders, and landed in Italy in 1944. The Polish ability to translate German tactical-level radio intercepts instantaneously provided a great improvement in Eighth Army intelligence. During the last stages of the battle for Monte Cassino one of Minski's intercepts established that a redeployment of the German para-troopers was to be preceded by a sneak single bomber raid against Cassino town. This gave Anders the critical timing for the final assault.

Minski commanded his unit until the end of the war. Based in southern Italy, it had the task of intercepting Russian radio codes as the Red Army advanced across eastern Europe.

Settling after the war in Britain where he was well known in the sound-recording industry, Josef Minski, like many expatriate Poles, lost touch with his family in Poland for many years, though he was able to make contact with his wife and children in later years. He visited his family in Poland, but by this time his children were adults and he preferred to remain in England.

b 1896   d 27.12.92   aged 96

GENERAL MATTHEW B. RIDGWAY

*General Matthew B. Ridgway, DSC,
DSM, commander of the US 82nd
Division during the second world war and
United Nations supreme commander in
Korea, 1951–52.*

MATTHEW B. RIDGWAY was an
adventurous and resourceful soldier who
pioneered the US Army's use of airborne
troops in the second world war. He later
went on to succeed Douglas MacArthur
as head of the United Nations forces
during the Korean war before reaching
the top of his profession as US Army
chief of staff. In all he did he had that
capacity to inspire his men with a
relentless desire to be at grips with the
enemy. From 1943 onwards he sought to
convince a sceptical US high command
that parachute operations could be the
key to unlocking enemy positions, and by
his personal example – he jumped with

his men on D-Day – he carried his point beyond argument.

He was, perhaps, continually involved in more fierce fighting during the war than any other Allied general. Sicily, Salerno, Normandy, the Ardennes counter-offensive and the crossing of the Siegfried Line all felt his hand, and, as in the Ardennes, he was frequently called in to restore situations in which things were not going well.

When he went to Korea, first as commander of the US 8th Army, it was in a similarly fraught situation. After a retreat conducted in bitter weather, morale amongst the men was low and the situation was worsened by the fact that many of them had lost faith in commanders who, they sensed, were not interested in sharing their hardships. Ridgway got his subordinate commanders out of their jeeps and onto their feet. "Get off your fat asses and get climbing hills" were his unambiguous instructions to one- and two-star generals who had forgotten what marching was, and had hoped to keep matters thus. Very soon the new commander had converted a dispirited rabble into an aggressively minded and tactically canny force.

His colourful personality endeared him not only to his own men but to the British, Canadian and Australian troops who came under his aegis after he replaced MacArthur as UN supreme commander. Patton had had his pearl-handled revolvers; Montgomery his assorted headgear; Wingate his beard and battered pith helmet. But Ridgway, who never went anywhere without one, or sometimes two, primed grenades attached to his chest, surely outdid them all. The ear-splitting siren which he had fitted to his jeep made sure that his arrival in the lines was never unannounced. And there were few of his men whose spirits did not acquire new mettle when "old iron tits" (as he was known from his grenade-adorned person) was near.

Matthew Bunker Ridgway, son of Colonel Thomas Ridgway, was born at Fort Monroe, Virginia. From the beginning he led an army life at the various posts where his father was stationed. After attending the English High School in Boston, he entered West Point, and in 1917 was commissioned into the infantry.

He served first with the 3rd Infantry in Texas, was an instructor at West Point and after a course at the Infantry School went overseas to command a company in China. After further overseas service in Panama and the Philippines, he went in 1933 to the command and general staff school. He then did a number of staff jobs until, in 1939, he was appointed to the general staff in Washington where he worked with the war plans division until 1942.

In March 1942 Ridgway became assistant divisional commander of the 82nd Division, and soon after took command. It became an airborne division in August 1942, and so began his close association with airborne operations, of which he became the US Army's leading exponent. Ridgway planned and led the airborne invasion of Sicily in July 1943. Here he displayed the front-line leadership for which he became renowned. He fought his way with his own advance guard to Trapani in the west of the island and subsequently took his troops into mainland Italy at Salerno.

In spite of mistakes in Sicily, Ridgway's belief in airborne forces was vindicated when on D-Day in June 1944 he jumped with his division in the assault on the Cotentin peninsula. He was next appointed to command the 18th Airborne Corps. As such he was involved in the Allied invasion of The Netherlands where fighting was still in progress when, on December 18, 1944, news came of the German breakthrough in the Ardennes. Ridgway's corps was immediately dispatched into the area and became involved in some of the heaviest fighting of the Northwest Europe campaign. In March 1945 he again distinguished himself, at the Rhine crossing where his corps broke through decisively in the Wesel area. He led it until it effected its junction with Soviet troops on the Baltic in May 1945.

In August 1945 Ridgway returned to the US and from October commanded in the Mediterranean until January 1946 when he went to be Eisenhower's representative on the military staff committee of the UN. Here he helped to produce the report which was a first step towards establishing an international police force. During this time he was also chairman of the Inter-American Defence Board, and then, after being C-in-C Caribbean Command in 1948–49 and deputy chief of staff in 1949–50, he once more embarked on active service.

In December 1950 Ridgway was appointed commander of the 8th Army in Korea. He took over at a time when it was defending roughly the line of the 38th parallel, and was virtually in command of all operations under MacArthur's direction. There followed a difficult period. The communist offensive at the beginning of 1951 caused UN troops to withdraw and Seoul was evacuated for the second time. But in a war such as this one Ridgway was simply not interested in ground won or lost. His aim was to inflict as many casualties as possible on the enemy and he was able to convince his men that the Chinese superiority lay only in their numbers. "All we've got to do is kill more of their guys than they do of ours. It's as simple as that. And we're going to win this war – that's for sure." It was an attitude which took the 8th Army back across the 38th parallel.

In April 1951 Ridgway replaced MacArthur as C-in-C UN Command, and in June began the negotiations which eventually led to the armistice. In these he displayed qualities which appeared to be antithetical to his character of battlefield fire-eater. As a negotiator he surprised many by his political wisdom and his far-sightedness. But in truth these qualities were merely a part of his view of the function of war-like operations as the hard-headed instrument of foreign policy goals. He was not a man to sacrifice life needlessly for aims which yielded diminishing returns.

Ridgway still had his two most responsible posts in front of him. In May 1952 he took over from Eisenhower as Supreme Allied Commander (SACEUR) in Europe. He held the post for only a year, but during this time held out resolutely for the strengthening of Nato's forces and refused to accept that nuclear weapons did away with the need for powerful conventional armies.

In July 1953 he handed over to General Gruenther, and returned to Washington to become Army chief of staff. In this, his last military post, Ridgway did not always see eye to eye either with the new doctrine of massive retaliation or with some of his military and political colleagues. But his restraining influence during the war in Indochina and the offshore island crisis made an indispensable contribution to the prevention of general war. In 1955 he retired from the Army, and from then until 1960 was chairman of the Mellon Institution of Industrial Research.

In his book, *The Korean War*, published in the 1960s when the Vietnam war was beginning to absorb America's military energies, Ridgway made comparisons with the two conflicts and expressed reservations – later to be more widely shared in the US military – about such a squandering of resources.

Three times married, Ridgway is survived by his third wife Mary and by two daughters of his first marriage.

b 3.3.95   d 26.7.93   aged 98

DAVID SHANNON

David Shannon, DSO, DFC, who flew on the celebrated Dambuster raid of May 1943.

A YOUTHFUL figure who could have passed as a 16 year-old, Flight-Lieutenant David Shannon was already a veteran bomber pilot by the time Guy Gibson chose him to join the newly-formed 617 squadron in the spring of 1943. Gibson himself did not know at that stage what the target for the special unit was to be. Secrecy surrounding the raid and its objectives was among the best of the war. Not until she saw his picture in the paper after it was all over, did Gibson's own wife know what he had been up to, and that two of the great Ruhr dams had been destroyed by a lone squadron in a single night. He had told her he was "resting" in a training squadron, after a hectic period on operations.

Shannon had already served with Gibson, who knew a lot about this 20-year-old Australian's superb qualities as a pilot. These were put to the proof during the raid itself when Shannon's was the first Lancaster to attack the second and largest of the Ruhr dams, the Eder, after the Möhne had already been breached.

This was the most difficult of the squadron's objectives. The Eder dam lay in a fold of hills which meant that the approach over water at 60ft was only possible after the steepest and most hair-raising of dives. To add to the hazard, a thick fog rolled over the surface of the lake. It was a test not only of skill but of heart. Five times Shannon attempted to claw his way down to the lake only to find himself flying too fast and too high at the crucial moment when the "bouncing bomb" devised by Dr Barnes Wallis should have been released, at a precise speed and height.

Shannon circled again to take stock of the situation while Maudslay, another of 617's pilots, had a go. He dropped his bomb but failed to get out of the valley afterwards and crashed into the hillside, killing himself and his crew. Steeling himself again, Shannon made a sixth and then a seventh approach and this time placed his bomb exactly where it should have been, snug against the dam wall, underwater. Gibson's formation had only one bomb left, carried in the Lancaster flown by Les Knight, another young Australian. After Knight, too, had made two failed attempts Shannon advised him over the radio: "Come in down moon and dive for the point, Les". Taking this cue Knight dropped his bomb perfectly. Suddenly the wall of the dam cracked; 212 million tons of water went racing down the valley at 30ft a second. The pilots, circling above in awed fascination, watched as a car, racing to get clear, was engulfed by the surge.

David Shannon was the son of an Australian farmer and MP. After leaving school he worked in insurance before joining the Royal Australian Air Force in 1941. He then came to Britain where he joined Guy Gibson's 106 squadron as his first operational posting. After flying on 26 raids he won his first DFC.

When Gibson, then expecting a rest from bombing operations after flying 173 missions, was told to form a new squadron at Scampton, Lincolnshire, for "something special", he had no hesitation in taking Shannon with him. In a squadron strong on glamour — which started at the top with the dashing Gibson — Shannon stood out. Tall, slim and elegant, he was a romantic figure. Very soon he added to this image by falling in love with one of the station's prettiest WAAFs, Anne Fowler. But he could be a venomed-tongued leader, ruthless in his chastisement of professional shortcomings among his aircrew.

Weeks of low level training now followed as 617 squadron accustomed themselves to flying at lower level than any squadron had done before. Finally, when, on the evening of May 16, 1943, Anne Fowler noticed that the crews for that day's "night flying programme" were being served with eggs — the tell-tale sign of an "op" — she realised that a raid was on.

Shannon flew with Gibson in the first of three formations which totalled 19 aircraft. Its first aim was to attack the Möhne Dam which it successfully breached, with three of its bombs as yet unexpended. When the codeword "Nigger" — a tribute to Gibson's black labrador which had been killed by a car the night before — had been flashed back to Grantham to signify the success of this first objective, Gibson flew on with Shannon and his remaining crews to attack the Eder. After only two bombs the dam wall broke open and the codeword "Dinghy" told headquarters that the second main objective had been achieved. Gibson and Shannon now turned for home leaving a third dam, the Sorpe, to be damaged by the mobile reserve commanded by 617's big American, Joe McCarthy. It was an astonishing success for such a small force. But the price was high: 56 men missing out of the 133 who had flown out on that night.

Back on the ground, breakfast for the survivors soon turned into a very alcoholic party which stretched on through lunch, dinner and beyond. At some point Shannon proposed to Anne and was accepted — but only after she had insisted he get rid of the magnificent moustache he had grown to make himself look older.

Shannon was awarded the DSO for his part in the raid. His medal was presented to him by the King on his 21st birthday, the monarch complimenting him on how "well preserved" he was for his age.

Gibson was rested from operations at that point, but for Shannon it was the beginning of a long association with 617, under Gibson's successors: George Holden, "Micky" Martin and finally Leonard Cheshire. Shannon flew on 617's toughest assignments — and most of them were very tough.

"Bomber" Harris had decided to use 617 as a "sniper" squadron, tackling low-level assignments other squadrons would have found impossible. Among these were the costly sorties to try to breach the strategically important Dortmund-Ems canal. From one of these raids only three out of eight aircraft returned.

When Leonard Cheshire took over 617 and perfected low-level marking techniques, Shannon became one of his most trusted pilots. He took part in the accurate surgical operations against the Gnome-Rhône factory at Limoges and the Juvisy marshalling yards. After D-Day he helped Cheshire mark for the devastating raids on the German E-boat pens. These used another Barnes Wallis invention, the 12,000lb Tallboy "earthquake" bomb, which created tidal waves in the pens, pulverising the E-boats and eliminating a dangerous threat to Allied shipping supplying the Normandy beachhead.

One operation Shannon was not sorry he could *not* participate in was Cheshire's humanitarian scheme to drop food parcels to PoWs in Stalag Luft III deep inside Germany on Christmas Day 1943. Cheshire's idea was that he, Martin and Shannon should sneak in over the camp, drop the parcels and nip out again over the Baltic before the *flak* defences woke up. Shannon and Martin were even less cheerful about the notion when Cheshire told them that the drop would take place in daylight and that the guns would be taken out of the aircraft to enable them to carry more food parcels. It was a recipe for suicide and Cheshire's two flight commanders hinted as much to their optimistic leader. Luckily for them the plan was utterly vetoed at a higher level. It was thought a certainty that the PoWs would be mown down by German guards as they rushed out to pick up the parcels since their captors would assume it was an arms drop. A crestfallen Cheshire simply could not understand Shannon's gasp of relief when this decision was announced.

Shannon ended his war with two DSOs and two DFCs. Thereafter he had a number of jobs: he worked in oil in Colombia and Kenya and farmed in Suffolk. He had been working on preparations for the 50th anniversary celebrations of the Dambuster raid, in May. He was senior member of the committee of the 617 Squadron Association.

His first wife predeceased him and he is survived by his second wife, Eyke and by a daughter of his first marriage.

b 27.5.22   d 8.4.93   aged 70

Lancaster bomber

HELEN KROGER

Goodbye to all that: the Krogers on their way to Warsaw in 1969

Helen Kroger, the spy who together with her husband Peter transmitted British naval secrets to the Soviet Union, and whose exchange for Gerald Brooke, the British lecturer imprisoned for smuggling anti-Soviet propaganda, caused a political storm in 1969.

TOGETHER with her husband Peter, Helen Kroger was a central figure in the Portland spy case of 1961, and half of one of the most successful partnerships in espionage history. When details of the spy ring emerged, two Admiralty employees, Henry Houghton and Ethel Gee, were found to have leaked naval documents to the Krogers, some concerning Britain's first nuclear submarine, *Dreadnought*. The Russians, lagging far behind in underwater warfare at that time, had decided to concentrate their efforts on the highly secret Underwater Establishment, at Portland, Dorset. They were to make considerable use of the information they received from the Krogers, and progress in developing new anti-submarine weapons was rapid from then on.

Helen and Peter Kroger were sentenced to 20 years each for their part in the spy ring. Their sentences were lighter than that of their colleague and fellow professional spy, Gordon Lonsdale, but

Helen was to serve only eight years of hers. Her release, together with that of her husband, came after that of Lonsdale and before that of the "amateur spies" Houghton and Gee.

Helen Joyce Kroger was born in America where she was known as Lona Petka, the daughter of a Polish immigrant. She became a librarian and later married Kroger, then known as Morris Cohen, a popular teacher with known communist sympathies. Together with her husband, she became part of the New York spy ring which included Ethel and Julius Rosenberg and Colonel Rudolph Abel. Shortly before their colleagues' arrests, the Cohens disappeared and were listed as missing persons by the FBI.

They covered their tracks with a series of forged passports through Canada, Austria, New Zealand and Japan, were re-briefed by the KGB and eventually resettled at 45 Cranley Drive, Ruislip, Middlesex, where they posed as New Zealanders. That they managed to pull off this absurdity says something for the parochial innocence of Ruislip in the fifties. Both had heavy Bronx accents. "It would have been a shame to waste them after all those years of training", explained an ex-KGB man, 20 years later, "especially as they were such excellent agents."

Helen Kroger and her husband settled into suburbia posing as antiquarian booksellers. Helen cut an exotic figure with her loud, boisterous manner and her habit of wearing trousers. With no children herself, and having come from a family of ten, she made friends with the local children.

But nothing about the charming Kroger household was as it seemed. After their arrest, a Ronson cigarette lighter was found to hold codes, an Ever Ready battery a KGB expense sheet and a tin of talcum powder was in fact a microdot reader. The radio transmitter used to send information to Russia was not unearthed until 1977 by the new owner, while digging in the garden, but in Helen Kroger's handbag was enough damning evidence to convict her − a film of microdots containing details of operations at Portland's naval research station.

Once in prison, the Krogers set about preparing the way for their release. Though American-born, they applied for Polish citizenship. Mrs Kroger was not too enthusiastic about returning to Poland, but she clearly had little alternative if she wished to be released prematurely. In Holloway, suffering from a nervous condition, she became involved in fights.

Meanwhile the Russians, after the successful exchange of Greville Wynne for Gordon Lonsdale, made approaches to Britain. They offered to exchange the Krogers for Gerald Brooke, a British lecturer imprisoned by the Russians for distributing subversive literature in the USSR. They also started to press claims that the Krogers were Polish (although during and after the trial no attempt had been made by the Polish embassy either to defend them or to gain consular access to them) and threatened to re-indict Brooke on further charges as soon as his five-year sentence had been served.

In 1969 the then foreign secretary, Michael Stewart, announced that a package deal had been agreed in which the Krogers were to be allowed to return to Poland in exchange for Brooke. His announcement provoked considerable criticism: some argued that the Russians would be encouraged to arrest further British tourists arbitrarily; others maintained that the Krogers, after only eight years, retained a definite espionage value for the KGB; while still more considered their release through the use of the Queen's Prerogative "wholly illegal". In 1969, however, in a blaze of publicity, the Krogers left London.

Their reception in Warsaw was a low-key affair and nothing was heard of them for some time, but letters to friends in London revealed the truth. Unable to cope with freedom, the couple put themselves into the hands of a series of medics and sanatoria, suffering from "nervous exhaustion" and a range of minor ailments.

In 1972 they disappeared into Russia, a country neither had seen before, and set up home in a KGB flat in Moscow. Years passed, and many people assumed they had died. But then, in 1991, a *Cutting Edge* documentary film crew, working for Channel 4 flew out to interview them.

Strange Neighbours showed a sprightly, animated 77-year old Helen, in contrast to her rather more listless husband, bearing up cheerfully under the strain of ill health. Both, of course, had endured intense isolation since leaving England. They had not seen their families for 40 years and in place of the usual domestic mementoes, the walls of their bedrom were hung with photographs of the KGB hierarchy. Asked if she felt trapped, Helen said "I feel perfectly free". Even with the communist system she had done so much to bolster crumbling around her, she had no regrets. Her work, she reasoned, had been inspired by peaceful motives: if both sides were equally well-armed, the possibility of another war became more remote. "I felt I was protecting them" she said of her old neighbours in Ruislip.

She is survived by her husband, now aged 82.

d December 92   aged 79

WOLFGANG LOTZ

Wolfgang Lotz, master spy of the Israeli secret service, who operated in Egypt during the 1960s.

WOLFGANG Lotz was a man of great charm with a taste for the good life which earned him the name of "The Champagne Spy" from his paymasters in the Israeli secret service. Married five times, he lived a life of adventure which gained him a reputation as an Israeli James Bond.

His mother was a Jewish actress and his father, a non-Jew, was a theatre director in Berlin and Hamburg. "I inherited a certain degree of acting ability from them

both — a vital asset in my profession later", Lotz wrote in his memoirs. His parents divorced in the early 1930s and his mother, realising there was no future for them in Hitler's Germany, went with her son to Palestine in 1933.

Lotz was sent to study at an agricultural school where he developed his lifelong love of horses, which later provided an important part of his cover as a spy. In 1937 at the age of 16 he joined the Haganah, the underground Jewish army in Palestine, undertaking mounted patrols through hostile Arab areas.

When the second world war broke out he forged the birthdate on his papers and joined the British Army as a volunteer. After commando training he was sent to Egypt where his linguistic skills in English and German (as well as Arabic and Hebrew) were used in behind-the-lines operations and the interrogation of German PoWs.

After the war he engaged in arms smuggling for the Haganah and in 1948 joined the fledgling Israel Defence Forces fighting in the Jerusalem area. By 1956 he was a major with an infantry brigade which fought in the Suez campaign.

Twice-married, and divorced by then, "life was beginning to grow dull when I was approached by the Israeli secret service" he recalled.

In fact it was Israeli military intelligence which had spotted Lotz, who had taken the Hebrew name Ze'ev Gur-Arieh, as a potential agent with just the right Aryan looks and qualifications for a planned insertion into Egypt as an ex-German army officer.

Lotz had dual nationality and so could use his genuine German name and identity papers. His cover story had him living in Germany from birth, serving in Rommel's Afrika Korps during the war and then moving to Australia where he had supposedly made a fortune as a racehorse owner and breeder before returning to Germany.

At the end of 1960, after a year in Germany to strengthen his cover, Lotz travelled to Cairo where his charm and big-spending won him entry into the fashionable Cavalry Club and gained him friends among Egyptian society and senior military officers, especially the club president General Ghorab — who was also head of Egypt's police force.

It was the general himself who suggested that Lotz establish a stud farm in Egypt and Lotz's position was cemented even further when a leading Nazi living in Egypt insisted that he knew the Israeli spy as a former SS officer.

On a return trip to Europe — ostensibly for business but in reality to meet his Israeli controller — Lotz was charged with learning about Egypt's fortifications and military build-up, and with acquiring information on the German scientists and experts in aircraft, rockets and biological warfare who were being recruited by the Egyptians.

Setting off on the Orient Express for a leisurely journey back to Egypt, Lotz met Waltraud, "a tall, extremely pretty blue-eyed blonde with the kind of curvaceous figure I always had a weakness for".

After a whirlwind courtship he married the German girl telling her he was a secret agent but only revealing some time later that he was an Israeli. His wife willingly helped him. Although not Jewish, she had a strong admiration for the Israelis.

But in February 1965, almost five years to the day that he arrived in Cairo, Wolfgang Lotz and his wife were arrested as spies. Egyptian security agents showed them the radio transmitter which they had found in his bathroom scales. Russian radio experts had helped the Egyptians trace the transmissions.

Lotz realised the game was up — almost. But he staunchly maintained that he was a German who had agreed to work for the Israelis only for money. The fact that he was never circumcised helped keep his cover intact, and saved him from being sentenced to death as an Israeli spy.

Lotz was given life imprisonment and hard labour while Waltraud was sentenced to three years in jail. Both were released together with four other captured Israeli agents in 1967 in an exchange deal for thousands of Egyptians taken prisoner in the Six-Day War.

Lotz and his wife, who converted to Judaism, settled in Israel and started a horse farm. But Waltraud was in poor health and died in 1973. Her death and a series of business difficulties affected Lotz badly.

Eventually he tried to settle in Germany, writing books (including a *Guide for Spies*) engaging in business activities, and marrying (and divorcing) twice more.

Wolfgang Lotz is survived by a son from his second marriage.

b 1921   d 14.5.93   aged 72

CAPTAIN ERIC NAVE

Captain Eric Nave, OBE, Australian naval cryptanalyst who specialised in breaking Japanese wartime naval ciphers.

IT IS doubtless one of the more fragrant fictions of the second world war that Churchill dragooned Roosevelt into the conflict by withholding from him British intelligence of the impending Japanese attack on Pearl Harbor.

But it was, understandably, thought intriguing enough to be thoroughly aired in Eric Nave's book (written with James Rusbridger) *Betrayal at Pearl Harbor: How Churchill lured Roosevelt into War*, published in 1991. In the book Nave and Rusbridger promoted Churchill from being merely a co-conspirator with Roosevelt in the catastrophe of Pearl Harbor (the previous "worst case" theory of the affair) to being the "onlie begetter" of the attack on December 7, 1941, which cost the Americans 18 warships, 349 aircraft and 3,581 soldiers, sailors and airmen killed or wounded.

The fact is that Roosevelt fully understood the gravity of the threat he had made to Japan in the summer of 1941 when he instituted an oil and steel embargo against her. It meant war sooner rather than later, as the President — several steps ahead of a still sleepwalking American people — well knew. He needed no help from Churchill. Certainly, a Churchill who could naïvely dispatch the *Prince of Wales* and *Repulse* to Singapore "to exercise that kind of vague menace which capital ships of the highest quality . . . can impose on all hostile naval calculations", only to have them sunk almost immediately by enemy aircraft, seems an unlikely plotter in a conspiracy involving, above all things, a thorough appreciation of the capabilities of Japanese naval air power.

The blame for Pearl Harbor is perhaps more plausibly laid at the door of that species of psychological paralysis which sometimes afflicts military machines even when they are well served — as America was — with intelligence about an obvious threat. Simply, the thing was thought to be impossible. As Admiral Kimmel, commander-in-chief of the US Pacific Fleet put it: "I never thought those little yellow sons of bitches could pull off an attack so far from Japan."

None of this detracts from the interest of Nave's theories, the undoubted truth in much of what he says, or from his truly remarkable achievements as a breaker of Japanese codes before and during the second world war.

Born and brought up in Adelaide, he had spent the early part of his working life, from the age of 16 when he left school, in the accounts department of South Australian Railways.

From this humdrum existence he escaped when an opportunity came to join the Royal Australian Navy. Compelled to learn one foreign language to pass his sub-lieutenant's exams he chose Japanese, a decision that was to have momentous consequences for him.

Far from regarding proficiency in languages in its sea-going officers as a somewhat superfluous qualification — as the Royal Navy has often seemed to do – the RAN allowed Nave to become thoroughly steeped in his chosen subject. He lived for two years in a small Japanese village, acquiring fluency in the language. Thereafter, whenever there was liaison work with Japanese squadrons to be undertaken, Nave was the RAN's natural choice as an interpreter.

Acknowledging its inadequacies in the Japanese department, the Royal Navy asked, in 1925, if it might borrow Nave to help it monitor Japanese naval radio traffic on the Far East station. He made his major break in coming at the key to Japanese codes by quick thinking on the occasion of the death of Emperor Yoshihito in 1926. Comparing the oft-repeated plain language broadcasts of pious sentiment with the coded versions of the same being relayed to embassies and naval headquarters throughout the world, he was able to gain valuable insights into how the ciphers worked. By the following year he was able to supply the Government Code and Cipher School (GCCS) in London with a comprehensive list of Japanese call signs.

He was now brought to London to start work on breaking Japanese naval attaché codes, through wiretaps on embassy and consular telephones. He also set up the Japanese code and cipher section at GCCS, and became its head. But by now the RAN wanted their valuable man back. After a short bureaucratic tussle the Admiralty won and Nave was formally transferred to the Royal Navy in 1930. From then on he worked for GCCS in London and the Far East. As international tension mounted he was posted to Hong Kong where, from June 1939, he was engaged in cracking the newly-introduced code known as Japanese Navy 25 (JN-25).

JN-25 was not a difficult code to break, merely a tedious one, and in the period leading up to the outbreak of war between Britain and the US and Japan the British and the Americans were fully acquainted with the substance of Japanese naval movements. Nave's subsequent claim, in *Betrayal at Pearl Harbor*, was that the British were acquainted with the most minute details of Yamamoto's advance with his aircraft carrier force towards the Hawaiian Islands in the December of 1941. "We knew that the Japanese would hit on a Sunday morning when the Americans would have fat heads after their Saturday night parties," he said. The British government's refusal to allow any of the relevant decoded signals to be made public, makes these claims difficult to assess, while the vexed question of the gulf between possession of intelligence and proper use of it is endlessly begged.

Nave was appointed OBE in 1946 for his services to cryptanalysis. In 1947 he retired from the Royal Navy and returned to Australia where he helped set up the Australian Security and Intelligence Organisation (ASIO). He worked for this for the next 12 years, retiring in 1959 as deputy director. Thereafter he lived quietly but his book brought him into the limelight in old age and he also, in 1991, took part in a BBC2 *Timewatch* programme on the intelligence aspects of Pearl Harbor.

He was a man who retained great clarity of mind into his nineties. Never content merely to live in the past he had an acute sense of the passage and significance of contemporary events. He made his home in Melbourne but liked to spend his winters in the warmer climate of Queensland, where he died.

He was twice married and leaves his widow Margaret and three children.

b 1899   d 23.6.93   aged 94

BRIGADIER
JOHN PACKARD

Brigadier John Packard, Army intelligence officer.

FOR a period of thirty years, in which the strategic threat changed from being Nazi Germany to our former wartime ally the Soviet Union, John Packard was one of the most valuable intelligence assets at the British Army's disposal. Had the cast-iron proof of Germany's military build-up on the Western front in 1940, which he made available, been listened to by Britain's political leadership, the disaster of the Battle of France might have been avoided. But though a string of distinguished visitors to the BEF and the French armies in the spring of 1940 was repeatedly told of the increase in German strength to well over a hundred divisions, neither Parliament nor the British people was informed.

Packard combined great brilliance as a linguist – he was fluent in German, French, Russian, Hindi, Urdu and Pashto – with an unusual ability to sink himself into the background of whatever national community he was operating in. In the 1930s he had been able to mingle unobtrusively with the fanatical enthusiasts who thronged the Nazi rallies. During the "phoney war" he chose to live in a French rather than a British army mess, a fact which led to close liaison and valuable intelligence exchanges between the two allies. Later, in Burma, his knowledge of Indian languages and his sensitivity to tribal politics created, likewise, intelligence of a very high order.

But his military career was not devoted purely to intelligence. He also thirsted for action and saw active service in both Burma and Korea.

John Packard was born in Belfast where his father was serving in the RAMC. When his father was posted to the Rhineland with the British army of occupation in 1921 Packard attended a local *Hauptschule*. There, over the next three years of his father's posting, he became fluent in German.

His own military career began in the ranks of the Middlesex Regiment. But he subsequently went to Sandhurst and was commissioned into the East Yorkshire Regiment. In the early 1930s during periods of service in various parts of India, including the North West Frontier, he acquired Hindi/Urdu as well as Pashto (one of the two principal Afghan languages) and Russian.

By the mid-1930s, however, the Soviet threat to the British Empire via Afghanistan was taking second place in military thinking to the Hitler menace. Packard had already spent six months leave from regimental service in Graz in 1935–36 observing the political climate of that pro-Nazi Austrian city. He was now employed by the War Office to report on Wehrmacht expansion under the Hitler regime.

For three months in 1938 he lived with a German family in Berlin, reporting what he saw to the British assistant military attaché. Not daring to commit anything to paper, he checked every garrison for troop movements, while at the same time attending many Nazi rallies. Later in Heidelberg where he went, ostensibly on a language course, he lodged opposite an SS barracks mingling with the unit's troopers in pavement cafés and learning a good deal from loose talk. With no other cover but that of a British officer on leave, he would not have had a leg to stand on had his real purpose been guessed at by the SS.

In the spring of 1939 he was able to abandon this cloak-and-dagger existence for that of an official observer at Hungarian army manoeuvres on the Czechoslovak border just before Hitler's entry into Prague. When the British Expeditionary Force went to France in 1939 Packard went with it as part of an intelligence team reporting on German army deployments. His standing as an authority on the Wehrmacht was such that he was asked to give daily briefings to the BEF's commander, Lord Gort, at General Headquarters at Arras. Living as he did in a French mess, he was able to bring to these briefings the best of French intelligence, greatly adding to their value since the French Army was in direct contact with the Germans on parts of its front. Alas, notwithstanding the steady stream of British government ministers who also attended these briefings, warnings of a massive German build-up in the west, after the defeat of Poland, went unheeded.

Back in Britain after Dunkirk, Packard led an investigation team which interrogated 200 German PoWs who had been captured during the Battle of France. Subsequently he went to Iceland where he set up and commanded a tactical school. Among his trainees were veterans of the recently lost Norwegian campaign to whom he taught modern infantry tactics and arctic warfare.

After further home service he was posted to Assam where Slim's 14th Army was preparing to sustain the Japanese thrust into India. As GSOI in Assam, Packard's knowledge of Indian languages was invaluable in organising weapon training and raising morale among the local tribesmen. During the desperate struggle for Imphal in the spring of 1944 he flew

several times into the beleaguered town.

But, though he was a fine staff officer, he pined for action and was, by the spring of 1945, allowed to take command of the 1st Battalion East Yorkshires just after the Battle of Meiktila. He commanded it on the advance to Rangoon until the end of the war in the Far East.

After the war he served in staff appointments on the Military Security Board in Berlin and Koblenz, and on the Allied Control Commission for Austria. But with the coming of the 1950s he was back on active service, and saw some brisk fighting in Korea.

His final army appointment was also one of the most delicate he had to undertake. In 1960 he was appointed chief of the British Military Mission to the Soviet commander in Germany, based at Potsdam. Although the mission was accredited to the Soviet forces, its cars were followed by East German Stasi agents wherever they went. This officiousness caused several unpleasant incidents. On one occasion Packard's car and an accompanying vehicle were blocked in, front and rear, by Stasi cars and then attacked by the East German agents with sticks and stones. Packard and his staff were pulled out and roughed up, while their cars were searched. On another occasion an East German border guard shot and wounded one of Packard's staff. Shortly afterwards Packard returned home.

In retirement Packard served from 1961 as head of information of Fison's in Suffolk where he was also active on the local district council. But in 1970, in poor health, he moved to London to a flat in the Barbican. He continued in public life as a Common Councilman of the City of London and was a sidesman at St Giles Cripplegate. He was also a member of the "Cogers" debating society in Fleet Street.

He leaves his widow Faith (who had served in the ATS in the war and been one of its youngest personnel to serve on the General Staff at the War Office) and their four sons and a daughter.

b 14.5.10   d 15.8.93   aged 83

SIR JOHN PRENDERGAST

Sir John Prendergast, KBE, CMG, GM, intelligence officer.

IT WAS hardly surprising – except to those who knew him – that John Prendergast should be written up during his lifetime as "the real life James Bond". He had the looks – he was often likened to Gary Cooper or Cary Grant – and experienced all the excitement and danger that people had come to associate with that of a spy. His career moved hand-in-hand with history, as one after another of Britain's colonies, strove – often violently – for independence, taking him to Palestine, Kenya, Cyprus, Aden and Hong Kong. He spent much of his time undercover in a succession of hot-spots and was awarded the George Medal for his bravery in the campaign against the Mau Mau in pre-independent Kenya.

Although born in Ireland, John Prendergast moved with his family to London when he was still quite young. He took an external degree at London University and began his working life in 1930 with the old Middlesex County Council, rising to the position of assistant clerk. But it was the second world war that was to dictate the direction of his future career. While with the Royal Sussex Regiment in mandated Palestine he was diverted to special duties with MI5 and took part in his first anti-terrorist operations against the Irgun and the Stern Gang, the extremist Zionist factions campaigning to turn Palestine into an independent Jewish state.

After the war he stayed on in Palestine as assistant district commissioner and had the first of many narrow escapes when he was in the King David Hotel, which was then being used as the British Army's headquarters, when it was blown up by the Irgun in July 1946. The following year he joined the Colonial Police, serving first in Palestine then moving on to the Gold Coast where he became a district head of Special Branch in the run-up to the colony's independence as Ghana. In 1952 he was seconded to the Army in the Canal Zone on special duties.

Then in 1953 came his big break when he was posted to Kenya as Director of Intelligence and Security against the Mau Mau. For his part in leading more than 30 patrols into terrorist strongholds in the Aberdare Forest, he received the George Medal. He also received the Colonial Police Medal.

He was then sent, in 1958, to Cyprus as Chief of Intelligence to take on a new enemy – EOKA, the underground organisation fighting for the island's independence and eventual union with Greece. This was the Cyprus of Murder Mile and Ledra Street, with British soldiers and their families being shot in the back in the tense period before the island was declared independent in August 1960. Prendergast was responsible for running Grivas to ground and then – on the instructions of Alan Lennox-Boyd, the Colonial Secretary – allowing him to leave the island rather than having him eliminated.

In the same year, Prendergast was awarded the CBE and posted to Hong Kong as Director of Special Branch. His targets this time were the agents infiltrating the colony from mainland China bent on subversion. He also renewed his links with MI5 for whom the colony provided the ideal "listening post" to monitor activity on the Chinese mainland.

In 1963 he was awarded the Queen's Police Medal. He retired from the Hong Kong police in 1966 with the rank of Deputy Commissioner of Police. But retirement was brief. He was sent as Director of Intelligence to Britain's next overseas trouble spot: Aden.

This time it was back to the dangerous world of the terrorist, trying to separate the various warring factions fighting for independence.

In 1968 he was awarded the CMG and retired, for a second time, to Malta where he and his wife Dolly converted an old farmhouse into a beautiful and comfortable home.

After five years however, following a flying visit by Hong Kong's governor, Sir Murray MacLehose, to their whitewashed farmhouse, Prendergast was persuaded to return to the fray just one more time. On this occasion it was to engage an entirely different kind of enemy: corruption in Hong Kong.

He was made Director of Operations for the newly formed Independent Commission Against Corruption and Deputy Commissioner of Police. What made this assignment particularly difficult for a man who had spent his life in the police was that the corruption took the form of graft within the colony's police force. What made it even more difficult was that graft was such an accepted part of the colony's everyday life that many had come to believe that it could not function without it. His achievement in getting Chief Superintendent Peter Godber back to Hong Kong to stand trial after he had made a suspiciously easy getaway to England, gave the fledgling anti-corruption commission just the boost it needed to convince doubters that it meant business.

In 1977, having seen the Commission become an effective and feared anti-corruption machine, John Prendergast retired again – this time for good – first to Wiltshire, and when the rural life began to pall, to London. He was appointed KBE in 1977.

Prendergast genuinely never understood people's obsession with spies – literary or real. If he had to be likened to any he would have chosen le Carré's Smiley to Fleming's Bond. Though without doubt a man of great courage his reputation was built as much as anything on the less glamorous qualities of integrity, hard work and an ability to get the most out of his staff.

As one might expect from someone in his line of business, he was a reticent man who preferred to let his achievements do the talking.

In London he indulged his love of books (he collected first editions); lunched at his club, the East India, and was constantly on the phone to his bookmaker and stockbroker.

One of his few regrets was that nothing useful could be found for him to do on his final retirement. However, not being one to sit around, he divided his week between acting as a porter at one local hospital, carrying patients' bags, and collecting funds for another.

When this became too much for him he worked three days a week at Heywood Hill, the bookshop in Curzon Street, sending out the bills and earning himself a welcome discount on the books. He also became a director.

He was a practising Roman Catholic, going to mass every Sunday wherever he was in the world. In his youth he had been a keen sportsman showing much talent at golf, tennis and particularly squash.

He was a workaholic, often taking time off at the weekends only to go to mass or to indulge his love of racing.

John Prendergast is survived by his wife, one son and one daughter.

b 15.7.02   d 23.9.93   aged 91

THE DUCHESS OF VALDERANO

The Duchess of Valderano, Duchess of Castel di Spanó and Marquesa de Rio Castel who was involved in the cloak-and-dagger operation during the Cold War.

FOR all her exotic-sounding titles, the Duchess of Valderano came of a thoroughly English background. She was born Honor Mary Langford-Sainsbury, the daughter of Air Vice-Marshal Thomas Audley Langford-Sainsbury, a much decorated first world war airman, and his wife Maude Hamilton Russell Mortimer. She was brought up in Somerset and, partly as a result of having rheumatic fever badly as a child, was educated at home.

She first met her husband – whose titles derive from Italy and Sicily – as a small girl, and encountered him again more seriously at her coming-out party. She and the then Lieutenant Ronald Waring were married shortly afterwards

in 1941. She accompanied her husband on his various domestic postings but when he was sent overseas to liaise with the Italian partisans in northern Italy she remained at Lymington with her two children. During the war she also served as a VAD, specialising in radiography.

Once the war was over she joined her husband in Italy, where what remained of the family estates existed. She spoke fluent Italian, French, Spanish, Portuguese and German, which made her a useful partner in cloak-and-dagger operations (this was the early, tense period of the Cold War). She played a major part in the escape of Count Almasy who had managed to get out of a communist prison in Hungary in 1948 and came through Rome with KGB agents in hot pursuit. This culminated in a 100 mile-an-hour car chase through Rome to Ciampino airport where she and her husband got Almasy onto a plane to

Cairo just as it was about to take off. She was also a first-class shot. One night, crossing the Futa Pass between Bologna and Florence, an attempt was made to hold up the staff car which her husband was driving. A bandit fired a burst from a sub-machine gun which went just over the top of the windscreen. Travelling at about 40mph she fired back instantly and, with a single shot from her pistol, succeeded in knocking the bandit head over heels into a ditch.

On another occasion she took part in the interrogation of a senior Hungarian Communist diplomat. She and her husband had had an old-fashioned wire recording machine flown out from London but had experienced great difficulty in getting it to work. After 24 hours of practising with it – for testing purposes their two children sang "Bandiera Rossa" (which they had been taught by the cook) and she recited "The Owl and the Pussy-Cat" – everything seemed satisfactory. In the interrogation the Hungarian was nervous and jumpy but the microphone had been duly concealed in a vase of flowers and, in some triumph, the wire was sent off via embassy courier to London. Alas, all that came out of it – when the top brass gathered to listen to it – were two piping children's voices singing "The Red Flag" and a woman reciting a poem about a bird and an animal going "to sea in a beautiful pea-green boat". A secret message promptly came through from London asking for the key to the code.

The years went by in Ireland, in Italy, in Spain and in Africa, in which continent she and her husband travelled very extensively. In 1961, 1962, 1964 and 1966 she was in Angola and the Congo with her husband later all over Mozambique and Zimbabwe. For 20 years, her home, however, was in Portugal where the Duke of Valderano, as Ronnie Waring became at the beginning of the 1960s, was an instructor at the Nato war college at Pedrouços, just outside Lisbon. After the Portuguese revolution in 1974 they moved between Rome, London, the United States and Brazil, with her husband again lecturing at various defence colleges and institutes.

The Duchess of Valderano had a great capacity for making friends in whatever country or company she found herself. There was also a marked caring, compassionate side to her, which could be displayed as much to animals as to human beings. More than anyone else, she was responsible for getting the cats which frequent the forum and the other classical ruins of Rome classified as being part of the monumental sites to which they belong and thus being entitled to protection under Italian law. She was appointed a Dame Grand Cross of the Order of St George and a Dame Grand Cross of the Order of St Ignatius of Antioch. She is survived by her husband, the 18th Duke of Valderano, and by a son and a daughter.

b 15.7.19   d 6.7.93   aged 73

SIR DICK WHITE

Sir Dick White, KCMG, KBE, former head of both MI5 and MI6.

DESPITE the secrecy which used to surround Britain's intelligence services, enough became known of Dick White's long and distinguished career for it to be accepted that he was the most notable and influential intelligence official of his time. His reputation stood as high abroad, among allied and overseas intelligence colleagues, as it did at home.

Born in rural Kent, Dick Goldsmith White was educated at Bishop's Stortford College and Christ Church, Oxford, where he was Fell Exhibitioner and winner of the Gladstone Memorial Exhibition. On leaving Oxford, he was awarded a Commonwealth fellowship and went to the United States where he graduated at the universities of Michigan and California. He had a natural aptitude for games and athletics. A notable "miler", he gained an Oxford athletics Blue, and represented Britain in the Olympic Games.

His first choice of career was teaching, and he taught scholarship candidates in the sixth form at Whitgift School. In 1931 he met Colonel Malcolm Cumming, then a regular Army officer, when both were appointed to help run an official pro-gramme of visits to the Dominions for English public schoolboys. When Cumming subsequently joined MI5 he provided the introduction that also brought the 30-year-old White into the organisation in January 1936.

White demonstrated a ready grasp of national and international political situations. He spoke a number of European languages fluently, including German and soon began to make a significant contribution to MI5's efforts to counter the mounting espionage and security threats from Nazism and Communism in the 1930s. As a member of the highly professional triumvirate of MI5 officers who directed prewar counter-espionage operations against the German intelligence organisation, he played a key role in assuring Britain's control over the German intelligence offensive against Britain.

These counter-espionage techniques were then extended to the Middle East and to India and Burma, thus giving the Security Service a very large degree of control over German intelligence operations directed against British interests throughout the second world war and enabling MI5 to pass false deception information before the allied landings in the "Overlord" operations in early June 1944. Deception information fed to the German High Command through MI5 intelligence channels caused the Germans to tie up seven divisions in the Pas de Calais area, where they were led to believe that a substantial invasion force would land, allowing the Allies to re-enter Europe through Normandy.

Many remarkable people contributed to the success of these intelligence and deception techniques and operations but, to the extent that there was a mastermind, it was Dick White's. Britain's allies readily recognised his contribution to victory and after the successful allied landings in France, he was seconded as "expert adviser on counter-intelligence matters" to General Eisenhower's staff. He was also awarded the US Legion of Merit and the French Croix de Guerre.

After the war he headed the intelligence

directorate of MI5 until, on the retirement of Sir Percy Sillitoe in 1953, he was appointed Director General. He immediately reorganised the Service to bring it into line with modern needs, a reconstruction which, albeit with certain modifications, has stood the test of time.

In 1956 he was transferred to become the first civilian head of MI6, replacing the bluff Major-General Sir John Sinclair. He thus became the only man ever to have led both MI5 and MI6. He deployed his deep understanding of the needs of intelligence to bring both services to a level of professionalism to meet his exacting standards. Although he did not have an easy ride – the private unmasking of Anthony Blunt and the escape of Kim Philby to Moscow both occurred during his period in office – it was a remarkable tribute to the balance of his decisions and the range of his knowledge that ministers, senior civil servants and the members of both services alike recognised and welcomed his leadership. He showed the same skills in reorganising MI6 for modern needs as he had shown earlier as head of its sister service.

On his retirement from MI6 he was appointed the first Intelligence Co-ordinator in the Cabinet Office, a post which enabled the intelligence community to continue to benefit from his unique experience across a wide range of intelligence-related affairs. He finally retired from the public service in 1972.

Dick White possessed a formidable intellect and a trenchant mind. He would unerringly and instantly identify the central issues and immediately make authoritative proposals to deal with them. Although he was firm and persistent in pursuit of policies which he knew to be right, it was not in his nature to be overbearing. His strength of mind and clarity of thought were compelling. There was a certain elusive quality about him that was hard to pin down. He was good company, told a story well but seldom revealed much about himself. He generated harmony, was always considerate and never grand with his staff. "One of those bustly days," he would cry as he sprinted from one high-level meeting to the next. Throughout his career both Labour and Conservative governments regarded him as a safe pair of hands, as did senior officials in Whitehall. His advice was sought around the world, within the Commonwealth and among Britain's closest allies.

Anxious that the truth should be told he went publicly to the defence of the reputations of two former senior colleagues, Guy Liddell, one-time Deputy Director General of MI5, and Sir Roger Hollis, a former Director General, who were both posthumously accused of having acted traitorously. On the strength of a long and close association with each, he was convinced that the charges – peddled by Peter Wright and Chapman Pincher – were untrue, and believed that he had a clear duty to do what he could to right what he saw as a great injustice. This relative openness made him more accessible than most shadowy presences in the Security and Secret Intelligence Services, and it was notable that he numbered among his friends figures as sceptical of the whole "spook" world as the late Malcolm Muggeridge, who had been once fleetingly in it himself, and Andrew Boyle, the author of *The Climate of Treason*. The latter at one stage even started to write White's biography but had not finished it at the time of his own death in 1991.

Dick White married, in 1945, Kathleen (Kate) Somers Bellamy, who supported him through a long illness. She survives him together with two sons of the marriage.

b 20.12.06   d 20.2.93   aged 86

CANON KEITH de BERRY

Canon Keith de Berry, Rector of St Aldate's, Oxford, 1952–74, and Canon Emeritus of Christ Church Cathedral, Oxford.

A CONFIDANT of bishops and students alike, a fearless preacher of the Christian gospel and an improviser to the last, Keith de Berry conducted a memorable ministry in Oxford for more than 20 years. From the early 1950s to the mid-1970s a huge, oblong notice always stood in term-time on the little piece of grass outside St Aldate's and opposite Christ Church. Taking a leaf out of the ways of the cinema, it proclaimed the church's forthcoming attractions – eminent churchmen appearing to preach on challenging themes.

But the names displayed there were by no means confined to orthodox Anglican clerics. Billy Graham and the late Malcolm Muggeridge were but two among many who found themselves being given this star, spiritual treatment. The St Aldate's of de Berry's day always very much saw the world as its parish.

Oscar Keith de la Tour de Berry was the only son of a prominent City of London figure, Oscar Berry, and his wife Nellie. Keith came at the end of a line of five sisters, Pearl, Ivy, Doris, Sylvia and Carol. All of them were brilliant evangelists, but the youngest of the six was the most prolific in terms of sheer evangelistic output, and the number of people reached. Many thousands of individuals from every walk of life attribute their Christian beginnings to his vigorous parochial leadership, spanning four decades, and a remarkable Wesley-like ministry, conducted in retirement, that was to range across Britain and even into America from 1974 until his death.

De Berry's own Christian pilgrimage began in earnest with his own call to commitment at the age of 11, five years after he had, with his sisters, waved off the *Titanic* from their home, then on the Isle of Wight. Education followed, at Marlborough and St John's College, Cambridge, where he gained a degree in history. After Ridley Hall, the low-church theological college at Cambridge, came Anglican ordination and a curacy at that power-house of the Evangelicals, St Mary's, Islington. There began a lifelong friendship with his fellow curate, Donald Coggan, later to become Archbishop of Canterbury.

It was now that the traits for which the de Berry family was renowned began to manifest themselves. They centred on an animated approach to life, a terrier-like refusal to let go of the main issue at stake, and a capacity for making something out of nothing – the last-minute improvisation of a visual aid for use in church, the turning of the most casual contacts into evangelistic opportunities, the trans-formation of the most trivial of events into an eloquent sermon illustration.

Incumbencies followed, at St George's Battersea, Immanuel, Streatham, and – lasting 23 years – St Aldate's, Oxford. All were characterised by an immense expenditure of energy, a passion for film evenings, a commitment to summer house-parties, open-air preaching, crowded "guest services" (late-comers at St Aldate's were fortunate to find a vacant window-sill) and, undergirding all, a cheerfully confident appeal to the authority of scripture. It was earnestness without intensity, a ministry achieved apparently without preparation or effort.

The platform, though, was solid enough. Its main planks were a life-long commitment to Bible study, a wide range of reading and a prayerful belief that no one was beyond the reach of the Christian gospel. De Berry might, as was said at his funeral, lose the debate against the Oxford University Humanists, but still ended up by winning his chief opponent to the faith.

It remains a mystery why (beyond being made an honorary canon in his last four years at St Aldate's) he never gained any preferment. The truth probably was that throughout the years of his active ministry Evangelicals remained unfashionable, and certainly his one book, *The Making of a Christian*, failed to do his gifts justice.

De Berry's main work was certainly not over when retirement finally came in 1974. From honorary curacies at St Paul's, Portman Square, and then at All Souls, Langham Place, he launched upon a ministry of "mini-missions", valued alike by schools, universities, parishes and overseas venues. A short, round-shouldered, unthreatening figure, he lacked all presence. But his words still seemed able to cut through the most formidable of defences. It is possible that in this period he won more hearts and minds than in all his previous years.

Unusual, but never eccentric, Keith de Berry will in part be remembered for an acutely enquiring mind, for his sherry parties at Wilton Place, for his hilarious explorations into the world of amateur cine photography, for his habit (developed since Marlborough days) of taking a cold bath every morning, and his contentment with the bicycle as a mode of transport. He is survived by his wife Betty, two sons and two daughters.

b 12.10.07   d 16.5.93   aged 85

CANON BRYAN GREEN

Canon Bryan Green, rector of Birmingham, 1948–70, and canon emeritus of Birmingham Cathedral.

"LOW and lazy" used to be the description applied to the Evangelical wing of the Church of England. The second adjective certainly never applied to Canon Bryan Green, in his time the leading exponent of the liberal brand of Evangelicalism within the Anglican Church.

A preacher of exceptional force and charm, he regularly led world-wide mission campaigns well before the era of Dr Billy Graham. His fame, indeed, was probably greater abroad, particularly in North America, than it was at home – where he received no higher preferment than that of being an honorary canon of Birmingham Cathedral.

He did, however, conduct three highly successful parochial ministries: first, before the second world war, at Christ Church, Crouch End, then, during the war and immediately afterwards, at Holy Trinity, Brompton (where he pioneered marriage reunion services), and finally for 22 years, at St Martin's in the Bull Ring, the parish church of Birmingham. The last was not, in fact, the pulpit of his choice. While still in the London diocese he made perhaps too little a secret of his longing to be vicar of St Martin-in-the-Fields; and it was only when that living, under the patronage of the then Anglo-Catholic Bishop of London, Dr J. W. C. Wand, went elsewhere, that he accepted the call to be rector of Birmingham.

But by then he had come a long way from his own strict Protestant origins. Born in Gipsy Hill, south London, he was brought up in an almost fundamentalist household. School at Merchant Taylors' did little to liberate him and he followed the approved Low Church path to the London College of Divinity. By the time, in 1924, he became a curate in New Malden he was, according to his own recollection in old age, "as narrow as they make them. Cigarettes, alcohol, dancing, the theatre — all were taboo. If people took to them, I prayed for their souls." (Twenty-five years later, a journalist interviewing him on his appointment to St Martin's, Birmingham, found him smoking merrily away, if through an elegant cigarette-holder.)

In Birmingham he had to work hard for the success that had come to him so effortlessly at the fashionable West End church of Holy Trinity, Brompton. Inevitably, although he had an effective team of curates, there were references to "our absentee rector" — for Green, like John Wesley, always liked to claim "the world is my parish". From 1947 onwards he regularly conducted at least two overseas missions a year, with the United States, Canada, South Africa, Australia and New Zealand providing his principal stamping-grounds.

The choice of countries to which he chose to take his essentially biblical message revealed perhaps that he was essentially the child of his time. Brought up in the age of the British Empire, he tended to identify with the white Commonwealth; and he played little or no part in the postwar development of such ecumenical organisations as the World Council of Churches. As the years

went by, this had the effet of leaving him in an isolated position even in terms of church politics (he served one term as a proctor in convocation for the diocese of London but found the Church Assembly, the predecessor of the General Synod, not to his taste).

The truth was that he was pre-eminently a mission preacher — probably the most striking of his generation — and he was only unusual in believing that this kind of ministry worked best if it had a parish base. His retirement from Birmingham in 1970 gave him a greater freedom to fill the role of a travelling evangelist and he took full advantage of it. He was still conducting evangelical campaigns at the time of his ninetieth birthday, while simultaneously serving as honorary curate of Thame. In a different age the Church of England would, no doubt, have made greater use of his gifts but for most of his career Evangelicals were regarded with suspicion while he himself, with his early support for women priests and advocacy of the selective remarriage of divorced persons in church, was hardly a fully representative figure among "the Protestant underworld".

In retirement, and in his eighty-fifth year, he was, however, awarded the signal distinction of an honorary Lambeth doctorate of divinity by the then Archbishop of Canterbury, Dr Robert Runcie. He had written three books — *The Practice of Evangelism* (1951), *Being and Believing* (1956) and *Saints Alive* (1959) — but none perhaps reflected his real ability, which lay in preaching as a dying man to dying men.

Bryan Green married in 1926 Winifred Bevan and they had a son and a daughter.

b 14.1.01   d 6.3.93   aged 92

CANON JAMES OWEN

Canon James Owen, vicar of Little St Mary's, Cambridge, and honorary canon of Ely Cathedral.

JAMES OWEN was of Welsh parentage but had a thoroughly English education. He went from St George's School, Windsor Castle, where he sang as a chorister in St George's Chapel, to Clifton College, Bristol. At Cambridge, to which he went in 1950, he read history at Trinity Hall in the days of the distinguished joint pastorate there of Owen Chadwick as dean and Tony Tremlett as college chaplain.

At Trinity Hall Owen was reputed on occasion to have sunned himself, with a rug and shawl around his feet and shoulders, sitting in a wheelchair at the bottom of his staircase — to the general bemusement of visitors, some of whom later looked back with pride on their conversation with so remarkable an old lady.

From Trinity Hall he went to Ely Theological College, only to return to Cambridge — after curacies at St Mary the Boltons, South Kensington, and All Saints, Clifton — as chaplain of Jesus College. This was in the heady *Honest to God* years of the early 1960s, and the younger Owen entered with zest into that whole theological debate. After a brief period as chaplain at Repton he moved in 1967 to the university chaplaincy at Nottingham.

There, in days of developing complexity in university life, he is remembered for a mature, personal ministry valued both by senior members and by students — the latter of whom especially rose to the seriousness with which he took their individual and corporate concerns, religious or secular. Throughout his life this was to be Owen's most distinctive pastoral gift.

To his immense pleasure, Peterhouse, as patrons of the living, brought him back to Cambridge as vicar of the Anglo-Catholic parish of Little St Mary's in 1974. At the same time, the Cambridge Union Society invited him to serve it in the secular-cum-pastoral office (for that was how he saw it) of steward. Few during the next two decades were to have a shrewder sense of what was in the university air — or more friends in colleges and town alike. The sure mark of his illness this year was his absence from Henley (he was, and looked, the quintessential cox) and the advertisement in *The Times* cancelling his annual summer party in the vicarage garden in Newnham Terrace.

The touch of brilliance about his return to Cambridge was, nevertheless, his attachment to a key parish to whose tradition of English Catholicism he was perfectly attuned. Little St Mary's, with its ordered and restrained beauty of liturgy and music, its measured preaching with its strong emphasis on Catholic teaching, and its warmth of fellowship, exactly reflected its vicar's own qualities. In a phrase of the great Bishop Charles Gore, the junior sister of the university church of Great St Mary's has always refrained from accosting the more reserved, and maintained its own native tradition of level-headedness. Owen believed, and probably rightly, that "our witness in this small place extends far into the Church of England".

Surprisingly, perhaps, to some who had not realised the very English dimension of his Catholicism, he supported in principle the admission of women into the ordained priesthood. This reflected the same Anglican openness to movement and disposition towards inclusiveness which, in his day, had made Owen's own great friend and inspiration, Archbishop Michael Ramsey (whose every tone of voice he could convey in brilliant, affectionate and sometimes devastating mimicry) so ardent a proponent of Anglican-Methodist reunion.

The proposed legislation nevertheless worried him. He pleaded for mutual understanding and a pragmatic trust. In this, as at all crucial personal moments, immediately below the surface of the brilliant host with all the *raconteur's* potential for anecdote and brisk exchange, could be detected the deeply serious and listening priest.

No one was ever more truly Anglican in his Catholicism, and it was from his sure perception of the historical tradition in which he stood that he reached out, carrying his parish with him, into a most successful reciprocal association with the Roman Catholic Church in Brussels. With the Friends of Little St Mary's, which, along with the Michael Ramsey Society and the Michael Ramsey Lectures, came out of his own energetic initiative, he visited Rome, Florence, Bruges, Luxembourg and was to have gone with them to Santiago de Compostela this summer.

He loved Ely, and was made an honorary canon in 1986. Henley regatta in the summer and the Welney Washes with their wintering Bewick swans were his annual delights. He was unmarried.

b 26.2.31   d 5.7.93   aged 62

HIS EMINENCE CARDINAL GORDON GRAY

Cardinal Gordon Joseph Gray, Archbishop Emeritus of St Andrews and Edinburgh.

ONE of the most outstanding churchmen of his generation, Cardinal Gordon Gray was for many years a patriarchal figure for Scotland's Roman Catholic community. Unbending in principle and uncompromising in belief, he espoused the simple charm of a friendly parish priest rather than the authority of his high office. Although he commanded a powerful presence, with a physique and facial features which seemed chiselled from granite, he was blessed with a gentleness which made him almost imperceptible, hewn from a natural modesty and simplicity. This was expressed in a soft yet strong voice well known to radio listeners over many years.

Gordon Joseph Gray was born to Francis and Angela Gray, the second son of four children. The Gray family were of Banffshire farming stock until his father turned engineer, rising eventually to a directorate in a paper-making firm. Educated at Holy Cross Academy, Edinburgh, the young Gray's path to the priesthood was unconventional for a Scottish seminarian: after education at St Joseph's Junior Seminary, Mark Cross, Sussex, and at St John's, Wonersh, he was ordained on June 15, 1935.

His first appointment took him to St Andrews in Fife where his distant predecessor as cardinal, James Beaton, was assassinated in 1546.

While assistant priest to his uncle, Canon John Gray, he undertook studies at the university and graduated with an honours MA in 1939 — the first Catholic priest to do so in modern times.

Two years later, he began to move steadily up the promotion ladder by taking charge of his own parish, SS Mary and David, Hawick. In 1947, after what one suspects were the happiest years of his life — in parish ministry — he was appointed Rector of St Mary's College, Blairs, Aberdeen.

Rectorate of the National Junior Seminary was a well-trodden path to the office of bishop. Nevertheless, even by today's standards, his appointment to the see of St Andrews and Edinburgh in 1951 at the age of 41 — making him the world's youngest archbishop — was exceptional, but part of a pattern which was to see him tot up a remarkable number of unique achievements.

A man of impressive and expressive spiritual depths, his considerable administrative and organisational gifts soon flowered. His 34-year reign as archbishop saw the opening of 30 new parishes and 37 new churches. One of his first projects was to found an archdiocesan senior seminary. St Andrews, Drygrange, opened on September 8, 1953. It remained on the Drygrange site until 1986 when it transferred to Edinburgh, taking the name Gillis College. Its closure this year, to pave the way for a new national seminary sited in Glasgow, was something of a disappointment to the cardinal who had earlier confessed to being "heartbroken" by the closure of the National Junior Seminary in 1986. Yet, despite his understandable sadness, his magnanimity shone through and was underlined by a recent appeal to Scots Catholics to support the new seminary.

He took part in the Second Vatican Council (1962–65) and, although prevented by guillotines on debates from making oral interventions, was steadily making a firm impression in papal circles.

Gordon Gray's reputation for caution and conservatism was deserved, but this did not mean a recipe for stagnation. His hand, at the helm of an 800,000-strong community, was steady. Certainly, his navigation helped weather the storms of change, both inside and outside the Church, of recent decades.

One of the first to respond to Pope Pius XII's appeal to bishops, in the letter *Fidei Donum*, to release priests to work in Africa, Gray established a link with Bishop John Reddington of Jos in Nigeria and undertook, in 1964, the responsibility for staffing and financing Bauchi Province, an area as large as Scotland. His missionary concerns also brought him into contact with Sergio Pignedoli, Nuncio to Nigeria and West Africa, who was previously auxiliary bishop to Milan's Cardinal Giovanni Battista Montini, the future Pope Paul VI. Pignedoli would subsequently become a high-ranking cardinal in the Roman Curia, as Prefect of the Congregation for the Evangelisation of Peoples, an influential Congregation on which Edinburgh's archbishop would also be given a seat.

One of the most notable features of Gray's relationships with others was his way with people and his ability to put everyone at ease. He enjoyed excellent relations with Cardinal Hume and his three predecessors at Westminster. Despite his long experience, he was never overpowering, never overbearing. He was a man without enemies. His non-threatening personality, and his ability to chair meetings efficiently, made him an ideal candidate for a quiet but effective international role in the life of the Church.

A member of the Vatican's Sacred Congregation for Divine Worship, he also served on the Pontifical Commission for Social Communications, the Church's central organisation for the mass media. He was in Rome to present, in 1971, the Pastoral Instruction on the Media, outlining the Church's future approach to newspapers, radio and television, which he helped to prepare.

In Britain, he was co-founder, in 1955, of the National Catholic Radio and Television Centre, Hatch End, Middlesex, and also served for 12 years on the Central Religious Advisory Committee for the BBC and the former ITA. According to his close friend, the late Bishop Agnellus Andrew, he had one of the finest broadcasting voices in the land.

One of his most important international roles was as chairman of the International Commission for English in the Liturgy (ICEL), charged with the translation of the Latin liturgy. It was a sensitive operation requiring massive consultation, impacting on the entire English-speaking world. Words with an innocent meaning in Britain could have had a very different meaning in parts of Africa. Yet the translations proved their worth, and have worn extremely well.

Gray also promoted the adoption of the Revised Standard Version of the Bible and became the first bishop to grant an *imprimatur* for Catholics to use it. The gentle force of his personality did much to break the shell of inter-denominational suspicions in Scotland. Inter-Church dialogue was always firmly on his agenda: as far back as 1964 he held discussions with members of the Church of Scotland's Church and Nation Committee on mixed marriages and in 1968 was the first Catholic since the Reformation to preach from the John Knox pulpit in St Andrews University.

In 1969, when Pope Paul VI named him cardinal, he became the first resident Scottish cardinal since the Reformation and only the third Scot to receive the Red Hat since 1546. Though he always insisted it was an honour for his native land, it remains unclear, because Scotland –

unlike England – has no primatial see, whether the honour was a purely personal one or not. What is certain is that news of his promotion was received with great joy by Catholics throughout Scotland and, indeed, by numerous fellow-countrymen of all religious persuasions and of none.

The undoubted highlight of his episcopate was the visit of Pope John Paul II to Scotland in 1982 when the Pope was a guest at St Benet's, the cardinal's residence in Edinburgh. A telling example of his homeliness and Scottishness could be detected when he greeted Pope John Paul at Edinburgh's Turnhouse Airport: preventing the Pope from kissing the airport Tarmac, he insisted that he kiss real Scottish soil instead. He was delighted when the commanding officer of RAF Turnhouse presented him with the sod of turf kissed by the Pope for replanting in his own garden.

A keen gardener, he liked nothing more than working with his hands, and was also an accomplished craftsman with wood. He also took immense enjoyment from repairing old cars, and was well known for picking up spare parts for his old Fiat whenever he had the opportunity while visiting Rome.

Cardinal Gray was the recipient of a number of honorary academic awards. A Doctorate of Divinity was awarded by St Andrews University in 1967 and he became the first Catholic prelate to be made an honorary fellow of the Educational Institute of Scotland in 1970. In November of 1981 the honorary degree of Doctor of the University of Heriot-Watt University was bestowed on him. It remained something of a mystery to many, at least within the Catholic community, that he was never so honoured by the University of Edinburgh.

Although he could display a pawky sense of humour, he was not someone whom it was easy to get to know at a first meeting. He was seldom inclined to small talk, preferring instead to discuss issues of the day, particularly within the Church. Reserved and retiring, he sometimes appeared to be a lonely man. But, particularly in retirement (since 1985), he seemed to enjoy visits by his fellow-priests, with whom he would generously share more than a dram of his favourite malt whisky, Antiquary.

In the twilight of his life, however, he was burdened with spondolitis, arthritis and curvature of the spine – which forced him to rely more and more on a wheelchair.

One of his last public appearances took place in June when he welcomed Mother Teresa to Edinburgh to endorse her "pro-life" appeal. He was an untiring defender of traditional morals and never sought to be considered a liberal churchman.

A measure of the esteem in which he was held by all Scots was seen when, already in retirement, he wrote a letter to a national newspaper lamenting the treatment of workers at Ravenscraig in Lanarkshire: his comments made national news and were quoted in the House of Commons. This was not perhaps surprising – after 34 years in office he had grown something of a Scottish institution.

Gordon Gray's mother lived to see him named a cardinal and he is survived by his brother George.

b 10.8.10   d 19.7.93   aged 82

JOHN CONNALLY

John Bowden Connally, former US Secretary of the Treasury, Governor of Texas, and unsuccessful presidential aspirant.

LIFE was a roller-coaster ride for "Big John" Connally – a man whose personality and driving ambition carried him from poverty to fame and fortune, and whose colossal ego led to ultimate disaster. Seriously wounded in the 1963 assassination of President Kennedy, when he was serving his first term as Democratic Governor of Texas, he went on to serve two more terms as governor in the 1960s before switching parties and making unsuccessful bids for the Republican presidential nomination.

Connally grew up in a small town near San Antonio, Texas, one of seven children of a poor farmer. Handsome and self-assured, he soon left his impoverished background behind. At the age of 21, after studies at the University of Texas at Austin, he was called to the Texas Bar and promptly became an aide to a freshman Congressman named Lyndon B. Johnson. The association between Johnson and Connally was to have profound consequences. In 1948, after serving a stint in the US Navy, Connally managed the campaign which carried Lyndon Johnson into the Senate. It was a bitterly fought election, widely alleged to have been won by fraud, but it set Johnson on the road to the White House.

During the 1950s, while LBJ was wheeling and dealing his way to control of the Senate, Connally was working as an attorney for a Texas oil billionaire, accumulating wealth and business contacts. He was already proving a less-than-loyal supporter of the Democratic party, campaigning for Dwight

Eisenhower against Adlai Stevenson in 1952, but he switched back to run Lyndon Johnson's vice-presidential campaign in 1960.

Johnson, though he showed his gratitude by recommending that President Kennedy appoint Connally to the post of Navy Secretary in 1961, had few illusions about his former protégé. He is quoted by James Reston in his 1989 biography of Connally, *Lone Star*, as saying: "John Connally doesn't have even the tiniest trace of compassion. He can leave more dead bodies in the field with less remorse than any politician I ever knew."

Johnson, who was talking at the time to Under-Secretary of State George Ball, added: "You know, George, I can use raw power — I can use raw power as well as anyone. You've seen me do it. But the difference between John and me is he *loves* it."

Connally's tenure as Navy Secretary did not last long. He resigned after 11 months to run for the Texas governorship, winning the 1962 election after a brilliant and energetic campaign. In the following November he was sitting in front of Kennedy in the presidential limousine when the president was shot. Connally was hit too. The bullet passed through his body, leaving him with scars on his back, chest, wrist and thigh. He always believed, in fact, that it was he, and not the president, who was the target of the attack.

The sympathy aroused by his narrow escape helped Connally to retain the governorship for two more terms, though his opposition to civil rights measures and social welfare legislation, plus his vehement support for the Vietnam war, had made him highly unpopular with liberal Democrats. This did not stop him, however, dabbling his toes in presidential politics. At the Chicago Democratic convention of 1968 he briefly joined in a bid to prevent Hubert Humphrey's nomination. This involved him in an improbable, last-minute alliance with the "peace candidate", Senator Eugene J. McCarthy, but it soon fell apart and Humphrey was duly nominated — only

to be defeated in the November election. In the light of this, it was not surprising that President Nixon nominated Connally as his Treasury Secretary in December 1970 — a move that left Lyndon Johnson, who had not been consulted by Connally before his acceptance, shocked and angry.

The year 1971 was a time of US recession and international monetary crisis. Connally took a highly nationalist stance, persuading Nixon to abandon the gold standard, place a 10 per cent surcharge on all imported goods, and devalue the dollar by 8 per cent. At meetings of the Group of Ten, and the International Monetary Fund, he adopted a hard bargaining position which did little to endear him to America's allies.

But his strategy worked. Ignoring contrary advice from the State Department, Connally kept up the pressure until, in December that year, he won greater currency revaluations from European countries and Japan than anyone had thought possible. Anthony Barber, then Chancellor of the Exchequer, remarked that "a lesser man, a man less tough than Connally, could not have done it".

Connally, though still nominally a Democrat, was now turning more openly towards identification with the Republicans and had moved closer to Nixon's inner circle of advisers. In May 1972, he resigned his post at the Treasury and began campaigning actively for the president's re-election, founding "Democrats for Nixon" in opposition to the Democratic candidacy of George McGovern.

Nixon won by a landslide and Connally, who had ambitions to run for the White House at the next election due in 1976, finally changed parties. Given that the Watergate scandal was already underway, a liberal joke of the time had it that his defection represented "the only known instance in recorded history of a rat swimming *towards* a sinking ship".

Connally had confidently expected to

be rewarded with the office of Secretary of State. It was not to be. Henry Kissinger moved from the White House to replace William Rogers, and the former Treasury Secretary had to be content with the post of "special adviser" which he left after only five weeks.

It may have been that Connally sensed the coming denouncement of the Watergate story. If so, he was too late to avoid all involvement. He had, after all, advised the president: "Have Ziegler (the president's spokesman) assemble, the White House press corps in the Rose Garden, pile up all the tapes, set a match to them, and let them then film the bonfire."

Congressional investigations found him to be involved in several examples of misdoings by the Nixon administration, and he was ultimately indicted by the Watergate grand jury on five counts of perjury, accepting a bribe, and conspiring to obstruct the course of justice, in connection with a $10,000 payment from dairy lobbyists.

Connally was acquitted on all counts in April 1975, but his presidential ambitions had been irreparably damaged. When he tried to seek the Republican nomination in 1980, he spent $11 million on a campaign that garnered him only a single delegate at the national convention.

"I reminded everyone of Lyndon," he explained.

Unabashed, Connally returned to Texas and, at the age of 63, set about making some real money. The state was booming, and he went into partnership with Ben Barnes, a former lieutenant-governor, to exploit the profits to be made in oil and real estate, borrowing vast sums to build houses, offices, condominiums and shopping malls. The two men even gave their personal guarantees for millions of dollars to fellow speculators. Extraordinarily, in view of Connally's legal training, they neglected to incorporate, accepting personal responsibility for every debt.

And then, in 1986, the bottom dropped out of the oil market and the boom went bust. In a welter of law suits, Connally declared bankruptcy with debts of $93 million. He never did anything in a small way.

One of America's last sights of John Connally came in January 1988: television images of an old man, still handsome, standing on the front lawn of his mansion while his personal possessions were auctioned off to pay his debts. He is survived by his wife Idanell, two sons, and a daughter.

b 27.2.17   d 15.6.93   aged 76

ROBERT ADLEY

Robert Adley, Conservative MP and railways enthusiast.

ROBERT ADLEY made no bones about his main contribution to parliamentary life. "I am a railways fanatic", he admitted. He will, therefore, be remembered chiefly for his obsessional interest in railways and his campaigns against his party's plans for privatisation. This, though, risks giving an incomplete impression of an increasingly independent-minded MP with a capacity to rebel against his party when he thought it necessary.

His father was Harry Adley, co-founder of the Pearl and Dean advertising organisation. Adley had a comfortable, middle-class Jewish childhood and was educated at Falconbury Preparatory School and Uppingham before travelling extensively in the Far East. His main business interest was in hotels but by his early thirties he was seeking a political career. He gained a seat on Slough Council before fighting the solid Labour seat of Birkenhead in 1966. He did sufficiently well there to be selected as candidate for marginal Bristol North-East which he managed to capture in 1970 by 462 votes. This was not enough to guarantee a seat for life and Adley was lucky in that redistribution came to his rescue (his constituency, though retaining its old name, was amalgamated with Bristol Central). He could thus afford to go off with a clear conscience in search of safer pastures.

At the first of the two 1974 general elections he won Christchurch and Lymington with the rather more reassuring majority of 14,634. By the time he died, the constituency – again as a result of boundary changes – had become simply Christchurch, and his 23,000 majority was one of the largest in the country.

In his early years in the House Adley was a dutiful party warrior, never straying from the party line and attempting, not always successfully, to score points off the third Wilson government. This was in contrast to his later, less orthodox attitudes when he was not afraid to support the Chinese government, even backing Chinese requests for Harrier jets on the ground that they were needed to fight Vietnamese aggressors. In 1985 he came out against the views of many of his colleagues on South Africa. When he visited the Republic as the guest of its government he was so concerned by what he witnessed that on his return he attacked it for provoking violence in the townships. He asked the Thatcher government to support the "legitimate views" of the black majority and later called for talks with the African National Congress.

He was against the poll tax, bus deregulation and the impact of the business rate on small companies, and frequently took his opposition into the voting lobbies. What he did support was a properly integrated transport system – and Concorde. His feeling for supersonic jets was a relic of his Bristol days and when Bishop Hugh Montefiore, like Adley a convert from Judaism to the Church of England, tried to kill off Concorde because of the stress its noise caused to the inhabitants of his then suffragan see of Kingston upon Thames, Adley had no hesitation in denouncing him as "the latest in a long line of crackpots".

The truth was that there was always a danger of his being categorised as a mere "rent-a-quote" MP. When he attacked Peter Jay, then the British ambassador in Washington, for seeking to turn the British Information Services office in New York into "a unit of Labour party propaganda" he infallibly hit the headlines, as he also did by accusing Sir Michael Edwardes, then running British Leyland, of adopting "bullying tactics" towards his workforce. He enjoyed being professionally mischievous, too. His long, running fight with Clive Jenkins over his right to belong to the union (ASTMS) Jenkins then led certainly added to the harmless stock of public pleasure, if only because it badly false-footed a rival self-publicist.

But all this activity was subsidiary to his ceaseless support for the railways. They had fascinated him since he was given *The Wonder Book of Trains* when he was three. He admitted that he once diverted an entire parliamentary delegation in China in order to inspect a rare example of the steam train (he had completed a book on his own experiences of steam just before he died). Inevitably he became chairman of the Conservative backbench transport committee and later chairman of the all-party Commons Select Committee on Transport. In these roles he proved one of the most effective opponents of the government's railway strategy.

Although he was not against competition – or some privatisation – he was convinced that the plans for British Rail, which included selling the freight division, creating a new track authority and offering franchises to operators, would not work.

As the privatisation proposals drag their way through Parliament the railways will know that they have lost their most devoted supporter in the Commons. No union-sponsored MP could have done more.

He was married in 1961 to Jane Pople. She survives him, with their two sons.

b 2.3.35   d 13.5.93   aged 58

JUDITH CHAPLIN

Judith Chaplin, Conservative MP for Newbury and former special adviser to John Major.

OF THE 21 new women MPs elected at the last general election, Judith Chaplin had perhaps the brightest future ahead of her. Very much a graduate of Whitehall — she had served both Nigel Lawson and John Major in the Treasury before moving to No 10 in December 1990 as head of the political office — she got to the House of Commons only at the relatively late age of 52. But she had a solid background in Tory politics, having been a member of Norfolk County

Council for 11 years, of the Conservative Research Department for three, as well as having run the policy unit of the Institute of Directors from 1986 to 1988. Few doubted that she would have been rewarded with ministerial office − and not necessarily merely at under-secretary level − in any summer government reshuffle.

A dental surgeon's daughter, Judith Schofield did not start out in politics. Educated at Wycombe Abbey and Girton College, Cambridge, her first job, as a young married woman, was to found and run an independent nursery and preparatory school. She never quite lost the aura of a brisk and businesslike headmistress − an aspect of her personality that served her well when, on party rather than official occasions, her duties at No 10 included the briefing of journalists. It fell to her to give the briefing on the prime minister's pro-Maastricht speech at the Welsh Conservative party conference held at Swansea in June 1991. Although John Major's language was necessarily coded − including, as it did, the first intimation that there would not, after all, be an autumn 1991 election − her exposition of it was a model of no-nonsense clarity and diplomacy.

Chaplin's degree at Cambridge had been in economics − she also subsequently took a diploma in economics from her local University of East Anglia − and, once she gave up running her school in Norfolk, she went to work for a firm of chartered accountants. At the time she also faced the task of bringing up four children as a single parent, her first marriage having ended in divorce in 1979. She headed the economics section of the Conservative Research Department from 1983 to 1986 before moving over in the latter year to the Institute of Directors.

It was from there that Nigel Lawson recruited her to be his political adviser at the Treasury. It was a move widely interpreted at the time as being intended to counterbalance the influence of Sir Alan Walters over No 10. But, if that was

its purpose, it failed. Within a year Lawson had resigned, specifically complaining against the role Walters was playing in second-guessing the Chancellor. Chaplin, however, was immediately re-appointed by Lawson's successor, John Major, with whom she established an instinctive rapport. (Significantly or not, her name is mentioned only once in Lawson's lengthy volume of memoirs, and then only very cursorily.)

Like David Owen, however, the prime minister has always had a penchant for strong, independent-minded women and Chaplin soon became an integral part of his team. She played a leading role in the preparation of the Conservatives' 1992 election campaign, being a regular member of the No 12 Committee (named after the whips' address in Downing Street where it met) established by John Major to co-ordinate the activities of government and party. She also attended the key strategy weekend meeting held at Chequers in November 1991 at which the groundwork for the manifesto was laid.

But by then she had, after some years of discouragement, succeeded in becoming a Conservative candidate herself, having been selected for the Berkshire seat of Newbury, which was already under threat from the Liberal Democrats. The need to nurse the seat involved some scaling down of her No 10 activities but Chaplin, despite grumbling from colleagues, held onto her post there until she was safely elected an MP less than a year ago. She made the always awkward transition from appointed to elective office with the aplomb only to be expected from someone who had already chaired a county education authority as well as serving on a number of departmental committees. She was one of the ablest women MPs on either side of the House.

Judith Chaplin was twice married, first to Robin (now Lord) Walpole, by whom she had two sons and two daughters, and then in 1984 to the architect Michael Chaplin, who survives her together with her children.

b 19.8.39 d 19.2.93 aged 53

ALEXANDER DUBCEK

Alexander Dubcek, first secretary of the Czechoslovak Communist Party during the reformist "Prague Spring" of 1968 and the consequent invasion by Soviet-led troops of the Warsaw Pact.

ALEXANDER Dubcek inspired the phrase "socialism with a human face" and became the figurehead of the movement to instigate cultural and economic reforms in Czechoslovakia. The fact that he envisioned these reforms being achieved within communist philosophy hardly lessened the enthusiasm with which they were observed in the West or the distrust with which they were greeted in Moscow and the other Warsaw Pact capitals.

This figurehead role was an unlikely one for Dubcek, however. The ideas that inspired the "post-January" reform programme were not his. It was an historic irony that, having been a compromise choice as party leader, he should have found himself in a position where he not only had to sponsor reforms more radical than he had

envisaged, but also had to try to save Czechoslovak independence from the aggression of the Soviet Union, which he had been brought up to regard and love as his fatherland.

For a man who had done his utmost to avoid provoking Moscow, and who constantly urged his own people to do nothing "precipitate", the invasion by Soviet-led troops of the Warsaw Pact, on the night of August 20, 1968, was the ultimate nightmare. It led to his being taken, manacled, to Moscow and browbeaten into accepting the Soviet presence. It led, too, to his being ousted from power and humiliated and ostracised for nearly two decades before the "Velvet Revolution" of 1989 brought renewed public adulation and partial restitution of his reputation as a national hero.

Remarkably, Dubcek's faith in Marxist-Leninism remained unwavering. He ascribed the responsibility for the Soviet invasion of 1968 to "neo-Stalinist totalitarian dictatorship". Like Mikhail Gorbachov, with whom he identified closely, he was, at heart, a party loyalist.

Alexander Dubcek's connections with Russia were very close. When he was four, his family moved to Russia to join the famous "Interhelpo" co-operative. Dubcek went to school first at Frunze and later at Gorki, and studied at the Communist Party College in Moscow. His father, Stefan, who was a carpenter and had spent two years in the United States, had joined the Communist Party of Czechoslovakia as soon as it was founded in 1921.

The family returned to Czechoslovakia in 1938 and Alexander, then 18, joined the illegal Communist Party of Slovakia.

Alexander became an apprentice fitter at the Skoda armaments factory near Trencin. Under the German occupation, Stefan became a member of the third illegal central committee of the Slovak Communist Party, which led the party until 1942, when he and the other leaders were arrested and sent to a concentration camp until the liberation. In 1944, during the Slovak Rising, Alexander Dubcek joined the Jan Zizka partisan brigade, and was wounded during fighting.

After the war, Dubcek worked for four years at the Trencin yeast factory. In 1951, he became a member of the national assembly. By 1953, he was chief secretary of the party's regional committee at Banska Bystrica, and from 1958−60 occupied the same post at Bratislava.

He was elected a member of the central committee of the Communist Party of Czechoslovakia in 1958 and in 1960 became one of its secretaries. In 1962 he became a member of the praesidium and a secretary of the central committee of the Communist Part of Slovakia. In the same year he was made a candidate member of the praesidium of the Communist Party of Czechoslovakia. The following year, he became a full member and was made first secretary of the Communist Party of Slovakia.

Alexander Dubcek was a hard worker − his only pleasures were reading, walking and swimming. He studied law as an external student at Bratislava and in 1958 graduated *summa cum laude* from the political high school of the central committee of the Communist Party of the Soviet Union in Moscow. In Russian eyes Dubcek was very much a Moscow man, and members of the Soviet praesidium used to refer to him as "Our Sasha". Dubcek was reputed to have close personal ties with Brezhnev, which accounted for the bitter disillusionment he voiced at meetings with the Soviet leader after the invasion.

Dubcek was an unknown quantity when appointed a secretary of the central committee of the Czechoslovak Communist Party in 1960. An Englishman who met him at the time took him to be a typical "Komsomolets" − young, smooth, cheerful, possibly somewhat cynical and, apparently, the blue-eyed boy of a party leader. He became first secretary of the Slovak Communist Party at a crucial time, on the eve of the dismissal of the leader of the Centralist Slovaks in Prague, the prime minister Vilem Siroky. The period of Dubcek's ascent to power in Slovakia coincided with rehabilitation of the Slovak "bourgeois" nationalists, the reappraisal of the Slovak Rising and a new-found love for the pioneers of Slovak national regeneration. Since it was the Slovaks in Bratislava who rocked the Czechoslovak boat by turning out the Slovak prime minister, it was perhaps appropriate that a Slovak should be chosen on January 5, 1968, to succeed the discredited Stalinist, Antonin Novotny, as first secretary of the Czechoslovak Communist Party; and that when Lenart's name was rejected, the position should be given to Dubcek.

This was a critical time. The country's economy was stagnant after 20 years of clumsy central planning. The Marxist-Leninist system had crushed the independent political and cultural life and the show trials of the 1950s had left a legacy of distrust. The crisis split the party between conservative diehards and a progressive wing. Dubcek was not among the radical thinkers drawing blueprints for change, but he saw the good sense of what the reformers were saying. He also inspired trust all round.

Addressing a rally in 1968

However, in April 1968, under Dubcek's leadership, an Action Programme was passed that called for economic decentralisation and guarantees of democratic freedoms of assembly and opinion. It represented the first buds of the Prague spring. Intellectuals and students throughout Czechoslovakia tested the limits of the new tolerance. Politicians faced hostile questioning at crowded public meetings. Censorship was abolished and criticism of the Soviet Union crept into the media. The country breathed an intoxicating air of national self-rediscovery after two decades of repression.

It was not to last. The disapproval of the orthodox Brezhnev leadership in Moscow, evident from the start, now loomed ominously. In May, the Dubcek leadership bowed to pressure and agreed to allow Warsaw Pact manoeuvres on Czechoslovak territory, fanning fear — at home and abroad — that Moscow might try to reassert its authority. In the middle of July came an alarming letter: five Soviet bloc leaders, meeting in Warsaw, said that there was a threat of counter-revolution. There were two more showdowns: the entire Soviet leadership travelled by train to the Slovak border town of Cierna-nad-Tisou and spent four days arguing with Dubcek; the rest of the soviet bloc, apart from Romania, joined them in Bratislava.

Dubcek emphasised to the other leaders his view that democracy meant a dignified discipline and respect for law and order. While reaffirming that his country was still socialist and a committed member of the Warsaw Pact, he remained firm on the fundamental point of national sovereignty and Czechoslovakia's right to pursue a democratic course. In vain, he said the quarrel could be resolved through discussion. He believed until the last, some would say against the evidence, that Moscow would not intervene. Warsaw Pact tanks rolling across the borders on the night of August 20 proved him wrong. He was accused by many of having been naïve.

As Dubcek frantically sought details of the extent of the invasion, the central committee building in Prague was surrounded by Soviet paratroopers. A Russian security officer and two soldiers burst into his private office, tore the phone from his hands and ripped the wire out of the wall. He was held at a secret military base in Slovakia while the Czechoslovak president, Ludvik Svoboda, was flown to Moscow and given an ultimatum: change the government and party leadership or face having Slovakia converted into a Soviet republic.

While Svoboda stalled, Dubcek and other detained members of the Czechoslovak central committee were flown to Moscow. All of them were held in isolation and prevented from learning of the extensive passive resistance of their countrymen to the invasion forces — which might have influenced their reactions to the pressure applied from the Kremlin.

Moscow's efforts to muster a new government failed and it reluctantly asked Dubcek to stay on as party leader, while insisting on a re-imposition of controls. Dubcek wept as he reported back to an anxious nation and appealed to Czechoslovaks to accommodate Soviet concerns. The Czechoslovak Communist Party, he said, had not always taken sufficient note of the strategic and general interests of the Soviet Union, "as a real, objectively existing and limiting factor of the possible pace and form of our own political development". The important thing, he said, was to restore Soviet trust in order to bring about the withdrawal of the Soviet troops.

His words were a bitter disappointment to his countrymen, many of whom felt that the unanimity of the response was such that it could have forced the withdrawal of the foreign troops. In spite of his efforts and his popularity among Czechoslovaks, Dubcek was in any case doomed. The Kremlin wanted him out. At the time of the invasion he was at the summit of his popularity, but by the following Christmas this had begun to wane. He had been regarded as the mouthpiece of national and popular aspirations, both Slovak and Czech. But after the invasion, in the eyes of the intellectuals at least, he seemed to be assuming more and more the role of the unwilling advocate of Soviet solutions. His policy seemed to be to postpone the implementation of the major reforms and, instead, to reconcile the people to what was euphemistically called "normalisation". This inevitably meant moving back towards the conformism of the Novotny era.

Anti-Russian sentiment led to a wave of violent incidents and these led, in turn, to Dubcek announcing his resignation at a plenary session of the central committee in April 1969. Initially he remained a member of the party praesidium and was elected chairman of the national assembly, but, as the first anniversary of the invasion approached, demands were voiced by the pro-Soviet opportunists who had taken over power that he should submit himself to "public self-criticism". At a central committee meeting in September, he was reported to have refused to confess to political errors, but he was dropped from the ruling praesidium and removed from the chairmanship of the federal assembly.

Surprisingly, he was appointed ambassador to Turkey, but this was a brief — as well as bizarre — respite, and, in January 1970, he was withdrawn from the diplomatic post and expelled from the party.

For the next 18 years, Dubcek worked as an official of the Slovak Forestry Commission in Bratislava, a non-person intently watched by the secret police and barred from public life. Years later he said he could not have survived the ordeal without the support of his wife and three sons.

In 1988 Dubcek's passport was suddenly returned and he was allowed to travel to Italy to accept an honorary doctorate from the University of Bologna. It seemed to be a first step to rehabilitation, but when he was invited by the French and Portuguese presidents to participate in a peace-conference in Paris along with Andrei Sakharov and Lech Walesa, travel approval was refused.

In 1989, heartened by what he saw as the similarities between the Gorbachov reforms in the Soviet Union and his own ideas of 20 years earlier, he began to emerge from the shadows. In November when, after ten days of mass protests, the communist regime in Prague began to collapse, Dubcek joined Vaclav Havel and the members of the Civic Forum reform movement in demanding the resignation of anti-reformist Communist leaders.

Dubcek's popularity had survived his years in isolation and there were calls for him to stand as a presidential candidate. But in December he stood aside in favour of Havel and ten days later was elected chairman of the federal parliament. In May the next year he visited Moscow again, paying tribute to Gorbachov and saying of the 1968 invasion: "It's no good crying over spilt milk." In June 1990 he was re-elected chairman of the Czechoslovak federal assembly, but his popularity was once again slipping and his actions, or lack of them, over the years were being questioned. He was criticised for failing to speak out in the 1970s for jailed dissidents; for failing to sign the

Charter 77 civil rights appeals and for failing to join the Civic Forum reform movement. Even so, in June 1992, he was returned to parliament as a deputy for Slovakia's Social Democrats and was a possible candidate for the Slovak presidency after the expected split between Czechs and Slovaks. He remained an unequivocal advocate of the common state.

Recalling 1968 in an interview in 1990, Dubcek admitted that he had not anticipated the Soviet invasion. "Of course we asked ourselves this question but the answer was always no. We felt that it would be too great a shock for the left movements of the world." He said that he had assumed that when the invasion occurred, the original plan had been to have him and his colleagues tried and executed. "The soldiers arrested us 'in the name of the Revolutionary Tribunal'," he said. "It was only our people's solid resistance and the worldwide protests against the invasion that saved our lives." But, he said, it was "neo-Stalinism" or "Brezhnevism" that disillusioned him, not communism.

Dubcek owed this popularity first and foremost to the fact that he replaced the hated Novotny and was thus seen as the man who let air into the stuffy Czechoslovak Socialist Republic.

He lived modestly and adopted a fresh approach to public office – unprecedented in the communist world – building up a popular image by greeting sportsmen, going to soccer matches and waving at crowds. He liked to swim in the public swimming baths where he would dive from the high board and afterwards sign autographs for youngsters.

In the 21 years between the crushing of the "Prague Spring" and the success of the "Velvet Revolution" there was much debate over whether Dubcek could have adopted any other course, short of resigning, which would almost certainly have opened the door to a more conformist succession. Dubcek's critics believed that at that fateful hour the country needed a leader of different metal. No one could say that Dubcek was

soft. The pluckiness he displayed in Moscow disproved that. He was, however, emotional, and perhaps somewhat naive. A man of subtler mind, of more penetrating acumen, and of greater political experience and diplomatic skill might have been more successful in handling the Russians and his own countrymen and in preserving more of what it was vital to preserve.

Dubcek was not a man of ideas. But he had a shining integrity that did indeed present a new kind of "socialism with a human face" and it undoubtedly inspired the aspirations of his countrymen.

Widowed in 1990, he is survived by his three sons.

b 27.11.21   d 7.11.92   aged 70

August 21, 1968 after the Warsaw Pact invasion

LORD GORMLEY

Lord Gormley, OBE, president of the National Union of Mineworkers, 1971–82.

JOE GORMLEY, the miners' blunt-spoken champion was a moderate by nature but was forced by circumstances to lead the National Union of Mineworkers in two big strikes that shook the country. The first, in 1972, saw the strategy of "flying pickets" – later outlawed – brought to perfection. The second, in 1974, led indirectly to the fall of the Conservative government headed by Edward Heath.

Often caricatured as "the battered cherub" (a description from which he took the title of his successful autobiography), Gormley was a much-loved figure in the coal industry and the wider trade union movement. He retained the respect of his members right to the end of an 11-year tenure of office at the top of Britain's toughest union. Behind the bluff, hearty exterior, however, was a calculating brain and a brisk appetite for hand-to-hand fighting in the strongly political world of the NUM national executive. "I'm not a very pleasant gentleman when the chips are down, and

I know how to put the boot in as well as anybody," he wrote in the story of his life.

Gormley came from a mining family, and followed his father underground at the age of 14 after leaving St Oswald's Roman Catholic School. He later recalled that as he collected his first wage, his father told him to pay threepence contribution to the Miners' Federation of Lancashire – a forerunner of the NUM. He worked in 11 different collieries as a face-worker for 28 years before winning full-time office as secretary of the Lancashire miners in 1961, beating a left-wing candidate for the job. "I have been an anti-communist all my working life," he said upon retirement.

His first years in the movement were mainly marked by an interest in political rather than trade union work, though he sharpened his negotiation skills in the days when piecework bargaining still prevailed. He became a Labour councillor in his early twenties and was elected to the party's national executive in 1963, remaining on that body for two years after winning the NUM national presidency.

Gormley's career really took shape in

1958, when he was elected to the NUM national executive while still a working miner at Bold colliery, near Wigan. The union leadership was (and still is) traditionally dominated by the full-time coalfield "barons", but he was formidable enough among the dominant moderate majority on the executive to capture the nomination of the right for the general secretaryship in 1968.

He was beaten in this contest, but his second chance came in 1971 when Sir Sidney Ford, veteran right-wing president of the NUM, had to retire prematurely. This time Gormley promised the miners he would fight to make them "the highest-paid industrial workers in Britain." In a two-horse race with the Scottish area president, Mick McGahey, he was an easy winner.

Gormley became president just in time to take the chair at the NUM's policy-making conference at Aberdeen in July 1971, which was a watershed in the union's history. At the conference, delegates voted to change union rules so that the majority for strike action required in a secret pithead ballot was reduced from 66 per cent to 55 per cent; and this led, six months later, to the first national pit strike since 1926, because the miners voted by 59 per cent to endorse industrial action.

Gormley did not want a strike, and used all his formidable powers of diplomacy and negotiation to avoid one. But, once launched upon the path of confrontation, he was determined to win. The miners did win after seven savage weeks in which Gormley ordered the blockading by pickets of all power stations and fuel dumps, a tactic that produced widespread power cuts.

The next big upheaval came after secret negotiations in the garden of 10 Downing Street and a West End hotel, and marked the high-point of trade union power in postwar Britain. After a long overtime ban, the miners struck again in February 1974, leading to the establishment of the "three-day week".

When a general election was finally called, Gormley feared that the Tories

would be returned with a thumping majority in a "who rules?" poll. But he was still unsuccessful in getting his executive to call off the strike.

His prophecy proved wrong, but for the duration of the 1974–79 Labour government he delivered the miners' backing for wage restraint under the TUC-Labour "social contract". He also negotiated with the government the expansionist *Plan for Coal* which pumped investment into the industry and slowed down the rate of job losses.

His other major achievement in those years was the introduction of locally-based incentive bonus schemes which repaid higher output with higher earnings. This reform, bitterly contested up to the Court of Appeal by his militant rivals, shifted the NUM's bargaining emphasis away from the annual pay battle which he believed was detrimental to the industry's long-term future. It also kept the miners at the top of the industrial wages league. Productivity rose sharply and absenteeism fell.

But over-production then became the major problem in the industry. With coal stocks growing, the first Thatcher government sought first to phase out operating subsidies to the industry, and then to accelerate the closure of uneconomic pits.

Miners in the traditionally militant coal fields began an unofficial "rolling" strike in February 1981 over the Coal Board's plan to shut 23 pits, but Gormley headed off an official national stoppage by negotiating £300 million in extra state subsidies. The government gave in to the miners within a matter of days, enhancing Gormley's position.

By this date the competition to succeed Gormley had already begun, and attention switched rapidly to Arthur Scargill. The ruling moderate faction was in disarray. At a meeting in Gormley's home in London in late 1980 the right wing could not agree on a single candidate to oppose the left, and Gormley despaired of finding a strong successor from among their number.

In fact, despite their obvious political differences, Gormley saw something of his own head-strong personality in Scargill, and did not discourage his presidential ambitions. He argued privately that the cares of office would diminish Scargill's revolutionary fervour.

In his last few years, Gormley became more isolated from his traditional followers on the union executive, but retained his popularity among the men. A *Daily Express* article he wrote just before he retired in April 1982, was widely credited with swinging a pithead vote against striking.

He also allowed his love of the turf freer rein in his declining years. He became a director of United Racecourses and in his pork-pie hat was a familiar figure at Epsom and Kempton. He refused a knighthood from a Labour government but accepted a life peerage under the Conservatives in 1982 as Lord Gormley, of Ashton-in-Makerfield.

Gormley had been appointed OBE in 1969.

His lively, if partisan and self-justifying, autobiography *Battered Cherub*, was published in 1982 and made the best-seller list. The following year, in a speech in the House of Lords, he urged the government to bring back the three-day week saying that in the winter of 1973–74 it had been "the finest period we ever had for productivity." Later that year he suffered two strokes, which affected his speech and left him partially paralysed, and he also underwent major heart surgery. In 1986 Gormley and his wife Nellie sold their home in Sunbury, West London, and returned to the North, settling in a bungalow near Wigan. Gormley is survived by his wife, whom he married in 1937, a son and a daughter.

b 5.7.17   d 27.5.93   aged 75

CHRIS HANI

Martin Thembisile (Chris) Hani, general secretary of the South African Communist party and a member of the African National Congress national executive committee.

SOON after returning to South Africa in 1990 after 27 years' exile, Chris Hani delivered what many might consider to be his own epitaph. "I've lived with death for most of my life," he said in a newspaper interview. "I want to live in a free South Africa . . . even if I have to lay down my life for it." But for others of his countrymen, particularly many whites, his recent statements condemning black-on-white killings was a belated conversion to peaceful change by a man who directed the ANC's guerrilla campaign in South Africa in the mid-1980s.

Hani had a powerful following among militants who oppose power sharing with de Klerk's white government. As leader of the Communist party, Hani had considerable influence in the ANC, whose top ranks include many Communists. He argued that the failure of communism in Europe had little relevance in South Africa where western style private enterprise had done little to raise the black community out of poverty. At times he seemed at odds with the more moderate approach adopted by Nelson Mandela, the president of the ANC. Hani's guerrilla background and commitment to communism made him a hero to young blacks who consider the ANC's older leaders too yielding to the white-led government and he was widely regarded as a possible heir to Mandela. He was the most popular candidate for the ANC's national executive at the party's congress in 1991 and was perhaps the biggest attraction at rallies and meetings across the country.

For years he had been portrayed by the government as one of the ANC's main "bogeymen" − a notoriety he accepted with good grace − and he enhanced this reputation when he first returned to South Africa under temporary indemnity from prosecution by declaring that, despite the launching of constitutional talks to end apartheid, a seizure of power could not be ruled out. Some of his most militant statements were delivered standing on platforms next to Mrs Winnie Mandela, the estranged wife of Nelson Mandela, as head of its armed wing, Umkonto we Sizwe (Spear of the Nation) − known by the initials MK. Their joint appeal to black youth, unschooled and unemployable after years of township upheaval, was powerful and regarded as dangerous by many inside as well as outside the ANC. Right wingers put a price on his head.

In recent weeks, however, Hani had called for reconciliation. Only days before his death he said that violence was hampering efforts to arrange the country's first election that would include blacks.

The conversion from hardliner to peace-maker was, in fact, gradual. In December 1991, Hani took over as general secretary of the SACP from Joe Slovo, in spite of objections by the ANC and its military wing, and the fiery rhetoric began to be replaced by criticism of the involvement in violence of ANC and SACP members. Hani called for a reappraisal of the control of township self-defence units, some of which, he said, were running wild among the communities they were supposed to protect. In April last year he quit as MK chief of staff.

He claimed not to be ambitious for personal power and recently said he preferred to be a political gadfly on the outside, criticising and prodding the government. When the ANC won power, he said, they might "jail the likes of me" as a troublemaker.

Chris Hani was a man of intellectual dynamism, a Latin scholar who also loved the works of Shakespeare, Keats and Shelley "to help me fly away from the trials and troubles of this world." One of six children of impoverished parents, he wanted at first, after attending a Catholic primary school in Transkei, to become a priest but his father opposed the idea and took him away.

He joined the ANC Youth League at high school and went on to Fort Hare University at Alice in the Eastern Cape province from which he was suspended for political activities. He graduated from the predominantly white Rhodes University in Grahamstown in Latin and English and in 1962, two years after the banning of the ANC, joined Umkonto we Sizwe and soon became part of the leadership.

Within months he was arrested under the Suppression of Communism Act and sentenced to 18 months' imprisonment but released on bail pending an appeal. When the appeal was turned down the following year he fled the country and joined other ANC exiles undergoing military training in the Soviet Union.

By the mid-1960s he had risen to the rank of commissar and saw action for the first time in the Rhodesian war, fighting with MK units on the side of Joshua Nkomo's ZAPU guerrillas. But he was arrested in neighbouring Botswana where he served two years of a six-year prison sentence for possessing weapons of war before being freed on parole.

In 1974, aged 32, he became the youngest national executive committee member of the ANC and was instructed to enter South Africa to establish a political infrastructure in the Cape province. He set up headquarters in independent Lesotho from where he directed guerrilla operations and continually infiltrated into South Africa.

Two attempts were made to assassinate him there in 1981. A bomb was placed under his car in Maseru, the Lesotho capital, but discovered before he got into the car, and shortly afterwards South African troops attacked ANC homes in Maseru killing 49 people. A statement was issued in Pretoria claiming that his wife had been killed but she survived and Hani, himself, was abroad at the time.

He was recalled to ANC headquarters in Lusaka, Zambia, where he was appointed army political commissar and deputy commander of MK and in 1983 was involved in the suppression of mutinies in MK training camps in Angola. But he always denied that he participated in the arrests, killings and torture that followed and which continue to be a matter of controversy inside and outside the ANC. The ANC has carried out its own investigations into the affair but so far has refused to name those responsible.

In 1987 Hani took over from Joe Slovo as MK chief of staff, with responsibility for its day-to-day operations and in South Africa his already fearsome reputation grew.

Of a wave of terrorist bomb attacks which claimed both white and black victims he said: "Our intention is to make them [white South Africans] see. When they are maimed and in hospital others will visit them and say: 'This is the price of apartheid.'

"A few blacks were maimed in a land mine blast in the Eastern Transvaal. Their response was: 'I am sorry I lost a leg but I know the action was not intended for me.'"

On his return to South Africa Hani went to live first in Transkei but moved last year into a modest home in Boksburg, east of Johannesburg, a town which became infamous in the late 1980s for its attempts to reintroduce petty apartheid but which was better suited to his position as one of the key figures in the constitutional negotiations for the ANC and the SACP.

He was popular among his white neighbours who were among the first to try to go to his aid after he was shot.

Chris Hani is survived by his wife, Limpho, and three daughters.

b 28.6.42   d 10.4.93   aged 50

Addressing a crowd at a rally in 1990

OLIVER TAMBO

Oliver Tambo, president of the African National Congress, 1978–91.

ALTHOUGH leader-in-exile of the ANC during its 30 years of guerrilla struggle against the white South African government, Oliver Tambo was hardly a firebrand revolutionary. He was a mild-mannered, gently-spoken, slightly-built man, usually wearing spectacles and a suit, who liked to surprise visitors by saying grace before meals. But he was strong-willed and adept at holding together the differing ideologies that existed uneasily within the ANC.

He suffered a stroke just before the 30-year ban on the ANC in South Africa was lifted in 1990 and, in the heady days following this event, there was criticism of the organisation's lack of direction and leadership. In 1991 he stepped down from the presidency to make way for Nelson Mandela, assuming instead the honorary post of national chairman. But during the lonely years of exile, underground activity and armed struggle, Oliver Tambo provided a remarkably steady, if unspectacular, hand on the tiller, while the imprisoned Mandela became the ANC's symbol.

Although he was more conservative than most of his colleagues, Tambo's authority was considerable and so was the respect with which he was regarded even among younger, more militant blacks. He was one of the ANC's old guard, a missionary-educated African nationalist, schooled in a tradition of non-violent protest. Yet he adapted himself to a more militant mission, campaigned vigorously for sanctions to be imposed on South Africa, railed against the West for its lack of meaningful action and never shirked the need for armed struggle.

Although sharing his authority with an executive committee, one-third of whom were communists, Tambo was considered by those outsiders who knew him best to be only mildly socialist in outlook. He advocated a multi-party system and a mixed economy; he disliked the inverted racism of Black Consciousness and was instrumental in bringing a multi-racial complexion to the ANC's executive committee. It was a sweet moment for him when, after 30 years of exile, he returned to Johannesburg in December 1990 to a tumultuous welcome from his countrymen, led by his comrade and former law-partner Nelson Mandela.

Oliver Tambo was educated at a mission school and at St Peter's Secondary School, Johannesburg, where he came under the influence of Father Trevor Huddleston, the English-born Anglican priest and anti-apartheid activist. Tambo went on to study at Fort Hare University, taking his BSc in 1941. He was studying there for a teaching qualification in 1942 when he was expelled with other students for taking part in a student protest.

He returned to St Peter's to teach and considered the priesthood for a time but turned instead to politics and the law. He joined the ANC in 1943 and was one of the founder members of its youth league, which was determined to stir into action a staid, conservative organisation. Another member was Nelson Mandela. In 1949 Tambo became a member of the ANC's national executive. He and Mandela had been friends at Fort Hare. They both became articled to a Johannesburg firm of attorneys and in 1952, after qualifying, set up an office together in the centre of Johannesburg, in defiance of the Group Areas Act.

In the 1950s, as well as working at his expanding legal practice − much of it involved in political cases − Tambo was at the centre of ANC activities, notably the campaign of defiance against unjust laws and the drawing up of a Freedom Charter. With the rest of the ANC ledership he was arrested on treason charges in 1956, but was released the next year (eventually the charges against everyone collapsed). He was repeatedly banned from attending meetings. He played a leading part in drawing up a new constitution for the ANC in 1957.

In 1960, during the emergency that followed the Sharpeville massacre, the ANC was declared an illegal organisation and the entire leadership arrested. Tambo escaped only because he was away from

home at the time. Carrying out an earlier decision by the ANC executive, he fled the country to continue the ANC struggle in exile.

With Mandela incarcerated, to Tambo fell the task of establishing an organisational structure. After settling his wife and three children in Muswell Hill, London, he shuttled endlessly between safe-houses in Dar es Salaam and Lusaka and around the other capitals of Africa and Europe, drumming up support. He lived with the ever-present danger of assassination. In 1967 after the death of Albert Luthuli, the ANC's president, Tambo became acting president and was formally appointed in 1978.

For the first two decades of his exile Tambo was treated as an uninvited guest in the West and his name meant little to the general public. What support the ANC attracted came from the Eastern bloc and non-aligned countries. But by the mid-1980s, as political unrest grew in South Africa, Tambo and the ANC began to find themselves courted by journalists, business leaders, liberal white South Africans and even by the governments of the Western powers.

In speech after speech Tambo criticised what he saw as the acquiescence of Western governments − in particular those of Britain and the United States − in Pretoria's racist policies; they were "co-conspirators in a crime of immense dimensions," he said, for their failure to impose effective sanctions on Pretoria. Although often regarded in some Western quarters as more moderate in private than his speeches indicated, Tambo had no scruples in escalating the guerrilla war against Pretoria, crippling the economy with sanctions and making the townships ungovernable.

A level of violence was being reached, he said in 1985, in which it was unavoidable that innocent people would be victims. At the same time he recognised that the organisation's refusal to renounce violence in response to partial reforms by Pretoria cost it support among white liberal opinion in South Africa and in conservative quarters abroad. He was sensitive to the ANC's dual need to retain its increasingly militant support at the grass-roots level while attempting to convince the West that the organisation was capable of providing South Africa with a reasonable and moderate alternative government.

As the violence worsened, the ANC continued its efforts to win greater support in the West by improving its image. Tambo said the organisation did not deliberately try to kill women and children. Civilian deaths, during attacks by ANC fighters on police and army personnel and installations, were regretted but considered unavoidable in a war situation.

Tambo believed it would take a combination of heightened conflict and increased international trade sanctions to make Pretoria seek talks with the ANC and he never abandoned his desire to negotiate a transfer of power. He continued to tour foreign capitals, calling on Western governments to boycott South Africa, and to canvass diplomatic support in the hope that the international community would come around to regarding the ANC as the only real representative of the South African people. He publicly dissociated himself from the views expressed by the leader of the ANC's military wing who said that South African judges, MPs and other prominent whites would become targets of attack.

In 1986, after months of assiduous backroom effort, Tambo achieved a diplomatic breakthrough by meeting formally, first with Lynda Chalker, then minister of state at the Foreign Office in June, and then with Sir Geoffrey Howe, the foreign secretary, at Chevening, in September.

Tambo followed this up the following year with a meeting with George Shultz, the American secretary of state, establishing the ANC's highest-level contact with the Washington administration. In the run-up to the talks with Shultz, Tambo spent more than a week meeting senior American politicians and businessmen, dining in the process with Henry Kissinger.

The ANC's more moderate stance in this period was indicated when Tambo marked the organisation's 75th anniversary with a speech aimed at dividing South Africa's white community by urging liberal-minded whites to breach their government's racial policies and join hands with blacks to create a non-racial society. At one such occasion in London he had meetings with Chief Buthelezi, the Zulu leader and former ANC member who headed the rival Inkatha movement, but was unable to forge a united approach.

In August 1989, with the prospect increasing of President P. W. Botha being replaced by the reformist-inclined F. W. de Klerk, Tambo suffered a stroke which left him partially paralysed. He was in Lusaka at the time but flew first to London and then to Stockholm for treatment. Still recuperating in a Stockholm clinic, he welcomed President de Klerk's announcement lifting the 30-year-old ban on the ANC in February 1990, but urged the world to do nothing to lessen the isolation of the apartheid regime.

A month later, still in Stockholm, he had an emotional reunion with the newly-released Nelson Mandela after a 28-year separation. Following his return from exile in December 1990 he resumed the ANC leadership and provided the first intimation of the organisation's change of stance over international sanctions when he said that, given the changing situation, there should be a careful revaluation of the advisability of insisting upon sanctions being maintained. In July 1991 Nelson Mandela succeeded him as president.

Oliver Tambo had few of the neuroses that might be expected from a life of exile. He recognised that the perils of post-apartheid South Africa might be as formidable as those already suffered, but he continued to espouse a multi-racial ideal.

He is survived by his wife, Adelaide, two daughters and a son.

b 27.10.17   d 24.4.93   aged 75

SIR PAUL HASLUCK

Sir Paul Hasluck, KG, GCMG, GCVO, PC, Governor-General of Australia, 1969–74.

IN JANUARY 1968, Paul Hasluck almost became prime minister of Australia. After the accidental drowning of Harold Holt he failed by only five votes to be elected leader of the Liberal Party and therefore prime minister. It was, perhaps, a failure which changed the course of Australia's political history. As Gough Whitlam told a farewell parliamentary dinner for the retiring Governor-General in July 1974, Hasluck would have been his "most formidable opponent" and Labour "might not have won" the 1972 election (which made Whitlam himself prime minister). At that dinner Whitlam said "there has not been a pro-consul of more diverse attainment since Cicero". Hasluck declined Whitlam's request that he extend his term as Governor-General and was succeeded by Sir John Kerr who later dismissed the Whitlam government.

Paul Hasluck was, at various times in his life, a journalist, poet, historian, career diplomat, politician and vice-regal representative. But he eschewed the politicking which would almost certainly have made him a prime minister. "I am available if the party wants me," he announced as five other Liberal contenders began lobbying to succeed Holt, and he added: "If it does not, I am not a particularly ambitious man".

Hasluck hardly canvassed his colleagues and did no deals, and John Gorton became Liberal prime minister. It was the same in 1966, after the retirement of Sir Robert Menzies, when William McMahon beat Hasluck for the Liberal party's deputy leadership by four votes. On both occasions Menzies supported the candidature of a man he much admired.

Hasluck had a fine mind which he used conscientiously in the service of Australia, and he brought his strong moral convictions into public life. He was respected on both sides of Parliament, where his rectitude could also be infuriating. In the early hours of one morning in 1964 even Whitlam threw a glass of water over Hasluck, then minister for external affairs.

As minister from 1964 to 1969 Hasluck was faced with formulating Australia's foreign policy during a critical period as Britain reduced her military strength in the Far East. He was a firm believer in the need to contain the spread of communism in Asia and criticised lack of interest in the region by the Western powers as "isolation in its most reckless form".

Hasluck worked hard in 1968 to ensure that Gorton did not follow the British example, arguing that Australia could not ignore "the great hopes, the rising nationalism, the great crises in Asia."

He strongly supported Australia's involvement in the Vietnam war. He encouraged the United States to prolong its own involvement, speaking out in 1968 against any unilateral decision to stop the bombing of North Vietnam. He warned that "the Americans must not forget that terrible Peking" and he saw the North Vietnamese as "Peking's puppets".

For a short period, 1963–64, Hasluck had been minister for defence. But his greatest service to Australia may have been as minister for territories from 1951 to 1963. This very long period enabled him to prepare Papua New Guinea for the independence which Whitlam thrust upon it in 1975. Hasluck had not expected such speed, but the new nation's stability owed much to his insistence that its tribes and regions, despite their differences, be developed at the same pace. In 1976 he recalled this stewardship in his book *A Time for Building*.

Paul Meernaa Caedwalla Hasluck was born into a Salvation Army family in Perth, Western Australia. His second name was an aboriginal one handed down by his grandfather who liked the sound of it while Caedwalla harked back to his Welsh ancestors. He went to Perth Modern School and, after graduating from the University of Western Australia, he joined *The West Australian* newspaper, then became a university lecturer in history, and in 1941 joined the Department of External Affairs. In 1942 he published *Black Australians*, a perceptive study of Aborigines.

In 1946 he became head of Australia's mission to the United Nations in New York. But, unable to work with his difficult minister, Dr Evatt, he resigned and returned to the university, writing two volumes of Australia's official war history. In 1949 he entered the federal parliament for Curtin, Western Australia. In 1977 he published *Mucking About*, an autobiography.

He leaves his widow, Dame Alexandra Hasluck, the writer, and a son.

b 1.4.05   d 9.1.93   aged 87

ALEX LYON

Alex Lyon, Labour MP for York from 1966 to 1983 and husband of the Labour MP Clare Short.

THROUGHOUT his 17-year career in the House of Commons which included two years as Minister of State at the Home Office, 1974–76, Alex Lyon was chiefly associated with immigration issues. Indeed, when he was dropped from his Home Office post by the incoming prime minister, James Callaghan in 1976, and his responsibility for race relations and immigration was divided among a number of other ministers, the event caused some controversy. At the time there was considerable public discussion on the question of whether the prime minister was, by this act, showing himself illiberal over race and immigration, or whether Lyon had been too zealous in aiding immigrants.

The decision certainly ended a controversial two years in office for Lyon, who at the turn of 1974–75 had gone to India, Pakistan and Bangladesh to enquire into delays in granting certificates of entry into Britain for dependants of people already settled. There was a clash when civil service procedures were criticised as amounting to a refusal of justice and in turn were defended – for instance, on the ground that patient enquiry into applications was better than hasty decisions over ill-founded documentation. Certainly, it happened that within a fortnight of Lyon's removal a quarterly report of the Ombudsman, Sir Idwal Pugh, called for simpler arrangements to speed entry of some immigrants from the Indian sub-continent.

It was the second occasion in his parliamentary career that Lyon had been deprived of a job. In May 1972 he had been dropped by the then leader of the Opposition, Harold Wilson, only a month after Lyon – a Labour front-bench spokesman on African affairs from 1970 and on home affairs from 1971 – had moved up to second spokesman on the latter, under Shirley Williams. The cause of Wilson's displeasure – based on reports by the whips and the Parliamentary Labour party, and spread alike over Lyon and over Maurice Foley – was that he had failed to observe a three-line whip on a vote in debate on the controversial Housing Finance Bill. Lyon's voting record was not of the kind to save him from dismissal.

There was to be no further Opposition role for Lyon, but in 1978 he was elected to succeed the Liberal peer Lord Foot as chairman of the United Kingdom Immigrants Advisory Service. This gave him much satisfaction enabling him to continue to scrutinise what he felt to be cases of unfair treatment to immigrants and would-be immigrants.

Lyon's actions often caused strong reactions – largely because he continually stood his ground as a zealot for what he saw as justice. Furthermore he was a zealot fortified with the trained professional skills and preoccupations of a barrister with years of practice behind him. He approached the legislative process with a sense of the injustice inflicted on some people under the law – "battered wives" for instance, many of whom he had represented in divorce hearings – and the accused in general when they seemed at risk from the rules of evidence and from the procedures over cautioning and taking statements.

He did not hesitate, after taking office, to speak out for a new deal under which a prosecuting service, independent of the police, might sanction prosecutions. He hoped such a service would look more sceptically on some cases than would the police themselves. If this made him less than popular with the police in his Home Office job at times, it was the clash with civil servants over immigration that he blamed for his early departure from office.

Alexander Ward Lyon was educated at West Leeds High School and University College London. He became a barrister in 1954 and practised on the North East Circuit. Once in politics, he joined, and later became chairman of, the Society of Labour Lawyers. He was also a member of the Committee of Inquiry on Privacy under Sir Kenneth Younger, which sat from 1970 and reported in two years. He was also a Methodist local preacher.

He won York in 1966 from the Conservatives when the notoriously close-fought constituency was for a time ignored by the Liberals, and he did well to hold it at the general elections of 1970 and in the spring and autumn of 1974. He barely managed it at the third contest, when the Liberals returned and his majority was cut to 831. But matters improved in the October 1974 election and his majority increased to 3,689. In 1969 he had been first an additional PPS to Treasury ministers and then PPS to the Paymaster General. He was a supporter of Britain's entry into the EEC and voted for the principle of entry in October 1971.

After his dismissal from the Home Office Lyon's career languished for a while – though he remained a vociferous spokesman on race and immigration issues. But his appointment to head the United Kingdom Immigrants Advisory Service, which had been set up in 1970 to advise and represent immigrants in difficulties with immigration control, gave him a new field for his concerns. In addition to his work with the service he

was, in 1981, a member of the Commons subcommittee which conducted an enquiry into the workings of the Commission for Racial Equality (CRE). As such he turned out to be one of the CRE's sternest inquisitors, accusing it in particular of virtually ignoring its law enforcement role. "What have you done with these powers?" he asked. "Out of 224 staff you have 53 in the equal opportunities division of whom only four are legally trained. In four years you have announced 45 strategic reviews of which you have completed ten, and those are the least important ones."

From 1980 to 1983 Lyon was chairman of the Parliamentary Labour party's Home Affairs Group. He was a vigilant scrutineer of the actions of the police, of whom he was often a stern critic. Here, too, he could be a stormy petrel, and on one occasion he was forced to retract remarks in which he had said that some chief constables appeared to think they were "above the law". He also took part in Labour delegations examining the state of human rights overseas.

Lyon was defeated for the York seat by the Conservative party candidate in the general election of 1983, when his wife Clare Short, whom he had married in 1981, was first elected to Parliament as Labour MP for Birmingham, Ladywood. The following year he relinquished his chairmanship of the United Kingdom Immigrants Advisory Service. He had periods of ill-health and in 1984 was diagnosed as having spinal muscular dystrophy. It was subsequently established that he was suffering from Alzheimer's disease. He continued to live with his wife at their home in Clapham until the summer of 1991 when his deterioration was such that he entered the Westbury Methodist Home at Milton Keynes.

Alex Lyon married, first, in 1951, Hilda Arandall, and they had two sons and a daughter. This marriage was dissolved. Clare Short and the children of his first marriage survive him.

b 15.10.31   d 30.9.93   aged 61

SIR MICHAEL McNAIR-WILSON

Sir Michael McNair-Wilson, Conservative MP for Walthamstow East, 1969–74, and Newbury, 1974–92.

MICHAEL McNair-Wilson was the first MP to be treated on a kidney dialysis machine and the first one to have a kidney transplant. These events, in 1984, transformed him from a mild, though critical, friend of the National Health Service to possibly its most enthusiastic supporter on the Conservative benches. He became president of the National Federation of Kidney Patients and diverted the energies he had previously devoted to skiing, riding and sailing into helping his fellow patients.

His health was the main reason for his decision before the 1992 general election not to fight the Newbury seat which he

had held for the previous 18 years. With his death Newbury has lost its previous MP and its sitting MP in the course of a few weeks, his successor, Judith Chaplin, having died on February 19.

Although a right-winger in some matters, McNair-Wilson was a notable Heath supporter after the second Conservative general election defeat in 1974 and he delivered a stern attack on Edward du Cann, then the chairman of the 1922 backbenchers' committee, for what he regarded as du Cann's failure to back Heath. McNair-Wilson was also parliamentary private secretary to Lord Walker when, as Peter Walker, he was Minister of Agriculture from 1979 to 1983 and one of the most prominent Tory wets.

McNair-Wilson was a first-class constituency MP and pleased his supporters particularly with his long-term opposition to the women protesters camped on Greenham Common.

He was a leading member of the Bow Group and in Parliament took a special interest in aviation.

Educated at Eton, Robert Michael Conal McNair-Wilson went from school into National Service and was commissioned in the Royal Irish Fusiliers. He served in Jordan, the Suez Canal Zone and in Gibraltar.

Back in civilian life, he farmed for three years in Hampshire, then took up journalism. He worked as a general reporter on several provincial newspapers before becoming a freelance. Between 1953 and 1955, he carried out important assignments for the BBC in Northern Ireland.

His next job was as press officer for Short Brothers and Harland, the Belfast-based aircraft company. This was his introduction to public relations, and he later joined Sidney-Barton, international public relations consultants, becoming a director in 1961.

McNair-Wilson had been an active worker for the Conservative party since 1958. He was prominent in the Young Conservative movement, serving on the executive of the Chelsea branch and later being elected chairman of the Westminster branch.

He served on the executive of the City of London and Westminster South Conservative Association. He had already made his mark as a propagandist in the Bow Group when he stood unsuccessfully against Dick Taverne, QC, then Labour, at Lincoln in the 1964 general election.

In 1967 he was adopted for Walthamstow East, which he won from Labour in the by-election of March 1969, turning a Labour majority of 1,807 into a Tory majority of 5,479. He was hard-pressed in the general election of 1970 but held on, with a majority down to 528.

In the February 1974 general election he was elected for Newbury, a constituency which includes the Greenham Common airbase. During the period of the anti-nuclear campaigners' attempt to blockade the base, he was deeply involved in efforts of local people to restore peace and quiet to their neighbourhood.

Between 1970 and 1974 he was variously secretary, vice-chairman and chairman of the Conservative backbenchers' aviation committee; for two years he was also joint secretary of the Conservative Greater London Members' Committee.

From 1973 to 1979 he was a member of the Select Committee on the Nationalised Industries, and of the council of the Air League from 1972 to 1976. He had been a member of the court of Reading University since 1979.

He was a joint author of *Blackshirt*, a biography of Mussolini (1959) and he also shared the authorship of a Bow Group pamphlet, *No Tame or Minor Role*, about Britain's future membership of the European Community.

He was the younger son of the late Dr Robert McNair-Wilson and Doris McNair-Wilson. He married, in 1974, Deidre Granville, and had four stepchildren and one daughter. His brother, Patrick McNair-Wilson, is Conservative MP for New Forest.

b 12.10.30 d 28.3.93 aged 62

IAN MIKARDO

Ian Mikardo, a Labour MP for 37 years and a former chairman of the Labour party.

THE Labour movement in Britain has traditionally consisted of two strands – the fundamentalists, always yearning to take the party back to the basics of socialism, and the pragmatists willing to make any sacrifice in order to attain office. From the moment that he wrote (with Dick Crossman and Michael Foot) the influential 1947 pamphlet, *Keep Left*, Ian Mikardo placed himself firmly in the former category. What, though, separated him from his more dreamy colleagues on the left was that he was in himself a very successful businessman. Starting out by running a laundry, he developed into a management consultant and eventually became a considerable entrepreneur in terms of East-West trade. (He was at least once sounded out about taking over the running of a nationalised industry – something he would have done supremely well.)

At Westminster "Mik" was very much a Commons character – genial, approachable and never in the least forbidding, for all his delight in demolishing opponents in argument. There was a racy side to his nature, reflected in the enthusiasm with which he served as the House's bookmaker: no election ever took place in any party on which he was not willing to quote a price. And he rarely lost money.

On the other hand, it may have been his political misfortune that in physical appearance he was the cartoonist's delight in looking the very image of a conspirator (and hardly a native-born one either). By Cummings in the *Daily Express*, in particular, he was regularly pilloried as someone out to undermine the British way of life – and in a famous witticism, Winston Churchill was once heard to murmur of him: "I'm told he's not as nice as he looks."

Born in Portsmouth of poor immigrant parents – his father from Poland, his mother from the Ukraine – Mikardo was proud to be a first-generation Englishman. As a child, his first language was Yiddish. A family story had it that his father, on arriving at the London Docks at the turn of the century, lived in the East End for four months before realising that he was in London and not in New York.

A bright boy, Mikardo thought of becoming a rabbi – he was to remain a committed Zionist all his life. But politics soon bewitched him and by 1944 he was prospective Labour candidate for Reading. At the time it seemed a safe Tory seat and an improbable vantage point from which a young socialist, however articulate, could make an impact on the national scene. But that year's Labour party conference set the tone for the election and at it the young Mikardo moved what came to be known as "the Reading resolution" calling for wholesale nationalisation once peace had arrived.

To the distress of the party leadership, the resolution was carried. As he left the hall Mikardo was accosted by Herbert Morrison, who ruefully remarked to him: "Young man, that was a good speech – but you realise, don't you, that you've lost us the general election."

In the event, Labour won a landslide victory just over a year later in July 1945 and Mikardo even gained Reading. It was to remain his political base for the next 14 years, with his triumph in holding onto it against an adverse national swing in 1955 being particularly notable. Predictably, Mikardo proved a first-class political organiser and "the Reading system" as his method of electioneering came to be known, soon became the envy of other constituencies. Even his campaigning resourcefulness could not, however, save him from defeat in Harold Macmillan's "You never had it so good" election of 1959 and for the next five years Mikardo found himself out of Parliament.

Worse than that, he virtually simultaneously lost his seat on the national executive of the Labour party to which he had first been elected in 1950. His supersession by Tony Benn was a particularly cruel blow as he was due that coming year to become chairman of the party – a post he had to wait to fill until 1970–71.

Within a year Mikardo was back on the NEC and four years later he returned to the House of Commons for the safe Labour seat of Poplar. Unlike other left-wingers, such as Barbara Castle, Dick Crossman and Tony Greenwood, he was not, however, offered any government post by Harold Wilson (something that increasingly seemed to rankle with him down the years). Certainly, he had all the ability to run a government department – but the truth was that he and Wilson had never got on. As it was, he could only display his gifts as a highly effective chairman of the Select Committee on Nationalised Industries, where he produced a widely praised report on the workings of the Bank of England.

To the Wilson governments of 1964–70 Mikardo soon became something of a thorn in the flesh. He was very critical of the party frontbench's stance on Vietnam, an outspoken opponent of all forms of incomes policy and a formidable antagonist to Barbara Castle over her trade union reform proposals as embodied in the famous white paper, *In Place of Strife*. By the time of the party's defeat in 1970, he had become – from his power base in the Tribune group – in effect the leader of the internal opposition to the government.

It was thus bad news for Wilson when, on his return to office in 1974, Mikardo was elected chairman of the Parliamentary Labour party. For the peace of mind of the Treasury bench his tenure of this office proved to be mercifully brief, a new chairman taking his place after the October 1974 election. The fact, of course was that Mikardo was now getting old – symbolically he was to lose his national executive seat in 1978 to Neil Kinnock – but he was still to enjoy one Indian summer, at least as a political organiser. Michael Foot's ten-vote victory over Denis Healey in the leadership election of November 1980 owed much to his ability as a campaign manager.

Mikardo had only a marginal sympathy for the constitutional causes that Tony Benn then took up, his personal loyalty remaining to his old Bevanite comrade, Foot. It was, in fact, partially re-selection, when he tried to bring in a compromise designed to preserve the rights of sitting MPs, that had cost him his seat on the NEC for the last time. His final years, both at conference and in the Commons, were slightly sad ones and it came as no surprise when he announced his decision not to contest the 1987 election. It was characteristic, though, of his love of Parliament that at the time he expressed a wish to serve as researcher to a young, incoming Labour MP. That never came to pass but instead he spent the early months of his retirement working on his autobiography which, when published in 1988, turned out to be aptly entitled *Back-Bencher*.

Mikardo married in 1932 Mary Rosette. They had two daughters.

b 9.7.08   d 6.5.93   aged 84

PATRICIA NIXON

Patricia Nixon, wife of the 37th President of the United States.

OF ALL the First Ladies who have recently occupied the White House, Patricia Nixon was perhaps the most stoic and the least pretentious. Despite the expression of rapt admiration with which she would watch her husband speak, she herself came to loathe the life of politics and more than once had urged him to give it up. It was, therefore, especially poignant that she should have had to share in the long drawn-out drama of Watergate which ended with Richard Nixon being the first US president forced to resign.

An intensely private person, "Pat" Nixon found herself thrust into national prominence as long ago as 1952. When under attack for his use of a "slush" fund in the first Eisenhower presidential campaign, the young Nixon, who was running for vice-president, did not hesitate to exploit his wife. Not only, as he delivered his notorious "Checkers" television speech, was she made to sit in camera shot with him in the studio; she was also the subject of perhaps the most mocked line in the broadcast — the one about her not possessing a mink coat but being the proud wearer of a respectable, Republican cloth one.

In the second of her husband's famous "six crises" Pat Nixon, who had some Irish blood in her veins, was, in fact, more inclined to battle things out than she was subsequently to be. Only a couple of years later she was in favour of her husband resigning the vice-presidency after only one term, feeling that Eisenhower had been less than fully supportive of him; and, after Nixon's narrow defeat by John F. Kennedy in the 1960 presidential election, she was passionately against him ever running for office again. Showing, for once, greater political acumen than he did, she argued particularly strongly against his disastrous bid for the governorship of California in 1962 and accepted with resignation rather than enthusiasm his decision to go after the presidency again in 1968.

Thelma Catherine Ryan — she later adopted the Christian name of Patricia, apparently because she had been born on the eve of St Patrick's Day — was the daughter of a German mother, who died when she was 13, and an Irish father. She was brought up in Artesia, California, a few miles from Richard Nixon's own home town of Yorba Linda. The two first met at an audition for an amateur theatrical production — and at the beginning it was the youthful lawyer, already the victim of one broken engagement, who made all the running. A good-looking woman with marvellous golden red hair, Pat Ryan was markedly more popular and poised than her suitor.

But one quality Nixon has never lacked is dogged determination; within a year, he had broken down the resistance of the 26-year-old schoolteacher he so much admired (he was later to say that, after he met Pat, he never looked at another girl again). The young couple became engaged in March 1939 and were married in June 1940.

The United States had not at that stage entered the second world war and at first they settled down to married life in Los Angeles. Nixon was angling at the time for a seat in the California state legislature but Pearl Harbor put all such plans on hold. He did not, though, immediately enlist, preferring to go as a civil servant to Washington, where he and Pat set up house in 1942. But six months later he had joined the US Navy, to the horror of his Quaker parents but to the relief of his wife, who was later to explain: "I would have felt mighty uncomfortable if Dick hadn't done his part."

If she did apply any pressure, Nixon afterwards should certainly have felt grateful for it. For, without his naval officer's uniform, it is highly questionable whether he would ever have been chosen as the Republican candidate for California's 12th congressional district at the end of 1945. With her all-American appearance – bright, blonde and neat – Pat Nixon soon proved the ideal candidate's wife, even managing to produce their first daughter well in time for polling day. At this stage of his political career she was always a tower of strength to her husband, not least in displaying the warmth and humanity – she was especially good with children – that Nixon himself, for all his efforts, was never quite able to show. Revealingly of her attitude at the time, she was among the strongest advocates of his following up his congressional victory of 1946 with a run for the senate in 1950.

What subsequently led to their drifting apart can only be a matter for conjecture – but if it remained a marriage, it soon ceased to be any form of political partnership. Indeed, as the years went by, Pat Nixon betrayed an increasing distaste for the intrusive demands of political life – whether as the wife of a senator, a vice-president or a president. One chilling story perhaps tells it all. On the day the Nixons had to leave the White House in August 1974, the disgraced president was about to deliver his final speech to his staff when his wife suddenly noticed three television cameras in the East Room where everyone had assembled. "Television?" she asked sharply, "Who authorised television?" A public man to the end, her husband had no alternative but to reply grimly: "I did – let's get in there." He then proceeded to make a rambling speech in which he went on at length about his dead mother and did not mention his wife once.

It says much for Pat Nixon's qualities that, in exile in San Clemente, she devotedly nursed the now officially pardoned ex-president through his recuperation after an attack of phlebitis in October 1974 that nearly killed him. She herself suffered a stroke in July 1976, allegedly as a result of reading Bob Woodward's and Carl Bernstein's *The Final Days* in which she was portrayed as a drunken recluse. She faithfully followed her husband in his moves back first to New York City and then to Park Ridge, New Jersey. She no longer, however, felt it necessary to put in many public appearances, seldom showing up even at the dinner parties for writers and journalists with which Nixon tried to further his quest for rehabilitation.

But she did make the supreme effort not only to be present, but actually to make a speech, when the Nixon presidential library was finally unveiled at Yorba Linda on July 19, 1990. Frail, unsteady on her feet, and already suffering from breathing difficulty, she was considered by many to be the star of the show.

Patricia Nixon is survived by her husband, who was ten months younger than she was, and by their two daughters, Tricia and Julie, the latter of whom married Eisenhower's grandson.

b 16.3.12 d 22.6.93 aged 81

LORD RIDLEY OF LIDDESDALE

Lord Ridley of Liddesdale, PC, Conservative politician who was a minister in all three of Mrs Thatcher's governments.

NICHOLAS RIDLEY claimed with truth that he was a Thatcherite before Margaret Thatcher and he remained resolutely and publicly Thatcherite after her fall from power. During the short period of his life which remained after that, he continued to proclaim the views he had held throughout the Thatcher years and, indeed, for all his political life. He was the most consistent advocate of the market as the one true liberating mechanism of society and he held to his economic convictions with the same sense of revelation which had sent his distant ancestor, Bishop Ridley, to the stake. He was once asked what he thought should be accomplished by a fourth Thatcher government and replied: "Nothing. That is the correct policy for a government." He was not being entirely flippant.

Despite his unrepentant Thatcherism he surprised some of his friends recently by doubting the wisdom of John Major-style rail privatisation, and as recently as a week before his death he was advocating in *The Times* taxing the better-off by raising the higher rate of income tax to 50 per cent. This was in the context of a warning from Ridley that a general increase in taxation was a prerequisite for economic recovery, and that the government should be "prepared to do unpopular things if the national interest demands them."

As he was one of Mrs Thatcher's leading ministers, at transport, at environment and at trade and industry, Ridley's beliefs have left their mark on the face of Britain. Contempt for the beliefs of others, however, contributed to the errors and even blunders which marked his career and culminated in the indiscretion which forced his resignation.

He had a well-justified reputation for intellectual arrogance and was not helped by his obvious distaste for the art of public relations. In the House he was abrasive, sometimes vitriolic. At news conferences he sat with a cloud of smoke over his head – he chain-smoked four packs of tipped cigarettes a day – and treated questions with almost insolent dismissiveness. In Whitehall he was truly formidable, respecting no hierarchy, remorseless with officials, questioning complacent quangos, providing floods of ideas, prepared to work 18 hours a day. To the Opposition, and to some members of his own party, he was the most unpopular of Mrs Thatcher's ministers. At close quarters, however, he generated a surprising and passionate loyalty, not least from his civil servants.

He could be charming as well as rude and some suspected that his public manner masked an element of private shyness. There was an elegance about his dogmatism, and his sharp tongue and sharper mind were qualities appreciated more in Whitehall than at the Palace of Westminster. He was at his best when things went wrong and it was noticeable that the leaving parties given for him at his various ministries all seemed marked by genuine, if wary, affection.

Ridley was the second son of the third Viscount Ridley. Inevitably, there were suggestions that his whole character was influenced by being a younger son. He maintained that any influence would have been for the good because it allowed him to do what he wanted. Still, his brother Matthew did inherit the viscountcy, the vast country house, some 10,000 acres and most of the family fortune. Ridley was left £10,000 and complained frequently about his lack of money. His circumstances must have contributed to many of his attitudes – opposition to all establishments ranging from consensus-seeking Tory governments to fat-cat trade unionists, contempt for those who had things too easy, appreciation for those who had fought their way upwards. He never passed through the Liberal or Labour phases of some of his colleagues. He was never even a left-wing Tory. He was saying that people should stand on their own feet long before it became a Thatcherite commandment. In the considerable Ridley vocabulary of invective there was no worse word than paternalism.

He was educated at Eton and Balliol. He wanted to be an architect, following his celebrated maternal grandfather, Sir Edwin Lutyens, who had created the Viceroy's House in New Delhi. But his father thought he should become an engineer. They compromised, Ridley reading mathematics and engineering at Oxford, before becoming a civil engineer and rising to managing director of his firm in the northeast.

Nine previous Ridleys had been MPs and Nicholas Ridley followed the family tradition. He started by fighting Blyth in 1955. This was a Ridley town, largely built by them and operated as a coal port in the past. If this was a gesture to his family it was a hopeless one. He lost predictably and massively but by the 1959 election had found a better constituency in the safe Tory seat of Cirencester and Tewkesbury, which he represented for the rest of his Commons career.

He made little impression in the House at first. Few recognised his promise. The only surprising thing was his spell as PPS to Sir Edward Boyle, the outstanding "wet" of his day. They had little in common except Eton and good conversation. In opposition Ridley was made a junior spokesman in various fields but he had to wait for the Conservative victory of 1970 before achieving anything of significance. He was briefly a junior minister at Technology before Edward Heath made him Parliamentary Under-Secretary for Trade and Industry. He left this post after two years, refusing the prime minister's offer of the arts ministry, claiming that he could not support the Heath government's industry bill U-turn. He had shown his colours before when he opposed the Macmillan plan to lend £500 million to the National Coal Board in 1961 and he had voted for Powell against Heath in the 1965 leadership election.

It was no surprise, therefore, when he found it impossible to remain in the government. His resignation was a well publicised affair, and with Jock Bruce-Gardyne and John Biffen he went on to fight Heath's counter-inflation plans from the back benches.

When the Conservatives lost the second election of 1974 Ridley's flat off Victoria Street was the scene of some of the meetings of the anti-Heath faction. Ridley's first choice as new leader was Sir Keith Joseph, and he settled for Margaret Thatcher with some reluctance as he thought she could not win. His pessimism proved unjustified, his career was modestly advanced and he became Minister of State at the Foreign and Commonwealth Office (he had hoped to be in the cabinet as Secretary of State for Trade). It was not an entirely happy experience – like so many of his appointments. Labour soon demanded his resignation when he announced the end of the arms embargo against Chile.

His time at the FCO is best remembered for his attempt to settle the Falklands dispute. He visited the islands first in 1979 and returned with a plan to yield Falklands sovereignty to Argentina in return for a lease-back agreement. He was booed off the islands and when he returned, utterly jet-lagged, and went immediately to the House of Commons, he took a hammering there. Tories, Labour and Liberals combined to attack Ridley personally and the plan. His warning that Britain must discuss sovereignty with Argentina or prepare effectively to defend the islands was ignored. By the time the invasion came, and he had been proved right, Mrs Thatcher had moved him to become Financial Secretary to the Treasury.

In 1983 he was made Transport Secretary. Almost immediately he went to the Motor Show in a French car. He defended his action by asserting the consumer's right to choice, turning his decision to buy a foreign car into a political act. It was not an argument which appealed to British manufacturers. His ministry continued to be controversial. Ridley began by announcing the intention to privatise British Airways. He expanded Stansted Airport after years of argument, allowed the Okehampton by-pass to cut through a national park, reduced rail and bus subsidies, spotted a way to start the

Channel tunnel without a public enquiry and pushed through bus deregulation against the opposition of 90 per cent of the industry. Protests were rebutted or ignored and the measures forced through with no regard for his personal popularity. For him, loyalty to the Thatcherite revolution came first.

After three years he was appointed Secretary of State for the Environment. Labour-controlled councils were his main target. He never had a taste for any sort of local government and he would have liked to strip down all councils until few, if any, of their functions remained. He made no secret of his views – or his intentions. Some Labour councils were singled out as "rotten", "stinking" or "totalitarian". Greens were described as "pseudo-Marxists". He went too far with his colourful phrases, however, when in the wake of the *Herald of Free Enterprise* disaster he quipped that William Waldegrave, his minister in charge of a bill, was not going out with his bow doors open. For this he made, unusually, an apology. He often had difficulty in distinguishing between affronting complacency and outraging human feelings. He faced more criticism – much from his own side – over water privatisation, over building on the site of the Rose Theatre and for giving permission to create a new town in Hampshire's green belt (to say nothing of granting permission to Peter Palumbo to demolish the Mansion House/Mappin and Webb site).

His action over the community charge also came under fire. The final consequences of his decision that the poll tax should be introduced immediately, instead of being phased in over ten years, came with Mrs Thatcher's resignation in 1990. As it was, 30 Tory MPs rebelled against his community charge bill when it had its second reading. He never sought to ingratiate himself with his colleagues and soon after the community charge revolt he mocked southeastern Tory MPs for their NIMBY (Not In My Back Yard) attitude to house building. It was, therefore, unfortunate that within weeks it became known that he had objected to an application to build houses at the bottom of his garden in the Cotswolds. Later there was more publicity when he attempted to divert a public footpath away from his cottage in Cumbria. He was not really created to be an environment secretary and it came as a relief even to his friends when he was moved to another department in 1989.

It is claimed that the first question he asked after arriving at the Department of Trade and Industry in 1989 was: "What is this place *for*?". The very idea of such a department offended his supreme belief that governments should not interfere in the running of commerce and industry. Controversy followed him again. There was trouble in the Commons when he took no action against the Al-Fayed brothers over the takeover of Harrods and the House of Fraser, even though an enquiry by his own DTI had accused them of deceit. This was followed by apparent floundering over the Iraqi supergun; a row when his department blocked a City takeover by mistake; and dispute over "sweeteners" (though this was really Lord Young's responsibility) paid during the British Aerospace-Rover takeover.

Then, in July 1990, after he had been resisting accelerated moves into the Exchange Rate Mechanism, he gave an interview to *The Spectator* that threatened to break the government's fragile unity on Europe. The interview, resulting from his underlying fear that Germany would dominate the pound in a fixed system, leading to higher inflation and greater recession, contained expressions obviously unacceptable in a cabinet minister in 1990. Ridley talked of monetary union being a German racket designed for it to take over the whole of Europe. The French were poodles. The European Commission was run by 17 unelected, rejected politicians. "I'm not against giving up sovereignty but not to this lot," he said. "You might as well give it to Adolf Hitler, frankly." Ridley was not anti-European. At one time he had seemed positively federalist – he even co-authored a pamphlet advocating a united

Europe in the 1960s – but ever since the publication of the Delors report he had become increasingly alarmed at the momentum driving Britain towards Euro-federalism.

He was in Hungary when the *Spectator* interview appeared and was seemingly unaware of the exact scope of the article or the fuss it would cause. Doubts were expressed at first about whether it would be necessary for him to resign. Mrs Thatcher's feeling was one of loyalty to an old friend, to one who shared her views and even influenced them and who had been prepared for ridicule, dislike and even hatred in order to sustain her revolution. Eventually, after an embarrassing delay, what should have been obvious in the first place was agreed. Mrs Thatcher, who had accepted so many other indiscretions from him, was forced to accept Nicholas Ridley's resignation.

THE SPECTATOR

Dominic Lawson meets Nicholas Ridley

Speaking for England

A.N. Wilson
Why I tell royal tales

Vicki Woods
The joy of sects

He was a man of great courage, sometimes subtle but never tricky, incapable of dishonesty, inflexible of purpose. He lacked one thing – a capacity to dissemble. He said what he thought, sometimes with disastrous results. He was a high-risk politician and in talking so frankly to Dominic Lawson, the editor of *The Spectator*, he took one risk too many. It was the job of Lawson's father, Nigel Lawson, that he had coveted after Lawson himself resigned in October 1989. He had many qualifications for the post but he had attracted altogether too much opprobrium to be given one of the great offices of state. In his July 1990 letter of resignation he revealed that even before *The Spectator* affair he had decided to retire at the next election. He hoped Mrs Thatcher would be there to win a fourth term but he had shrewdly concluded that he would have a diminishing influence even on a future guided by her.

After Margaret Thatcher's fall, he wrote the best of the post-1990 ministerial memoirs (apart from Nigel Lawson's), *My Style of Government: The Thatcher Years*, as well as starring in a memorable edition of *Panorama* entitled "Mr Ridley's Europe". He was also a journalist of some distinction − contributing a number of articles to *The Times* and latterly (even more remarkably) to *The Spectator*.

Made as a life peer in the 1992 Dissolution Honours, and taking the title Lord Ridley of Liddesdale, he returned to his native Cumbria and resolved that he would devote himself to writing and to art − he was a water colourist of professional standard. Outdoors, perhaps he would create another masterpiece like the water garden he had created at his home in the Cotswolds. He might choose to change his life but, like Bishop Ridley, he would not change his beliefs. If his final illness prevented him from being conventionally active in the House of Lords, he nevertheless continued to make his political presence felt through his writings.

He married, in 1950, Clayre, daughter of the fourth Baron Stratheden and Campbell and they had three daughters. The marriage was dissolved in 1974 and five years later he married Judy Kendall, who survives him.

b 17.2.29   d 4.3.93   aged 64

Collecting litter with Mrs (Lady) Thatcher in Parliament Square (1988).

LORD WINSTANLEY

Lord Winstanley, former Liberal MP and chairman of the Countryside Commission, 1978–80.

MICHAEL WINSTANLEY, a family doctor by profession, enjoyed two brief spells in the House of Commons. He was the surprise victor in the Tory seat of Cheadle at the 1966 general election, overturning a previous Conservative majority of 8,691. Eight years later (having lost Cheadle in 1970) he succeeded in representing, if only for a period of seven months, the newly created seat of Hazel Grove, in which some of his old constituency had been incorporated. His Commons career terminated at the second general election of 1974 but at the end of 1975 he was created a life peer on the nomination of Jeremy Thorpe, the then Liberal leader.

In truth, though, Winstanley's career was made as much in medicine as in politics. Even before he entered the Commons he was chairman of the Liberal party's health panel and was well known as a general practitioner in the northwest. There were some, indeed, who ascribed his striking victory at Cheadle in 1966 to his having been Granada TV's screen doctor for a number of years (much as Charles Hill owed his initial political success to having been the BBC's "Radio Doctor" in the 1940s). Winstanley was an accomplished broadcaster, as he demonstrated in the years that he "fronted" Granada's social action programme, *This Is Your Right*, and though his presenter's role was interrupted by the IBA the second time he became an MP in 1974, he continued to take an active interest in all questions of broadcasting policy, serving at one time as a member of the BBC's General Advisory Council. In 1978 he was appointed chairman of the Countryside Commission but his tenure there proved short-lived as the Thatcher government put in its own nominee in 1980.

Michael Platt Winstanley, himself the son of a doctor, was educated at Manchester Grammar School and at Manchester University, where he was president of the union as well as captaining the university cricket team and editing the student paper. In accordance with the wartime custom, he was given deferment in order to qualify as a doctor and did not enter the forces until 1946, when he joined the Royal Army Medical Corps. From 1948 to 1966 he practised in Urmston, Greater Manchester, combining his family practice with being a Treasury medical officer and an Admiralty surgeon and agent from 1953 onwards. He played a full part in local medical politics being the Manchester divisional spokesman for the BMA and serving for a number of years on the Lancashire executive council of the NHS.

By contrast, his political career sometimes seemed less than fortunate. His victory in Cheadle in 1966, though impressive, was the result of a lot of quiet work the Liberals had already put into the constituency and Winstanley's loss of it four years later (admittedly to a new Tory candidate) was a bad blow to the party in the generally gloomy 1970 election. Being out of parliament helped him, however, with his television work and there can be no doubt that the fame in

the northwest of the tea-time programme, *This Is Your Right*, assisted him in gaining the new seat of Hazel Grove in February 1974. Had the IBA not banned him from continuing with the programme in April 1974 on the curious, nanny-state, ground that being associated with it might give him "an undue political advantage", it is perfectly possible that his Commons career would not have been as abruptly amputated as it was.

Winstanley found time, however, to identify himself with a number of forward-looking causes. He was a pioneer of the notion of a register of MPs' business interests, an early advocate of fixed-term parliaments, a stout champion of the environment (particularly of national parks) and always a staunch defender of the National Health Service. Ill-health had latterly restricted his activities in the Lords but in his early years there he was an energetic and articulate member who saw no difficulty at all about the Liberal party's merger with the Social Democrats. He had been a front-bench spokesman on broadcasting, health and social security.

A competitive sportsman all his life – some of his friends believed that the highlight of his career in his own eyes lay in captaining the Combined English Universities Cricket Team in 1941 – Winstanley for a time wrote a sports column for the *Manchester Evening News*.

He was also the author of five books, *Home Truths for Home Doctors* (1963), *The Anatomy of First-Aid* (1966), *The British Ombudsman* (1970), *Tell Me Doctor* (1972) and *Know Your Rights* (1975).

He was twice married and is survived by his wife Joyce, their son and daughter and one son of his first marriage.

b 27.8.18   d 18.7.93   aged 74

SIR DAVID BROWN

Sir David Brown, industrialist and chairman of Aston Martin Lagonda, 1947–72.

DAVID BROWN was not only one of Britain's leading industrialists, but a man who was passionately interested in the sport of motor racing. In the late 1940s he purchased Aston Martin and Lagonda and, by investing a considerable amount of money into the companies, was largely responsible for the return of these two famous marques to international race circuits. His initials, DB, were used in the names of a succession of Aston Martin models.

Brown had a knack of mixing business with pleasure, whether it was by taking over a company he loved, or aggressively expanding into a competitor's territory: "To begin with, one works hard to achieve a decent standard of living. Then the real pleasure is the game of business itself, the accumulation of money doesn't enter into one's calculations — it is incidental. But my biggest kick is watching the business actually grow."

His was not a rags-to-riches story. He was born into a well-established Yorkshire manufacturing family whose future had already been assured by his grandfather's success in the gear manufacturing industry. Brown's father, Frank Brown, passed on to his son an astute appreciation of big business and from a young age David was determined to make money, buying his first shares when he was a schoolboy with £5 saved from his pocket money. He was educated at Rossall Scnool and at Huddersfield Technical College.

He joined the family firm, David Brown and Sons (Huddersfield), as a 17-year-old apprentice in 1921 and was deliberately treated no differently from any of the other apprentices. After a grounding in various sections of the works Brown progressed from foreman, assistant works manager and works manager to director and, in 1932, managing director.

Almost at once the company began to advance on a broader, more ambitious basis. Brown soon absorbed a considerable amount of engineering experience and in 1928 was sent on an extended visit to the United States, South Africa and Europe to study factory conditions and business methods.

At the age of 28 Brown started a new bronze and steel foundry in Penistone where unemployment was severe. The introduction of a new, easily learnt technique in steel casting manufacture enabled him to make quick use of the labour available and at the same time bring much-needed relief to the town.

In addition to serving associated companies, the foundry produced steel and bronze castings, including air frame and engine components for modern aircraft, heavy components for electrical plants (including nuclear power installations), oilfields and oil refinery equipment and precision castings for innumerable industries.

Seeking an end product of his own, Brown then turned his attention to tractor production. In 1936 he collaborated with the pioneer Harry Ferguson in the production of a revolutionary tractor – the first machine to incorporate the now universal hydraulic lift principle.

Their association ended in disagreement, but Brown continued with his own research among British farmers, and came up with the first all-British tractor, shown for the first time at the 1939 Royal Agricultural Show, which was immediately dubbed the Rolls-Royce of tractors. As a result of this success, a separate tractor manufacturing plant was established at Meltham, near Huddersfield.

However, the outbreak of war interrupted plans for the tractor's full-scale production and Brown's factories were harnessed to the national effort. Gears and steel castings for aircraft, tanks and ships were the company's main contribution. At the height of the Battle of Britain in 1940, the factory at Meltham was the only one producing Spitfire engines and supercharger gears (all the others had been bombed out of production). Meltham also produced gearboxes for Churchill tanks.

In 1951, 30 years after joining the company, Brown merged the parent company with his many subsidiaries and associated companies into the David Brown Corporation.

Second only to business, cars were the great passion of Brown's life. After his first motorcycle, Brown had gone on to build his own motor car, buying a Meadows engine and gearbox, a Timken axle and two pieces of steel for the chassis, and constructing a wooden frame, with aluminium body panels. His love of motor racing dated from his days as an apprentice, when he first met Amherst Villiers, who approached Brown's company for a blower-type supercharger to be fitted to his car.

Brown later raced on the beach at Southport in 1929 and won his class at Shelsey Walsh. However, he was forced to give up racing and put business first after his father had a stroke in 1930. As he could not bear to go near motor-racing circuits without competing, he decided to concentrate instead on horse-racing. He became a natural horseman, playing polo and hunting, and was Joint Master of the South Oxford Hounds for many years.

Then, in 1947, Brown saw a small-ad notice in *The Times* offering a defunct car business for sale. Having made enquiries, he found it to be none other than Aston Martin, which he duly bought for £20,000. At that point the company consisted of little more than a shed at Feltham, a few rusty lathes, a prototype car called "The Atom" and an engine. The following year Brown bought Lagonda for £50,000.

Brown was largely responsible for the company's success in racing and many great names of the track – Eric Thompson, Dennis Poore, Peter Walker, Reg Parnell, Roy Salvadori, Peter Collins, Stirling Moss, Carroll Shelby and Tony Brooks among them – drove for Aston Martin. Brown's proudest moment came in 1959, when Roy Salvadori and Carroll Shelby from Texas won the Le Mans 24-hours race in an Aston Martin (Brown had to be dissuaded from driving the car himself).

His decision then suddenly to withdraw from the track was based primarily on a conviction that he had strayed too far from his original idea — which was to see sports car racing more closely related to a production car which the public could buy. In the larger scheme of things, the company made very few cars. Since Aston Martin was founded in 1914, less than 12,000 cars have been built — 9,000 of which are still on the road. But those few they did make became among the most sought-after of production cars and Brown was delighted to supply the now famous Aston Martin DB5 fitted with various gadgets and an ejector seat for the James Bond "007" films *Goldfinger* and *Thunderball*, based on the books by his friend Ian Fleming. Brown was knighted in 1968.

By the early 1970s, however, tractor production had increased to 1,000 a week, unfortunately conciding with a sudden slump in agriculture. Management differences arose and in 1971 Brown, by then described as the "non-executive chairman" was told by a consortium of bankers to keep out of the running of the David Brown Corporation (the banks' continued support for the by-now heavily indebted corporation was conditional on this promise). The tractor company was duly sold off to a Houston company in 1972, and Brown's beloved Aston Martin was sold later the same year. In 1978 Brown's shipbuilding company, Vosper Thornycroft, was nationalised. Brown did not feel adequately compensated for its assets of £30 million, and left the country in disgust the same year.

Leaving behind his second wife, he settled in Monte Carlo as a tax exile and later married his former personal assistant, 47 years his junior. His last years were lived in the sun and devoted to yachts, jetsetting and visiting friends. He remained fit and active and, well into his eighties, could still bound up six flights of stairs and play a game of tennis.

He was married three times, first in 1926, to Daisie Muriel Firth by whom he had a son and a daughter. That marriage was dissolved and in 1955 he married Marjorie Deans. They were divorced in 1980, the same year in which he married Paula Benton Stone. He leaves his widow and his two children.

b 10.5.04   d 3.9.93   aged 89

Aston Martin assembly line (1957)

SIR JOHN DAVIS

Sir John Davis, CVO, former chief executive, chairman and president of the Rank Organisation.

JOHN DAVIS was one of the most forceful businessmen of his time, exercising autocratic power over Britain's postwar film industry, which he pruned ruthlessly, and going on − by means of a brilliant investment in the Xerox copying machine company − to build the Rank Organisation into one of the country's most successful conglomerates, controlling cinemas, hotels, holiday-camps and bingo-halls.

An ebullient, dictatorial figure who acknowledged four marriages but was reputed to have entered into six, Davis ruled the Rank Organisation as a personal fiefdom and was directly responsible both for its successes and its failures. He was loathed as much as he was admired and was notorious for the way he bossed around the Rank Organisation's contract film stars and starlets; and for the cold-blooded manner in which he axed executives, dispatching around 70 during his tenure of office. His most spectacular boardroom battle occurred in 1975 when, at the age of 68, he was chairman, but, reluctant to delegate authority, he sacked Graham Dowson, the company's chief executive. It was a messy and public affair in which Lord Goodman was called in for legal advice by Rank and a former governor of the Bank of England, Lord O'Brien, played a pivotal role as a non-executive director.

John Henry Harris Davis was educated at the City of London School and started his business career with the British Thompson Houston Electric Group. In 1938 he became chief accountant to the Odeon cinema chain, at that time run by a Birmingham metal merchant, Oscar Deutsch.

In 1942 J. Arthur Rank (later Lord Rank) bought control of Odeon Theatres, and made Davis joint managing director, along with Deutsch. That Davis remained in senior management for so long was due in no small part to the personal confidence Rank had in him, and which he continued to have throughout the subsequent controversies.

Davis was promoted to managing director of the Rank Organisation in 1948. As such he was responsible for more than 500 Rank cinemas in Britain and scores more throughout the Commonwealth. More significantly, although his name never appeared in any film credits, he exercised supreme power over which films were made, at which studios and with what budgets. He also controlled the careers of such bright film stars of the time as Jack Hawkins, Kay Kendall and Anthony Steel and the dozens of others who were contracted to Rank, even instructing them on the way they should dress for official Rank functions.

In the 1950s, however, the British film industry was facing a slump. Not only was the industry encountering intense competition from often superior Hollywood productions, but the duty which had previously protected the domestic product from American imports had recently been scrapped. Public taste in entertainment was also changing, particularly with the advent of television. The company was in debt to the tune of £16 million and Davis felt justified in initiating a process of "rationalisation" of interests: a euphemism for the closure of cinemas and the making of fewer films. Although this was strongly criticised at the time, it made a complete restructuring of the organisation possible. The company was broken into 20 divisions, each with its own responsibility and accountability to a divisional director.

Under Davis's control, Rank began to diversify, extending into television set manufacture, hotels and scientific equipment, as well as leisure activities such as ten-pin bowling and ballroom dancing. In the 1970s Davis brought City Wall Properties, Butlin's and Oddenino's Property and Investment Company into the organisation.

Over the two decades that Davis was in control, the Rank Organisation grew into an enormous conglomerate and became one of the country's star performers in terms of exports. Davis's financial management was certainly competent, but what really tipped the scales as far as profits were concerned was his decision to enter the xerography market (the photocopying process). Davis was no engineer and was making a decision to back an unproven technical product. It was a gamble that paid off. The Rank Organisation jointly with Xerox corporation of Rochester, New York, formed Rank Xerox in 1956, and in 1969 began to manufacture a range of other scientific products including computers. Rank Xerox performed just as well outside America, and xerography eventually came to account for over 40 per cent of the group sales turnover.

By 1969 the organisation's total profits had reached £60 million, and by 1972 over £80 million. Partly through good fortune, partly through management prowess and "hunch", Davis had become known as one of Britain's most formidable businessmen, as well as one of the most ruthless. There was, it was noted, an unusually high turnover among senior management staff closest to him: "I eat managing directors for breakfast", he once said. His business as well as his personal life was marked by squalls and acrimony, most of which arose from his unwillingness to delegate authority.

Over the years Davis's strength within Rank had been underpinned by the 53 per cent holding that the Rank Foundation (of which he was a trustee) held in the company. This "undemocratic" capital structure was the cause of much contention with ordinary shareholders. In 1972, however, American shareholders in the organisation (who held only non-voting "A" shares) managed effectively to stop Davis's take-over bid for the brewery concern, Watney Mann, after bitter exchanges at semi-public meetings. The Americans were concerned that Rank Xerox's profits would be diluted by the takeover.

In September 1975 disputes between Davis and his chief executive and heir apparent, Graham Dowson, erupted into a serious boardroom row. The main points of the dispute were over Davis's diversification plans and general management style. But Dowson was not backed up by the rest of the Rank board, which was made up almost entirely of non-executive directors, and whose responsibilities for the day-to-day running of the firm were not entirely clear.

Although Dowson was forced to leave, subsequent criticism from shareholders and the press over the sacking brought matters to a head for Davis. In 1976 it was announced that votes would be given to the nearly 140 voteless "A" shares held in the organisation, and that Davis would retire as chairman in March 1977. He went on to hold the position of president until 1983.

John Davis was knighted in the Birthday Honours of 1971. The last year of his chairmanship of the Rank Organisation was clouded by disappointing financial results for the shareholders, but more important was the damage done to the "image" of business by the chairman's domineering management style, which had become more obsessive with age. The flamboyance of his personal life did not improve matters. Nevertheless, the early decisions he took with regard to the structure of the British film industry helped to ensure the survival of the Rank Organisation.

His judgment was vindicated by the development of the xerography business, in which he took a bold lead after others had faltered. He also devoted much time and enthusiasm to encouraging the arts, supporting charities and promoting business professionalism, especially in the advertising industry. He was chairman of the fund raising committee of the Westminster Abbey Appeal, 1973–85, and was appointed CVO in 1985.

The wives whom John Davis acknowledged were Joan Buckingham, whom he married in 1926 and by whom he had one son; Marian Gavid, whom he married in 1947 and with whom he had two daughters; Dinah Sheridan, the actress, whom he married in 1954; this marriage was dissolved in 1965 and in 1976 he married Mrs Felicity Rutland.

b 10.11.06   d 27.5.93   aged 86

RAUL GARDINI

Raul Gardini, Italian entrepreneur and yachtsman.

RAUL GARDINI turned the Ferruzzi group – once a provincial family business – into Italy's second largest private company, after Fiat. In a country where a few powerful families have traditionally dominated the business landscape, the hitherto obscure Ferruzzi clan became, in a space of ten years, celebrities on the scale of the Pirellis. But Gardini's cavalier expansion drive during the mid-1980s' equities boom eventually left the company saddled with $20 billion of debt.

Gardini was known in Italian finance as *Il Contadino*, translated as "the

farmer" or "the peasant". While, in his company's heyday, Gardini was said to enjoy the epithet – "it symbolises many of our values" – the suggestion earlier this year of sharp business practice led the Italian press to change it to the less complimentary *Il Corsaro* – "the pirate".

But in the late 1980s Gardini was seen as a symbol of successful modern Italy. Expensively dressed, permanently suntanned and never without a Camel cigarette, he enjoyed living in a style calculated to provoke comment. He commuted from apartments in Rome and Milan, and a palace on the Grand Canal in Venice, to the firm's headquarters – a Renaissance palazzo in Ravenna on the Adriatic coast – which he had decorated in the style of an English country house (Barbours, tweed caps and Burberrys in the entrance hall). Photographed at the helm of some of the world's fastest yachts, Gardini went on to spend $100 million on one – *Il Moro di Venezia* – intended to win the America's Cup.

Gardini's father was a wealthy, authoritarian Ravenna landowner and his son determined to do things differently. Business was always in his blood but he did not excel at school, never gained a mathematics qualification and quickly dropped out of Bologna University. He was taken on instead by his father's best friend, Serafino Ferruzzi – a successful grain-merchant who made his fortune trading in cheap barley and wheat from Algeria and the Soviet Union after the second world war – and, in 1957, married his employer's daughter, Idina. Like Alan Bond, whose marriage gave him the collateral to start in property, Gardini was made by the match: Ferruzzi's own son had no head for business, and for 20 years Gardini was his employer's right-hand man and heir apparent.

Their relationship was not always smooth: after one argument, Gardini turned Ferruzzi out of his car and left him stranded by the roadside to hitchhike to a meeting. But when Ferruzzi died in a plane crash in 1979, his will unequivocally named Gardini as his successor.

The Ferruzzi company's roots were in agriculture: it owned two and a half million acres of land in Europe and America – growing corn, sugar beet, coffee, rubber and citrus fruit, as well as raising 100,000 cattle a year. With Gardini as chairman, the company – fast becoming a one-man empire – launched a series of aggressive take-over bids, including, in 1986, a successful one for Montedison, the chemicals and financial services group. That year Ferruzzi's revenues topped $8billion and the company became Europe's biggest sugar conglomerate, grain and cereals trader, and its largest producer of corn starch.

But as the empire grew, so did Gardini's arrogance. In 1990, with company debts spiralling out of control, family shareholders stepped in to prevent him from taking over the state share in Enimont – a joint venture between the state-owned Enichem Chemicals Company and Montedison. Montedison's share was sold instead to ENI – Enichem's parent company – at a considerable profit, but Gardini was furious at being sidelined in this way. The following year, in what looked like a calculated insult to the Italian political establishment, he resigned as chairman of Ferruzzi, appointing his 22-year-old son, Ivan, as his successor.

Gardini had always turned to the sea to escape the pressures of the business world. Now he left for San Diego to launch a campaign to win the America's Cup. A sailor from the age of 12 when he began racing Lightning and Finn dinghies, he graduated to become the Maxi world champion in 1988 and to win the right to challenge for the America's Cup in 1992.

Sponsored by Montedison, he launched an extravagant campaign to win the cup and make the chemical giant a household name in America. Three million dollars was spent on the launch of the first of five America's Cup yachts (all to be called *Il Moro di Venezia*). And, though the campaign cost over $100 million, the family group spent more buying up the best technology companies within the marine industry and setting up the most advanced composite manufacturing plant in the world at Venice, where his boats were built.

The axe on the boat-building company fell shortly after *Il Moro di Venezia III* won the America's Cup world championship in 1991 – a warm-up for the main event in 1992 – beating the favourites from New Zealand and the US. Had Gardini's crew not won, then the axe would almost certainly have fallen on the project, too. Gardini, however, was allowed to continue leading his cup campaign into the finals. The Ferruzzi family, however, cut off all extra spending. For the last year of the campaign the designers went unpaid and all research and development was halted.

Remarkably, Gardini's crew came from behind in the Challenge finals to beat the New Zealanders for the right to race against Bill Koch's *America* but lost the series.

Gardini had returned to Italy in 1991 with a new business plan, which would have put him in sole control of the Ferruzzi empire. The family rallied together and rejected the plan – only Gardini's wife supported him. She then sold her 23 per cent stake in the business and the couple walked away with a deal worth, in cash and assets – including the yachts – $500 million. Gardini set up a new company, trading in food stuffs and mineral water. The Ferruzzi group was forced to put itself into the hands of the banks.

Since February the "Clean Hands" corruption investigation has been looking into allegations that Enimont was overvalued in 1990 when the transaction with Gardini took place, and that the company paid out $40 million in bribes to the Christian Democrats and Socialists.

Raul Gardini is survived by his wife, a son and two daughters.

b 7.6.33   d 23.7.93   aged 60

FERRUCCIO LAMBORGHINI

Ferruccio Lamborghini, founder of the high performance car company which bears his name.

THE mythology of the Lamborghini car company begins somewhere in the late 1950s with its future founder, then a manufacturer of oil heating systems, powering a Ferrari along the Autostrada della Serenissima in the direction of Venice. Suddenly, ahead of him he espies another high performance sports car. Determining to overtake, he puts his foot down and begins to overhaul it. But with the race almost won, in those hazardous mechanical regions somewhere above 9,000rpm his clutch disintegrates, throwing bits in every direction. In disgust he pulls over on to the hard shoulder. At that moment he determines to challenge the long assumed supremacy of the great Enzo Ferrari at the pinnacle of Gran Turismo motoring.

Ferruccio Lamborghini's first mechanical productions were at a distant remove from the GT cars with which his name was to become inseparable throughout the world. A graduate in industrial engineering, he had picked up a living after the war repairing farm machinery. But noting the mass of military matériel left in northern Italy by the Allies, he decided to try his hand at manufacture. He bought Morris 6 engines at scrapyard prices, mounted them on chassis and suspension units hybridised from spare Ford and General Motors parts (even abandoned German tanks sometimes had their uses) and produced a robust and workmanlike air-cooled tractor which he was able to market at a competitive price.

Within ten years from 1948 his firm Lamborghini Trattori was a power in Italy and he next diversified into oil heating systems. In 1960 he founded Lamborghini Bruciatori which had, within three years, become the second largest firm in the Italian heating sector. By now Lamborghini was an immensely wealthy man. He also had a truly Italian passion for fast cars. Products from both the Ferrari and Maserati stables found their way into his domestic garages. But Lamborghini was loud in his criticism of what he saw as their mechanical unreliability. He had many heated personal exchanges with Enzo Ferrari who is reported to have made it clear that he did not relish having the reputation of his darling creations besmirched by a lowly heating engineer.

In the early 1960s the market for high

performance cars was booming. Lamborghini tooled up in a brand new factory at S. Agata Bolognese – provocatively close enough to Ferrari's Modena HQ to constitute a visible throwing down of the gauntlet. He poached shamelessly from his rivals, notably Maserati's Gian Paolo Dallara, whom he enticed over to become his technical chief.

It was on Dallara's expertise that the success of the whole project ultimately depended. Lamborghini was aware that his first effort had to be mechanically spectacular. Certainly, when the first Lamborghini, the 350GT, was unveiled at the 1963 Turin motor show it won no accolades for appearance. A rather ugly two-seater coupé, it had none of the grace of the great Ferrari Testa Rossa or the spectacular gull-winged Mercedes-Benz 300SL of the previous generation. But its V-12, 3.5 litre engine, developing 350bhp, was a revelation and delivered a road performance that confounded the critics.

Lamborghini would not rest there. Performance and style, he decreed, must be merely components of a homogeneous entity. Bertone of Turin was drafted in to work on a body shell while Dallara worked ceaselessly to place his already brilliant engine beyond the reach of competition. In March 1966 at the Geneva motor show the Lamborghini Miura (the name is that of a Spanish fighting bull) was rolled out, to stake an unassailable claim as one of the great GT classics.

Inside Bertone's sleek two-seater coupé body the engine had been enlarged to 3,929cc and now delivered 370bhp. More important, it was now transversely mounted in the middle of the car between the seating and the rear wheels. Experts were sceptical. The concept seemed far-fetched. Yet chassis and suspension translated these mechanical advances into a road speed for the later marks of the Miura of 186mph, simply the fastest production car in the world at that time. Furthermore, because the design released the whole nose for stowage space – as well as giving some more in the tail behind the transmission – the Miura was revealed to be no mere plaything, fit only for jaunts between neighbouring casinos, but a practical tourer for the rich man who liked to go far and fast. True, with the carburettor intakes only inches from the occupants' ears, this was not a car for those who required a silk-lined insulation from the stresses of high-speed driving. Indeed, the Miura's muscular passage about the world's highways was all part of the car's animal image. It is reckoned one of sports car racing's great losses that Lamborghini would not permit race-tuned versions of his car to show their paces against their great competitors.

It seemed hardly possible for Lamborghini to improve on the Miura, yet in 1971 the Countach, with an even sleeker body shell, was producing road speeds of well over 190mph from a power unit unchanged in size, although its V-12 engine now ran fore and aft. In the year 1979, when it was rated second fastest GT car, the later Countachs were capable of 196mph.

By this time Lamborghini had been forced to sell a majority stake in his car company which was finally acquired by Chrysler in 1987. With the onset of the energy crisis in the 1970s he also sold his tractor company and retired to a 740-acre estate in the Umbrian countryside overlooking Lake Trasimeno. There he devoted himself to the production of wines of denominazione d'origine controllata (DOC) standard. He also established the Museo Lamborghini where all models and marks of machines and vehicles created by him can be seen.

In spite of the competitive nature of the high performance car business, Lamborghini was a relaxed individual. Tractors and heaters had made his money; fast cars were his hobby. He had no intention of being a slave to them. He liked to deprecate the Milanese non-stop work ethic in a wryly amused way to visitors to S. Agata, who seemed surprised when he left the plant for lunch at midday, vowing not to return until the morrow.

b 28.4.16   d 20.2.93   aged 76

SIR JOHN MOORES

Sir John Moores, CBE, founder of the Littlewoods Organisation, and its chairman, 1924–77, and 1980–82.

JOHN MOORES was as close to the archetypical self-made north countryman as one might find north of the Trent. He was the founder and life president of the Littlewoods Organisation, the largest family-owned company in Britain, whose activities include football pools, a mail order division, chain stores and credit data marketing services. Even in "retirement" Moores was actively involved in sport and the arts, and in helping the young people of Merseyside.

He was the son of a building tradesman and the eldest child of a family of eight. He left school at 14 to be a GPO messenger boy at six shillings a week, but by his early thirties had made his first fortune, out of football pools. He did the same thing with an early form of mail-order (this part of Littlewoods is now among the largest business of its kind in Britain), and with chain stores.

He built a rigidly self-financing private empire and died probably the richest commercial giant in the country, with a fortune popularly estimated at £1.5 billion. Yet through it all he remained modestly provincial, intent on doing good – as with handicapped children and a boys' association – in and around Liverpool where the JM Centre, headquarters of the Littlewoods Organisation, became a prominent feature on the city skyline. Caution, thrift, an insatiable appetite for work and a distaste for personal publicity were the hallmarks of his personal style.

He finally stepped down as chairman

of Littlewoods Organisation in 1982, but took on the office of life president. His only regret, he said at the time, was that he could not see his way to continuing in the post for another 50 years. His interest in the affairs of the company remained unabated. As one journalist who interviewed him in the 1950s remarked, John Moores was a good-natured busybody as well as everything else. But if he cast a long shadow over the JM Centre it was because he had the stature, albeit in the patriarchal and paternalistic mould.

After Moores' first job as a post office messenger he trained as a telegraph operator. He joined the Royal Navy in 1916 as a wireless telegraphist and was stationed at Aberdeen. After the war telegraphy took him in 1921 to County Kerry with the Commercial Cable Company. His mother had inculcated in him the habit of thrift and with what he saved from his various jobs he started his first business in his spare time. At first he supplied equipment to a local golf club before forming a company to sell general goods, including books and stationery.

The year 1923 saw him setting up business in Liverpool — a football pool, run with two partners, whose first ever dividend was £2 12s (£2.60). The venture lost money and Moores bought out his partners, persevering into the 1924–25 season, helped by one girl assistant and one of his sisters. Then his brother Cecil came in as manager.

The business was so successful that by 1932 he was able to disengage himself sufficiently from pools promotion to start up Littlewoods Mail Order Store. This exploited the idea which he had first tried out in Ireland of getting customers to save over a period of weeks in a club until there was sufficient money to buy whatever goods the customer wanted. It was only later that the concept of credit, now so much part of the mail order business, was developed.

By 1936, with the club's business booming, he was starting up the Littlewoods Chain Stores Division and opened his first store in Blackpool in the following year. Three years later, not only

had he a highly profitable pools and mail order business, but there were 24 chain stores operating in various parts of the country.

During the war various Littlewoods buildings were turned over to producing munitions, barrage balloons, parachutes and other safety equipment. By 1944 there were 16 Moores factories involved in war work, employing some 44,000 people.

The Moores drive after the war went into development of the retailing empire. In 1960 he relinquished his association with the pools, dominant in its field, leaving it in the control of his brother Cecil.

There are now six companies in the mail order division which is the second largest mail order business in Britain. There are also well over 100 stores in this country, with a progressive expansion programme which has, over the years, added new and much larger stores. The Littlewoods Organisation now employs some 30,000 people — a third of them in the northwest of England — with another 5,000 in the pools division.

Moores was reckoned to be the second wealthiest man in Britain and ninth wealthiest in Europe. But he lived in a modest four-bedroomed house in Merseyside. Sport was one of his great interests: he was twice chairman of Everton Football Club. Among many local interests he was chairman of the Liverpool Motorists' Annual Outing for Physically Handicapped Children. He also organised biennially, together with Liverpool's Walker Art Gallery, a national painting competition for which he put up the prize money. Painting, with modern languages, were his other main interests.

John Moores was appointed CBE in 1972 and knighted in 1980. In 1923 he married Ruby Knowles, daughter of a Liverpool shipping clerk. She died in 1965. There are two sons, one of whom, Peter, is a director of the organisation, and two daughters.

b 25.1.1896   d 25.9.93   aged 97

SIR GEORGE TURNBULL

Sir George Turnbull, chairman and chief executive of Inchcape, the international business services and marketing group, from 1986 to 1991.

GEORGE Turnbull, who was, for five years, at the helm of one of Britain's leading car dealing and marketing groups, with a staff of more than 40,000, will be best remembered for the key roles he played in the 1960s and 1970s, first as the, not entirely to be envied, managing director of the strike-ridden British Leyland Motor Corporation and later in establishing the new and rapidly-successful South Korean motor industry.

Under his watchful eye the South Korean car name, Hyundai, suddenly became a force in the world motoring market, in spite of the somewhat quaint name "Pony" with which the first models were christened. True, the first Hyundai cars reminded their drivers, who bought them, often at heavily discounted prices, of the somewhat faded virtues of the old Austin/Morris qualities on which they were based. But they improved in time to become an important component of Korea's export penetration of western economies.

George Turnbull was born in London, but his career followed closely that of Standard Triumph, based in Coventry. He was educated at King Henry VIII School, Coventry, from where he won a Sir John Black scholarship to Birmingham University where he graduated with a BSc in mechanical engineering. From 1950 his career developed within Standard Triumph and in 1959 he was appointed general manager.

In 1973, after the company's merger with the British Motor Corporation (BMC) to form the British Leyland Motor Corporation (BLMC) under Sir Donald (later Lord) Stokes, Turnbull was appointed managing director of this last-ditch effort to save Britain's only surviving mass producer of cars and trucks. Years of bitter warfare with militant shop stewards, resulting in almost continuous strikes, led to extensive reorganisation of management at the highest level and an influx of top executives from Ford, then the most successful British-based car maker.

Turnbull, who was still operating from the group's Midlands headquarters at Longbridge, became increasingly opposed to what he regarded as "stifling bureaucratic controls" being imposed by the newcomers based in London, far from the scene of the real action. Late in 1973 he caused a sensation by resigning and leaving.

He was wooed by many would-be employers, including car makers in Britain and overseas, but there was still widespread surprise when, in 1974, he chose to join the little heard-of Hyundai Motors in Seoul, South Korea, as vice-president and director. At that time Hyundai was assembling a few Ford Cortinas from kits of parts exported from Britain. But by the time Turnbull left three years later he, and a team of British specialists whom he had recruited, had established a huge car plant on a green field site and had seen the first truly Korean car, the Pony, on its way to export markets.

From 1977 to 1979 he worked with the Iran National Motor company in Tehran first as consultant to the chairman and later as deputy managing director. In 1979 he returned to Coventry as chairman of Talbot UK, the former Rootes Group, which had been acquired by the French Peugeot concern. He held this position until he joined Inchcape on September 3, 1984, as group managing director. He was appointed chief executive on January 1, 1986, and six months later became chairman and chief executive.

Although Inchcape is best known for its wide-ranging business it also brought Turnbull back into the automobile fold. Inchcape sells more than 180,000 cars a year in more than 20 countries. Ironically for one whose first love, the British motor industry, suffered extensively from the inroads of Japanese cars his new company became the sole distributor for Toyota in ten countries, among which Britain was a conspicuous customer. Illness eventually forced him to stand down from his positions at Inchcape last year.

It is perhaps a fair summary of Turnbull's career that his one great regret was that he was never given a real opportunity to make BLMC into a major force in world markets. To him the notion was almost a crusade.

He was knighted for his services to industry in 1990.

He married, in 1950, Marion Wing. They had one son and two daughters.

b 17.10.26   d 22.12.92   aged 66

George Turnbull with Rover prototype car 1969

SIR ROY WATTS

Sir Roy Watts, CBE, chairman of Thames Water since 1983 and a former joint deputy chairman of British Airways.

ROY WATTS, whose tragic disappearance followed his diagnosis as suffering from Parkinson's Disease, was a quietly competent, energetic and forward-looking administrator in the fields of air transport and of major water supply and distribution. At a time when both of these industries were being subjected to much political upheaval, Roy Watts brought a calm and skilful management style to the creation of workable operating procedures and organisation — all based on good personal relationships.

He had come to the Thames Water Authority, as it then was, in 1983 with the reputation of being a tough accountant in the aviation world where he played a key role in setting British Airways on the path to commercial stability. After Lord King of Wartnaby was recruited by the government to the top job at British Airways in 1981, with the aim of privatising the company, it became clear that there could not be a place for Watts in the senior management of the company indefinitely. Nevertheless he was one of the few top executives to survive the energetic reorganisation that followed in the wake of King's arrival; indeed, Watts' own vision of BA and its future was very much one which espoused the privatisation imperative (and the acquisition of other competitors).

As he left the company to go to Thames Water at the end of 1983 he made it clear that he saw BA's future as being that of the only privately-owned national flag carrier, one which would take British

Caledonian under its wing – as in fact happened.

At the Thames Water Authority, to which he was appointed to bring more business expertise to the lumbering statutory water industry in the run-up to privatisation, he proved, equally, a restless presence. He came to an industry which he found hidebound by legal restraints and suffocating from lack of innovation. He did not shrink from conflict with ministers over government plans to force water-rate increases on the industry, and he always described his "Don't tax water" campaign as a fight against government abuse of monopoly power. He oversaw the authority's privatisation as Thames Water in 1989.

Educated at Doncaster Grammar School, University College, Oxford and Edinburgh University, Roy Watts was, at 18, commissioned in the 8th Royal Tank Regiment before a spell of five years as a qualified accountant in local government. With valuable experience of the importance to good order of discipline, the efficient maintenance of essential machinery and of a close control of costs, Roy Watts in 1955 joined British European Airways in its Organisation and Methods Branch as head of its Systems Study Section, moving on to become the airline's chief internal auditor.

From 1958 to 1961 he was sent overseas as BEA's area manager in Sweden and Finland before returning as the airline's fleet planning manager. Marked for advancement, he was appointed, in 1967, as general manager, North and Eastern Europe and, in 1970, became director of the airline's BAC One-Eleven Aircraft Division where he brought in, with success, the concept of domestic shuttle services with guaranteed seats, when necessary backed up by extra aircraft.

When, in 1972, BEA's chief executive, Kenneth Wilkinson, became managing director of the recently nationalised Rolls-Royce (1971) Ltd, Roy Watts succeeded him under Sir Henry Marking's chairmanship. Those were, however, times of rapid change, with the politically motivated merger of BEA and BOAC to form British Airways. In this new organisation Roy Watts became, in 1977, its director of commercial operations under Sir Ross Stainton, with special responsibilities for finance and planning, going on to become chief executive from 1979 to 1982 and – in the following year – group managing director and deputy chairman as well as chairman of the Association of European Airlines.

When, in 1983, fundamental changes were brought about in the water supply industry, Watts was appointed chairman of the newly-formed Thames Water Authority, relishing the challenges of a new span of activity and perhaps welcoming the chance to get out from under Lord King's shadow.

At Thames Water, Watts will always be remembered – among other innovations – for the design and completion, under his chairmanship, of London's remarkable Water Ring Main, completed at less than estimated cost and ahead of time; it ensures adequate water supplies in London for years to come.

Watts, however, retained a link with his old love – air transport – by accepting the deputy chairmanship of a new, independent airline, Brymon Airways of Plymouth, of which his old BEA associate Charles Steward was chairman and chief executive.

Among his other enjoyed activities Roy Watts – in company with his former BEA and BA colleague Stephen Wheatcroft – was for many years a trenchant and lucid lecturer to the Royal Aeronautical Society's annual international air transport course at Oxford, while taking up also, from 1991, the chairmanship of the Frank Graham Group and of International Business Communications. He always appeared to enjoy his weekend country life with his family at Charlbury in Oxfordshire – walking, gardening and watching cricket. Watts was appointed CBE in 1978 and knighted in 1992.

Roy Watts leaves his widow Jean and a son and two daughters.

b 17.8.25   d 5.5.93   aged 67

SIR HUGH WONTNER

Sir Hugh Wontner, GBE, CVO, president and former chairman and managing director of the Savoy hotel group, Clerk of the Royal Kitchens and a former Lord Mayor of London.

FOR MORE than three decades Hugh Wontner presided, with dramatic flair, over four of Europe's most illustrious hotels — the Savoy, Claridges, the Berkeley and the Connaught — with an unashamed commitment to excellence, style and luxury, regardless of the cost. In doing so he ensured that his hotels attracted the most prestigious clientele and remained London landmarks as famous as Nelson's Column and Buckingham Palace. He also beat off attempted take-overs from Sir Charles Clore, Harold Samuel, Victor Matthews of Trafalgar House, Sir Maxwell Joseph of Grand Metropolitan and — the most persistent of all — Lord Forte whose marathon efforts lasted eight years and have still not ended.

Wontner's business philosophy was that standards should never be compromised simply for an extra penny of profit. The Savoy, he said, could satisfy every whim of the most exacting guest as satisfactorily at 4am as at 4pm. There were always enough rich people, he argued, willing to pay for the best.

The success of this strategy was effectively summed up, during the heat of Lord Forte's campaign to gain control of the Savoy, by a letter writer to *The Times*:

"I have never had to carry my own luggage at the Savoy, which is more than can be said for Trusthouse Forte hotels."

Hugh Walter Kingwell Wontner was the son of a distinguished actor, Arthur Wontner. His mother was an actress but gave up the stage after her three children were born. Home was in Bedford Park, Chiswick, and then Regent's Park. Wontner was educated at Oundle and in France but was not, he said later, an academic pupil. On his return to London, not yet 20, he joined the secretarial staff of the London Chamber of Commerce.

In 1933, at the age of 25, he was appointed general secretary of the Hotels and Restaurants Association of Great Britain.

It was in that position – and as secretary of the Coronation Accommodation Committee, set up by the London hotels to cope with the rush of bookings at the time of George VI's coronation – that Wontner came to the attention of George (later Sir George) Reeves-Smith, who had been managing director of the Savoy group since 1900.

Reeves-Smith was impressed by Wontner's administrative abilities. But the young man had other qualities, also, which appealed to the veteran managing director: a discerning palate for wines, a taste for travel and a consuming passion for the theatre. To Reeves-Smith, whose own brother Harry was a fine actor and whose hotel had been founded by and was still closely associated with the D'Oyly Carte family, Wontner must have seemed ideal Savoy material. In 1938 he invited Wontner to join the group as his assistant.

Wontner came to the Savoy at an exciting time. War was looming and the elegant lines of the public rooms were being obscured by steel girders and sandbags. Staff were doing double duty as air-raid wardens and nurses. Soon the hotel's air-raid facilities were in greater demand than its suites and as the war progressed the chefs laid aside steak tartare and began to improvise with spam and dried eggs.

Throughout this period Wontner remained as imperturbable as his mentor, Reeves-Smith, and the two of them strained every nerve to ensure that, even in the most difficult circumstances, the hotel should offer its guests efficiency, courtesy and as much comfort as it could muster.

In May 1941 Reeves-Smith died at the age of 86. When Rupert D'Oyly Carte, the Savoy chairman, came to look for a replacement for the man who had guided the group's fortunes for more than 40 years, he had no doubts about the succession. He appointed the 32-year-old Wontner as managing director.

The prospects for the Savoy looked rather bleak when the new managing director took over. Bookings were sparse and many of the key personnel were in the services. But this slack period did not last long. When America entered the war business picked up sharply as officers, diplomats, trade officials and journalists vied with one another for rooms and suites. The hotel became a meeting place for war leaders. Lord Mountbatten, Charles de Gaulle, Jan Masaryk, the Czech leader, and General Wavell were among the regular Grill Room diners and the hotel's air-raid shelters were the smartest in London.

Wontner proved a resourceful hotelier during the war years. Irked by a court case in which the Savoy was accused, but absolved, of buying chickens at above the controlled price, the new managing director decided to set up a poultry farm in Surrey which not only met all the hotel's needs but provided, in addition, large numbers of eggs which were sold to an eager public.

Wontner made himself indispensable during this period and in 1947, on the death of the chairman, Rupert D'Oyly Carte, the board appointed Hugh Wontner to the post. He was the first person to fulfil the dual roles of chairman and managing director since Richard D'Oyly Carte, Rupert's father.

Under his delicate control Claridges became a home in London for numerous statesmen, from President Tito and King Husain to Gandhi, while the Savoy attracted such showbusiness stars as Frank Sinatra and Sophia Loren.

During the next three decades Wontner led the group through a period of consolidation and expansion. In 1956 he purchased the Connaught and in the early 1960s decided to move the Berkeley. When the new Berkeley eventually opened in Knightsbridge in 1972 Wontner was immensely proud of his handiwork, describing it – perhaps controversially – as the last really de-luxe hotel to be built in Europe. He was careful to achieve a size somewhere between going over into mass production and being so small that it would be impossible to make money.

The original Berkeley was at the centre of the first major takeover bid faced by Wontner, who over the years was to prove himself resourceful and cunning at fighting off such unwelcome approaches.

In 1953 the entrepreneur Charles Clore began buying shares in the Savoy which he then sold to Harold Samuel, the property tycoon. When a Board of Trade enquiry revealed that it was Samuel who was building up a stake in the group Wontner guessed that his real target was not the Savoy itself but the Berkeley, whose Piccadilly site would make a remarkable acquisition for the property developer.

Wontner devised a simple but effective defence. He transferred control of the freehold of the Berkeley to the Savoy Staff Benevolent Fund, making it virtually impossible to acquire. Samuel soon backed off and offered his shares to Wontner. The freehold was then transferred back to the Savoy and subsequently sold at a large profit, the proceeds being used to finance the new Berkeley in Knightsbridge.

Wontner changed the share structure of the group in 1955 in an effort to fend off further bids, but this did not stop several groups making attempts. He successfully fought off Trafalgar House in the early Seventies and almost a decade later engaged in a furious battle with Sir Charles Forte, whose Trusthouse Forte group made several, acrimonious and unsuccessful raids on the Savoy. Wontner, at 6ft 1in, was not averse to enjoying the comparison of size in his battle with the diminutive Charles Forte.

THF eventually gained 69 per cent of the Savoy's equity but only 42 per cent of voting rights. As a result, a legal settlement was reached three years ago, under which the Savoy consented to give Lord Forte's son Rocco, chief executive of Trusthouse Forte, and Donald Main, its finance director, seats on the main board in return for which it undertook not to buy any more shares in the Savoy for at least five years.

Throughout his career Hugh Wontner was admired by business associates for his acumen, integrity and loyalty while being accused by his critics of aloofness and arrogance. Beneath a genial manner there certainly lay steely determination and a fair degree of ruthlessness. He admitted the aloofness which, he said, probably stemmed from the fact that he preferred the company of women to men. He had no close male friends, he said, and found the softer approach of women more congenial.

Wontner was closely associated with the Royal Household over many years. He was appointed a Catering Adviser in 1938 and in 1953 was appointed Clerk of the Royal Kitchens, a post which was revived specially for him, having lapsed in the early days of Queen Victoria's reign.

Like his predecessor, Reeves-Smith, Hugh Wontner always looked at home in formal or ceremonial garb, and he had more opportunities than most to don it, being a member of several livery companies, the recipient of a string of foreign orders, and the holder of a number of distinguished offices in the City of London, most notably that of Lord Mayor in 1973–74.

But perhaps the group of which he was most proud of being a member was The Old Stagers, the world's oldest amateur dramatic society, to which he was elected in 1937 and in which he was still playing an active part more than forty years later.

His devotion to the Savoy Theatre, its bricks and mortar, its decor and what played on stage, was complete. He was chairman and managing director of the theatre from 1948. He was devasted when it burnt down in 1990 and personally supervised its reconstruction. The topping-out ceremony, conducted by Prince Edward, gave him immense pleasure and only a few days before his death he was talking about presiding over the re-opening next year.

Hugh Wontner was appointed CVO in 1969, knighted in 1972 and created GBE in 1974. He is survived by his wife Catherine two sons and a daughter.

b 22.10.08   d 25.11.92   aged 84

SIR JOSEPH CANTLEY

Sir Joseph Cantley, OBE, High Court Judge, 1965–1985. Blunt Mancunian who was the Old Bailey Judge in the prosecution of the former Liberal leader Jeremy Thorpe.

Joe Cantley, a Mancunian to the bone, possessed all the Lancastrian qualities — of directness of thought and language, common sense, and balanced judgment — that made him an effective advocate, a sound lawyer and a model High Court trial judge, particularly skilled in handling a jury.

Cantley was educated at Manchester Grammar School and Manchester University (which years later honoured him with an LLD). He became a pupil of Denis (later Mr Justice) Gerrard who died prematurely in office in 1955 and whose widow in 1966 married Cantley. He was called to the Bar by the Middle Temple in 1933 and began a busy junior's career — interrupted only by war service in which he ended up as a lieutenant-colonel — on the Northern Circuit.

He was noticeably less successful as a Queen's Counsel, partly because the immediate postwar flood of litigation had tapered off in the 1950s and partly because his blunt, and often unpalatable, advice to law clients reduced the volume of leaders' briefs that came his way. His elevation to the Bench in 1965 was widely predicted and applauded. There then began 20 years of solid judicial achievement, mostly conducted on circuit. He made infrequent appearances in London courts; but one of them was memorable to him and to the public.

In June 1979 he was the trial judge at the Old Bailey in the prosecution of Jeremy Thorpe, the former leader of the Liberal party (with three others), on the charge of conspiracy to murder and a separate charge against Thorpe of inciting one of the three to murder a former male model who had claimed a homosexual relationship with Thorpe. Mr Justice Cantley's summing-up unmistakably favoured an acquittal. He had described the alleged victim of the conspiracy as a "crook, a fraud, and a sponger".

The judge's approach to the case throughout was to seek to rid the minds of the jurors of surmise and prejudice, and direct them solely to the evidence adduced in the court and not to what other facts might point to. But Joe Cantley's friends and acquaintances detected in him a deep revulsion to the thought that, if Thorpe were convicted, any judge would have been duty-bound to have imposed a very substantial term of imprisonment, even on someone of such a high reputation and impeccable public record. In the event Cantley was spared this unpleasant task.

A few months earlier Cantley's sense of undiluted even-handedness in the judicial process had been shown in a case which was to hit the headlines (and has never ceased to arouse acute public controversy) when it went to the Court of Appeal. He was the judge in chambers who dismissed the application by the Chief Constable of the West Midlands to have struck out the civil action brought by the Birmingham Six for assault by police officers on them. Professional opinion to this day much prefers Cantley's rational decision (which, had it stood unchallenged, might have led to the revelation a decade earlier of the gross miscarriage of justice) to the emotive language and irrational legal policy propounded by Lord Denning in preventing the action by the Birmingham Six from going ahead. No one could conceivably have accused Cantley of softness towards terrorists. In February 1977, in sentencing to life imprisonment four Provisional IRA men who had waged a campaign of bombings and shootings in England in 1975, he recommended that they should serve a minimum of 30 years in prison.

His recreations were golf and music. But he had a penchant for baking bread, and could regularly be seen in Covent Garden purchasing yeast and flour. He is survived by his wife Hilda, now aged 92, and his stepson.

b 8.8.10   d 6.1.93   aged 82

PETER CONI

Peter Richard Carstairs Coni, OBE, QC, a Recorder and chairman of the Amateur Rowing Association, 1970–77, and of the Henley Regatta, 1977–93.

FOR 15 years Peter Coni masterminded the Henley Royal Regatta, maintaining its traditions – including a ban on mini-skirted women spectators and a ten-year-long ban on women rowers – while transforming it into one of the few major events on the British sporting calender to thrive, financially, without sponsorship. His legal training and his interest in sport came together in the field of drug use in 1982, when, with the support of the athletes and coaches, he set up the first programme of random drug testing of athletes in training. Six years later he chaired an independent panel of enquiry into allegations of drug use by British athletes, which made far-reaching recommendations to improve the testing system in Britain and to develop an educational programme to cut abuse.

With a carnation in the buttonhole of his blazer, pink socks and, usually, smoking a hand-rolled Balkan Sobranie through a tortoise-shell cigarette holder, Peter Coni was a colourful figurehead for the sport he administered so enthusiastically. He took an ebullient delight in being controversial, dismissing mini-skirted debutantes as "ghastly" and imbibers at the riverside hospitality tents on the other side of the river as "those blasted folk who block every ruddy land and road". For a time he wore a lapel badge declaring his support for "Gay Whales Against The Bomb", and at the 1990 regatta caused a modest stir by stripping to his underpants and diving into the river to retrieve a walkie-talkie radio.

Peter Richard Carstairs Coni was educated at Uppingham School and St Catharine's College, Cambridge. He was called to the Bar in 1960 and became a QC in 1980. In 1985 he was appointed a Recorder, and in 1986 became a Bencher of the Inner Temple.

In February 1988 he was chosen to chair the enquiry committee set up by the British Amateur Athletic Board and the Amateur Athletic Association to investigate allegations of drug abuse in British athletics following allegations published by *The Times* that some British officials had aided British and other international competitors to avoid testing. The committee did not substantiate the allegations but came to the conclusion that there was a serious level of drug use in athletics, estimating that 10 per cent of leading competitors were taking drugs.

At Cambridge Coni became an enthusiastic oarsman. He lacked the physique to reach the very top, yet went on to row for London Rowing Club in the Grand Challenge Cup at Henley Royal Regatta for seven consecutive years (1960–66), playing a leading role in keeping the London flag flying during a period when that great club was in the doldrums.

In retrospect it is hard to believe that he was regarded at the time as something of a rebel by the rowing establishment, who were inclined to equate rebelliousness with a disregard for sartorial convention. It must be conceded that Coni never wholly overcame his preference for informal footwear, even on royal occasions. But his acute brain and ability to communicate were soon recognised as invaluable in the committee room.

In 1962 London Rowing Club appointed Coni as their representative on the council of the Amateur Rowing Association. In 1968 he was elected to the executive committee, serving as chairman from 1970 to 1977.

In the meantime he had become a steward of Henley Regatta in 1974, and after only two years apprenticeship was elected to the committee of management in order that he could take over as chairman in 1977. The following year he was appointed to serve on the executive committee of the Central Council for Physical Recreation, and also on the Thames Water Authority.

At that period the Royal Regatta was struggling with economic problems caused by a relentless rise in costs and the membership limitations imposed by lack of space. Coni would have been the first to give credit to his predecessor as chairman, John Garton, for sowing the seeds of recovery. But it fell to the newly-elected chairman to transform Henley from a costly regatta into a profitable £1 million-per-year business with the minimum damage to its traditional charms.

As chairman of the management committee of the Henley Regatta he admitted to having virtual dictatorial powers. These extended even to being able to choose the music to be played at the regatta by the Grenadier Guards (he thus had "boring old Souza marches" replaced by Beatles music). He maintained, however, that he wielded his powers benevolently.

Coni strongly disapproved of the commercialisation of sport arguing that, once big money came into play, the advertisers, the agents and the sponsors followed. "Once you sell your soul you are lost," he told one interviewer. "The tail begins to wag the dog. When you depend on a sponsor, there's nothing to stop them telling you the deal's off unless their *can-can* girls are allowed into your enclosure." Following the turning away of one mini-skirted woman from the regatta, Coni made no excuse for rigidly upholding the rules of dress.

"We manage to keep things as they used to be. If people want to wear the height of fashion, do themselves up like a dog's dinner, they come in on our terms. We maintain a level of dignity and do not allow the rowing to become a sideshow." He also imposed equally rigid standards of behaviour on the participating oarsmen, summoning any deemed to have celebrated too ostentatiously for a severe dressing-down. Wimbledon, said Coni, "should have stopped the rot when they had the chance to – with McEnroe – and they should have insisted that Agassi cut his hair, not just wear white."

As chairman of the Henley Regatta, Coni was responsible for first allowing women to row at Henley in 1983 but the occasion was regarded as an experiment and deemed a failure with the result that they were excluded and only admitted again in 1993. Coni maintained the ban on the ground that, although there were one or two fine women rowers, overall the quality of their entry was indifferent. And he scornfully dismissed the outcry the ban provoked saying the "women's squealing" was "more noisy, stupid and harmful to their cause than anything I can think of."

From 1983–89 Coni served on the committee of Leander Club. In 1986, when the World Rowing Championships were held in Britain, he was at the head of the organising committee. Shortly before the opening he suffered a minor heart attack while driving from London to Nottingham. Typically, after a few days in hospital he discharged himself to attend the championships.

In 1987 he was appointed OBE for his services to rowing, and was awarded the Medal of Honour of the Fédération Internationale des Sociétés d'Aviron. In 1988 he became president of London Rowing Club, and in 1990 further added to his duties, membership of the National Olympic Committee and the treasurership of FISA. He was a member of the Court of Assistants, Needlemakers' Company, a Freeman of the Watermen's Company and a member of the Athenaeum and Garrick clubs. He used to be a leading light in the City of London Philatelic Society and he had a considerable collection of Hockney prints.

If Peter Coni had a weakness it was his reluctance to delegate; he never took a back seat, which of course was precisely why he was pressed into so many activities. In coping with these he was aided by an astonishing ability to focus his mind at two levels simultaneously. In committee he would work on a set of unrelated papers, apparently oblivious of his surroundings, yet monitoring and analysing all that was being said. When deadlock was reached he would look up from his papers and, as often as not, offer the carefully worded conclusion which all had been seeking.

Coni admitted that his interest in rowing generally and Henley in particular was fairly obsessive. In that respect, he said, it was convenient that he was a bachelor and did not have "seven sprogs to keep at expensive private schools".

He will be remembered, not least, for having persuaded the Port of London Authority to vary their by-laws so as not to enforce the International Starboard Hand Rule to crews rowing on the London tideway, a measure which would have put an end to rowing on the championship course from Putney to Mortlake.

b 20.11.35   d 13.7.93   aged 57

LORD EDMUND-DAVIES

Lord Edmund-Davies, PC, High Court Judge, 1958–66; Lord Justice of Appeal, 1966–74; and a Lord of Appeal in Ordinary, 1974–81.

AMONG the most distinguished criminal lawyers of his generation, Lord Edmund-Davies will be remembered by the public at large — and by a grateful police force

– for his achievements in three widely differing judicial spheres. He first caught the popular imagination in 1964 when he presided at the trial of those charged with what has gone down in the annals of crime as The Great Train Robbery, and the sentences he handed down to the 12 men convicted of stealing £2½ million from a Glasgow-London mail train have acquired something of a mythological status for their uncompromising severity.

He next came before the public in a very different light. As a Welshman it was a peculiarly poignant matter for him to be appointed to chair the Tribunal of Inquiry into the Aberfan Disaster in 1966 – doubly so as he was himself a native of nearby Mountain Ash and had affinities with those who found themselves so cruelly bereaved when slag from a coal tip buried a village school.

Edmund-Davies's third difficult judicial task arose from his chairmanship of the Home Secretary's Police Inquiry which sat between 1977 and 1979. On the question of police pay, the most important and contentious part of the committee's deliberations, Lord Edmund-Davies was generally acknowledged to have done right by the force when he recommended substantial pay rises for police officers – indeed to have acted with some courage in making those awards both more generous and more speedily to be implemented than the government of the day might, strictly speaking, have wished them to be.

But these were merely three particularly emotive milestones in a career which took Edmund-Davies from school in Mountain Ash, through a distinguished career at the criminal Bar, war service in the legal branch of the Army and recorderships in his native Wales to eight years on the criminal bench, eight years as a Lord Justice of Appeal and finally seven years as a Law Lord.

Among his peers Edmund-Davies was remarked not only for the wisdom of his judgments but for a brilliancy of intellect which had shown itself from his earliest days, and which would have guaranteed him a career in academe had he not chosen the cut and thrust of the outside world and the criminal courts.

He was born Herbert Edmund-Davies, the third son of Morgan John Davies and Elizabeth Maud Edmunds. After attending Mountain Ash Grammar School he went first to King's College, London, and then to Exeter College, Oxford. He took his LLB (London) and became a postgraduate research scholar in 1927. He was placed first in the first class in the Bar finals examination. He became LLD (London) in 1928 and BCL (Oxon) and Vinerian scholar in 1929, the year in which he was called to the Bar by Gray's Inn. He also lectured and examined in law at LSE for the year 1930–31. As a barrister he built up a thriving practice in Swansea in the 1930s.

With war clouds gathering, he joined the Army Officers' Emergency Reserve in 1938 and in 1940 he was commissioned into the Royal Welch Fusiliers. But he was soon seconded to the Judge Advocate General's department and spent the latter part of the war as Assistant Judge Advocate General with, from 1944, the rank of lieutenant-colonel. In tandem with his military duties he had also been Recorder of Merthyr Tydfil from 1942 to 1944 and he was subsequently Recorder of Swansea from 1944 to 1953 and of Cardiff from 1953 to 1958, the year in which he became a High Court Judge, Queen's Bench Division.

At the Bar on the Welsh circuit the forensic skills as a defence lawyer of Mr Edmund-Davies (as he then was) often made the headlines; in 1952 he successfully defended Widow Roberts in the locally-celebrated "Weedkiller Trial" at Swansea, while in the following year, at Glamorgan Assizes held at Cardiff, he represented the defendant against a colourful prosecution for a murder committed at Laugharne. This was enlivened by the poet Dylan Thomas having a word to say for the good character of the accused. The trial was the more remarkable for the fact that the accused, who was a deaf mute, did not, when the not guilty verdict was rendered, at first realise that Edmund-Davies's advocacy on his behalf had been successful.

On the Bench Mr Justice Edmund-Davies became as noted for the incisiveness of his judgments as he had been for the shrewd nature of his pleadings at the Bar. To this were allied qualities of tact, patience, lucid intelligence and stamina which made him the ideal man to preside over long, complex trials. As a judge he expressed his philosophy thus: "There are those who speak and write as though the sole object of punishment is the reform of the accused. I think this is so exceptionally benevolent as to be capable of being positively mischievous." This might seem to place him on the conservative wing of the judiciary, but he always felt that the concern he genuinely had for the rehabilitation of prisoners ought to be balanced by a concern for society at large and the damage suffered by those of its members who were victims of crime.

This showed itself in what was his most famous trial, at Aylesbury, that of 12 men charged with stealing £2½ million from a mail train in Buckinghamshire in August 1963. In sentencing the 12 convicted men to a total of 307 years imprisonment − seven of them for 30 years each − Mr Justice Edmund-Davies made it clear that he felt the men ought not to be allowed to benefit from the ill-gotten gains of their crime, which they might, if given only short sentences. This approach raised eyebrows in some quarters, but it was based on a deeply-meditated philosophy of sentencing and not on an emotional reaction. Indeed, the judge's evident understanding of the psychology of the leading members of the accused in this case won him wide admiration.

One of Edmund-Davies's first tasks on being appointed a Lord Justice of Appeal in September 1966 was to head the public enquiry into the circumstances of the Aberfan disaster in which 144 people, including 116 children, had been killed. This was an emotive task for a man who had been brought up in the ethos of the valleys, but the choice of someone from such a background was welcomed as a sign that there would be no whitewash.

In the event the report of the tribunal placed the blame for the disaster squarely on the National Coal Board and its officials and concluded that the tragedy "could and should have been prevented". The tribunal, in a report which pulled no punches, accused coal board officials of repeatedly disregarding warnings about the safety of the tip, even though a bad slide had already occurred there.

The tribunal recommended a national tip safety committee to coordinate research, an inspectorate of qualified civil engineers and fresh legislation to protect the public. In all, his stewardship of the tribunal strengthened Edmund-Davies's reputation as a man of compassion as well as of forthrightness.

This sense of fairness continued to be in evidence when he became a Law Lord. His forthright approach to the problem of police pay was much admired as being the only honest solution to the problem. Settlements which in some cases meant rises of 45 per cent over two years for individual officers drew hardly any public or press criticism even in a period of extreme economic hardship for the country at large during the twilight of the last Labour government; this was a tribute to Edmund-Davies's grasp of the deep-seated nature of the police grievance over pay. The ladies on the force were not quite so impressed when, in the following year, Edmund-Davies came down against too great an increase in the number of women police officers on the grounds that the fair sex was not strong enough to carry out its duties as effectively as the male.

Retiring in 1981, Edmund-Davies continued active, not relinquishing the pro-chancellorship of the University of Wales which he had held since 1974, until 1985. He was a life governor and fellow of King's College, London, and an hon fellow of Exeter College, Oxford.

His wife, Eurwen, whom he married in 1935, died in 1992. He leaves three daughters.

b 15.7.06   d 29.12.92   aged 86

LESLIE CHARTERIS

Leslie Charteris, author of popular thrillers and creator of The Saint.

LESLIE CHARTERIS was one of the world's most popular thriller-writers. Later generations may have known the Saint mainly from television, but for anybody who grew up in the 1930s the original stories are powerfully nostalgic. They were translated into 15 languages, constantly reprinted in cheap editions and made into a number of indifferent films. Even in retrospect their success is not hard to understand. Charteris gave his fast-moving plots a light veneer of sophistication, literary elegance and humour, which, although it soon attracted imitators, distinguished him sharply from his more leaden contemporaries. Subsequently, however, the Saint passed through a curious variety of transformations. In 1992, twenty years after publication of the last authentic Saint novel and fifty years after the peak of the author's productivity, the Crime Writers' Association gave Leslie Charteris its Diamond Dagger Award for a lifetime's achievement.

Leslie Charles Bowyer Yin was born in Singapore. His father, S. C. Yin, was a Chinese surgeon, a descendant of the Shang emperors: his mother was English. Although Chinese and Malay were his first languages, he was brought up on authors such as Rider Haggard, Conan Doyle and E. W. Hornung and was particularly fond of the pirate stories in *Chums*. When he was ten, he tried his hand at writing and illustrating a magazine of his own. He was sent to England at the age of 12, to preparatory school and then to Rossall, which he did not much enjoy. He went on to King's College, Cambridge, but came down after a single year, because, as he put it, "I figured I'd been educated enough"; he had decided to become a writer. His father, who wanted him to be a lawyer, was furious. They were afterwards reconciled by letter but never met again.

Deprived of parental support, he took an exotic range of temporary jobs, which included gold mining and pearl fishing in Malaya and spells in Britain as a bartender, professional bridge-player and auxiliary policeman. He changed his name by deed-poll to Leslie Charles Charteris Bowyer-Ian, the Charteris being borrowed from Colonel Francis Charteris, an 18th-century gambler, duellist and founder-member of the Hellfire Club.

His first book, *X Esquire*, about a fiendish plot to destroy Britain with poisoned cigarettes, was published in 1927. He followed it with several other quite lively but unremarkable thrillers. His third novel, *Meet the Tiger*, in 1928, featured a debonair hero called Simon Templar, known from his initials as the Saint. It made no special impact, but when, the following year, Charteris began writing for a new twopenny weekly, called *The Thriller*, this was the character which struck Monty Haydon, the brilliant controlling editor of boys' papers for the Amalgamated Press, as worth developing.

At around the same time Charteris moved his books to Hodder and Stoughton, which, with Edgar Wallace, E. Phillips Oppenheim and Sapper on their list, were then the leading publisher of thrillers. The Saint was relaunched with a tremendous fanfare of publicity. Seven hardback volumes, containing stories which had originated in *The Thriller*, were published within the next two years. The haloed "sign of the Saint" was derived from the stick-man figures with which Charteris had illustrated his boyhood magazine.

Charteris himself spent much of the 1930s in either Hollywood or Florida and, in 1946, became a naturalised American citizen, although he returned eventually to live in England. He wrote comic strips and radio scripts and mixed socially with the Hollywood film community. "We had fun," he said, "and the money was good." He worked on a number of films, including not only some of the Saint series but *Lady on a Train*, with Deanna Durbin, and *Tarzan and the Huntress*.

Being in America when the war broke out, he stayed, and took the Saint across the Atlantic as well. *The Saint in Miami* (1941) is an anti-Nazi thriller; by implication, a plea for America to join the war. After Pearl Harbor he deliberately sobered the Saint down, because he thought the old swashbuckling style no longer appropriate. Instead the Saint became a semi-official counter-spy, and, after the war, an amateur detective drifting around the glamour spots of the world, more anxious now to help friends in distress than to lift boodle from the ungodly. "The Saint has matured," said Charteris, "like me. He's become respectable." He wrote a monthly short story for *The Saint Mystery Magazine*, and published collections of these instead of new novels. They were never as good as the full-length books but they kept the market turning over. He founded the Saint Club, which raises money for a children's hospital and for a youth club in the East End of London.

The Saint in New York, featuring Louis Hayward, was the first and most accurate screen representation: later films, with George Sanders, became indistinguishable from routine private eye thrillers. There were three television series: in the 1960s starring Roger Moore, in the 1970s starring Ian Ogilvy and in the 1980s starring Simon Dutton. Charteris quite liked the first two series: the producers of the third failed to consult him, though they were pledged to do so. Some of the better scripts were "novelised" ostensibly by Leslie Charteris but actually and admittedly by other hands. Charteris did, however, supervise these hybrids carefully, arguing that popular characters were frequently revived after their creator's death, and, by allowing it to be done while he was still present, he could at least ensure that the *ersatz* version stayed reasonably faithful to the original. "For an old Saint fan," sighed one critic, "reading them is like chewing plastic." The last book written by Charteris himself was *The Saint in Pursuit* (1971), with a plot adapted from one of his comic strips.

Many people, he would acknowledge, thought that the 1930s had been the Saint's best period. They were right. Those early tales had a gaiety and a gusto which no one else quite matched. They contained plenty of violence but of a cheerful kind ("Saturday night is bath night, brother", says the Saint as he knocks a villain from a bridge into the river) but with no hint of sadism or squalor: nor was there any sex beyond an occasional, and purely formal, romantic interest. They were appreciated by schoolboys but well enough written to be enjoyed by intelligent adults. These standards at least were scrupulously maintained throughout the later years when the fashion in thriller writing had changed. He addressed himself, he said, "to upright citizens with furled umbrellas and secret buccaneering dreams".

He was married four times: to Pauline Schishkin, who bore him a daughter, and from whom he was divorced in 1937; to Barbara Meyer, from whom he was divorced in 1941; to Elizabeth Bryant Borst, from whom he was divorced in 1951; and, in 1952, to Audrey Long, a former actress, who cared devotedly for him and for the Saint.

b 12.5.07   d 15.4.93   aged 85

MONICA DICKENS

Monica Dickens, MBE (Mrs R. O. Stratton), author of a score or more of highly readable and often very funny novels that were read by the million.

THE fact that Monica Dickens was a great-granddaughter of Charles Dickens probably did not hinder her rise to become one of the world's most successful fiction writers of her day. Her work, if never in the first rank of literature, had something of his flair for opening windows on parts of the world – the world behind the scenes, the world below stairs, and often the squalid world – that readers liked to look through if they could be persuaded by writing that was attractive enough.

Monica Dickens was a shrewd reporter with a sense of atmosphere that caused John Betjeman, for instance, to call her "one of the most affectionate and humorous observers of the English scene." She was to develop into a shrewd observer of the New England scene, too, after moving there when she married a US Navy officer, and she was a founder of the Samaritans movement in the United States.

Monica Enid Dickens was educated at St Paul's Girls' School, from which she claimed to have been expelled for throwing her school uniform off Hammersmith bridge into the Thames. A self-confessed "fat, rebellious girl," she had apparently taken exception to the box pleats of the official skirt, which did nothing for her figure.

If it is true, as cynics say, that the sure-fire formula for a best-selling romantic novel is the doctor-nurse relationship, she gave herself a head start by training as a nurse during the war. This led to *One Pair of Feet* (1942), a loosely autobiographical story, often comic but with a true feeling for the sadness of hospitals.

It was a sequel to her first, dramatically successful, essay in fictionalised biography, *One Pair of Hands*, an account of her experiences as a freelance "cook general" at the tail end of the cocktail party era between the wars when everybody with middle-class pretensions had somebody to do the housework, at least some of the time. First published in 1939, it went through edition after edition, became a set book for school examinations and was still in print half-a-century later.

One Pair of Hands, although written in the light, gosh-jolly-hockeysticks style of the Thirties, was nevertheless regarded as a slightly daring book, if only because it was a daring thing for a girl of her background – she was a prewar deb – to have ventured through the green baize door to the servants' quarters. Sometimes there were parties where there would be somebody she knew, she would recall: "I had to hide behind a palm, or keep my head down as I cruised the crowd with my tray of Sidecars and White Ladies."

The classic Monica Dickens version of

the doctor-nurse love story – with a mature humour that put it far above pulp fiction – was *Thursday Afternoons* (1945). The theme, the tragi-comic romantic fantasies of a heroine past the first flush of girlhood, was one she was to return to.

Her nursing training was followed by training as a journalist. This led to *My Turn to Make the Tea*, which remains possibly the truest picture ever painted of life in the office of a local weekly paper. She had an eye for what was funny, but also what was sordid and petty. (The joke in the title was that since she was the only girl in the office, it was *always* her turn to make the tea.)

For 20 years she wrote a column for *Woman's Own*, continuing to write it when she went to live in Cape Cod, Massachusetts, after marrying Commander Roy Stratton of the US Navy in 1951. As a columnist she had that rare virtue of not taking herself *too* seriously, weekly dispensing, in her own words, "oceans of facile wisdom".

To Americans she was indulgent ". . . Oh my, Miss Dickinson," they always seemed to be saying. "So Shakespeare was your uncle . . ." She followed the obvious course of going on the American lecture circuit. Much of the content of lectures, she admitted, was textbook stuff about her great-grandfather, presented as family secrets. It had never occurred to her to question her grandfather about the great man. But she did remember her grandfather at the grand Christmas assemblies of the clan, giving his impersonations of his father reading from the novels. The family tradition was almost that writing had stopped with Dickens' death. Hence the disapproval in the air when she started out as an author.

In 1970 Monica Dickens moved into children's literature with *The House at World's End*, including some of her memories of her own, full childhood. (She had it "translated into American" so that children in the United States could read it. The subtle differences of meaning and nuances of English words in America constantly fascinated her.)

There followed the horsey "Follyfoot" stories, which became a television series. Animals, particularly horses, were one of her passions, a fact that had much to do with the childhood weekends she had spent at a cottage in the Thames Valley where she had kept her own pony. *Cobbler's Dream*, about cruelty to animals, was one of several books with a serious message. She did her homework diligently. *Kate and Emma*, about cruelty to children, followed months of observing NSPCC inspectors at work. *The Room Upstairs* was about the plight of old people.

Her interest in the Samaritans arose from her reporter's curiosity. She interviewed the movement's founder, Chad Varah, and worked alongside him during several spells in London. On this she based *The Listeners* (1970). She went on to open the Boston Samaritans' branch in 1974 and it became the busiest in the world. Her autobiography, *An Open Book*, appeared in 1978.

Her husband died in 1985 and she then returned to England to live in a secluded Berkshire cottage. This was in no sense a retirement from literary activity. If anything the move seems to have stimulated her creative impulses and in 1988 she published *Dear Doctor Lily*, her first novel for eight years. Describing experiences in both England and America over a period of 20 years it arose very directly out of the events of her life up to that date, some of which were recent and painful. Roseate nostalgia was never for her and for *Enchantment* (1989), a novel about a mentally-isolated figure which was suggested to some extent (though she was careful to distance her protagonist from violence) by the psychology which underlay the events of the Hungerford massacre, she went on a survival course. She continued to produce a book almost yearly until her death and her latest novel, *One of the Family* is due to be published in the spring of next year.

She leaves two daughters.

b 10.5.15   d 25.12.92   aged 77

JEAN PLAIDY

Jean Plaidy (Mrs Eleanor Hibbert), prolific and successful author of popular historical, romantic and Gothic novels under various pseudonyms.

AMONG the plethora of aliases — Victoria Holt, Philippa Carr, Eleanor Burford, Ellalice Tate, Elbur Ford, Kathleen Kellow — under which Mrs Eleanor Hibbert wrote, Jean Plaidy was the best known. Plaidy it was who launched an author who became as respected for the breadth of her historical knowledge and the solidity of her research, as she was for her knack of concocting a plausible yarn. Yet, for every two Plaidy histories there was, each year after 1961, a production from the gothicist Victoria Holt.

Holt was launched 14 years after Plaidy's first appearance in print, with her precise identity concealed to heighten the mystery. But she was soon drawing her own armies of fans through a series of novels in which a thick encrustation of Cornish names and titles such as *The*

Bride of Pendorric, added the chill of remote, granite moorlands and gaunt, flagstoned manors, to this fluent author's armoury of settings and situations. In a Plaidy novel the female protagonist was generally expected to behave with a simulacrum of historical versimilitude. Her lot might even be a somewhat stodgy one as her lord mounted his charger to ride off to the wars. Holt's heroines had far less protection from the *mores* of their times. They might well find themselves captured by pirates, thrown into harems or otherwise exposed to various types of male caddishness.

The output of these two ladies was prodigious. Even so there was to be a third substantial incarnation in Philippa Carr, who somehow managed a perfect amalgam of the personae of her two predecessors. In Miss Carr fantastic romance and history combined in an undemanding mélange, which, if it was never the runaway success of Plaidy's and Holt's works, nevertheless seldom failed, like them, to appear among the year's 100 top-selling novels. The achievements of Mrs Hibbert's other noms de plume were more sporadic, on an altogether less spectacular level from that of their great competitors. The early effusions of Eleanor Burford (Mrs Hibbert's maiden name) were frank Mills and Boon in quality. She did not persist in this vein once the successes of Plaidy and, particularly, Holt had begun to dominate her life.

Eleanor Burford was born neither on wind-blasted moor nor in moated manor, but in Kennington, London. Her father was something of an odd-job man, but, luckily for his daughter, was of a bookish bent. She read from the age of four and thereafter consumed books avidly. She left school at 16 and went to work for a jeweller in Hatton Garden. In her early twenties she met and married a leather merchant twenty years her senior. He, too, was an ardent reader. Most important, her marriage to him gave her the freedom to write.

This she did prolifically, producing novels in the manner of most of the great

European novelists she had absorbed: Dickens, Hugo, Tolstoy. "In those days one wanted to put the world to rights," she used to laugh. Publishers did not share her early idealism and the rejection slips piled up. She did not repine. The *Daily Mail* and the *Evening News* were running short stories and she adapted to this genre with some success. When the literary editor of the *Mail* set up as an agent he encouraged her to write romantic novels. She read fifty, to get the hang of it and then started writing a few herself. Her first publications, under her maiden name, were tales of young love whose titles reflect their subject matter: *Passionate Witness* (1941); *Married Love* (1942); *So The Dreams Depart* (1944); and *Not In Our Stars* (1945).

By this time she was living in Cornwall. The nearby beach was called Plaidy. The name Jean appealed to her for its brevity. The marriage between them caught the eye of an agent and, after being rejected by a number of publishers, *Beyond the Blue Mountains* was published in 1947. Success on a very different scale awaited its author. Though Eleanor Burford kept writing (her last title appeared in the early 1960s) and Kathleen Kellow and Ellalice Tate, too, remained on duty at the typewriter keyboard, the swelling stream of Plaidy's output eclipsed them both (Elbur Ford's career was a mere four-book affair, between 1950 and 1953). Plaidy titles such as *Gay Lord Robert* (1955): *A Health Unto His Majesty* (1956); *Daughters of Spain* (1961) and *Sweet Lass of Richmond Hill* (1970) were interspersed with books for children, among them *Meg Roper, Daughter of Sir Thomas More* and *The Young Elizabeth* (both 1961).

Most important, America approved. It was to do so even more wholeheartedly with Victoria Holt, who made her debut with *Mistress of Mellyn* in 1961. Though the number of Plaidy novels − 90 in all − far exceeded Holt's 31, Mrs Hibbert's second incarnation was to prove her biggest money spinner. *Mistress of Mellyn* − by Wilkie Collins out of the Brontës, and well shaken and stirred at that − was a *Reader's Digest* Book Society Choice and was serialised in *Ladies Home Journal*. It has recently been estimated that Holt's sales in 20 languages have exceeded 75 million.

Philippa Carr was launched in 1972 with *The Miracle at St Bruno's*. Her career was, necessarily, less prolific than those of her precursors, but her skilful blend of their chief characteristics proved popular and she was closing on the twenty book mark at the time of her death.

In all this Eleanor Hibbert remained an enigmatic figure, never wanting to challenge her fictional success by larger-than-life behaviour herself. The scorn of Fleet Street's literary editors had little power on her naturally self-effacing nature. Queenie Leavis might fulminate against her and her kidney ("fatally persuasive", "pernicious") from the grove of academe, but it would never have occurred to her to be taken so seriously. When asked if she wrote to "help people switch off" she seemed surprised that the question had needed to be asked at all: "Oh yes," she replied, "and there's no reason why they shouldn't." To the end, she took a simple pleasure in the sheer fun of being able to entertain.

Her husband, to whom she was devoted, died during the 1960s. They had no children.

b 1910   d 18.1.93   aged 82

SIR WILLIAM GOLDING

Sir William Golding, CBE, English novelist and winner of the Nobel Prize for Literature (1983).

WILLIAM GOLDING was one of only five English authors (the others are Kipling, Galsworthy, Bertrand Russell and Winston Churchill) to receive the Nobel Prize for Literature. Some felt it might justly have gone to Graham Greene, Anthony Powell or James Hanley, but none questioned Golding's suitability for the award, as is so often the case.

He was a "big" novelist, most of whose work could usually carry the weight he put into it. He lived outside literary coteries, struggled with grave and ponderous themes, and took risks which lesser writers could not dare to take. As is the case with all such writers there is general disagreement about which is his masterpiece − but no doubt as to whether he produced one. Is it *Lord of the Flies* (1954), *The Inheritors* (1955), *The Spire* (1964), *Darkness Visible* (1979) − or the last trilogy consisting of *Rites of Passage, Close Quarters* and *Fire Down Below* (1981−89)? This is in any case a formidable list and some would add to it.

William Gerald Golding's father, a Quaker turned atheist, was a master at Marlborough Grammar School where William was educated. He then went on to Brasenose College, Oxford, from which he graduated in 1935. While still at Oxford he published, as "W. G. Golding", a volume *Poems* (1934) with Macmillan in London, and in New York (1935). What reviews this received were indifferent, and of the book he later declared that he made "furtive efforts to conceal, destroy, or at any rate disclaim that melancholy slim volume of my extreme youth". For some years, indeed, there was no copy of it in the British Museum Reading Room. However, slim and melancholy though it may have been, some have found in it vital clues to his later struggles and achievements.

From 1935 until 1940 − and again, part-time, from 1945 to 1954 − Golding worked in small theatre companies in Wiltshire as writer, actor and director. Some of his impressions of this work may be gathered from his novel *The Pyramid* (1967), not one of his best books. In 1940 he joined the Royal Navy which he admired and enjoyed "because it worked". During his service he became officer in charge of a rocket ship and (and as a schoolteacher) instructed naval cadets. In 1945 he returned to Bishop Wordsworth's School, Salisbury, whose staff he had joined in 1939. He remained there until 1961 when the success of *Lord of the Flies* enabled him to resign.

This novel was the fruit of half a lifetime. Golding was 43 when he published it. Its knowledge of youth in particular and of human nature in general was immediately apparent. Yet, anthropologically, this story of boys who, isolated from adult supervision, become brutal and self-destructive is "wrong": studies have shown that boys who are actually thus isolated do not behave as Golding had them behave in *Lord of the Flies*. The force of his fable rose from its being, not based on "fact" but on what any sensitive and highly-imaginative schoolmaster might dream up while performing his duties on a wet afternoon. It was R. M. Ballantyne's charming Victorian tale, *Coral Island*, turned on its head; but its "boys" are really terrible little men − as in Kipling's *Stalky & Co* − which Golding rewrites with the venom its author was unable to put into it.

Read like that, *Lord of the Flies* is the story of adults (at least males) in the 20th century with its politicians and its "experts" and its wars. Yet Faber's reader had originally famously said of it: "Rubbish and dull. Pointless." The public disagreed and the book quickly acquired a cult reputation, especially in the United States, where it succeeded *The Catcher in the Rye* as the most popular novel for young Americans. By the mid-1960s it had been widely translated, had sold over two million copies and had been made into a successful film (this success was part of the reason why Golding could eventually give up teaching).

Golding liked to change his style and mood with each book: his gear changes were never those of a "minor" writer and his fiction covered an enormous range of subject matter − from prehistoric man to 19th-century sea voyagers, from ancient Egypt to Britain during the Blitz. *The Inheritors* (1955) is one of the most remarkable *tours de force* in postwar fiction of any nationality. It tells of the defeat of a group of Neanderthals at the hands of *homo sapiens*. Some would say this is Golding's greatest novel.

His work had at all times a pronounced

sense of the religious, but nowhere more so than in his next magnificent novel, *The Spire* (1964) set in medieval England: a priest, Jocelin, tries to crown his cathedral with a four-hundred foot spire, even against the laws of gravity. He, a "flesh dog", is inspired by angels and tempted by demons at every step.

Golding always waited until he was ready, and this meant long periods of comparative silence. The 15 years from 1964 to 1979 saw only the relatively minor *The Pyramid* (1967), a collection of three novellas called *The Scorpion God* (1971), and a book of essays *The Hot Gates and other Occasional Pieces* (1965). During this period Golding had almost drowned his family and himself in the English Channel while pursuing his most beloved recreation, sailing. It was, he said, "a traumatic experience which stopped me doing anything for two or three years".

In other respects, however, he made good use of his time. He kept a journal, travelled widely and developed his love of music, particularly the piano. His reputation was by now intact: he had been appointed a CBE in 1966, and throughout the 1960s and 1970s academic articles continued to pour out. As a novelist, however, he was silent but not forgotten.

He returned triumphantly with *Darkness Visible* (1978) and dispelled any lingering doubts among his followers that he was a one, or at most two, novel writer. *Pincher Martin* (1956) had not provoked uniformly good reviews and critics continued to quarrel over the respective merits of *Lord of the Flies* and *The Spire*, and to interpret the latter in various wild ways as anything from a Christian allegory to a Freudian phallic fantasy.

Darkness Visible is set in England from 1940 to the late 1970s. It has a relatively simple, thriller-like plot at its centre, but its complex characterisation (of the boy Matty, in particular), its moral seriousness and dense symbolism attracted critics who, although they could not agree about it, recognised that they had a real, and a really tragic, book on their hands. Golding was no help: he refused interviews and was himself profoundly disturbed by what he had produced.

Of the final trilogy and the separate novel, *The Papermen* (1984), perhaps the latter, a grim parable about the trials and tribulations of a writer's life, is the more powerful and satisfying. The trilogy, beginning with *Rites of Passage* (which won him the Booker prize in 1980), is less intense, although it is a profoundly interesting work by a man by no means written out. Its first half is Golding's most exuberant and humorous work, and the one which best reveals his love-hate relationship with the sea. In the work as a whole, Golding tried to express his curiosity about, and sympathy with, homosexuality, and to portray the nature of male sexual desire as distinct from female. It was, as always, highly unusual.

"Miss Pulkinhorn" a short story published in *Encounter* in August 1960 and adapted for radio by Golding in that year, should be mentioned as one of Golding's outstanding uncollected works.

William Golding was a private man who was careful to stay well outside the literary politics of the metropolitan world. That independence of spirit lay at the heart of his fictional achievement. But he was also genial and courteous with friends, and those who knew him spoke warmly of him.

He had been well before his sudden collapse. He leaves a widow, Ann, whom he married in 1939, and a son and a daughter.

b 19.9.11   d 19.6.93   aged 81

LORD WILLIS

Lord Willis, playwright, politician and author.

LORD Willis, brought up in a bug-infested house possessing only an outside lavatory shared with another family, decided at the age of nine that he wanted to become a writer. The summit of his early ambition was to work as a reporter on the *Tottenham Herald*. Instead, he went on to write plays, novels, film scripts and television series. His most famous creation was *Dixon of Dock Green*, which ran on television from 1953 to 1975.

His early work was influenced by his working-class upbringing and left-wing political views; later, while continuing to write sympathetically and with insight about ordinary people, he tended to sacrifice social and political comment in favour of well crafted entertainment that would appeal to a wide audience. His view of the human race was essentially optimistic, warm and a little sentimental. Like his policeman hero, George Dixon, he believed honesty and decency would eventually win through. Willis also sat in the House of Lords for nearly 30 years.

Willis was born in Tottenham. He always claimed that he only existed because his mother failed in an attempt to induce a miscarriage. On learning that she was pregnant with her third child she apparently took copious amounts of margarine and gunpowder as well as indulging in the more usual remedies for her condition which prevailed at the time – hot baths and gin. These measures did not produce the desired result and on a cold January day Ted Willis duly arrived in a draughty tenement in Stanley Road, Tottenham.

His mother – according to the mythology about his life which he was never slow to propagate – relented. "Oh well, I'll hang on to him," she is reported to have said after one look at the latest addition to her family.

Willis grew up as one of five children. His father had a drink problem which did not help his employment prospects during the depression period before the war. Willis was educated at Tottenham Central School and worked as an office boy, a baker's roundsman and a bookie's runner.

But he spent most of his adolescence fighting fascism and advocating socialism. A brawl with Sir Oswald Mosley's Blackshirts ended on one occasion with Willis spending a weekend imprisoned in a police station. He became national leader of the Labour Party's League of Youth and in 1939 caused a sensation by defecting to the Young Communist League which he saw then as a more effective force against fascism. One who followed him into the Communist party was Frank Chapple. Forty-five years later, when they had both become peers, it was Willis who was one of Chapple's sponsors when he entered the House of Lords.

Willis joined the Royal Fusiliers in 1939 and subsequently served with the Army Kinematograph Service. There he was able to develop his talent for writing by producing scripts for documentary films; he helped with War Office films and wrote documentaries for the Ministry of Information. His first play, *Buster*, was produced at the Arts Theatre in 1944. He was still a communist and became theatre critic of the *Morning Star*, and was closely involved with the left-wing Unity Theatre.

Buster, a comedy of East End life before and during the war, set the pattern for later work. Throughout the 1940s Willis continued to be involved, as writer and producer, with the Unity Theatre. Of his early plays, the most notable was *No Trees in the Street*. A harsh examination of the London slums and their social effects, it was produced at the St James's Theatre in 1948.

The following year Willis and an Australian collaborator, Jan Read, sent an unpublished play about the London police to Ealing Studios, suggesting it might be adapted for the screen. This was *The Blue Lamp* and it introduced the character of Constable Dixon. In the film Dixon was killed half-way through but, resurrected by Willis for *Dixon of Dock Green* on television, he proved indestructible.

The series started in 1953 and ran for 22 years and 430 editions. Helped by the sympathetic playing of Jack Warner, Dixon became a national father figure, the shrewd, kindly, ordinary copper. Indeed, when the constable was shot dead in one episode by a villainous character played by Dirk Bogarde the outcry was so great that he had to be resuscitated to plod the beat again. (Ironically, Willis had previously been fired as a scriptwriter from radio's long running soap, *Mrs Dale's Diary*, for getting rid of the protagonist and her friends by having them reverse their car over Beachy Head while out on a day trip.)

Long before *Dixon of Dock Green* ended, Willis had handed over to other writers – but it remained very much as he had created it. Even the arrival in the early 1960s of *Z Cars*, with a more critical and less cosy view of the police, failed to shake *Dixon*'s popularity.

In addition to launching *Dixon*, Willis wrote many single plays for television during the 1950s and was, at one time, the medium's leading playwright: his "poetic realism" invoked comparisons with the American writer Paddy Chayevsky. He also brought realism to the British cinema, with *Woman in a Dressing Gown* which charted the break up of a middle-aged marriage, a film version of *No Trees in the Street* and *Hot Summer Night*, a stage and television play with an underlying theme of race prejudice. In 1959 Willis helped to found the Screenwriters' (later Writers') Guild of Great Britain and was its president for the first ten years.

The success of *Dixon* tended to overshadow Willis's other television series but *Sergeant Cork*, *Mrs Thursday* and *Hunter's Walk* were all, in their different ways, skilfully written and popular dramas with well drawn characters. Among later plays for television were *The Four Seasons of Rosie Carr*, a four-part cycle tracing the life of an East End barmaid, and *The Ballad of Queenie Swann*, written in rhyming couplets and about a widow in search of a husband; this was also produced as a stage musical.

He was one of the earlier life peers when Labour sent him to the Upper House in 1963. His maiden speech in the Lords was, appropriately, about relations between the police and the public. As president of the Writers' Guild he also helped to lead the fight for legislation on authors' Public Lending Rights and in the Lords he backed Sunday theatre opening and the abolition of stage censorship. He also sought to end the statutory and common-law offence of blasphemy.

In 1970 he inaugurated a television award for outstanding services to the media. Thirteen years later he received the award himself in recognition of 40 years of television and screen writing. In 1970 Willis published an autobiography covering his early years called *Whatever Happened to Tom Mix?* Surprisingly, it was his first book but he soon made up for lost time with a succession of deftly plotted thrillers, which virtually established a new career. The first, *Death May Surprise Us*, centred on the kidnapping of the prime minister; *Man-Eater* had tigers loose in the English countryside; *The Churchill Commando* imagined Britain taken over by right-wing extremists; and *The Buckingham Palace Connection* speculated on the fate of the last Russian Tsar.

Willis remained perennially modest about his great success. Interestingly, although he was, to a greater degree than any of his much more "angry" writing contemporaries, a product of an unsparingly poverty-stricken background, bile seldom infected his writings. He never gave the impression of having resented his upbringing. He saw nothing to regret in the details of a childhood which might have left serious scars on a less robust constitution. In later life he was to say (again with the self-effacement which was characteristic): "I think one of the reasons I'm not a better writer is that I had nothing in my childhood to make me angry. It didn't occur to me to question such things. Now, I think perhaps that I *should* have been angry that we didn't have much to eat and that my mother should have had to take in washing."

Willis was also active as a businessman, in film-making, television and commercial radio and he was a member of the Sports Council from 1971 to 1973.

He was a fellow of the Royal Television Society and was also elected a fellow of the Royal Society of Arts.

He married, in 1944, Audrey Hale and they had a son, a producer of television documentaries, and a daughter.

b 13.1.18   d 22.12.92   aged 74

ALEXEI ADZHUBEI

Alexei Adzhubei, Soviet journalist who was Khrushchev's son-in-law.

DURING the five years of Khrushchev's supremacy as Soviet leader, Alexei Adzhubei, too, enjoyed power and influence unparalleled by any Soviet journalist. Through his lively editorship first of *Komsomolskaya Pravda* and then of *Izvestia*, he shook the Soviet press out of its uniformity and dullness, making the papers more accessible to the readers to whom they were supposed to be appealing.

But he also acted in that period of greater cordiality in relations with the West almost as a roving ambassador for the Soviet Union. He travelled extensively abroad, hob-nobbing with the likes of President Kennedy and the West German Chancellor, Ludwig Erhard. In this role he often smoothed the path for subsequent official visits by Khrushchev himself. It was even rumoured at one time that Khrushchev intended to make Adzhubei his foreign minister.

This unique position of course owed almost everything to his marriage to Khrushchev's second daughter, Rada. The truth of a rhyming couplet, in wide circulation in the Soviet Union in those years, which ran cynically:

Why have a hundred friends, they say,
You've just got to marry like Adzhubei . . .

could scarcely be denied. Yet it must be conceded that Adzhubei made the best of having married the boss's daughter. His personality went down well in the years of the Khrushchev thaw, when a greater openness in the exchange of ideas seemed, briefly, to herald a more human Soviet state. With his stocky form seemingly bursting with energy, and his vivid blue eyes and blond hair, Adzhubei appeared to radiate goodwill wherever he went.

Alexei Ivanovich Adzhubei was born into a worker family. When he was still a child his father died and his mother brought him up in Moscow where he went to school. Towards the end of the war he served in the Soviet Army and afterwards attended the Moscow Arts Theatre Studio School before graduating from Moscow University's faculty of journalism. At the university he met and, in 1947, married Rada Khrushchev.

While still at university he had become student correspondent of *Komsomolskaya Pravda*, the newspaper of the Communist Youth League. After graduating he joined the overseas department of the paper and it was not long before he was on its editorial board. In 1957 he became chief editor and initiated a journalistic revolution which, of course, had the blessing of authority at the highest levels. Bulganin and Khrushchev were still in harness as, respectively, premier and Communist party first secreatry at this point, but it was Khrushchev who was to triumph in the following year, deposing Bulganin and assuming both offices.

In the meantime at *Komsomolskaya Pravda* innovations of unimaginable sauciness were taking place. Pictures of pretty girls replaced the stolid shop floor matrons who had until then been the paper's nearest approach to sex appeal. Dramatic headlines broke up the grey deadness of format. ''Personal confession'' columns and cartoons all became part of an attempt to make the paper more attractive. The pent-up talents of journalists, stifled by years of enforced drabness, were suddenly released as their new editor sent them out into the field in search of stories which they were encouraged to tell in simple and human terms. In three years *Komsomolskaya Pravda*'s circulation soared from 1.5 million to 3.5 million.

These developments continued at the government newspaper *Izvestia* when Adzhubei went there in 1959. Intensely interested in the outside world from which he had been excluded for so long, he travelled widely, to Britain, France, Italy, Australia, the US and Latin America. In the US during the course of several visits he conducted an exclusive interview with John F. Kennedy and was wined and dined at the White House. In West Germany his role was virtually that of emissary and he used his influence to create more fruitful relations between Khrushchev and Chancellor Erhard. In Italy he was the first representative of the Kremlin to visit the Vatican officially.

Adzhubei enjoyed himself hugely in the process, surf-riding near Sydney, playing roulette at Reno and developing a taste for haute cuisine and fine wines which was soon to be reflected in an increasingly ample girth. The byline "A. Adzhubei, Our Special Correspondent" could be expected to appear over articles of previously undreamed-of diversity. The subjects on which he wrote were treated with a refreshing absence of dogma. The American businessman could, for the first time, be seen as a man trying to survive in a hostile environment, and not always simply as an exploiter of the proletarian masses. Even Russian *émigrés* were allowed their say in an Adzhubei interview – though at the last ditch, they were dismissed as the dinosaurs of a bygone political age. Certainly the Bear did not suddenly change its coat because of Adzhubei's arrival. Beneath his sophistication he retained the classical ideological standpoint of Marxism-Leninism. But he had the wit to see that criticism of American foreign policy, for

example, had to be presented as more than mere propaganda, if it was not to weary *Izvestia*'s readers.

The effect of all this on the newspaper's circulation was dramatic and it doubled its circulation to 4½ million in the first two years of his stewardship.

Such success inevitably bred resentment in the Kremlin. Though a member of the central committee, Adzhubei had no real standing within the party and his professional experience had been exclusively journalistic. Many Praesidium members resented the fact that *Izvestia*'s editor so often short-circuited them through his family connections. Khrushchev himself did not help to assuage this resentment by frequently backing up arguments of his own by citing his son-in-law's opinion on the matter.

When, on October 15, 1964, Khrushchev was deposed it was the end of his place in the sun for Adzhubei, too. He was forced to resign from his editorship of *Izvestia* next day and the following month he was expelled from the Communist party Central Committee for what were termed "errors committed in his work". He was, finally, relieved of the general secretaryship of the Soviet journalists' union in October 1965. The fine French cognacs which had been introduced by him, as its secretary, to the bar of the Moscow Journalists' Club, were withdrawn, and the old staples of vodka and Crimean wine reigned once again supreme.

Thereafter he went into virtual eclipse. After being forced out of *Izvestia* he went to perform lowly editorial duties for *Soviet Union* a propaganda magazine published in several languages for circulation abroad. He drank heavily and in 1967 narrowly escaped prosecution when a car he was driving struck and seriously injured a woman. In the period after Mikhail Gorbachev came to power his by-line did occasionally appear but his career never really recovered.

He leaves his widow Rada.

b 1924 d 1993 aged 68

GEORGE CANSDALE

At the Boys' and Girls' exhibition, Olympia (1956)

George Cansdale, television's "Zoo Man" during the 1950s, and superintendent of London Zoo, 1948–53.

KNOWN by millions simply as the "Zoo Man", the big, bluff and tweedy George Cansdale made an unlikely television star. He was employed as superintendent of the London Zoo when he made his first television appearance in 1948, only months after starting his new job at Regent's Park. Three years later the BBC gave him his own show, *Looking at Animals*, and Cansdale was being unofficially dubbed television's "Man of the Year".

Cansdale went on to be the Johnny Morris of his day, hosting such television series as *All about Animals, Pets Parade, Studio E, Sunday Specials* and *Focus*. Usually pictured with a python or a chimpanzee clinging to his neck, his benign features became known to some two milliion viewers over the next decade and, unusually, the programmes went down equally well with adults as with children. For the first time on television, zoology was being presented not as dry classroom stuff, but as one man's practical observation of animals gleaned from 15 years of living in Africa.

Cansdale was not easily fazed by anything the animals decided to do on camera, and frequently found his best television performers not among the elephants and hippopotami but amid what he called the "small stuff". In his first series he placed a tortoise and a jerboa (or desert rat) together in a sandpit. The jerboa, apparently offended at having to share his space with a tortoise, proceeded to bury the tortoise with sand, stopping every now and then to inspect his progress.

Viewers were delighted and Cecil McGivern, the television programmes chief, thought it one of the funniest pieces of television he had ever seen. The jerboa was asked back for a return date, but failed to repeat its first night success.

Other animals were less eager to face the cameras, and television crews at Lime Grove became adept at rounding up stray performers (although when a poisonous puff adder escaped, a zoo attendant had to be called in).

Cansdale's popularity stemmed not so much from his zoological learning – which was immense – as from his obvious love of animals. Talking to the camera, he would absent-mindedly stroke whatever creature was to hand, referring to it warmly as "little fellow". Even when bitten, which he often was, he refused to blame the animal for its ill-temper. He would point cheerfully to one finger, minus the tip, and explain: "Snakebite, in Africa. I found it was a mistake to meddle with a burrowing viper."

Despite his sudden popularity at the age of 40, Cansdale was not a man who actively sought the limelight. On the question of money, he used to say: "Pay me what you think I'm worth."

George Soper Cansdale was educated at Brentwood School in Essex, and St Edmund Hall, Oxford, where he read forestry. In 1934 he joined the Colonial Forest Service in the Gold Coast (now Ghana). It was here that he fell in love with the local wildlife, first squirrels and then bushbabies.

His association with zoos began as an animal supplier. Before he left Africa in 1948, he was responsible for introducing a handful of new animals to Britain including a pygmy flying squirrel, the size of a mouse (he was an expert on forest squirrels), and had captured the longest specimen of a cobra ever recorded, measuring 8ft 8½in.

During the second world war he was, as a civilian, in charge of the production of timber, firewood, charcoal and cordage needed for the British and later American troops stationed in the Gold Coast. Afterwards he resumed dispatching monthly shipments of animals to zoos and, in this way, his name became well known in zoological circles.

In 1948 Cansdale was appointed superintendent of the London Zoo in Regent's Park. There he quickly displayed an ability to enlist the help of the public and media. When Lien-Ho, the giant panda, fell sick in 1950 through vitamin B deficiency (caused by a shortage of bamboo shoots), Cansdale put out a public appeal and was duly inundated with bamboo. His reluctant decision to put down Rajah, an Indian elephant who attacked his keepers, was covered by the press in heart-rending tones.

But despite his subsequent high profile on television as the "Zoo Man", and the attendant welcome publicity for the zoo, Cansdale later became embroiled in arguments with his employers, the council of the Zoological Society, and in 1953 was sacked from his post for what were termed "reasons of economy". It was understood that several members of the council disapproved of his television appearances, and felt he should spend more of his time actually at the zoo.

The dismissal caused an outcry, not only with the public but among many of the fellows of the Zoological Society. Cansdale at first maintained a dignified silence over the row, but later spoke out against what he saw as the zoo's declining standards.

His broadcasting career was not badly affected by the sacking. Commercial zoos and private collectors continued to lend him animals to work with, and Cansdale became a regular on the schools' lecture circuit. He would take with him a private menagerie – pythons, bushbabies, flying squirrels and tortoises – which he kept in the garden at his home in Hampstead. His television career wound down by the early 1960s, but he continued to be a frequent guest on *Blue Peter* from 1962, appearing four times a year on the show for the next twenty years.

Away from the camera, Cansdale was an active evangelical Christian and churchwarden at All Souls, Langham Place. He also wrote a number of books and was a regular contributor to publications such as *The Field* and *Zoo Life*.

He married Margaret Williamson in 1940. They had two sons.

b 29.11.09   d 24.8.93   aged 83

W. D. FLACKES

W. D. Flackes, OBE, political correspondent for BBC Northern Ireland, 1964–82.

"BILLY" Flackes was perhaps Ireland's most respected journalist. When he retired from the post of political correspondent with BBC Northern Ireland in 1982, fellow professionals North and South went out of their way to salute his remarkable achievement. He was soon to be invited to become a member of the Radio Telefis Eireann Authority. The Ulster MPs at Westminster, not exactly noted for cross-community co-operation, nor indeed for their admiration of reporters, combined to give him a special farewell at the House of Commons to convey unanimous admiration and affection.

Flackes was born in Donegal a month or so before the creation of the Free State.

His family later moved to Belfast and it was at the Belfast Technical College that he studied book-keeping and engineering to prepare himself for an unlikely career in telephone rentals. Restless and energetic, he was soon offering copy to local papers. Engineering was abandoned in favour of a succession of reporting jobs with papers whose names echo Ulster's strident history – the *Armagh Guardian*, the *Fermanagh Times*, the *Derry Standard*, the *Northern Constitution*. Even so early in his career it took just six weeks for him to produce, along with Michael Magill, a substantial and well-received biography of Field-Marshal Montgomery. He was later to become a spare-time, science-fiction writer – his publisher gave him the preposterous pseudonym, Vektis Brack.

By 1945 he had moved to Belfast's *News Letter* and was covering Stormont politics. Two years later he joined the Press Association as a parliamentary reporter at Westminster. His reputation for reliability, meticulous accuracy and painstaking fairness was building and when he returned to Belfast it was to be news editor and chief leader writer at the *Belfast Telegraph* from where, in 1964, he joined BBC Northern Ireland as its first political correspondent.

Flackes had no thoughts of adapting to the conventions of microphone technique. He would write for broadcasting as he had written for print. Those who demanded elocution would have to live with it. They did, and their affection for the Flackes style would grow. Thus, when the infamous Ulster "Troubles" erupted in 1968, W. D. Flackes was an already established and widely-believed commentator. But would that unbending North Irish accent be acceptable to the mainland and beyond? There need have been no doubt about it. It easily withstood mildly unkind impersonation. Implacable truth and authority shone through.

Off-screen Flackes was twinkling, perpetually smiling, ever ready for gossip but even his gossip had balance and it always fell correctly short of criticism of individual politicians whose integrity he respected and frequently defended. He took no risks with their trust. Many a politician or public figure would conclude a private diatribe against the media by conceding that when "W. D." left a message they would always ring him back. No one begrudged him the OBE to which he was appointed in 1981. For Billy Flackes (or "Flakjacket" as he was sometimes irreverently known) was an honest broker, his office a mecca for broadcasting mandarin or junior researcher alike. He made time to assist and advise. He had too much enthusiasm to keep just to himself.

Of lasting value to every Ulster-watcher has been, and will continue to be for a long time to come, his *A Political Directory to Northern Ireland*, a unique compendium of Ulster's Byzantine politics, written in collaboration with the political scientist Sydney Elliot. The fourth edition is just about to be published. It reflects Flackes's flair for detail, his total recall, his deft use of understatement, his unique encyclopaedic knowledge of his subject.

He is survived by his wife Mary and one daughter.

b 14.3.21   d 1.8.93   aged 72

BILL GRUNDY

Bill Grundy, television presenter and journalist.

OF ALL the professional casualties produced by television, Bill Grundy was among the more notorious. But in his day he was a journalist of trenchant style and considerable appeal. In the first decade of Granada Television, his was the persona most closely identified with Sidney Bernstein's concept of a place called Granadaland. He brought to any studio in which he appeared a Lancastrian no-nonsense spirit which was entirely his own.

Grundy's invariable habit of addressing the camera, slightly side-on, eyebrow cocked, offered an indication of what the viewer might expect. He was sceptical and challenging with an unerring eye for the phoney and the meretricious. He cared little or nothing for reputation and was one of the first television interviewers to make politicians quake at the thought of an encounter. All this was in the early

1960s, when television was politely feeling its way into society. Most interviewers at the time were content to adopt an ingratiating demeanour, unctuously rolling titles like "Your Grace" or "Prime Minister" around their tongues.

Grundy would have none of that. What you saw was what you got and, although what the audience sometimes got was brusque and bad-tempered — occasionally even rude — it was never boring. There was always a whiff of danger attached to Grundy's appearances on the small screen and this, no doubt, played its part — as with Gilbert Harding — in his undoubted capacity to hold his viewers' attention.

A geologist by training and initially a schoolmaster by profession, Grundy was with Granada from the time of its launch in May 1956. His TV debut was in Granada's first drama production — a play about football called *Shooting Star* — in which he played a humble "extra". He came into his own, however, when

Granada started its nightly local news programme entitled *People and Places* in 1958. Its fame soon spread well beyond Granadaland and Grundy's relaxed chairing of it — at first shared with Gay Byrne (later to join RTE) — soon established his reputation, at least within the television community. He was also the anchorman for the first-ever TV coverage of any by-election, that of Rochdale in March 1958. That, with his decade and more of commentating on party conferences, provided him with a national identity that in serious television at the time was perhaps matched only by that of Richard Dimbleby.

When Dimbleby died in 1965, there were those who believed that Grundy was the man to take his place on *Panorama*. It would certainly have been a different programme if he had (as it was, Robin Day succeeded to Dimbleby's chair). It might also have made a great difference to Grundy's own future career, which tended from the 1970s onwards to go downhill. Announcing his departure from Granada in 1968, Grundy somewhat grandiloquently remarked that he suspected the trouble, from the company's point of view, was that his own name had become "practically synonymous" with that of Granada. The truth, alas, was that it had become far too closely connected with increasingly bizarre behaviour both in and out of the studio.

An habitué of hospitality suites, Grundy was to fight a long battle with alcoholism. Even during the years of his greatest celebrity there were regular stories of stormy scenes in the company flat above Granada's canal-side headquarters in Manchester. Producers tended to quail before him, and it was sometimes left for the most senior company executives to bring him to order — though his greatest come-uppance was reputed to have been delivered by Elizabeth Douglas-Home when he presumed to insult her husband during a social gathering at a Tory party conference.

Grundy's later years in television were sad ones. He was the co-presenter, with Eamonn Andrews, of Thames TV's local early evening current affairs programme — quaintly called *Today* — during most of the 1970s; but it was an association that came to grief fairly soon after his famous studio encounter with the Sex Pistols in December 1976. This was a programme that instantly went down into television folklore, with Grundy being accused of having incited his guests to "turn the air blue" at an hour when children were still having their tea. Although Grundy's defence was that he was merely trying to show what "a foul-mouthed set of yobs" the members of this particular rock-group were, it did him little good with his employers. He was immediately suspended from duty and, a year later, did not get his contract renewed.

He remained, however, a considerable writing journalist — contributing regularly to William Davis's *Punch* and (earlier) to Nigel Lawson's *Spectator*. His early training as a teacher gave him a real enthusiasm to share what he knew — and this was also true on the box where he remained a particularly effective presenter of *What the Papers Say* (a programme he was to present more than 80 times).

Towards the end of his career he increasingly only wrote about television — frequently giving the impression that it had turned sour on him. But, by then, of course, not just television but the whole of broadcasting had more or less given up on him. One of his last appearances in any form of studio came at Radio Piccadilly in Manchester some ten years ago when he walked out on his own son. As the producer of the commercial station's early morning programme, he had dared to criticise his father's delivery. At least, it was an uncharacteristic gesture on Bill Grundy's part — for in general his entire maverick record proved that he cared as little for his own fame and reputation as he did for that of others.

He is survived by his wife, Nicky, two daughters and four sons.

b 18.5.23 d 9.2.93 aged 69

BRIAN INGLIS

Brian Inglis, journalist, author and television presenter.

IT WAS characteristic of Brian Inglis that he should have called the autobiography he published in his early seventies *Downstart*. He was a self-depreciating man, sometimes shy and always loth to remind people that he was one of the most familiar faces in the land when he was presenting programmes such as *What the Papers Say* and *All Our Yesterdays* on independent television. He rarely talked about the three golden years from 1959 to 1962 when he edited *The Spectator*. Bernard Levin was the political correspondent, Cyril Ray castigated any number of institutions and their chairmen, while a young music critic called David Cairns was beginning to attract attention.

Inglis enjoyed working for the media and was highly successful at it. But his first love was books. He gave up *The Spectator* to write more of them. And he used to claim that Granada TV's *All Our Yesterdays* was the ideal programme because it provided some research for him and allowed him plenty of time to do the rest himself.

Books filled his tiny garden flat in Belsize Park. And books came in a steady stream from Inglis himself in a period of over thirty years. At first he dealt with Irish subjects, including a notable study of Roger Casement (1973) which authenticated the homosexual diaries, much to the fury of some of the diehard Irish. (This was neither the first nor the last time Inglis upset some of those in the land of his birth.) Then after studies of psychosomatic diseases and homeopathic medicine – the latter prompted a number of articles by him in *The Times* – he became more and more interested in the paranormal. Again he restricted his views mainly to print, rarely inflicting them on unwilling listeners, although he did once ruefully remark that none of his books sold more than 4,000 copies.

His work in this field attracted much scorn from those who were terrified at the thought that there could be "more things in heaven and earth, Horatio, than are dreamt of in your philosophy". His critics, though, found it difficult to pick holes in his logic, so thoroughly researched was all his work in this field, as in everything he did; he had a great deal of amusement from the outrage he provoked by challenging head-on many of the orthodox beliefs.

Brian St John Inglis was born in Malahide, co. Dublin. His father was Sir Claude Inglis, who saw to it that his son had a proper *English* education, which meant the Dragon School, Shrewsbury and Magdalen College, Oxford. Inglis by upbringing was very much part of the Anglo-Irish upper-middle class, known as the West Brits. And with good reason he called his first autobiographical work *West Briton* (1962).

During the war Brian Inglis served with

Coastal Command, flying Sunderlands and Catalinas and rising to the rank of squadron leader. After demobilisation he fell in naturally with Dublin's intellectuals and started writing for *The Irish Times* in various capacities, which included reporting on the Dail. Inglis's Dublin was the Dublin of Patrick Campbell, Brian O'Nolan (Flann O'Brien), of the Pearl Bar, the Palace and O'Dwyer's. At the same time he managed a PhD at Trinity College. But the connection with *The Irish Times* did not last all that long. The editor decided to sack him on the grounds that he gathered around him "too many shady characters", but the parting was amicable.

And, fortunately for Inglis, there was another job waiting in London on the *Daily Sketch* as a feature writer. From there he moved swiftly to Ian Gilmour's *Spectator*, which was always on the look-out for lively, clubbable writers, as assistant editor. Inglis swiftly made his mark by bringing in Bernard Levin as political commentator. Levin was an unknown quantity so it was decided to take the precaution of running the column under the pseudonym of Taper. Such wariness was unnecessary: Levin quickly became as well known as Inglis and the two remained lifelong friends.

What the Papers Say began on television in 1956 and was enough of a success to allow Inglis, as a regular performer on it, to offer his resignation to *The Spectator* a couple of years later. Gilmour responded by proposing the editorship instead and this Inglis took over from him in 1959. He made the magazine essential reading for journalists and brought in both big names and names that were later to be big. But relations with Gilmour soured and Inglis threw in the sponge. There was certainly a feeling that *The Spectator* had become too lightweight, but Inglis and his staff preferred to believe that it had become too liberal (Gilmour was soon to become a Conservative candidate). In any event, John Freeman's *New Statesman* was steadily increasing its lead over it in terms of circulation.

Inglis left in 1962 and again there was a job waiting. James Cameron was about to give up presenting *All Our Yesterdays*, a weekly look at the news of 25 years ago, for Granada in order to have more time for journalism and Brian Inglis moved into his seat. There he was to stay for the next 11 years. The flow of books resumed, most notably the biography of Casement. His interest in medicine, and especially fringe medicine, which had begun in the Dublin days, was resumed.

When *All Our Yesterdays* eventually closed in 1973 (it was later to be revived) Brian Inglis devoted nearly all his time to studies of alternative medicine and the paranormal and had a regular output of books to show for it.

In 1958 he had married Ruth ("Boo") Langdon, who also worked in Fleet Street. They had a son and a daughter, but their sets of friends were different and, in Inglis's own words, they gradually drifted apart. The marriage was dissolved.

But as he grew older Inglis became more and more dependent on female company. The days of pubs in Dublin and around Gower Street had vanished and he preferred his Black Velvet on weekends in his Belsize park flat surrounded by a harem of women, usually much younger than he, often unattached if only temporarily and almost invariably having some connection with the media. They did the talking, Inglis did the listening.

Yet this surprising man had one more surprise for his friends, and indeed for himself. His last association, with Margaret van Hattem, political correspondent of *The Financial Times*, was plainly destined to endure; visiting them, his friends remarked upon the nature of the relationship – a gentleness that was new on his part, signalling a deeper feeling. By a terrible irony, Margaret discovered that she was incurably ill; Brian's solicitude reached ever greater heights as she wasted away. For their five years together, he made a privately-printed book, recalling her and their love.

b 31.7.16   d 11.2.93   aged 76

LORD BERNSTEIN

Lord Bernstein, founder of Granada Television.

SIDNEY Bernstein was a complex personality whose life and career embodied several apparent contradictions. He was a committed socialist and a millionaire capitalist, a businessman who was also an intellectual. He combined a connoisseur's appreciation of fine art with an instinctive feel for mass taste. In public he was a brilliant showman, in private, often reserved and shy. Granada Television was the crowning achievement of a many-faceted career that had included building up a successful cinema chain, using film in wartime propaganda and making features with

Alfred Hitchcock. Created very much in Bernstein's image, Granada was the most adventurous of the early ITV companies, the longest surviving and, after a shaky start, the most consistently profitable.

Sidney Bernstein was born into a large Jewish family headed by a Swedish father and a mother who was the daughter of immigrants from Russia. His father owned quarries in Wales and was a property dealer who built some of the first cinemas in the East End of London. Sidney grew up first in Ilford and then Cricklewood. He left school at 15 to follow his father into the cinema business. At 22 he inherited the family's four theatres fortuitously on the eve of the arrival of "talkies".

From this base he developed the Granada cinema chain, choosing the name in fond memory of walking holidays in Spain. A year later he shrewdly engineered a merger of his own chain with Gaumont British, becoming managing director. Then, starting in Dover in 1930, he opened a series of super-cinemas seating thousands which were further distinguished by their exotic decor and aggressive publicity. Bernstein believed cinema-going should be an event, so he brought in the Russian theatre director, Komisarjevsky, to design the interiors, which combined eye-catching elements of gothic, Renaissance and Moorish architecture. Bernstein's most flamboyant creation was the Granada at Tooting in south London.

In 1927 he went into theatrical management with Komisarjevsky and Arnold Bennett, putting on a season of plays at the Court Theatre in London and giving Charles Laughton his first break. Three years later he built the Phoenix Theatre in the West End and opened it with the first production of Noël Coward's *Private Lives*. Though he sold the Phoenix in 1932 he continued to take a close interest in the theatre and, from the 1930s, he joined the campaign to establish a British National Theatre.

Bernstein joined the Labour party in his teens and in 1925 was elected to Middlesex County Council, one of the youngest councillors in the country, serving for six years. He was particularly concerned at the rise of Hitler and his involvement in anti-fascist causes earned him a place on the Gestapo blacklist.

During the second world war Bernstein was film adviser to the Ministry of Information, making an important contribution to Allied propaganda and handling with skill and sensitivity relations between Britain and the United States over the cinema's wartime role.

In 1944 he became head of the film section of the Psychological Warfare Division attached to Supreme Head-quarters Allied Expeditionary Force and he brought over from Hollywood his friend Alfred Hitchcock to make two French-language shorts as a tribute to the French Resistance.

In the following year Bernstein decided to produce a film based on footage taken by Allied cameramen of the German concentration camps and he invited Hitchcock to supervise it. Bernstein intended the film as a permanent reminder of Nazi atrocities for German and world audiences. But the authorities decided not to show it and its existence was not made public until nearly 40 years later.

After the war Bernstein and Hitchcock formed a production company, Trans-atlantic Pictures, for which Hitchcock made *Rope*, with its controversial experiment of the ten-minute take, and the disappointing *Under Capricorn*. In 1952 Bernstein produced a third Hitchcock film, *I Confess*.

Bernstein was initially opposed to the concept of commercial television but, as its arrival became inevitable, he changed his mind and was granted one of the first ITV franchises. (Later he was equally slow to welcome the advent of colour.) Based in Manchester and serving the north of England, Granada went on the air on May 3, 1956.

The possibilities of television drama and social documentary programmes were clear to Bernstein from the start and the idiosyncratic style of Granada's output in these fields came largely from

the authority he exerted and the guidance he supplied. He disliked an over-academic approach to the production of programmes as much as he detested the sensational or the vulgarising of issues in a documentary programme. He would never starve any worthwhile idea of the money it needed to become a good programme but neither would he tolerate what he regarded as waste. His high view of the influence and responsibility of the medium was combined with a business-man's realism in the fields of adminis-tration and organisation.

Although in its earliest months, Granada had severe cash-flow problems, forcing it to reach a secret arrangement with the London franchise-holder, Associated-Rediffusion, by which the London weekday company supplied it with the bulk of its production costs in return for the lion's share of its advertising revenue, it very soon became a money-spinner. By 1963, when it still covered both Lancashire and Yorkshire, Granada had higher advertising revenue than any of its rivals. Asked why, as a southerner, he started television in the north, Bernstein said he had made his decision after tooking at two maps, one showing population density and the other measuring rainfall.

Though not a man of the north (he never owned a cinema north of Oswestry and his country home remained in Kent rather than Cheshire), Bernstein was keen that Granada should reflect the culture and talent of the region and he made a point of encouraging northern writers and artists. At the same time he aimed to reach wider than a purely northern audience. He succeeded beyond his wildest expectations with *Coronation Street* (masterminded by Derek Granger who went on to make *Brideshead Re-visited*), which transcended its working-class Lancashire setting to become the nation's favourite television programme and the longest-running drama series.

During the 1960s Granada's dramatic output was consistently better than that offered elsewhere on ITV and Bernstein's other main achievement was to raise the quality and incisiveness of television journalism, even if this meant brushes with the Independent Television Authority and the courts over contentious programmes. His bold approach was epitomised by the trenchant current affairs series, *World in Action*.

He contended that the best way of losing money in television was to assume a moronic level of intelligence among the public. And he objected to the term "highbrow" arguing that it was "impolite to talk to people in terms they do not understand". He preferred to talk of extending his viewers' experience and said that the only way art and entertainment should be divided was between good and bad. Critics sniped that this was a convenient approach that enabled Granada to transmit wrestling as happily as the plays of D. H. Lawrence providing the cameramen knew their jobs.

He also encountered criticism for what was seen as a failure to play a stronger role in pushing through artistic and social developments in the North such as the creation of an arts centre. Granada TV did create the Stables Theatre in Manchester, with a permanent company of actors, but it was not a success. However, the universities of Leeds and Keele found in Bernstein a supporter of their departments of politics and communications and he created a chair of Landscape Architecture at Sheffield University. He was also an ardent supporter of the North West Trust and its plans for cleaning up the North of England.

Bernstein was a tall and elegant man with immense vitality and a forceful personality which he stamped indubitably on Granada television. Not for nothing was the picture of Phineas Barnum, the American showman, hung in his offices. Bernstein regarded himself first and foremost as a showman. Respected in the studios and the cutting rooms as well as in the marketing and accounting departments, he surrounded himself with a youthful and enthusiastic band of loyal professionals. He made a point of being familiar with most of his programme-makers and their programmes and displayed a remarkable, some said obsessive, attention to detail.

He liked to imagine Granada operated as a democracy and was mystified by suggestions that it was more of a mildly tyrannical autocracy. He once shouted at one of his drama producers: "I'm not trying to steam-roller you. I just want you to agree with me." On another occasion he and Derek Granger were bawling at each other because two writers had defected to another company. "It's your fault," Bernstein yelled. "You didn't oppose me strongly enough."

In 1969 Bernstein was created a life peer and, having reached the age of 72, resigned the chairmanship of Granada Television while remaining chairman of the Granada Group. Though television was Granada's best known activity, it had come to represent only 16 per cent of the company's income as Bernstein had diversified into television rental, publishing, bingo, bowling alleys and motorway service areas. He remained chairman of the group until 1979, when he handed over to his nephew, Alex Bernstein, and became life president of the company.

Aside from television, perhaps Bernstein's greatest interest was friendship. His list of friends was enormous and eclectic, and he kept his friendships in good repair, speaking out for those who needed defending, encouraging others. His munificence was very remarkable; he never forgot a kindness and was lavish in helping, surreptitiously, those who had fallen on hard times. Shy he may have seemed, but he was also gregarious, a connoisseur of wine and food, an attentive listener and a sparkling talker; dinner at his table was an exhilarating experience.

Bernstein's first marriage, to a *Daily Express* journalist, Zoe Farmer, was dissolved. In 1954 he married Sandra Malone, a Canadian, who predeceased him. The son and two daughters of his second marriage survive him.

b 30.1.99   d 5.2.93   aged 94

JOYCE HABER

Joyce Haber, one of the last of Hollywood's powerful gossip columnists.

IN THE tradition of Hedda Hopper, whom she succeeded as a columnist for the *Los Angeles Times* in 1968, Joyce Haber wielded her typewriter to make and break careers in Hollywood.

Time magazine, where she had begun her journalistic career as a researcher from 1953 to 1963, once labelled her "Hollywood's No 1 voyeur." She was, said the article, "more intelligent, more accurate — and often more malicious — than her predecessor".

The accusation was well founded. Haber had a cruel touch, once describing Melina Mercouri as having "wall-to-wall hips, an ear-to-ear smile, and more teeth than a pretzel has salt".

Julie Andrews, she wrote, had "a kind of flowering dullness about her" to which the actress retorted that Haber "needs open heart surgery, and they should go in through her feet".

But it was Haber's "blind" items, using merely initials to protect herself against legal retaliation, which proved most deadly.

The most notorious example came in 1970, when she wrote about "the baby Miss A is expecting." "Papa," the column went on, "is said to be a rather prominent Black Panther". "Miss A" was identified three months later by *Newsweek* as the actress Jean Seberg, against whom the Federal Bureau of Investigation under J. Edgar Hoover had plotted to plant the rumour in order to discredit radical causes she supported.

On reading the story, Seberg went into premature labour and lost her baby. She and her husband, French novelist Romain Gary, sued *Newsweek* and settled for several thousand dollars, but she became despondent and made several suicide attempts on the anniversary of the baby's death. Seberg finally killed herself in 1979, and Gary followed suit a year later.

Haber always denied knowledge of FBI involvement in the affair, saying that the report was based on a letter given to her by an editor whom she refused to name.

A child of the movie industry, having acted in three "Our Gang" features at the age of six, Haber received an expensive education at Brearley School, Bryn Mawr and Barnard College. She worked briefly in summer stock theatre, as a political campaign aide and in an advertising agency before turning to journalism. In 1976 she retired as a columnist to write *The Users*, a best-selling novel centred on the exploits of some 70 real and fictional Hollywood characters.

The allegations in the book were said to have disturbed some of her friends and sources. She subsequently worked as a freelance writer, contributing articles to many leading American magazines.

Joyce Haber was divorced in 1972 after six years of marriage. She is survived by one son and one daughter.

b 28.12.32   d 29.7.93   aged 60

JOHN HERSEY

John Hersey, American war correspondent and novelist.

IN MAY 1946 *The New Yorker* sent the Pulitzer prize-winning journalist John Hersey to Japan to find out what actually happened in the city which had sustained the world's first nuclear attack. When he returned and delivered the typescript of *Hiroshima* the magazine did something it had never done before. The original intention had been to serialise Hersey's findings. But in a flash of inspiration *The New Yorker*'s managing editor, William Shawn, saw that this would not do and persuaded the editor, Harold Ross, to a radical departure from normal practice. A whole issue of the magazine was cleared of all but essential advertising. For the first time in its history it carried no satire, no cartoons, no smart quips, no shopping notes.

When on August 31, 1946, *The New Yorker* appeared on the streets, there was nothing on its innocuous looking cover to prepare the reader for what was in store. Only an editorial introduction to the opening feature apprised the reader that this was to be the *only* feature in the issue. "*The New Yorker* this week devotes its entire editorial space to an article on the almost complete obliteration of a city by one atomic bomb, and what happened to the people

of that city. It does so in the conviction that few of us have yet comprehended the all but incredible destructive power of this weapon, and that everyone might well take time to consider the terrible implications of its use."

Within a few hours the issue was sold out. For weeks afterwards tattered copies were being passed from hand to hand or mailed to friends and relations of its original readers throughout the United States. More than fifty American newspapers applied to serialise it.

Hiroshima's reputation spread to Britain where it provoked a publishing crisis. Paper was still being rationed and *The New Yorker* would permit no cutting for serial use. But Penguin Books struck a deal with Alfred A. Knopf, who had acquired the rights, and *Hiroshima* appeared complete in a paperback edition of a quarter of a million. Marketed in the drab grey covers of Penguin's "World Affairs" series, that, too, soon sold out.

The dropping of the A-bomb was a story that was a year old. The world knew that in sheer destruction terms something colossal had happened. Yet, neither the statements of scientists nor the explanations of technical journalists could really convey to the layman the horror of the event. Figures like 20 kilotons, even when translated into such dramatic headlines as: "The Power of Two Thousand Ten Ton Bombs!", could give no idea of the scale of human misery such a notion represented.

By interviewing half-a-dozen survivors of the bomb and distilling their memories, Hersey brought the event vividly alive as a human catastrophe which readers – especially those in Britain who had suffered so much from bombing – could re-live themselves. *Hiroshima*'s great strength lay in the dispassionate manner of its narrative. A reporter by instinct and training, Hersey, wisely, made no attempt to occupy the high ground of moral indignation. He let the unvarnished facts speak for themselves. They did so with terrible eloquence.

Hersey had an eye for detail – often of a quizzically humorous nature –

which might well have escaped another: a group of survivors gratefully share a hot pumpkin which has been done to a turn by the nuclear flash; a girl sits among stinking piles of dead and wounded at a river's edge, painstakingly mending a tear in her kimono with needle and thread; at night doctors are glad of the light from the blazing city which enabled them to continue operating; immobilised on his hospital bed with a temperature of 104F, a priest worries about all the funerals he should be conducting. In more sombre vein, a crazed young mother, vainly trying to suckle her dead baby at her breast while she begs passers-by to look for her soldier husband in the wreckage of the city's barracks, is one of the book's ineradicable images.

In Hersey's barely 30,000-word account the very word "Hiroshima" became the ultimate symbol of the horrors of modern warfare. It was a book which confronted the reader with the notion that with the A-bomb something unspeakable had entered into the vocabulary of man's capacity to inflict suffering on himself.

John Hersey was the son of a YMCA missionary, working on famine relief in China. At ten he was brought back to the US and after leaving school went to Yale where he graduated in 1936. He then spent a year at Clare College, Cambridge, before returning to America where he became secretary to Sinclair Lewis from whom he learnt a great deal about writing.

He started in journalism by joining the staff of *Time* magazine as an editor. From 1942 he was a war correspondent for *Time* and *Life* and his rovings around the battlefields of the Pacific and of the European theatre, gave him a wealth of material for subsequent volumes of reportage and novels. His first book *Men on Bataan* (1942) was a graphic description of the courageous American attempt to hold the Philippines against the Japanese in the spring of 1941. While reporting for *Life* on Guadalcanal in 1942 Hersey was commended by the US Navy secretary for his bravery in helping the wounded out of the fire zone. From this experience he produced *Into the Valley* (1943) which described the bitterly-contested, five-month battle between the Americans and Japanese for control of the island.

In the novel *A Bell for Adano* (1944) the scene shifted to Europe, in a tale of problems encountered by occupying American forces, personified by an Italian-American officer, in a Sicilian village. For this he won the Pulitzer prize and was therefore already a writer of renown by the time *The New Yorker* hired him to go to Japan. Certainly his performance there set the seal on his reputation.

But Hersey never rested on his laurels. He continued prolific thereafter. As *Hiroshima* had indicated, he was best as a recorder of fact and incident. A tendency towards a more literary approach in his later novels, could sometimes act to their detriment. Best known among them are: *The Wall* (1950), a painstaking account of the destruction of the Warsaw ghetto, done in diary form; *The War Lover* an air force novel in which the intrusive anti-war sentiment was so much less effective than its almost complete absence had been in *Hiroshima*.

Blues (1988) was something in a different vein, an account of the bluefish which throng the seas off Martha's Vineyard in summer time, their vast shoals sometimes covering thirty square miles. Not just a nature or fisherman's book, it was consciously cast in the venerable piscatory form of Izaak Walton's *Compleat Angler*.

John Hersey married, in 1940, Frances Ann Cannon. There were three sons and a daughter of the marriage which was dissolved in 1958. In that year he married Barbara Day Kaufman, by whom he had a daughter. His wife and daughter survive him, as do the children of his first marriage.

b 17.6.14   d 24.3.93   aged 78

LEONARD PARKIN

Leonard Parkin, former ITN newscaster.

ALTHOUGH never quite a television megastar – he lacked the popular touch of a Reggie Bosanquet or a Sandy Gall – Leonard Parkin was for 20 years one of the most valuable frontmen that ITN possessed. He himself would have resented that label: he was proud of his solid journalistic origins and he had a much greater claim to have been a working reporter than most of his colleagues.

Before graduating to Wells Street, then ITN's headquarters, he had been a reporter and feature writer for various Yorkshire newspapers, a foreign correspondent for the BBC in Canada and the United States and (briefly) a member of the *Panorama* team in the days of James Mossman and Sir Robin Day. He left the BBC for ITN in 1967 taking over from Robert Kee as the main presenter of its *First Report* lunchtime bulletin in 1976 and moving from there to its highly popular *News at 5.45* in 1978, staying with it until 1982. He retired from ITN, where he was by then back on the lunchtime beat, in 1987.

Leonard Parkin was born in Yorkshire and educated at Hemsworth Grammar School. From there he went straight into local newspapers, serving his apprenticeship on the weekly *Yorkshire Observer* and then on the *Telegraph and Argus* in Bradford before graduating in 1954 on to the *Yorkshire Evening News* where he worked as both a reporter and a sub-editor.

Tall and blessed with striking Cary Grant good looks, he soon attracted the interest of BBC Television and was recruited by them when TV news was really in its infancy, going on to report from such far-flung places as Algeria, Australia and the Congo. It was in covering the assassination of President Kennedy in 1963, though, that he made his name. His work on that story led to an overture from *Panorama*, then still very much the BBC's flagship programme, which he later joined in 1965. His tenure as a *Panorama* reporter was, however, cut short by a car accident in Ireland in which he not only damaged his right hip, leaving him with a permanent limp, but suffered severe facial injuries. It took six months for his face to heal and during that time his berth on *Panorama* had been filled. His last year with the BBC was spent none-too-happily with *24 Hours*, the current affairs programme that succeeded the legendary *Tonight*. The one job that he never did for the BBC was to read the news, believing that the BBC's emphasis on the primacy of editors made this a singularly unrewarding task.

Things, however, were different at ITN. When Parkin arrived there in 1967, *News at Ten* had just started, Sir Geoffrey Cox having won his battle to get a guaranteed half-hour of prime time every weekday evening (this, of course, was in the days of the old ITA and long before the advent of the new toothless ITC). Parkin almost immediately joined such presenters as Bosanquet, Gall and Andrew Gardner as one of those who launched the new venture. When, however, *News at Ten* became more of a star vehicle — with Sir Alastair Burnet very much as *primus inter pares* Parkin was happy to move to the other new bridgeheads that ITN had opened up. He was never anything but a highly professional newscaster, taking a particular pride in the part he played in shaping each bulletin.

His career in television had spanned three decades and in 1987 it was announced that, at the age of 58, he was taking early retirement. It was typical of the gentlemanly air that the brought to the screen that he went gracefully (though he cannot but have been aware that ITN's lunchtime news was losing out badly in terms of viewers to the BBC's rival version then presented by Martyn Lewis). Parkin read his last bulletin on national television on June 17, 1987, though he went on in retirement to do some documentaries for Yorkshire Television.

He moved back to Yorkshire from Hertfordshire on leaving ITN and took up what had always been one of his greatest passions, fly-fishing. He had been ill with cancer of the spine for some time and had been looked after by his wife Barabara whom he married in 1955 and from whom he had briefly been separated. She survives him together with one son.

b 2.6.29   d 20.9.93   aged 64

NOEL WHITCOMB

Noel Whitcomb, Daily Mirror *columnist who brought the high life to millions.*

FOR more than 30 years Noel Whitcomb was one of the most famous journalists in Britain. At one point his column appeared every day in the *Daily Mirror*, while he contributed with equal success to several women's magazines.

His picture was displayed on buses and hoardings all over the country with the slogan "Buy the *Daily Mirror* and go gay with Noel" – the times were more innocent then – and at the height of the *Mirror*'s circulation more than five million people did that every day. He also founded and organised the *Daily Mirror* Punters' Club and was responsible for bringing on-course experience of racing to many thousands who had never been to a race meeting before.

The Punters' Club provided the happiest phase of his career for, unknown to his readers, Whitcomb despised his style of journalism, disliked the *Mirror*'s Labour politics and claimed to hate his publicity. He maintained that he only worked for the *Mirror* because of the high salary – he was certainly one of the best-paid journalists in Fleet Street – and his legendary expenses.

He once explained: "From the time I joined the *Daily Mirror* at ten guineas a week in the mid-1940s to the time in the late 1970s when the paper was paying out well over £150,000 a year to cushion my life from needless discomfort, and thereby ensure my continuing loyalty. I always felt that part of the money was compensation for living in a goldfish bowl." His verdict was that "most of the columns I wrote were as shallow as a puddle".

Whitcomb began his journalistic career with the cinema trade press during the war. After joining the *Mirror* as a general reporter he made his name with a typical tabloid story of the time: the discovery of a talking dog that appeared to speak well enough for the story to be followed up by all the rival papers.

Soon he had his own column and was mixing with the great and the famous. Unlike many columnists – he hated to be called a gossip columnist – he actually was on reasonably intimate terms with many of the subjects of his articles. He really did take the Shah of Iran night-clubbing in Rome, he certainly advised Herbert Morrison personally about the Festival of Britain of 1951 and there is good reason to believe his claim that he was instrumental in the career switch which took Noël Coward to the Café de Paris and on to Las Vegas.

His most envied exclusive, however, came from one of the great romances of the 1950s when the youthful Jimmy Goldsmith, now Sir James Goldsmith, eloped with Isabel Patino, daughter of a Bolivian tin millionaire. Whitcomb had come to know the couple in Paris and when Patino forbade his daughter to marry she fled to London, was sheltered first in Whitcomb's house and then went into hiding in Scotland, where Whitcomb proudly helped to stage-manage their secret wedding.

His career, and his salary, moved steadily upwards until he was involved in a serious traffic accident after he had left his Paris hotel (which typically, was the Ritz). It was thought he would never recover completely and he was offered a post on the Mirror Group's women's magazines. Only a few months later, however, he was well enough to be reassigned to the *Mirror*, though he was still writing for *Woman and Home*, for instance, more than 20 years later.

Now he was sent abroad on big international stories but not enough to satisfy him. "More often I was wearing the old top hat and watching the tiaras go by," he complained in his autobiography. He was, therefore, delighted to be offered a transfer to the old IPC, pre-Murdoch *Sun* which had been created by the Mirror Group from the ruins of the loss-making *Daily Herald*. Whitcomb spent five years there, satisfied to be writing three times a week for a more up-market paper.

As the 1960s ended, however, the IPC *Sun* sank and Whitcomb was recalled to the *Mirror*. Bored with the prospect of years more of gala celebrations and royal weddings he had his great inspiration: a club for racing people who did not go racing. Intended as a mild circulation booster, the success of the Punters' Club amazed *Mirror* executives.

Its inauguration was pure Whitcomb – in the ballroom of the Dorchester Hotel, with the Duke of Devonshire and other senior stewards of the Jockey Club present, and a letter of encouragement from the Queen Mother.

Soon there were 200,000 members. The club took punters by coachloads and trainloads to courses all over Britain. It gave ordinary readers the chance to experience the grandstand and Tattersalls, and the original misgivings of some leading racing figures were overcome as the punters arrived, properly dressed, prepared to enjoy a day out and, incidentally, spend a great deal of money. At one late summer Ascot meeting there was even a Punters' Club special enclosure – and that at the suggestion of the late Duke of Norfolk. The club started to own horses, first in Whitcomb's name and then in the name of the club when racing's rules changed. The punters went abroad – to Longchamps, to Bombay, to Caracas. At its peak there were 600,000 members.

Then Robert Maxwell arrived at the *Mirror*. He told Whitcomb he was costing the paper a million pounds a year. Whitcomb protested, disputed the figures, pointed out the club's publicity value to the paper but then decided not to argue. He wound up the club, completed his contract and retired. On the day he left the paper the doorman called out as usual: "Goodnight, Mr Whitcomb." But, as Whitcomb pointed out, nobody said goodbye.

He is survived by his wife Sally – they married in 1947 when they were both working on the *Mirror* – and by their daughter Kate.

b 25.12.19 d 11.6.93 aged 73

LIEUTENANT-GENERAL SIR IAN JACOB

Sir Ian Jacob (centre) with Marmaduke Hussey and Sir Michael Checkland

Lieutenant-General Sir Ian Jacob, GBE, CB, Director-General of the BBC, 1952–60.

ALWAYS an outstanding administrator, Sir Ian Jacob's career fell into two sharply defined halves. As a soldier, he rose to be military assistant secretary to the war cabinet. As a civilian, he was director-general of the BBC from December 1952 until he was succeeded by Sir Hugh Greene in January 1960. In both careers his analytical approach, his forthright manner and his no-nonsense attitude brought outstanding achievements – and some controversy.

To those who did not know him well he could appear as a mere efficient bureaucrat. But he had the good officer's care for his men, mixed easily and, though of an Establishment cast of mind, fought a doughty battle in defence of the independence of the BBC at the time of Suez. Probably the most courageous deed of his career was committed not while he was a soldier but when he was in command of the great battleship in Portland Place. It was he who decided that Hugh Gaitskell, as leader of the Opposition, was entitled to a right of reply to Sir Anthony Eden's prime ministerial broadcast defending the Anglo-French invasion of Egypt in November 1956. This stand on principle was all the more notable as Jacob, a fifth generation product of the Indian Army, did not himself at all sympathise with what Gaitskell had to say.

The son of Field-Marshal Sir Claud Jacob, GCB, GCSI, KCMG, Edward Ian Claud Jacob was educated at Wellington and at the then Royal Military Academy, Woolwich. He was commissioned from Woolwich into the Royal Engineers in 1918 and in 1923 was one of the first to take the young officers' course at Cambridge, obtaining his BA at King's College. It was natural, with the Jacob family record of long service in India, that he should be posted to Roorkee to join the Sappers and Miners.

He joined the 3rd Field Company KGO

Bengal Sappers and Miners commanded by Captain Brian Robertson (later General Sir Brian Robertson). His father was about this time successively CGS India and C-in-C Northern Command. In 1922 the company was sent to Waziristan to work on the Razmak road in the Waziristan campaign. While working one day with his company on the sides of the Barani Tangi, the Hazara Pioneers marched past and cheered their founder's son.

He returned to Britain after five years in India and in 1931 went to the Staff College in one of the best terms of the interwar years. It produced 15 generals of whom four became members of the Army Council. He was good at all games, especially at hockey and cricket, and passed out among the leaders of his term. From 1934 to 1936 he was a GSO3 in the War Office and then went to Egypt as brigade major in the Canal Brigade, returning in 1938 to join the Committee of Imperial Defence as a military assistant. This decided how he would spend the war years, for it was clear that he was an outstanding staff officer and his services were asked for in 1939 as military assistant secretary to the war cabinet. He remained in this appointment throughout the war until he retired in 1946.

Ian Jacob was never the type of *fonctionnaire* who was content to carry out his duties with machine-like docility; he was much too strong a character for that. He could, however, dictate the most complicated report in the minimum of time and with complete clarity. He was a very quick worker, but his judgment was absolutely reliable and, however great the pressure, he remained calm and collected. He won the total confidence of the prime minister, the chiefs of staff and of General Ismay, soon making himself indispensable in the war rooms of Whitehall.

Many of his friends regretted that he was never given the chance to show his qualities in battle, for he had all the attributes of a great commander. He had a good brain, sound judgment,

strength of character, self-confidence and a delightful, quiet sense of humour: with reasonable good fortune he could have gone to the highest commands in the field. Fate, however, ruled otherwise. His consolation was that, in the particular post he held, he rendered outstanding service towards winning the war.

It was in connection with the preparations for D-Day that Sir William Haley, then editor-in-chief of the BBC, first came into contact with Jacob. The contact was only brief, but its effect was that when the BBC was looking round for new blood after the war Haley, by then in sole executive charge, invited Jacob to become the BBC's director of European Services. A reorganisation was at that time already in hand and when the European and Overseas Services were merged Jacob became head of the combined operation as director of External Services.

When Winston Churchill returned to power in 1951, becoming minister of defence as well as prime minister, he asked the BBC to second Jacob back to him as a personal assistant. The Corporation was reluctant to do this. It knew that it would be losing a key man at a critical time. But the prime minister was insistent and for the greater part of 1952 Jacob was back in his old world. (The arrangement continued when Earl Alexander of Tunis was appointed minister of defence.) The BBC, though, had always insisted that it could reclaim Jacob's services if an imperative need arose. When its governors were faced with selecting a new director-general in the autumn of 1952, following Haley's appointment as editor of *The Times*, their choice fell on Jacob, he being the first member of the Corporation's staff to be fully and permanently appointed to that post.

Jacob's initial task as head of the BBC was to meet the challenge of commercial television which, by 1953, had been decided upon by the Conservative government. Internally, he needed to complete the BBC's coverage of the country for television. He had also to preserve sound broadcasting, both by bringing in the VHF system, which had been submitted to the government years before, in order to extricate listening from the almost impossible medium wave jumble; and he needed to ensure, in face of the challenge of television, that radio's audience could be preserved and its needs financed.

Whatever methods he chose to do all these things were bound to be criticised. In the event, the criticism was very heavy indeed. His cutting back on the hours of broadcasting on the Third Programme was denounced as a mortal blow at the BBC's most significant contribution. And his decision to make the Light Programme almost unrelieved entertainment, and to have no inter-relation between the three networks, which could have led listeners from one to the other, was held to be an abandonment of the BBC's self-imposed, long-standing aspiration to raise public taste.

Another controversial area in which his practical mind achieved more conventional success was in his dealing with political broadcasts. He secured the abolition of the absurd 14-day rule (which prohibited broadcast discussion of any topic due to come up in Parliament within the next fortnight) by the simple expedient of applying it with such rigour that public opinion was led to say that it was intolerable. He followed this by using the rise of commercial television — the pace here was forced by Granada TV — to introduce the reporting of general elections and to release other political broadcasting out of the straitjacket the major parties had forced it into. He also widened the BBC's broadcasting of public affairs. All this deserves to be set against what was, perhaps rightly, criticised on the cultural side.

Less forgivable, at least from the perspective of the 1990s, was his old-world, intolerant attitude towards attacks on established institutions. When in October 1957 Malcolm Muggeridge, then working with *Panorama*, published an

article in the American magazine *The Saturday Evening Post* which was critical of the monarchy, Jacob had no hesitation in immediately banning him from the air-waves. According to his own account, he briskly told the BBC television service: "No, on no account. Why should we give this chap a national platform?" After Muggeridge leaked a story about the personal reprimand he had received from the D-G, Jacob only made matters worse by declaring: "This chap will never go on the air as long as I am director-general" (a prophecy, or rather a threat, that was fulfilled).

The fact that he had thereby amply vindicated the charge that Muggeridge — during the earlier debate over the coming of the commercial television — had frequently brought against the BBC's use of "the brute force of monopoly" never seemed to bother him. Indeed, 20 years after he had left the Corporation, Jacob was still prepared to defend the decision he had taken: "You may say that I was abusing my position — but I felt very strongly." It was not perhaps surprising that many saw the news of the appointment in 1959 of Hugh Greene to be Jacob's successor as amounting to "an opening of the BBC's windows".

Jacob spent his retirement for the most part quietly in East Anglia. Although he was once lured by an editor of *The Listener* to review a BBC drama production called *Churchill and the Generals* (1979) he, on the whole, zealously abided by Stanley Baldwin's advice to those who have left office not to "spit on the deck or speak to the man-at-the-wheel". He served as a governor of Sherborne School, played a conscientious part in the affairs of Chatham House and sat for a number of years as a county councillor — first on the East Suffolk and then on the Suffolk county council — for his home town of Woodbridge.

He married in 1924 Cecil Bisset Treherne, who predeceased him. He is survived by their two sons.

b 27.9.99   d 24.4.93   aged 93

KING BAUDOUIN OF THE BELGIANS

At a Guildhall function in 1963

King Baudouin of the Belgians.

KING Baudouin of the Belgians was a kind, inconspicuous monarch for 42 years. Known as "Le Roi Triste," he was one of the few unifying forces in the political struggle between Flanders and Wallonia, and his death leaves a power vacuum in a country that lies on the brink of division.

Baudouin was the model of the modern European monarch. When he visited his local golf club, he would habitually walk up to whoever he found on the first tee and ask to play a round with them. The colourful crowd of Belgians from war veterans to sun-tanned teenagers, gathering outside the palace yesterday was testimony to his widespread popularity.

His reign was dignified, conscientious and marked by tragedy; he was the understated monarch whose influence was subtle but pervasive in a comfortable, inward-looking country not noted for strident nationalism but where tradition and the Roman Catholic Church are still powerful forces.

The son of Leopold, Prince of Brabant, and Princess Astrid, the immensely popular and beautiful daughter of Princess Ingeborg of Sweden, he was pre-baptised, on the day of his birth, Baudouin Leopold Albert Charles Axel Marie Gustave, and was given the title Count of Hainaut.

Baudouin became crown prince at the age of three, when his grandfather, King Albert I, was killed in a mountaineering accident. It was the first tragedy in a life strewn with sadness; two years later, his mother Astrid was killed in a car crash. In the years before the war the young prince and his brother Albert and elder sister Josephine-Charlotte lived sheltered lives, educated in the Royal Palace at Laeken north of Brussels and spending holidays in Noordwijk in the Netherlands; he quickly became bilingual, an attribute vital to his future success as king.

On the outbreak of war in 1939 the children began a peripatetic existence, sheltered by governesses and shuffled around southern Belgium and France before heading south for Saint Sebastian in Spain. Then they returned to Belgium, where the German invasion of 1940 shattered the lives of the royal family. The palace of Laeken was guarded by the Wehrmacht during the war, Leopold having surrendered to the Germans, ignoring the advice of his generals to fight or flee to London. Baudouin spent the rest of the war either as a German prisoner or as a refugee on foreign soil, while his father, who remarried in September, 1941, was spirited out of Belgium by the Germans to an "unknown destination".

In June 1944 the family was evacuated, crossing the Ardennes and into Luxembourg. They then travelled south to the castle at Hirchstein, on the Elbe, where they were reunited with Leopold. With its high walls and trellis, the castle was a virtual prison. In April the following year the family was moved to a chalet, less austere, in Austria, where it was liberated by a detachment of the American Seventh Army. While war-torn Belgium debated whether it wanted the family back, Baudouin completed his studies at the Calvin college in Geneva.

In March 1950 Belgium held a referendum on "la question royale". Fifty-eight per cent of the population favoured Leopold's return. But the deep enmity that now divided the country, with Flemings openly accused of conspiracy with the Nazis, gave little chance to a king who had effectively bowed to Hitler without resistance. Belgium was suddenly on the brink of civil war, with the police shooting dead thirty demonstrators at an anti-royalist rally.

Leopold abdicated in August 1950, and the bespectacled Baudouin succeeded to the throne on his 21st birthday in 1951, the youngest monarch in Europe and the fifth King of the Belgians since independence from the Netherlands in 1830.

The young king was a quite different creature from his fiery and moustachioed forebears, who had ruled over Belgium's colony of Congo with iron fists. Known as *Bwana Kitoko* on the African contient, or the "good chief", Baudouin found himself powerless to prevent the newly-independent Zaire from falling into bloody civil war in 1960. The country troubled the king for the rest of his reign, and his good relationship with the dictator Mobuto Sese Seko was of questionable value in international terms. He made his last visit to Africa, to Rwanda, another former colony, in 1987. "Baudouin the African: the heart and the distance," commented the leading daily *Le Soir* yesterday.

In 1960 Baudouin married Dona Fabiola de Mora y Aragon, the tall, auburn-haired daughter of a line of the Spanish royal family, and two years his senior. The marriage was always happy, but punctuated by great sadness that visibly reflected itself in the king's demeanour. Fabiola suffered three miscarriages, and the couple remained childless.

"For many years we struggled to fathom the meaning of this sorrow. But gradually we came to understand that, having no children ourselves, we have more room in our hearts for loving all, truly all, children," Baudouin told the nation some years ago. Fabiola's deep Catholicism and her strong influence over her husband led the country to the brink of constitutional crisis in 1990 when parliament tried to legalise strictly limited abortion. The king abdicated for 24 hours to allow parliament to pass the new law. "I would sooner abdicate than legalise abortion," he said at the time. "Does freedom of conscience apply to everyone except the King?" Polls in popular newspapers like *La Dernière Heure* showed that over 75 per cent of Belgians believed Baudouin had acted correctly.

Baudouin, by now a frail and stooped figure, did not enjoy the best of health. Speculation that he might pass the throne on to his brother Albert began two years ago, when he underwent a successful operation for prostate cancer. Six months later he received heart by-pass surgery in Paris, from which he also appeared to have made a full recovery. In the same year he celebrated forty years on the Belgian throne.

Much of the king's energy in the last years was devoted to preventing the split up of his country, where high-tech Flanders believes it is paying too heavily for smokestack Wallonia's social security bill. Yet most Belgians distrust their politicians, whom they believe guilty of playing games with federalism; they have sided with Baudouin and held colourful pro-Belgium marches through Brussels over the past months.

In his independence day speech last year Baudouin compared those seeking to break up Belgium with the war-mongers in the former Yugoslavia, and called for a federal but united country. Such a Belgium, he said, would be an example for a future federal Europe. "He was the symbol of Belgian unity, which he worked passionately, discreetly but very influentially to preserve," Jacques Delors said yesterday. "He was also an activist for European construction."

Recent television images of Baudouin showed the king where he wanted to be, close to Belgium's people and far from its petty politicians; talking with garbage collectors in the streets, welcoming Belgium's first astronaut, Dirk Frimout, to the Royal Palace, shaking the hands of children and joking with naval officers.

He is survived by Queen Fabiola.

b 7.9.30   d 31.7.93   aged 62

The King and Queen of Belgium visiting the Cutty Sark *in 1971*

QUEEN ALEXANDRA OF YUGOSLAVIA

Queen Alexandra, widow of the last King of Yugoslavia. She was born, a princess of Greece and Denmark, in Athens.

ALEXANDRA, a great great granddaughter of Queen Victoria and a cousin of the Duke of Edinburgh, was fated to be an exiled royal. Her father, Alexander, who died before she was born, was briefly King of Greece, four years before the monarchy in Athens was overthrown in 1924. And Alexandra was, herself, Queen of Yugoslavia for only 20 months between her marriage to King Peter II in March 1944 and November 1945 when the monarchy was abolished by a constituent assembly dominated by

Marshal Tito's communists. Her life continued to be marked by tragedy. Twice, in 1953 and 1963, she attempted to commit suicide following marital problems with ex-King Peter.

The recurring saga of exile first affected Alexandra's family during the first world war. Her grandmother was a sister of Kaiser Wilhelm of Germany and, because of this, the Western Allies feared that the sympathies of her husband, King Constantine, would lie with Germany rather than Britain and France. The Allies demanded his abdication and that of his son, the crown prince. As a result, Constantine's younger son, Alexander, became King of Greece, reigning from

1917 to 1920. At the time he was only engaged to Aspasia, the daughter of a noble Greek family.

To avoid complicating the royal line of succession, the couple gave their promise that they would not marry until after the war. Following the armistice, they married in November 1919. Then, in the summer of 1920, the king was walking in the gardens of the royal palace at Tatoi when his dog was attacked by a pet monkey belonging to the vineyard keeper. He tried to separate the two animals and was bitten on the leg by the monkey. A month later, after a series of high fevers and 11 operations, he was dead. He and Aspasia had been married only ten months and Aspasia was five months pregnant.

With both her own and her husband's families in exile, Queen Aspasia returned to Athens alone for the birth of her daughter Alexandra, who was granted the rank of royal princess. Had she been born a boy her name was to have been Philip. As it was, her great-aunt Alice and great-uncle Andrea, Prince and Princess Andrew of Greece, gave the name to their son Philip who, at Westminster Abbey in 1947, married Princess Elizabeth. In a book which she wrote about her cousin in 1959, Alexandra recalled that, as babies, they had shared prams and, in their teens, the possibility of their marriage had been discussed.

Alexandra spent her early years in exile with her mother in Italy, but moved to England when she was seven to live near Ascot and to attend a local boarding school. The Greek royal house was not rich and, with the fall of the monarchy, had lost all its possessions in the republic. Alexandra's mother had only a modest pension, paid to her in Swiss francs, and a small capital sum left to her by her husband.

Through her relationship to Queen Victoria, Alexandra was related to most of the royal families of Europe and, as a child, two of her favourite cousins were Prince Philip and Michael of Romania. She was unhappy and insecure at boarding school and at 13 was taken by her mother to Switzerland and then, in 1935, to Paris, where the two shared a rented apartment on the fifth floor of the Hotel de Crillon while Alexandra attended a Paris finishing school.

When Alexandra's romance with King Peter II of Yugoslavia developed, it was not universally popular among the king's supporters. Some of his advisers deemed his wish to marry inopportune, provoking a split among the disparate political groupings who had hoped that, once Yugoslavia was liberated from German occupation, the king could be a symbol of survival for a unified state. The couple married in London and 19 months later Peter lost the throne. They lived afterwards mostly in France in relatively impoverished circumstances. Peter worked but money was always tight. On one occasion a Paris dress house seized Alexandra's furs saying she owed them £5,000. Financial difficulties appeared to be at least partially responsible for the problems they encountered in their marriage. Rumours that the couple would separate were denied but in 1953, Alexandra was found with her left wrist cut after being told that her husband had decided to proceed with a divorce. Ten years later she made a second and more serious suicide attempt in Venice, lapsing into a coma after taking a drug overdose. Her husband died in Colorado in 1970. Alexandra is survived by their son, Alexander, the crown prince.

b 25.3.21   d 30.1.93   aged 71

DON JUAN DE BORBON Y BATTENBERG

Don Juan, wearing the uniform of an admiral of the Spanish navy, standing before a portrait of his son, King Juan Carlos

Don Juan de Borbon y Battenberg, Count of Barcelona, who was for many years the Pretender to the Spanish throne.

DON JUAN was both the son and the father of a king of Spain. His father was Alfonso XIII, the last king before the declaration of the Second Republic in 1931. His son was King Juan Carlos. Yet Don Juan himself was never king, and spent many years of his life in exile, during the Republic, the civil war and the Franco dictatorship.

For much of that time he was engaged in an unequal struggle with Franco over the future of the monarchy. Franco was not opposed to the notion of monarchy, but wanted it to be on his terms, and after he had left the scene. After the second world war he offered to allow Don Juan to return to Spain with the title of Prince of Spain, and to grant him the right of succession.

Don Juan refused, partly because such submission was outside his character, and partly because he believed in constitutional monarchy and thought that too close an association with the Franco regime would damage the royal appeal. But he did allow his elder son, Juan Carlos, to be educated in Spain and to be groomed for the succession by those who hoped to continue Francoism after Franco.

Once Franco had died in 1975 and Juan Carlos had become king, it was Don Juan's idea of a constitutional monarchy which prevailed. In spite of his education, the new king, discreetly supported by his father, threw his weight behind those who wanted to restore democracy in Spain; and in 1977 Don Juan showed his approval by formally renouncing his claim to the throne in favour of his son.

Don Juan was the third son of King Alfonso XIII of Spain and Queen Victoria Eugenia, Princess of Battenberg and grand-daughter of Queen Victoria of England. He was a cadet at the naval academy in Cadiz when the second Spanish Republic was proclaimed in April 1931. He escaped via Gibraltar to France, and thence came to England to finish his naval training at Dartmouth.

In 1935 the prince, by this time a lieutenant in the Royal Navy serving aboard HMS *Enterprise*, received a letter from his father naming him his heir: his elder brothers had renounced their heriditary claims to the throne of Spain, the one because he was marrying a commoner, and the other because of a physical handicap. He accepted the nomination, but his wish to continue in the Royal Navy was thwarted by a regulation introduced by Ramsay MacDonald's government, in spite of protests by King George V, Don Juan's cousin. After abandoning his naval career he studied European history and law at the universities of Florence, Lausanne and Geneva and married his cousin, the princess Maria-Mercedes Borbon-Orleans.

In August 1936, believing that the military rising against the Republic had as its object the restoration of the monarchy, Don Juan crossed into Spain to fight on the nationalist side, assuming the name Juan Lopez. He was quickly escorted back to the French frontier. General Franco subsequently refused the offer of his services and Don Juan was to say later that as a young man he had been "too impetuous . . . too trusting".

In 1937 Don Juan and his wife returned to Italy, living in Rome where their son Juan Carlos was born.

After the death of his father in 1941, the Alfonsist monarchists referred to Don Juan as John III of Spain. He preferred his older title, Count of Barcelona. Over the next three years he repeatedly urged Franco to keep Spain out of the second world war and to work for the reconciliation of the two sides in the civil war. In January 1944 he released to the press a letter he had written to Franco: dictatorships could only bring ruin to nations; no government could be stable if it lacked the support of the people; a legalised opposition was as necessary to a state as a conscience to an individual.

In March 1945, from Lausanne, he issued, what was in effect an appeal to the Spanish people to oust Franco. He called on Franco to give up his powers and proposed the replacement of the regime by parliamentary government under a constitutional monarchy. But he had miscalculated his strength and Franco remained. Fearing, however, foreign intervention in Spain once the war in Europe was over, Franco offered to install Don Juan in the Zarzuela Palace in Madrid and, under the title of Prince of Spain, to concede him the right of succession.

In 1947 Franco's controlled parliament passed a Law of Succession, which declared Spain a monarchy. It "legalised" Franco's retention of complete power till death and his choice of a succesor: there was not to be a restoration of the monarchy, but an *instauracion*, or establishment of a new one. Don Juan, who had moved to Estoril, issued a new manifesto denouncing the law as a fraud, and reiterating his appeal for the institution of parliamentary democracy under a king. In reply the government-controlled press denigrated Don Juan as a "foreign sailor who hardly speaks Spanish" and as "a red, a mason and a drunkard" who had asked the Allies after the war "to occupy Spain".

Don Juan thereafter concentrated on the long-term future of the monarchy. As he himself put it "the institution is more important than the person".

He met Franco in 1948 to arrange for the education in Spain of Juan Carlos, then 12 years old, and there were further meetings on the matter in 1954, 1960 and 1968.

Franco was reported to have again offered in 1968 to nominate him as his successor and again the offer was rejected. Then in July 1968 Juan Carlos announced that he was prepared to accept Franco's terms, and he did it formally in July – publicly to the chagrin of his father, yet perhaps privately with his approval; for it was probably the only bloodless way that Spain could come to be the constitutional monarchy and parliamentary democracy which Don Juan had outlined in his 1945 and 1947 manifestos.

When Franco died in November 1975, Don Juan spoke neither for nor against his son's assumption of the throne. He stood on the political sidelines watching with approval the way Juan Carlos provided the motive force behind the dismantling of the Franco regime. However he made clear his commitment to Spain's need for democratic rule. From his home in Portugal he paid several visits to the royal palace in Madrid to discuss with his son, family and political matters including his requirement that Spain should be clearly on the path to democracy before he would renounce his right to the throne.

On May 14, 1977, two weeks after the dissolution of the *Movimiento*, Franco's principal instrument for the control of political thought and action, Don Juan formally renounced his hereditary claim to the throne of Spain in favour of his son in a simple and moving ceremony in the Zarzuela Palace attended by members of the royal family and intimate friends. Juan Carlos was thus King of Spain by right of inheritance and not merely by grace of Franco. Don Juan went to live in Spain and in his remaining years was entrusted with various missions of state.

Don Juan would have made a good constitutional monarch. He not only looked the part – he was 6ft 3ins tall, affable and dignified – he had a great sense of duty, but no thirst for power. A Battenberg rather than a Borbon, he loved the sea. He continued sailing into his seventies, frequently posing casually in seagoing attire, cigarette in hand for photographers. Four children were born to him of his marriage with the Princess Maria, who survives him: King Juan Carlos, Prince Alfonso who was killed in an accident in 1956, and the princesses Maria Pilar and Margarita.

b 20.6.13   d 1.4.93   aged 79

RUTH LADY FERMOY

Ruth Lady Fermoy, OBE, Woman of the Bedchamber to Queen Elizabeth the Queen Mother since 1960 and founder of the King's Lynn Festival.

RUTH Lady Fermoy was one of the Queen Mother's oldest allies, a lady-in-waiting since 1956 and a hovering presence at the royal side on many a walkabout. She was also the maternal grandmother of the Princess of Wales. When the Prince's engagement was announced in February 1981, speculation in the press was rife that the two grandmothers had somehow engineered the match.

There is no doubt that Lady Fermoy gave her granddaughter some tips on royal etiquette, but anything else she hotly denied: "When two young people fall in love and decide to marry that is there decision, not that of their grandparents." In fact, Lady Fermoy was of the opinion that duty to one's country, and particularly to the royal family, should come before any personal wishes.

Certainly in her own life, her loyalty to the Queen Mother tended to override any bond she may have felt towards the Princess of Wales or her own family; in recent months she was horrified to find herself being sucked into all the speculation that surrounded the Waleses' crumbling marriage. It was reported that she felt her granddaughter had let down Prince Charles, and that grandmother and granddaughter were not, for a period, on speaking terms.

Lady Fermoy was also a great believer in the sanctity of marriage, and was devastated by the relationship of her daughter, Frances – then the Countess Spencer – with the businessman and *bon viveur*, Peter Shand Kydd. In 1968 she decided to give evidence in the Spencers' divorce case, testifying against the suitability of her own daughter as a mother, thus helping the Earl to secure custody of his four children. She attended his funeral last year.

As the young wife of the fourth Lord Fermoy, Lady Fermoy was first drawn into royal circles as a near neighbour of the family at Sandringham. A gentle and softly-spoken girl, she quickly became a favourite of Queen Mary and of her daughter-in-law, the Duchess of York. On the very day – January 20, 1936 – that King George V died, Lady Fermoy was giving birth to her daughter, Frances. Despite her personal grief, Queen Mary still found time to send a note of congratulations to her neighbour.

Ruth Sylvia Gill came from a solid middle-class background in Aberdeenshire, the daughter of a retired colonel and landowner from Bieldside. Having shown exceptional musical talent as a child, she was packed off to Paris in the 1920s to study for four years under the great French pianist Albert Cortot at the Paris Conservatory. The high-point of her career came when she performed before the royal family at the Royal Festival Hall. But what looked likely to be a promising career was cut short when she met the fourth Lord Fermoy.

This was a man who many considered at the time to be one of the most eligible bachelors in England. Maurice Fermoy had been brought up in America as the heir to his maternal grandfather whose one curious, condition to Fermoy inheriting his money was that he remain in America. But when Fermoy inherited his father's Irish barony in 1920, he made sure that his benefactor's conditions were upset by the courts, and early in 1921 came to Britain, wealthy, titled and a graduate of Harvard.

Fermoy quickly threw himself into the ways of his newly-adopted country, and became great friends with the Duke of York (later George VI). As a favour to his son, King George V granted Fermoy the lease of Park House, an enormous place originally built to handle the overflow of visitors to Sandringham. Fermoy was a fine shot, and as a neighbour and tenant of the royal family, ended up spending a great deal of time with them.

He was also a figure of some standing in the Norfolk community in his own right. Having built up a good reputation locally he was able to win the 1924 election as Conservative candidate for King's Lynn, and was re-elected with growing majorities in the subsequent two elections. He retained his seat until 1935 and was elected mayor of King's Lynn in 1932.

Having successfully courted Miss Gill, he married her at St Devenick's, Bieldside, Aberdeenshire, in 1931. Lady Fermoy found being the wife of an MP a full-time occupation, and stopped practising the piano so conscientiously. But she eventually found her musical niche as patron of the arts in the local town of King's Lynn, and organiser of the King's Lynn Festival, an annual cultural festival of music, plays, films and poetry readings.

This came about when she and her husband set about raising funds for the restoration of the 15th-century Guildhall at King's Lynn. That accomplished in 1951, Lady Fermoy had the idea of using the hall as an annual festival centre, and established the Fermoy Centre Foundation.

Queen Elizabeth the Queen Mother agreed to become the festival's patron, and would think nothing of driving the eight miles from Sandringham to King's Lynn every evening and sometimes twice-a-day at festival time. Lady Fermoy stepped back onto the platform herself every year in an amateur capacity.

The event quickly became known on the international, as well as local, arts circuit and attracted such distinguished performers as Yehudi Menuhin, Peggy Ashcroft, Richard Rodney Bennett and Rostropovich. But Lady Fermoy was also keen to seek out and promote local talent and, as a warm-up to the festival, introduced the practice of monthly lunch-hour concerts for shoppers in King's Lynn. Having been made a JP in 1944, she was granted the freedom of King's Lynn in 1963, as recognition of her services to the town.

After 25 years as chairman of the festival, she resigned in 1975, and became its president. Her fund-raising activities for the festival continued unabated and in 1987 she was to be seen on the streets of King's Lynn selling 50p-lottery tickets for a Skoda, which, she tried to convince customers, was a "very nice" car. But after another 14 blameless years, she resigned, in 1989, in a flurry of acrimonious and well-publicised exchanges with the festival's new management.

Lady Fermoy declined to give a reason for her resignation, which was generally thought to centre on a disagreement over funding for the by now loss-making festival. Instead, she continued to promote local musical events, sometimes enlisting the support of Prince Charles. Her contribution to music was recognised by the University of East Anglia in 1975, when they made her an honorary doctor of music.

Lord Fermoy died in 1955 and, widowed at the age of 46, Lady Fermoy turned for support to her wide circle of friends. She often came up to London, where she kept a flat in Eaton Square, and continued to entertain on a modest basis.

In 1956 the Queen Mother appointed Lady Fermoy as an Extra Woman of the Bedchamber and promoted her in 1960 to Woman of the Bedchamber. She was, with Lady Hambleden and Lady Elizabeth Basset, one of the Queen Mother's closest surviving friends, and continued to accompany her on a punishing schedule of royal duties despite increasingly frail health. Behind her gentle nature lay a strong-willed and principled woman, fond of children and eager to put people at their ease.

She was fiercely loyal to the Queen Mother throughout all the royal family's recent troubles. Her death comes only six weeks after that of the Queen Mother's private secretary, Sir Martin Gilliat.

Ruth Lady Fermoy is survived by Mrs Shand Kydd and another daughter. Her son, the fifth Lord Fermoy, died in 1984.

b 2.10.08   d 6.7.93   aged 84

MARGARET MacDONALD

Margaret "Bobo" MacDonald, LVO, former nursemaid and dresser to the Queen, died at her home in Buckingham Palace.

OVER a period of more than 60 years of devoted service to the Queen — first as nursemaid, then as dresser and finally as a retired retainer who continued to live at Buckingham Palace — Margaret "Bobo" MacDonald built up an exceptionally intimate relationship with the sovereign which was unrivalled by any other member of the Royal Household staff. She was, in effect, a life-long friend.

An essay written by the Queen at the age of 11 provides the first written reference to this remarkable closeness. Tied up with pink ribbon and preserved in the royal library at Windsor, it reads: "The Coronation 12, May, 1937. To Mummy and Papa. In Memory of Their Coronation. From Lilibet Herself. At five o'clock in the morning I was woken by the Band of the Royal Marines striking up just outside my window. I leapt out of bed and so did Bobo. We put on dressing-gowns and shoes and Bobo made me put on an eiderdown as it was cold and we crouched in the window looking onto a cold misty morning. . . ."

As nursemaid to the royal princess, Margaret "Bobo" MacDonald shared the young princess's bedroom; later, as her dresser, it was her duty to wake the Queen with a cup of tea each morning and, over the years, she accompanied the monarch on more than 40 foreign tours. Equipped with a rather dour Scottish manner she struck the right balance of deference and dignity; she was commonly believed to be the only member of the Royal Household staff who was allowed — in private, at least — to call the Queen by her pet family name, Lilibet, and was held in not a little awe by others in the Royal Household.

According to Robert Lacey in his 1977 biography of the Queen, Bobo was prepared, as none of the Queen's other servants were, to tell her mistress when she had made a poor showing on television or had not spoken at her best. "Unsentimental and severe, she has come to provide a unique sounding board, the closest contact Queen Elizabeth can have with the world she looks out at through limousine windows."

Such was her apparent influence that Bobo was sometimes held responsible for the Queen's fashion sense. "Possibly if she had had a French maid as a dresser instead of Bobo, she would have been smarter, but not so serene," wrote Elizabeth Longford in *Elizabeth R.*

Margaret MacDonald was born on the Black Isle, north of Inverness. Her father was a coachman-gardener who became a railway surface worker, living in one of a pair of stone-built cottages at Killernan Crossing, a mile from Redcastle Station, north of Aberdeen. Her mother came from a fishing village in Sutherland. Her first job was as a chambermaid in a Scottish hotel, after which she was employed by the Marchioness of Linlithgow at Hopetoun House, near Edinburgh, as a nursery cleaner. It was a friend of the marchioness, Lady Rose Leveson-Gower, who recommended the shy, 22-year-old nursery cleaner as a prospective assistant nursery maid to her sister, the then Duchess of York, now the Queen Mother, when she was pregnant with her first child.

Margaret MacDonald joined the Yorks' household at 11 Bruton Street, Mayfair, in 1926, a few months after the birth of Princess Elizabeth, working under the senior nanny, Mrs Clara Knight (who had been the Queen Mother's own nanny), and two years later moved with them to 145 Piccadilly. As the young princess began talking, the name Margaret proved too long for her to pronounce so, in accordance with the royal family's custom of adopting affectionate nicknames, Margaret MacDonald became Bobo.

In 1930, when Princess Margaret was born, Mrs Knight concentrated on the new baby and Bobo took charge of Elizabeth. Throughout what was perhaps inevitably a secluded childhood and a restricted adolescence for the princesses, with their parents often away, Princess Elizabeth grew particularly fond of Bobo who became the most constant of her daily contacts.

She accompanied the Queen and Prince Philip on honeymoon and was cleaning her mistress's shoes at the Sagana Hunting Lodge in Kenya when, only yards away, Prince Philip was breaking the news to his wife that her father had died in his sleep and she was now Queen. And she was with the Queen during the hours leading up to the birth of each of her four children.

John Dean, Prince Philip's valet found her to be "a rather peremptory Scotswoman". When they first met, "she asked me my name and I told her, adding that everybody called me John. She replied: 'Well, to me you will always be Mr Dean. We have to keep up a certain standing in the house.' She was good fun with a nice sense of humour, but even when we were staying in some village and were out socially in a local pub, she always addressed me as 'Mr Dean' and referred to Princess Elizabeth as 'My Little Lady'."

In the 1970s when an economy drive was instituted in the Royal Household, the controller decreed that none of the staff could in future be served meals in their rooms. Bobo promptly took to her bed with a cold which was so bad and lingered so long that, regulations or not, her food had to be taken to her by one or other of her two assistant dressers. Therafter Bobo was the only member of staff whose food was served to her in her own room.

Bobo was always given preferential treatment and on board *Britannia* was the only staff member to have her own private cabin, which was locked-up and not used when she was not on board.

When she completed 50 years service, the Queen had a special commemorative brooch made for her by Garrard, the royal jewellers, in the shape of a flower with 25 diamonds, representing the crown, and 25 gold stamens, representing the good that Bobo had brought to the Queen's life. In retirement she continued to live in her own suite of rooms above those of the Queen and as she became increasingly frail the Queen ensured that she was well cared for.

In 1953 the Queen had made her a member of the Royal Victorian Order and in 1986 advanced her to a Lieutenant of the Order.

Bobo MacDonald, who was unmarried, is survived by her sister Ruby, who is also a member of the Royal Household staff and who used to work for Princess Margaret.

b 4.7.04   d 22.9.93   aged 89

THE EARL OF WESTMORLAND

With King Faisal (1967)

The Earl of Westmorland, GCVO, former Master of the Horse and Chairman of Sotheby's.

DAVID Anthony Thomas Fane was the elder of the two sons of the 14th Earl of Westmorland (a keen amateur rider and sportsman and one of two men whose company the Duke of Windsor claimed to have really missed in his long exile following the Abdication).

His mother, Diana, was immortalised in a book, *A Portrait of My Mother*, by the younger son, the novelist Julian Fane. She was the daughter of the elegant Edwardian peer, Lord Ribblesdale, and was thrice married and thrice widowed. Her first husband was Percy Wyndham (killed in the first world war) and her second, the dashing "Boy" Capel best known as the lover of Coco Chanel. In later life Diana made a gallant effort to maintain her lovely Gloucestershire home, Lyegrove, near Badminton, and earned the reputation of a legendary

gardener. Here her young family was raised, both her sons serving as pages at the Coronation of George VI. The 14th Earl died in 1948, and his widow in 1983.

David Westmorland was educated at Eton. As Lord Burghersh, he served in the Royal Horse Guards in the war, was wounded in North Africa and retired in 1950 with the rank of captain. In the same year he married Jane Findlay, the beautiful daughter of Colonel Sir Roland Findlay, Bt. They had two sons and a daughter.

Thereafter Westmorland's career was two-fold. He had a royal life and he was a partner and later, briefly, chairman of Sotheby's. His connection with the royal family stemmed from his proximity to Badminton, and he served from 1955 until 1978 as Lord in Waiting to the Queen. He — and particularly his wife — were considered close friends of the royal family and, indeed, his daughter Camilla was one of many young women tipped as a bride for the Prince of Wales, especially after she accompanied him to Royal Ascot in 1977.

When the later Duke of Beaufort retired as Master of the Horse in 1978, David Westmorland, an experienced horseman, was his natural successor. Both Duke and Earl had kept their figures and so easily did Westmorland slip into the role, that he also fitted "Master's" uniform. His appointment was doubly appropriate since his ancestor, the 10th Earl, had served as Master of the Horse to George III from 1795 to 1798.

As Master of the Horse, he was the third most senior figure in the Queen's Household with overall responsibility for the Royal Mews (the day-to-day work being done by the Crown Equerry). He took part in the annual Trooping the Colour, riding in the Queen's procession, and the State Opening of Parliament. Unfortunately he did not hold the job as long as he might have hoped, resigning in 1991 through ill-health and handing over to Lord Somerleyton. Though one of the great officers of the Royal Household, the Garter that might have come to him eluded him. He was promoted GCVO in October 1991 having been KCVO since 1970.

Among many other important equestrian interests Westmorland was president of the British Show Jumping Association and the British Horse Society.

His business career seemed set to follow a traditional patrician role. He rose through Sotheby's and after a year as deputy chairman in 1980 he succeeded his cousin, Peter Wilson, as chairman. Wilson had built the company up to a position where their annual turnover was £181 million. He proved a hard act to follow and unfortunately things did not run smoothly. Westmorland served for only two years, during which time there were rumours of a takeover bid, shares began to slip, and 400 employees were laid off. Profits for 1981 were down £58,000 and following a vast expansion programme, the firm's worldwide overdraft stood at £13 million. The year 1982 saw a sizable decrease in sales, and Westmorland was held personally responsible for the unpopularity of the introduction of the buyer's premium on sales.

But the end came with the appointment of jewellery expert, Graham Llewellyn, as chief executive, a newly-created post, generally deemed to be a polite way of shifting Westmorland aside. At the time, it was announced that this appointment would enable Westmorland to devote more time to "the development of new business for the group worldwide". Soon afterwards he resigned, though remaining a director.

During his time as chairman he made a spirited attempt to break up the system of "the ring" by which certain dealers made private arrangements not to bid against one another. In 1980 he wrote a letter to various dealers' associations reminding them of the Auction (Bidding Agreements) Acts of 1927 and 1969, which outlawed such procedure unless the auctioneer is warned in advance.

His heir is Lord Burghersh, a sports consultant with interests in St Moritz.

b 31.3.24   d 8.9.93   aged 69

LIEUTENANT-COLONEL SIR MARTIN GILLIAT

At the Epsom Derby 1985

Lieutenant-Colonel Sir Martin Gilliat, GCVO, MBE, Private Secretary to the Queen Mother.

MARTIN GILLIAT, soldier and courtier, would have inspired a magnificent Spy cartoon. Tall, with wisps of hair spiking upwards, whimsical of expression, his eyes half-closed, he stood in his later years in the shape of a question mark, head forward, knees bent, as though from half a lifetime of bending his ear to the lesser height of his royal mistress. On the Queen Mother's more important public engagements, Gilliat was always a pace or two behind, protective, benign and helpful. He succeeded Captain Oliver Dawnay as Private Secretary to Queen Elizabeth the Queen Mother in 1956 and for the next 37 years was the mainstay of her Household, particularly after the death of Sir Arthur Penn in 1960. Gilliat was in the best tradition of the bachelor gentleman courtier, polite, brave, the scion of two rich, landed families; combining his executive role with a deep personal friendship with the Queen Mother.

Gilliat was the second son of Lieutenant-Colonel John Babington Gilliat, DSO, DL, JP, a Hertfordshire landowner. The Gilliats (Sir Martin's grandfather was Governor of the Bank of England) were seated at Chorleywood Cedars, Rickmansworth and Frogmore Hall, Hertfordshire, but moved to the Manor House, Welwyn, which was Sir Martin's home, though latterly he moved to Appletrees, Welwyn. His mother, Muriel Grinnell-Milne, also came from a banking family.

Gilliat's elder brother, a lieutenant in the Royals, fell foul of a tiger in India and died of his injuries in 1935, leaving Martin as heir. Gilliat was educated at Eton (where he was a Rambler), and proceeded via Sandhurst to the King's Royal Rifle Corps in 1933.

He served in the British Empire Force in the second world war, and was mentioned in dispatches, but from 1940 to 1945, he was imprisoned at Colditz. Gilliat was appointed MBE in 1946. Modestly he never liked to expand on his Colditz days.

From 1947 to 1948 he was Deputy Military Secretary to Lord Mountbatten, when he was Viceroy of India. On the night of September 9, 1947, he was making a routine inspection of the sentry guard arrangements at a hospital in Delhi in the company of the author, Alan Campbell-Johnson. Later, possibly somewhat conspicuously dressed in white dinner-jackets, they visited the Pahargunj area, a particular trouble spot. Though the streets appeared deserted, their car was suddenly fired upon at point-blank range. Gilliat was wounded behind the right ear. Their Sikh driver was killed instantly, and only by the initiative of Mountbatten's personal security officer, Inspector Elder, was the car prevented from plunging over a bridge. The party was rescued and Gilliat was delivered to the Willingdon Hospital. Though he suffered considerable loss of blood, his head wounds proved superficial.

From 1948 to 1951 Gilliat served as Comptroller to Malcolm MacDonald, Commissioner-General for the UK in Southeast Asia. Their headquarters were in Singapore, but they were constantly travelling between Malaya, Singapore, and the three British Borneo territories. These were difficult years, with a great deal of communist terrorist activity in Malaya.

Gilliat then served as Military Secretary to the Governor-General of Australia from 1953 to 1955. He was in effect the right-hand man to Field-Marshal Sir William Slim. This was an era when the high standards of protocol, absorbed from Viceregal Lodge in Delhi, were applied to Government House, Canberra, and tacitly welcomed by the Australians. Bill Slim had Gilliat in mind when he joked: "Here I am a grammar-school boy surrounded by Old Etonians".

Gilliat was much to the fore when the Queen and the Duke of Edinburgh spent five days at Yarralumla in February 1954, during which time there were never less than 24 for lunch and 50 for dinner. Gilliat was later appointed CVO.

In 1955 Gilliat joined the Queen Mother's Household at Clarence House, and the following year took over as Private Secretary and Equerry. For nearly forty years he was responsible for all the Queen Mother's official duties, and there was little reduction in these as the years went by. The Household at Clarence House was run in the style of an old world court, everyone breaking for tea at the appropriate hour to mull over the matters of the day. The efficiency, and occasionally military precision, never stood in the way of a spirit of friendliness and courtesy. A sense of kindness and fun, that life was to be enjoyed, permeated all levels of Clarence House, and emanated directly from the Queen Mother. To Gilliat fell the pleasant task of assisting her in the spreading of this aura of bonhomie. Visitors to Clarence House were always given the impression that they were being allowed a glimpse of a special world, and, if they needed to be loosened up a little, Gilliat was the pourer of no mean gin-and-tonic.

Gilliat − he was advanced KCVO in 1962 and GCVO in 1981 − was also responsible for the many private interests of the Queen Mother. He could occasionally be spotted waving a catalogue at Christie's or Sotheby's. He shared and encouraged Her Majesty's passion for the turf. He was himself a keen racehorse owner, training with Ryan Price, and running his stable in light blue, black cross-belts and gold cap.

He assisted the Queen Mother in the buying of her stable, and maintained a complete record of all her horses in a series of blue-bound volumes. He could be seen in many a royal box, clad in grey morning suit, binoculars to hand, and nor was he averse to placing a bet. But the *Private Eye* story that he was spotted in a betting establishment in St James's, placing a substantial sum on the as-yet-unannounced Christian name of the infant Prince William, is surely too unsporting to be true.

It was Gilliat's custom, along with other members of the Household, to invite his "employer" (as he called the Queen Mother) to the theatre on her birthday. This outing required numerous advance reconnaissance visits, as Gilliat, an "angel" in the theatre, eliminated the possibility of happenings on stage deemed unsuitable for the Queen Mother's public observance.

He was often at Royal Lodge, acting as *animateur* of the party, and fighting a not entirely successful rearguard action to protect the Queen Mother from over-doing things. During her weekend parties, she was never particularly keen to go to bed. Gilliat was never off-duty. When playing croquet after luncheon, he would cast frequent glances at the door lest the Queen Mother emerge after her siesta.

Every year an American prelate (now deceased) spent a weekend there. He was known to have a fondness for dry Martinis, after which he was less than his normal stimulating company. One Sunday evening, the Queen Mother urged Gilliat "on pain of dismissal" to ensure that the bishop had but one dry Martini before dinner.

Alas, he succeeded in securing a second, as a result of which, in the dining room he stood silent − interminably − when he should have said Grace. Gilliat said later that in those few moments his whole career passed before him. He went through Ludgrove and Eton and was halfway through Sandhurst, when the bishop recovered himself and intoned: "For Her Majesty's kindness in bringing us together in this place, O Lord, and for thy bountiful mercy . . ."

With such incidents and many more were Gilliat's later years fulfilled. He continued to serve the Queen Mother until cancer laid him low. On the occasion of her 90th birthday he paid tribute to her on television, and when he was asked about the decade to come, he said he was confident she would be around, but (with a genial laugh) was less confident about himself and some of the others who served her.

Martin Gilliat was appointed a Deputy Lieutenant for Hertfordshire and Vice-Lieutenant in 1971. He became an honorary Bencher of the Middle Temple in 1977. In the same year the Queen Mother bestowed on him an honorary LLD at London University.

b 8.2.13   d 27.5.93   aged 80

DIZZY GILLESPIE

Dizzy Gillespie, jazz trumpeter.

ALONG with Louis Armstrong and Miles Davis, Dizzy Gillespie was the most influential trumpeter in the history of jazz. A spectacular virtuoso, he helped to usher in the bebop era in the 1940s. In his later years he became an affable father-figure on the international festival circuit.

John Birks Gillespie was the youngest of nine children. His father, a bricklayer, was an amateur musician who died when his son was only ten. Gillespie did not begin to take music seriously until he was 14 when he took up the trombone. Some months later a neighbour loaned him a trumpet.

After his family moved to Philadelphia in 1935, he joined a band which included the trumpeter Charlie Shavers. From him, Gillespie acquired a passion for the great swing player Roy Eldridge, faithfully copying his phrasing. It was also around

this time that his tomfoolery earned him the nickname "Dizzy".

By the late 1930s Gillespie had moved on to New York where he first held down a job with the bandleader Teddy Hill, and then joined the big band of Cab Calloway, with whom he stayed until 1941. They eventually fell out when Calloway accused Gillespie of throwing spitballs during a concert.

By this time he was beginning to experiment with the music that would become known as "bebop". Along with Charlie Parker, Thelonius Monk and other like-minded players, he took part in late-night jam sessions on 52nd Street. The young iconoclasts baffled the older swing musicians by their use of shifting rhythmic patterns, unconventional chords and rampant tempos. Many of the early bebop standards were based on the harmonic structure of old songs such as "I Got Rhythm" and "How High The

Moon''. Who actually deserved most credit for the innovations remains hazy, partly because of the American Federation of Musicians ban on instrumental recordings, which lasted from 1942 to 1944.

A breakthrough came when Gillespie and Parker joined a big band set up by the singer Billy Eckstine, who was prepared to give the young innovators a relatively free hand. The band became an important vehicle for the beboppers. From there the two men moved on to their own small group, which began a celebrated engagement at the Three Deuces venue on 52nd Street. Gillespie's studio recordings from this period included "Hot House", "Groovin' High" and "Shaw Nuff". The new movement began to generate media interest. The name "bebop" stuck simply because it seemed to capture the basic sound of the music. Gillespie's style was marked by a much lighter use of vibrato than was typical among swing era trumpeters. Quality of tone was less important than the urgency and inventiveness of his soloing, resulting in a stream of splintered notes rising into the stratosphere. Unfortunately, the low-quality recordings made in the late 1940s did not always do him justice: he sounds at his most majestic and full-bodied on albums – including the orchestral session *Gillespiana* – made well over a decade later.

While Parker's harmonic innovations poured out as if they were almost beyond his control, Gillespie's approach was more studied: it was often left to him to sit at the piano with a sheet of paper and explain the complexities to the other musicians. As for the public, the reaction was either exultation or baffled dismay.

The swing era had brought jazz a mass audience. Gillespie and his colleagues were less willing to make compromises. "First I play for myself," he once commented, "next I play for the musicians and then I hope that the audience likes it. It's in that order."

Audiences did. In 1945 Gillespie won *Esquire* magazine's new star award and

three years later his band was named *Metronome* magazine's band of the year.

Gillespie's relationship with Parker came under intense strain during their 1946 residency in Los Angeles. Debilitated by drugs and alcohol, Parker frequently missed engagements. At the end of the six-week stint Gillespie returned East; Parker stayed put, eventually suffering a nervous breakdown which led to his confinement in a sanatorium.

After the parting from Parker Gillespie went his own way, forming a big band. This was arguably his best-ever unit, with brilliant sidemen such as vibraphonist Milt Jackson and arrangements by John Lewis and George Russell. The latter contributed the drum suite "Cubana Be''/"Cubana Bop" which highlighted Gillespie's innovative use of Latin American rhythms. The Latin influence was also evident in "Manteca", and in Gillespie's most famous tune "A Night In Tunisia". The postwar years were a difficult time for big bands. Financial pressures forced Gillespie to break up the orchestra in 1950.

He formed his own record company, Dee Gee, the following year, partly with the aim of making somewhat more commercially acceptable music. The venture was short-lived, but it did yield a number of enjoyable recordings. "Birk's Works", "Tin Tin Deo" and the humorous vocal number "Swing Low Sweet Cadilla".

Gillespie's musical development was more or less complete. The one new development from this period was the introduction in 1953 of his distinctive 45 degree trumpet. Typically, this came about completely by chance, when his instrument was accidentally knocked over on the bandstand. Gillespie found that he preferred the tone produced by the new shape. His other visual trademark – his ballooning cheeks – always intrigued onlookers. He was to recall that a NASA scientist once offered to carry out X-rays to investigate the phenomenon. Unfortunately Gillespie missed the appointment.

Bebop was running out of steam. By now Gillespie's work was overshadowed by the cool, understated approach of Miles Davis, but he continued to work steadily with small groups under the aegis of the impresario Norman Granz. In 1956 the controversial Harlem congressman Adam Clayton Powell cajoled the State Department into funding a big band tour to south-eastern Europe and the Middle East. It was the first time Washington had sponsored such a venture, and Gillespie's trip was so successful that another one was swiftly organised, this time to South America.

His support for the civil rights campaign and his opposition to American involvement in Vietnam – not to mention his mischievous sense of humour – prompted a half-serious presidential campaign in 1964. His manifesto included a pledge to deport the arch-segregationist Governor George Wallace, and to appoint Ray Charles to administer the Library of Congress.

The 1960s were a generally fallow period, but the following decades saw him re-emerging as an elder statesman. A certain predictability crept into his public performances, and the clowning and play-acting were not to everyone's taste. There was certainly a limit to the number of times audiences could listen to his familiar pay-off: "Thank you, ladies and gentlemen, for your magnificent indifference". He continued to record at regular intervals, notably for Granz's Pablo label. Live appearances tended to bring out the best in him, and sometimes the worst. Always keen to encourage new talent, he did much to further the career of young trumpeters such as Jon Faddis and the Cuban virtuoso Arturo Sandoval. By the time he celebrated his 70th birthday in 1987, he was understandably reluctant to indulge in too many high-note extravagances.

The following year he set off on a world tour with his self-styled United Nation Orchestra, an all-star unit which featured Sandoval, Paquito d'Rivera, Slide Hampton and Gillespie's long-time friend James Moody. While his own contribution was carefully rationed, the tour was a reminder that he was at his most content when surrounded by a roaring big band. He kept up a gruelling touring schedule until the last year of his life. Reviewers noted that he was having increasing difficulties with his intonation, but there were still nights of inspired playing, and his avuncular stage presence normally made up for any shortcomings.

There was one last surprise, a live album of trumpet-and-drums duets with his old bebop partner Max Roach. This exposed setting, with no rhythm section to act as a safety net, conveyed the same sense of risk as the vintage recordings. Gillespie was in ebullient form, too, on one of his last studio sessions, a collaboration with the West Coast-based group Bebop and Beyond.

His survival in the turbulent world of jazz owed much to the support of his wife Lorraine, whom he married in 1940. He was also a follower of the Baha'i faith. His autobiography, *To Be Or Not To Bop*, was published in 1979.

b 21.10.17   d 6.1.93   aged 75

IVY BENSON

Ivy Benson, bandleader of the pioneering All Girls' Band.

ONE of the forces' favourites during the second world war, Ivy Benson compelled men, by the sheer longevity of her career, to take women seriously as popular musicians. Despite providing a constant source of amusement for northern comedians, her twenty-girl band managed to keep in touch with the changing musical fashions for over fifty years.

Five hundred girls passed under her baton, along with bebop, the jitterbug, jive and samba. In later years the repertoire included pop hits from the Top Thirty along with Benny Goodman and Glen Miller. Benson never minded taking requests for the old favourites, but she was adamant that they should keep up to date in their arrangements.

If Benson was an early feminist of sorts, she was not blind to reality. She knew that men came to see the band — twenty women glamorously decked out in full evening dress — for visual as well as musical reasons, and liked to employ pretty girls, preferably between 18 and 24 years old. The fall-out rate, however, in the days when most girls wanted to be married by the age of twenty, was high and Benson lost many of her best trombonists to GIs. Because of this she was never happy unless there were several girls (up to six in the 1940s) waiting in reserve.

Recruitment was another problem. Where a male bandleader could pick from a hundred outfits to find the trumpeter he needed, Benson had to find her own market, and provide the training. New girls would arrive competently trained from schools or brass bands, mostly from colliery districts or the Salvation Army, with a certain amount of technique but little flair. Benson would have to teach them to listen to their own rhythm and "swing".

Musically, although she could coax a big brassy sound from her girls, she never felt that becoming a good trombonist should be a woman's true vocation. When a good lung capacity is an asset, she argued, a woman could not be expected to blow like a man.

This doyenne of the Mecca ballroom circuit had found it initially very hard to break into the male-dominated dance-band world of the late 1930s. At a time when many male musicians were out of work, the bandleaders openly set out to sabotage her efforts.

After Jack Hylton had taken Benson under his wing, securing her a radio booking for the BBC in January 1943, the other bandleaders, held a meeting in London to discuss tactics for her removal. Despite an underhand campaign — musical arrangers deliberately put wrong notes in the girls' scores and the bandleaders sent a petition to the BBC — Ivy Benson's All Girls' Band was a success, and was receiving 300 fan letters a week from servicemen by the end of the war.

A musical career for the young Ivy Benson seemed inevitable from the start. Her father had played in the orchestra pit of the Leeds Empire and intended Ivy to become a concert pianist, giving her piano lessons from the age of three. When she was nine she won a talent contest at the Empire for her rendition of "Yes, We Have No Bananas". She later learnt the clarinet, the saxophone and the trombone.

Having left school at 16, her first job was in a shoe shop, followed by piecework at the Montague Burton's factory. Benson supplemented her slender income by playing in bands such as Edna Croudfoot's Rhythm Girls during the evenings. Although there were numerous all girl bands in those days, the standard of musicianship was not high.

It became Benson's ambition to lead a girl orchestra which could really play. In 1940 she formed her 20-piece All Girls' Band. Their earliest venues were London tea shops, but as the second world war began to take its toll, creating a drain on bandsmen, the girls stepped into the breach and began to play in the increasingly packed dance halls.

Although Benson was very much the professional bandleader, turning to fix her audience with a warm smile every 16 bars or so, she would regularly put down her baton, pick up her saxophone, and join in.

The band's big break came with a contract with the Mecca Ballroom in Manchester. After the BBC booking — playing alongside broadcasting bands like Henry Hall, Jack Payne, Geraldo and Joe Loss — came a 22-week stint at the London Palladium.

Benson's was the first band into Berlin in May 1945 — Montgomery himself requested they play in the victory celebrations — and the girls represented British entertainment during the 1948 Olympic Games. They spent the next three years touring and entertaining the troops in the Middle East, the Far East and Germany.

Benson used to say that the exploits of Tony Curtis and Jack Lemmon in *Some Like it Hot* were as nothing to some of the situations her girls found themselves in. At Checkpoint Charlie, they found the only way to get past some peculiarly obstructive Russian border guards was to charm them with an impromptu performance of *Il Silencio*, while in the Sahara Desert the girls were put under armed guard to protect them from the amorousness of troops who had not seen women for several months.

Bookings in the top hotels and ballrooms of Europe followed, together with seasons at the Palladium and numerous television appearances. Every summer the girls took up residence at Douglas in the Isle of Man. However, their popularity was never backed up with the sort of financial rewards that the men's bands could expect.

In the 1960s and 1970s the ballrooms and theatres began to close and the big-band era came to an end. Benson still kept a pool of 30 girls in reserve for the round of masonic balls and civic dances that were now her staple. But in the early 1980s she retired to a bungalow in Clacton-on-Sea, Essex. She continued to play the electric organ at venues along the seafront most evenings, introducing herself with the signature tune, "Lady Be Good", which she had first used in 1944.

Benson's unashamed popularising approach on stage concealed a more thoughtful woman who could speak French, German, Spanish and some Russian and Italian. One of her unfulfilled ambitions was to give an orchestral recital of symphonic jazz music by Gershwin and Constant Lambert. In later years she worked tirelessly for charity.

Benson always held that big bands and husbands did not mix, and her own two brief marriages ended in divorce.

b 11.11.13   d 6.5.93   aged 79

SAMMY CAHN

Sammy Cahn, popular song lyricist who won four Academy Awards.

SAMMY Cahn was the despair of his good Jewish mother. The second of five children and her only son, she had him pegged to become a doctor or a lawyer. But she had made the mistake of teaching him to play the violin, and Samuel Cohen, as he was born, had other ideas about his career. After setting a record for truancy he began working as a violinist in Bowery burlesque houses. He was just 15 years old. Between "musical engagements", the young Cahn worked as a porter, elevator operator, tinsmith, usher, and restaurant cashier. He became a proficient violinist, playing in various semi-professional bands around New York and at the "borsch belt" resorts in the Catskills Mountains.

With Saul Chaplin he published "Shake Your Head from Side to Side" in 1933. This failed to earn them any royalties but they succeeded in 1935 with "Rhythm Is Our Business", composed for the bandleader Jimmie Lunceford. It became a hit record and subsequently Lunceford's signature tune.

In 1936 they wrote "Shoe Shine Boy", a hit for Louis Armstrong, which he used as a finale piece for his review at the Cotton Club. Jack Kapp, a record executive from Decca, commissioned the pair to compose for Ella Fitzgerald and Andy Kirk. It was their composition, "Until the Real Thing Comes Along", which helped to establish Kirk's band. Kapp also asked for an English-language version of a Yiddish song called "Bei Mir Bist du Schon" (1937), for The Andrews Sisters. This became their first million-seller and was the premier novelty song of the year earning over $3 million.

The team was given a contract by Warner Brothers to work at the Vitaphone studios in Brooklyn. Cahn said of Warners that their motto was "We don't want it good – we want it by Thursday!"

Following the closure of Vitaphone in 1940 the pair travelled to Hollywood where, eventually, they dissolved their partnership after failing to secure any further work. At this time Cahn met, and married in 1945, Gloria Delson, a former Goldwyn girl.

By this time Sammy had changed his name to Kahn, to avoid confusion with a comedian named Sammy Cohen, and then changed it again to Cahn to distinguish himself from another lyricist, Gus Kahn.

Cahn attempted to enlist in the US army following Pearl Harbor but was turned down on medical grounds (he suffered from ulcers for most of his life). Instead of going to war, Cahn formed a new partnership with Jule Styne. The team worked mainly on films, including *Romance on the High Seas* (1948) which included the memorable, "It's Magic" sung by Doris Day. They also wrote the songs for *The Toast of New Orleans* (1949), which gave Mario Lanza his first million-seller, "Be My Love" (written with Nicholas Brodszky). Perhaps their most famous song was "Three Coins in a Fountain". This won an Oscar for best song of 1954: Cahn claimed that it was written in under an hour. The Four Aces' version became a multi-million hit, although in the film it was sung by Frank Sinatra.

Sammy Cahn had met Sinatra through the bandleader Tommy Dorsey. They had become friends immediately and the Cahn-Styne partnership began to produce a string of songs for him. These included "Saturday Night is the Loneliest Night of the Week", "I Fall in Love Too Easily", "I Walk Alone" (which was nominated for an Academy Award) (1944), and "Five Minutes More" (1946). Cahn and Styne frequently wrote within other teams. Cahn worked with Sammy Fain on

numbers for Walt Disney's *Peter Pan*, with Sylvia Fine on Danny Kaye's *The Court Jester* and with Bronislau Kaper on *Forever Darling*.

Cahn teamed up with Jimmy Van Heusen in 1955, writing the major hit title song for Frank Sinatra's film *The Tender Trap*. The partnership was tremendously successful and heralded a long association of producing dazzling uptempo hits. These included "Love and Marriage" (1955), "All the Way" (1957) and "High Hopes" (1959). Cahn turned this into John F. Kennedy's presidential campaign signature in 1960. Song classics followed including "Come Fly With Me" (1958). For this Cahn had written the lyric about a "bar with exotic views", Sinatra changed it to "exotic booze" at the recording session.

At the suggestion of Broadway producer Alexander Cohen, Cahn compiled a one-man show retrospective of his work, *Words and Music* which opened in 1974. Cohen received the Outer Circle Critics Award for Best New Talent on Broadway. Ironically this qualified him for membership of Equity for the first time. The show also ran in London (from September 1974), under the title *Sammy Cahn's Songbook*, the same year his autobiography was published: *I Should Care*.

Cahn was a natural and witty raconteur and during the early 1980s appeared regularly in television chat-shows in London. He was given a place in the Songwriters Hall of Fame in 1972. He always maintained that his favourite recreational activity was to simply sit and type – anything at all. He was a naturally gifted writer who had a mind for comedy that might have just as easily earned him a career as a gag writer. It was this mastery of the punch-line that earned him such respect for his lyrics. The prodigious canon of lyrics Sammy Cahn produced over six decades have become woven, durably, into the postwar popular psyche.

He is survived by his wife, a son and a daughter.

b 18.6.13   d 15.1.93   aged 79

BORIS CHRISTOFF

Boris Christoff, the Bulgarian-born bass.

FEW singers could create such an arresting impression on stage as Boris Christoff. His imposing features and penetrating, almost demonic eyes ensured that he was noticed immediately he came on stage, and his formidable, not to say melodramatic, acting made certain one never forgot he was there even when another artist was singing. His voice, not the largest or most beautiful of instruments, was utterly distinctive in character and, once heard impossible to forget. It had great powers of projection and, above all, an amazing variety of colour and nuance. Both in the opera house and on the recital platform, he evinced an innate feeling for character and for the meaning of what he was interpreting. He was the most sought-after Boris Godunov and Philip II (in Verdi's *Don Carlos*) of his day and was distinguished in a number of other Italian and Russian roles – quite apart from the huge service he did for the dissemination of Russian song.

He was helped to success by his upbringing. (He was born in 1914, as he latterly admitted, not 1919 as most books of record have it.) His father, who always encouraged his son's talent, sang in the local church choir, and the young Boris was a member of his local children's choir. He became an opera fanatic after seeing *Der Freischütz* when he was only ten. Thereafter he would sit spellbound in the gallery of the Sofia opera house watching performances and wanting to emulate them. On holiday in his teens he would go off into the peace of the mountains and try out his fledgling voice. At 18 he joined the famous Gusla Choir, which toured Bulgaria and surrounding countries, while at the same time studying law.

Although he qualified as a lawyer he continued to sing in his spare time, as a soloist in the Alexander Nevsky Cathedral Choir in Sofia. King Boris III invited the choir to sing at the Royal Palace and Christoff sang a solo – a folksong. So impressed was the king that he persuaded Christoff to abandon the law and arranged for him to have a scholarship to study in Italy. In 1942 he went to Rome to work with the famed baritone Riccardo Stracciari from whom he learnt the virtues of line and singing off the text.

The two established a rapport, but war interrupted their fruitful relationship. After many vicissitudes, including imprisonment, Christoff managed to get back to Rome in 1945 and resume his studies with Stracciari, who had despaired of seeing his star pupil again. Christoff made his professional debut singing Wotan's Farewell at the Santa Cecilia Academy in Rome in 1946. His debut in opera came the following year in *La Bohème* as Colline at the Teatro Argentina. He was an instant success and had to repeat the Coat Song twice. Appearances at la Fenice in Venice and La Scala in Milan confirmed his new-won fame.

On November 19, 1949, he made his debut at Covent Garden as Boris Godunov, which he was singing for the first time. It was a role he was to make his own. Yet disputes with the producer Peter Brook and an insistence on Christoff's part that the Rimsky-Korsakov version, rather than

Mussorgsky's original (then, as now, current at the Royal Opera House) should be used nearly caused him to cancel. Only soothing words from David Webster (then administrator of Covent Garden) saved the day. Christoff was already proving an awkward, even recalcitrant, colleague because of his invincible conviction that his was the only way of doing things.

There could be no argument about his superb interpretation of the tortured Tsar, a reading that he was to refine and perfect over the succeeding thirty years, repeating it frequently at intervals at covent Garden. He recorded it twice, most notably under his mentor the conductor Issay Dobrowen in 1952.

He first sang Philip II at the Maggio musicale in Florence in 1950, and it is the role in which he will perhaps be most gratefully remembered in this country. He took the part in the first performances of the now-legendary Visconti production at Covent Garden in 1958, conducted by Giulini and with Christoff's brother-in-law Tito Gobbi as Posa. He returned several times to repeat his riveting interpretation. He seemed to peer, dramatically and vocally, into the tormented king's soul in the private scenes while exuding authority in the public ones. His other Covent Garden part was Fiesco in Verdi's *Simon Boccanegra*, another commanding performance. He also appeared with the company at the Edinburgh Festival as Don Basilio, disclosing the lighter side of his all-consuming art.

Among other roles in which he made an indelible impression were Mephistopheles in both Boito's and Gounod's operas based on Goethe's *Faust*; Ivan Susanin in Glinka's *A Life for the Tsar*; Galitsky and Khan Konchak in *Prince Igor*; Dosifei in Mussorgsky's *Khonanshchina*; the title role in Rossini's *Mose*; and Henry VIII in Donizetti's *Anna Bolena* (which typically he wanted re-titled after the king's name). In Verdi he sang Zaccaria in *Nabucco*; Silva in *Ernani*; Procida in *Vespri Siciliani*; and Padre Guardiano in *La Forza del*

Destino. In all of these he always attempted to create a specific character based, where relevant, on historic precedent.

Early in his career he sang such roles as Leporello (*Don Giovanni*), Pizarro (*Fidelio*) and Agamemnon (Gluck's *Iphigénie en Aulide*). He also assumed – once, for a broadcast – the role of Gurnemanz in *Parsifal* with Callas as his Kundry, and Vittorio Gui as conductor. Off-the-air records show this to have been a most unusual and exceptionally revealing occasion.

His greatest legacy may prove to be his long succession of discs of Russian song, an achievement not equalled before or since. His complete set of Mussorgsky's songs, now on CD, demonstrates the extent of his understanding of the genre, each piece given with exceptional insights, not least the *Nursery* cycle where he reduced his bass to a child-like timbre. These were recorded between 1955 and 1957 after a lengthy period of study. He also left single records of songs by Glinka, Borodin, Tchaikovsky, Balakirev, Rimsky-Korsakov, Cui, Rachmaninov and Gretchaninov, as a whole a unique achievement.

Off the stage Boris Christoff remained larger than life, a jovial, forthright companion who, his friends often felt, might at any moment assume one of the many characters he portrayed on stage and in song. After the war he lived most of his life in Italy where he became naturalised, with his wife Franca, sister of Tito Gobbi's wife Tilde. Franca was adept at curbing the excesses of temperament to which Christoff was prone, and smoothed over many a ruction in the opera house, when Christoff was on the point of quitting over some difference with a producer. It has to be said, in Christoff's defence, that most of his disputes arose, as they did with Callas, from his high regard for his art and for the maintenance of artistic standards.

His wife survives him. There were no children.

b 18.5.14   d 28.6.93   aged 79

BILLY ECKSTINE

Billy Eckstine, singer and bandleader.

THE rich, resonant timbre of Billy Eckstine's bass-baritone voice, and his sophisticated treatment of popular melodies, brought him huge success as a singer of romantic ballads in the 1940s and 1950s. Some of his records – in particular "I Surrender Dear" and his duet with Sarah Vaughan on "Passing Strangers" – have become classics of their style, and he had an influential impact on the next generation of popular vocalists. He was also, for a brief spell in the late 1940s, a bandleader whose orchestra proved to be an intensive breeding ground for the creators of bebop jazz, featuring the early work of Charlie Parker, Dizzy Gillespie and a host of other musical innovators. As such Eckstine was a pivotal figure in jazz history.

In the 1940s when he first achieved national prominence he was the first male black singer to reach a mass multi-racial audience, singing romantic popular songs, preceding – by a short head – and paving the way for another musician turned singer, Nat "King" Cole.

Nicknamed "Mr B", Eckstine was voted America's most popular vocalist in 1949 and 1950. A handsome and elegant man, he was the first black singer to be featured on the cover of *Life* magazine and to become something of a sex and fashion symbol. The youth of America – whites as well as blacks – imitated his dress style, particularly the rolled "Billy Eckstine" shirt collar and draped jackets.

William Clarence Eckstine grew up in Washington. He began singing at the age of 11 but won a sporting scholarship to Howard University and it was not until his late teens that he abandoned hopes of being a footballer to concentrate on a career as a vocalist. After winning a talent competition singing in the style of Cab Calloway, he worked initially as a master of ceremonies and singer in nightclubs until, in 1939, he was hired as a vocalist by the jazz pianist and bandleader Earl Hines.

While with Hines he developed a modest talent as a trumpeter and valve-trombonist and became a talent spotter, helping to recruit Charlie Parker and Sarah Vaughan to the Hines band. His first recordings were with the band in 1940: two blues hits, a raunchy number entitled "Jelly Jelly" and "Stormy Monday".

Three years later Eckstine left Hines and spent a year as a solo nightclub singer before forming his own big band. Although it was active for only three years, from 1944 to 1947, it became the nucleus of the emerging bebob style of jazz. At various moments during its three-year existence the band's personnel included, in addition to Gillespie and Parker, Fats Navarro, Miles Davis, Kenny Dorham on trumpets; Gene Ammons, Dexter Gordon, Lucky Thompson on tenor saxophones, Leo Parker on baritone, John Malachi on piano, Tommy Potter on bass and Art Blakey on drums.

With this star-studded line-up Eckstine made a series of recordings featuring his own singing, effectively showcased by powerful and sometimes complex orchestrations, and began extending his reputation as a ballad singer of distinction. However, the band was ahead of its time as far as public tastes were concerned and it failed commercially. Later he commented: "It didn't last forever but we had a hell of a band."

When the big band folded, Eckstine fronted a septet with Wardell Gray on tenor and then began touring internationally with jazz-based accompanists.

Eckstine's singing was marked by its radiant warmth, carefully controlled vibrato, immaculate diction and a sensitive attention to the meanings of the lyrics. At a time when American audiences were still largely segregated, these qualities broke through racial stereotyping and crossed the colour barriers. In 1947 he was signed by MGM Records, becoming the first black singer to record for a mainstream white label. His first hits included: "Fools Rush In" and "Everything I Have is Yours".

Recalling the racial breakthrough in a 1984 interview, Eckstine said: "Until then they weren't ready for black singers singing love songs. It sounds ridiculous but it's true. We weren't supposed to sing about love, we were supposed to sing about work or blues."

Between 1945 and 1951 he had a series of recording hits including "A Cottage for Sale", "Prisoner of Love", "I Surrender, Dear", "Blue Moon", "My Foolish Heart", "Caravan", "Body and Soul", "Laura", "Tenderly" and "I Apologise" and his style inspired many singers including Tony Bennett, and Carmen McRae.

Eckstine's recording of "None But You" reached number three in the British hit parade in 1954 and his "Gigi" was number eight in 1959. "Passing Strangers", which he and Sara Vaughan recorded in 1957, reached 17 in the British charts 12 years later. More than a dozen albums featuring his singing were released, the latest of which, *Billy Eckstine Sings with Benny Carter*, appeared in 1986.

Eckstine toured Britain as a member of the George Wein jazz package in 1974 and last visited in 1984 when he appeared at Ronnie Scott's Club.

In spite of his widespread popularity, Eckstine's colour prevented him from enjoying the usual attributes of such success in America – his own nationally-networked radio or television shows or a career in films – while he was at the peak of his success. When he did appear in a cameo singing role in the 1953 film *Skirts Ahoy!* he was instructed not to look at any of the white women in the scene.

Eckstine was married and divorced twice. He used to remark, wryly, that Bobby Tucker, the pianist who worked with him for 40 years, had outlasted both his marriages.

He is survived by his seven children.

b 8.7.14   d 8.3.93   aged 78

REGINALD GRENFELL

Reggie and Joyce Grenfell in 1934

Reginald Pascoe Grenfell.

REGINALD Grenfell, who trained as a chartered accountant, and later worked for British Consolidated Non-Ferrous Metals, was the husband of the *diseuse*, Joyce Grenfell, whom he married in 1929. Grenfell was the elder son of Arthur Morton Grenfell and his first wife, Victoria, the eldest child of the 4th Earl Grey of Howick, who died when Reginald was five.

Grenfell met his future wife, Joyce Phipps, at Ford Manor in Surrey when she was 17. She was then about to go to RADA where, she recalled: "I lasted exactly one term, before Reggie took my mind off the stage and I left." But just as Reggie had been instrumental in curtailing his wife's early theatre career, so he was to encourage it when Joyce took to the stage again in 1939. He was also responsible for secretly editing her first volume of autobiography, *Joyce Grenfell Requests the Pleasure* in 1976, spiriting off early chapters, which he photocopied and rearranged with Sellotape. Thereafter he edited all her work.

Reggie Grenfell was certainly no sleeping partner in the highly successful show-business career of his wife. All Joyce Grenfell's professional decisions were taken in consultation with Reggie, as she readily admitted: "Helped? He did everything for me." With his Frank Muir say-nothing-smile, and his somewhat lanky frame, Grenfell's tastes were most decidedly "ordinary". An expert "twitcher" and cricket fan (he would become addicted in later years to the BBC's *Grandstand*), he was a house-husband before his time – although he fell short of doing the cooking. Not that he did not need a certain amount of wifely organisation: "Reggie, left to himself, might be a last-minute man, but long years of living with me have trained him the other way."

The couple were only really parted during the war – in which Reggie had a distinguished career in the 60th Rifles, rising to the rank of lieutenant-colonel. Herself on tour entertaining the troops, Joyce would write him long and often hilarious letters describing her latest adventures. At such times, she would be reminded of her husband's qualities: "Funny thing the way I long for him more and more as a lasting, enduring, darling and real person," she wrote when in Egypt in 1944. "He's the linchpin in my life all right. I am one of the lucky ones." Reggie accompanied her to New York in 1956, when his duties included delivering Joyce to the *Ed Sullivan Show*, there to be met by hordes of screaming teenagers: not Joyce Grenfell fans, alas, but there to see Elvis Presley, who was sharing the bill.

In 1950, Grenfell's cousin Harold Grenfell, chairman of the Messina (Transvaal) Development Company, invited him to join the board as a director. Joyce often went with him on his annual visits to South Africa, staying at Harold Grenfell's ranch and, with the chairman's wife, enjoying the swimming pool; not so her husband, as she recalled in a voice reminiscent of her own monologues: "Reggie never plunges except in a hot bath."

The Grenfells led a quiet social life, much preferring entertaining at lunch – favourite guests would be Noël Coward or Athene Seyler – rather than at dinner and invariably going to matinées rather than to evening performances at the theatre. They enjoyed, though, their grand Christmases at Cliveden with the Astors (Nancy being Joyce's aunt), and occasional royal balls at Windsor: "Reggie and I dance a little and stare a lot." But black-tie did not come naturally to Reggie, who was happier in grey flannels on more casual Somerset visits to his niece Susan and her husband, Marmaduke Hussey.

It was partly the wit of her husband – an extremely funny, if very modest and private man – which helped Joyce to make her observations of everyday life into the wonderfully comic monologues that became her trademark. Without Reggie's stable presence, it is doubtful if Joyce's talent would have been able to flourish in the manner in which it did. In later years, when she became a television star, Reggie would sit down to enjoy – with six million others – his wife's witty appearances on *Face the Music*. His pleasure and pride in her achievements was untainted by any form of envy.

After Joyce's death from cancer, Reggie agreed to allow Maureen Lipman to revive her monologue in *Re: Joyce!*, a show written by James Roose-Evans. Lipman was honoured when Reggie told her after the first night: "It was wonderful to see her again." Joyce Grenfell died in 1979, two weeks before their golden wedding. They had no children.

b 1.11.03   d 31.3.93   aged 89

LADY GLOVER

Greeting Margaret Thatcher Zurich (1983)

Lady Glover, political hostess and widow of the former Conservative MP, Sir Douglas Glover.

THE death of Lady Glover at her home in Switzerland brings to an end an era of a great hostess with devoted worldwide friends. Schloss Freudenberg became synonymous as a home from home to royalty, prime ministers, and international leaders of finance and business from all over the world.

Lady Glover was the elder daughter of the Rev Richard Ridge, of Ridge in Shropshire. The Ridge family had long historic connections as squires in Shropshire.

Educated privately, Eleanor Ridge moved with her parents from Stepney, East London, where her father was vicar of St Matthew's church, to Doddington, Cambridgeshire, in 1922, when her father became incumbent of this country living.

During the war she joined British Military Intelligence and in 1945 was posted to Vienna under the command of Colonel Charles Beauclerk (later the Duke of St Albans), where she worked closely with Graham Greene and the journalist and historian, Gordon Brooke-Shepherd.

After the war Eleanor Ridge returned to Doddington and helped nurse her father until his death in 1949. She led an active social life in London and frequently visited Freudenberg to stay with her godmother and her future husband, Erwin Hurlimann.

The family friendship between the Ridges and the Hurlimanns dated from before 1914. Eleanor's father had assisted at St Andrew's Anglican church in Zurich; the Hurlimanns were outstanding supporters of the church.

Erwin Hurlimann was already a senior figure in world finance, having brought rapid expansion to Swiss Reinsurance. In 1927 he purchased an estate on Lake Zug and commissioned the Scottish architect Howard Robertson to prepare plans for Freudenberg. Eleanor's father laid the foundation stone and a unique house in a perfect setting was created.

In 1951, a year after the death of his first wife, "Hurl" Hurlimann married Eleanor Ridge. Despite his international reputation as a financier, Hurl was a man of great natural charm and modesty. They complemented each other.

Following their marriage, Eleanor and Hurl travelled extensively and Freudenberg soon became a centre for all their friends to be entertained. Never ostentatious, but with perfection in every respect, you could find yourself sitting next to Nancy Mitford, a prince, a prime minister, or a curate. Many of their friends from England spent happy summer afternoons in the wonderful gardens and park at Freudenberg.

There was always the finest food and drink, hospitality, and friendship, which was orchestrated by Eleanor Hurlimann. Never flamboyant, but always beautifully and immaculately dressed, Eleanor entered a room and brought a complete sense of chic and elegance to a party or just a meeting with a personal friend.

Because of her religious roots and deep spiritual convictions, Eleanor Hurlimann, from an early age, had a natural ability to give a helping hand to people from every walk of life. She was always the first person to whom people turned – not for financial reasons but because she listened to problems, brought them into perspective, showed sympathy and gave outstanding advice.

The death of Hurl in 1968 brought to an end a life-long friendship which culminated in a most loving, devoted, and intensely loyal partnership. Eleanor remained much of the time at Freudenberg, occasionally visiting her small home in Paris, to see close friends. After six months, she quietly returned to the scene at her table at Claridges. Her many loyal friends brought her back from her deep mourning.

Early in 1976 she met Colonel Sir Douglas Glover again. She had known him as Colonel Glover in Vienna in 1945.

The decision to remarry was not easy. Sir Douglas, who was a widower, had retired from Parliament six years earlier after being MP for Ormskirk for 17 years and rising to be chairman of the National Union of Conservative and Unionist Associations, the voluntary arm of the Conservative party organisation.

The next six years, before they were all-too-abruptly ended by Sir Douglas's death, became an intensely happy period for both the Glovers. They had many mutual friends, and enjoyed entertaining and travelling.

It was during this time that Freudenberg became the summer retreat for the Thatchers. Eleanor Glover ensured that the family and political friends of the prime minister were always made welcome during these stays.

Although known as hostess to the then prime minister, this did not preclude an endless stream of other visitors. Her great religious belief and support of the English church in Zurich brought bishops and clergy together with politicians at her table.

Much of Eleanor's life was devoted to nursing members of her family. She gave herself selflessly to both her parents during their final illnesses, and the nursing of both her husbands took a heavy toll on her health.

Until her final illness, which started a year ago, she continued to travel between Freudenberg, Paris and London.

A close friend who was invited to stay only five weeks ago was amazed by her immense courage, finding her standards had never changed, and that her sense of humour remained unimpaired.

She will be remembered as an intensely warm and loyal friend, who brought comfort, happiness, and enjoyment to people from all over the world.

Lady Glover is survived by her only nephew, Richard Raynar, sole child of her younger sister, Margery.

b 1908   d 20.3.93   aged 84

REGINALD HAMLIN

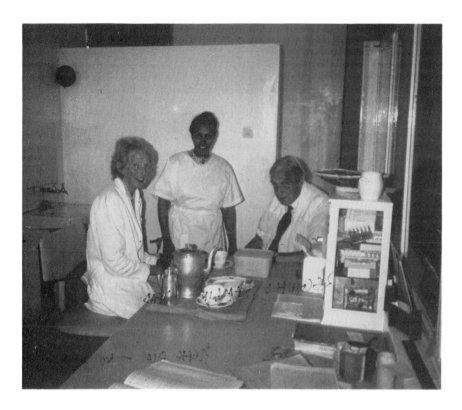

Dr Reginald Hamlin, OBE, joint founder with his wife Catherine of the Addis Ababa Fistula Hospital for Poor Women with Childbirth Injuries.

UNTIL the arrival of Reginald and Catherine Hamlin in Ethiopia in 1959, the lot of a pregnant woman in the remote fastnesses of the country might, if she were unlucky, be one of horrific and unrelieved suffering. To begin with, she would be entirely without access to even the most rudimentary medical care. If the delivery was obstructed the baby would most probably die. In doing so, its head, eroding through the bladder and rectum would generally cause a fistula – a suppurating rent – in one or both. The result would be infection, unspeakable pain and grotesque tissue damage.

To encounter a young wife, thus cruelly and humiliatingly maimed, filthy and foul-smelling, is a deeply harrowing experience. Probably still in her teens; grieving the loss of her first and only child; incontinent of urine and faeces, spurned by her husband; without friends and without hope, such a woman is expected to bear her rejection in silent shame.

Reginald and Pat Hamlin had left a thriving gynaecological practice in Sydney in 1959 to go to Addis Ababa. They were on a three-year contract, their task to set up a school of midwifery at the Princess Tsehi Memorial Hospital. The hospital had been named after a daughter of the Emperor Haile Selassie, who had died in childbirth.

They never returned home. What they saw in Ethiopia made the couple determine to devote the rest of their lives to alleviating the plight of the outcast wives they encountered and to ameliorate the appalling sufferings that go hand in hand with childbirth in that country.

Born in New Zealand, Reginald Hamlin embarked on his medical career in Australia, as an obstetrician and gynaecologist at the renowned Women's Hospital, Crown Street, Sydney. In the second world war he served in the Royal New Zealand Navy.

When the Hamlins arrived in Addis Ababa in 1959 they were soon made aware of the magnitude of the problem facing the service they had been charged with setting up. Patients with fistulas came to them from all over Ethiopia, often arriving only after the most arduous journeys which might be on camel, mule, donkey, or on foot. One had begged for years at the roadside, to raise the £1 bus fare. Another arrived almost blind but besought the couple to repair her fistula before she would consent to any treatment for her sight. Simply, before that damage was made good no one would come near her.

It became clear to Hamlin and his wife that the sheer scale of the problem they faced could not be coped with in a single department within a general hospital. The establishment of a separate, specialist institution was vital. Skill and energy as fundraisers now went in tandem with their surgical expertise. To the end, Hamlin was always happy to describe himself as one of the world's greatest beggars. Campaigning tirelessly, the couple raised money in New Zealand and Australia, the United States and Great Britain to build a hospital on land donated by Haile Selassie.

The Fistula Hospital for Poor Women with Childbirth Injuries was eventually opened in 1975. Since then it has treated over 15,000 women free of charge. Some 700 women a year are now being treated. When discharged, patients are told to tell other women in their village that free treatment for their injuries is available. Some stay on to help in pre-operative care such as physiotherapy to straighten the legs of women who have often lain curled up in the corner of their hut, too ashamed to move outside.

When they arrive the women are accommodated in the grounds of the hospital while awaiting surgery. After the operation they are given new clothes and money to get home.

Fistula surgery is a complex and delicate business, which requires a meticulous technique and innovative skills. Hamlin had both, and as a result was in great demand as a teacher. He was generous with his knowledge to those who came from all over the world to learn the art, and to take the necessary skills to other developing countries where fistulas are very common.

For many years young Ethiopian doctors training to become gynaecologists have been seconded to the Fistula Hospital to learn these difficult operations. One of Hamlin's most rewarding successes was Mamitu Gashe, a skilled fistula surgeon. She had arrived in Addis Ababa on a stretcher, doubly incontinent, in 1963. After receiving treatment and achieving a successful recovery she determined to devote her life to the hospital and has become one of its most remarkable practioners.

The work of Hamlin, his wife and Mamitu was recognised by the Royal College of Surgeons of England with the award of its Gold Medal. Hamlin was appointed OBE in 1972 and was given the Ethiopian Nobel Prize and Gold Medal. Though an Anglican, he was presented with the Papal Award of the Order of St Gregory the Great. Earlier this year the work of the Hamlins and the hospital was featured in a BBC television programme, *Walking Back to Happiness.*

During Hamlin's final illness, Catherine carried an increasing burden of surgical work. This she will continue, aided by Mamitu and the Ethiopian doctors they have trained.

Hamlin leaves his widow and a son, as well as a hospital which is a memorial to one of Africa's greatest and most compassionate surgeons.

b 21.4.08 d 4.8.93 aged 85

KATHLEEN HILL

Kathleen Hill, MBE, Winston Churchill's secretary during the second world war and later, for 23 years, the curator of Chequers.

THROUGHOUT nine of the most crucial years in British history, Kathleen Hill sat close to the heart of power and government. Yet she died with her store of secrets still intact. She was the model of model secretaries.

She was at Churchill's side at times of triumph and disaster: when he replaced Neville Chamberlain at 10 Downing Street; at the time of the Allied victory in Europe; and when he lost the 1945 general election. She was with him on early visits to President Roosevelt, her notebooks and typewriter at the ready.

She recalled in later years his evident distress on hearing that the battleship *Prince of Wales* had been sunk in the Far East and graphically described the "buzzing" atmosphere whenever the great man was in full flow.

She took dictation from him in his car, while he paced up and down his wartime bunker and even in his bedroom – where she would sit at the foot of his bed, a typewriter on her knee. She typed some of the most famous speeches in the language, on at least one occasion while Churchill was on his feet in the House of Commons, the pages being passed forward to him as he spoke. Her shorthand and her typing were impeccable and Churchill never troubled to check her copy – though he dictated at great speed.

Yet the woman who knew so much

never kept a diary or tried to capitalise upon her memories. She divulged only the most trivial information – and usually only to set the record straight after some journalist or historian had erred. Her reward for such professional discretion was that Winston Churchill trusted her implicitly.

Kathleen Hill's job came through a secretarial agency. An accomplished violinist, who had made broadcasts and played in public, she had hoped to be given a post in a girls' school, where she could make an input to its musical curriculum. She never regretted, however, the chance decision which took her to Chartwell and changed the future course of her life.

She was born Kathleen Spratt in Portsmouth, where her father worked for the Royal Navy in the dockyard. She began work there as a 17-year-old secretary in the first world war, developing the skills which were later to take her to the top. But she left for India after the war was over, to marry George Hill, an official of the Bengal-Nagpur railway. Their wedding, which took place despite opposition from their families, was held in Bombay Cathedral in 1924. The new Mrs Hill became a Girl Guide district commissioner and subsequently took a job as secretary to the Chief Commissioner of Girl Guides in All-India, Lady Linlithgow.

Her marriage ended unhappily, however, and she returned to this country where she began working for Churchill in 1937. Based at Chartwell, she was chiefly involved, at first, in Churchill's journalism and literary life.

She later moved with him to Downing Street as his personal private secretary, heading a team of three who worked a shift system during the war, sleeping and working in Downing Street itself or in its so-called annex.

Following Churchill's defeat in the 1945 General Election, however, the curator at Chequers retired and she was offered the job by the Chequers Trust. She accepted, commenting to friends that one could be a secretary for too long, and spent the next 23 years running the prime minister's official country residence for six more holders of the office. The six included Churchill in the early 1950s, though as he normally continued to use Chartwell he gave her and her staff (traditionally drawn from the three services) an easy time.

To all of them, from Clement Attlee to Harold Wilson, she devoted the same qualities of loyalty, efficiency and discretion until her retirement in 1969. Her signed photographs of all of Britain's prime ministers over a period of 30 years must be among the rarest collections of that kind.

But her signed copies of all Churchill's books were sold in Sothebys earlier this year when she had to enter a nursing home after a fall.

Her former husband inherited a Cromwellian baronetcy 12 years ago, becoming Sir George Hill, 9th Bt. Their son Richard was made the 10th baronet on his father's death, but he died last March and Mrs Hill is survived by two grand-daughters.

b 20.8.00   d 16.11.92   aged 92

CAPTAIN JOHN TREASURE JONES

Captain John Treasure Jones, the last master of the Cunard liner Queen Mary.

A LONG career at sea, beginning in a Cardiff tramp steamer and including being sunk in the second world war, culminated for John Treasure Jones in the last voyage of the *Queen Mary* in 1967. By that time the magnificent three-funnel 81,000-ton Cunard liner, once holder of the Atlantic Blue Riband, was already a creature of a former era. In the 33 years of her working life thousands of pounds had been gambled in her smoke room. Her vast promenade lounge, with its splendid grotesqueries of marble fire place, velvet drapes and onyx Grecian urns, had seen the rich, the royal and the otherwise famous, tango to the music of its dance band. But by the egalitarian Sixties air travel had turned her into an unaffordable luxury. The frenetic pace of modern business could no longer tolerate four days and more spent on

what could be accomplished in seven hours.

For her master it was the end of the line, too, as a sea-going mariner. When the *Queen Mary* was sold to the Californian city of Long Beach, as a floating hotel, he came onshore and into retirement.

John Treasure Jones was one of eight children, the son of a Welsh hay and corn merchant. But there was a strong maritime tradition in the family, as with so many West Wales families. His maternal grandfather had skippered a windjammer and three uncles had also done sea time.

At 16 Treasure Jones was apprenticed as a deck-hand on a tramp steamer sailing out of Cardiff in the years immediately following the first world war. Conditions in such vessels were grim and life was tough. Moving to Newcastle he took his second mate's certificate and joined the White Star line. But when the Depression descended he found himself out of a berth and was forced to go back home and work on the land. After that he went to Liverpool where he worked as assistant superintendent stevedore in the docks.

By the time he was able to get back to sea in 1937 his old company, White Star, had been merged with Cunard and he served in its big ships. During the war all liners were pressed into service either as troopships or armed merchant cruisers. The latter suffered heavy losses as they vainly – and often valiantly – tried to engage German surface raiders or, without proper Asdic apparatus, fell victim to U-boats. Treasure Jones was serving in the Cunard liner *Laurentic*, then doing convoy escort duty as HMS *Laurentic*, when she was torpedoed off the aptly-named Bloody Foreland, Donegal, in November 1940. He spent ten hours in the water before he was rescued. Once recovered, he went back to convoy escort duties and ended the war in command of the 49th Escort Group.

Returning to Cunard after the war, Treasure Jones was master first of the *Media* and then of the *Saxonia*. In the latter he gave a demonstration of his superb seamanship during a strike of Canadian tugmen, when he took her out of Montreal and into the St Lawrence Seaway without assistance. In 1962 he was given command of the *Mauretania* and captained her until 1965. He was her last master, too. When she arrived back at Southampton on November 10, 1965, it was the end for her of 27 seagoing years during which she had steamed more than three million nautical miles. No such reprieve as the *Queen Mary*'s was available to her, and she finished up in a Firth of Forth scrapyard.

There followed one round trip across the Atlantic in command of Cunard's flagship the *Queen Elizabeth*, before Treasure Jones became master of the *Queen Mary* for the last two years of her working life. In August 1966 he coaxed her to her fastest crossing of the Atlantic since the Blue Riband passage of 1938, when the *Queen Mary* averaged 29.68 knots over four days and three hours. It was a remarkable achievement for her, by then, 32-year-old boilers and steam turbines.

Her final round trip in September 1967 was an affair of unashamed nostalgia, with the Countess of Brecknock, the film mogul Michael Havas and Princess Maria d'Ardia Carraciolo among her passengers. In the following month Treasure Jones sailed the *Queen Mary* to her final resting place at Long Beach, where to this day she remains as a tourist attraction and hotel.

He retired in August 1968 to his home in Hampshire, but not before he had seen his daughter Susan married, an occasion for which Cunard lent him the main lounge of the *Queen Elizabeth* for the bride's reception.

John Treasure Jones leaves his widow, three sons and a daughter.

b 18.8.05   d 12.5.93   aged 87

Queen Mary

SUNNIE MANN

Sunnie Mann, the wife of the former British Beirut hostage and second world war hero, Jackie Mann.

SUNNIE Mann's huge blue-framed spectacles became a distinctive feature on numerous television chat shows after her former Spitfire pilot husband, Jackie, was kidnapped in May 1989 and held hostage in Lebanon until September 1991. She campaigned with determination to gain her husband's freedom and, once that goal was attained, basked in the attention paid her by journalists, diplomats and minor royalty at the whirl of cocktail parties and receptions that followed his release. She viewed this as a fitting reward for the 29 terrifying months spent waiting alone in west Beirut through some of the worst shelling in Lebanon's civil war.

In many ways, while they were devoted to each other, the Manns were not well-suited as a couple, as both freely admitted. She was out-going, he was retiring. He loved planes, she loved animals. They often fought like cat and dog and, for years in Beirut, even lived in separate — but adjoining — apartments.

They had been the last British couple living in Moslem west Beirut. They stayed on, they said, because they hated the British climate, lacked the funds to live elsewhere abroad and considered themselves too old and insignificant to be in any danger of kidnapping. Sunnie's book *Holding On*, published in 1990, described the privations of her solitary life after her husband's capture as she struggled to make ends meet. A heavy smoker, she would lug heavy containers of water up five flights of stairs to their apartment in Raouche, which was often without running water or electricity.

With no word from the kidnappers until just days before Jackie's release, she never knew if she was waiting in vain. Seven months after his abduction, her dog Tara was stolen which was another traumatic incident for a woman who was an ardent pet lover all her life.

Sunnie Mann's courage and single-mindedness was present from childhood. Born into a reasonably well-to-do family in Weston-Super-Mare, she was sent to a private girls' school, which she hated. At 16, she rebelled and ran away to London. A year later she married one of her father's closest friends, a wealthy man 22 years her senior. It was a disastrous marriage that ended after less than three years leaving her with a daughter, Jennifer. She had no more children.

During the second world war Sunnie Mann worked as a volunteer driver for the St John Ambulance Brigade, experiencing some of the worst of the London Blitz. A shrapnel wound abruptly ended this career. She loved the heady atmosphere of war-time London, counting actors like Basil Rathbone as close friends and going to pubs popular with pilots and other servicemen. In her mid-20s, she married her second husband, a Royal Marines officer called Keith McWhirter, whom she had met just three days before. Months later, he was killed in action.

Encouraged by one of the great pioneer plastic surgeons, Archie McIndoe, Sunnie Mann began helping to rehabilitate fighter pilots and bomber crews who had sustained severe burns. This was how she met a 26-year-old sergeant pilot, Jack Mann, at the Dorchester Hotel. He had suffered terrible burns when his Spitfire landed in flames in a field in Kent.

They married at Croydon registry office in 1943 but were separated by work for much of the last two years of the war. Sunnie was employed in the fur department at Harrods and lived in a large apartment in Knightsbridge where she took in lodgers.

The end of the war left them free but rudderless. Her daughter, Jennifer, was living in the country with her grandmother. Jackie used his demobilisation pay to buy a 60-foot decommissioned boat hoping to smuggle cigarettes from France into Britain. But they gave this up after a narrow escape on their first trip to Le Havre. In the summer of 1945, the Manns made their first trip to the Middle East. A year later, they moved to Beirut, where Mr Mann was offered a job with the fledgling national carrier, Middle East Airlines.

The couple loved the Lebanese capital from the beginning and they lived there for the next 45 years. During Beirut's heyday as the Paris of the Middle East in the 1950s and 1960s, they enjoyed a hectic social life and had a wide circle of friends. Sunnie Mann became the first woman in Lebanon to run a riding club. But the quality of their lifestyle rapidly deteriorated with the first rumblings of civil war in the early 1970s. They became trapped between ever-shifting front-lines, spent days at a time in underground shelters and lived in constant fear of car-bombs. Palestinian gunmen wilfully killed several of Mann's horses. Twenty-two more died in an Israeli air raid during the 1982 invasion, which Sunnie Mann always described as being worse than the Blitz.

Following Jackie's release from captivity — he had been the eldest of the Western hostages held by pro-Iranian kidnappers in Beirut — and his spell of recuperation in England, the couple settled in Cyprus. He was at her bedside for much of the two weeks she was in hospital before she died.

Sunnie Mann is survived by Jackie and her daughter Jennifer.

b 19.7.13   d 7.11.92   aged 79

C. NORTHCOTE PARKINSON

Professor C. Northcote Parkinson, author, historian, business economist and originator of Parkinson's Law.

THE satirical author of over sixty books and propounder of numerous "laws", Parkinson was fond of stating that he did not invent his most famous dictum — "that work expands so as to fill the time available for its completion": he merely "discovered it". The truth of the law, and its sting, applying principally but not exclusively to government departments, was seized upon with relish in numberless countries where the citizens felt the heavy hand of bureaucracy. Published in 1958, *Parkinson's Law* went down particularly well in China, where it sold out in two days in Shanghai.

As presented by the author, with supporting figures, the dictum demonstrated that work expands not only to fill the time available, but also to occupy the people available for its completion. Hence staff tend to multiply regardless of the amount of work produced. The idea had its origins in wartime Britain, where Parkinson learnt something of administration for the first time, under the Chief of the Imperial General Staff in London. "I observed, somewhat to my surprise, that work which could be done by one man in peacetime, was being given to about six in wartime. I think this was mainly because there wasn't the same opportunity for other people to criticise. You could always riposte: 'Don't you know there's a war on?' "

Behind Parkinson's droll manner lay serious intentions. As with his friend and literary mentor, G. K. Chesterton, he believed that humour in general and paradox in particular were the proper means by which to communicate strong opinions. He first put his formula into words in 1958 in a piece for *The Economist* for which he contributed occasional articles. He had ruled out offering it to *Punch*, as some people thought he should, because he felt that a serious article in a humorous publication goes unnoticed, whereas a humorous article in a serious one makes its mark.

Not that Parkinson fully foresaw the impact the article would have. Although he considered his law a self-evident truth, it was the particular, timely and imagination-catching words he used to express it that were so perfect for Britain in the late 1950s with its spores of rampant bureaucratic growth.

In the event, Parkinson became one of Britain's most frequently cited men. The BBC produced a musical version of the law, with an overture scored for typewriters, and the Institute of Directors threw a party for him. While he enjoyed both, he was somewhat surprised that the victims of his satire should have taken it so well.

Plucked from relative obscurity as Raffles Professor of History at the University of Malaya, Parkinson toured American universities for two hectic years, lecturing to audiences of up to 8,000. He was made visiting professor at Harvard in 1958, and at the universities of Illinois and California in the following year. Although he regarded most Americans as illiterate, Parkinson made an exception of Walt Disney whom he considered a genius "not a very well-educated genius, but a genius all the same". His attempts to interest Disney in film rights to a screenplay based on the law foundered because no part could be found in it for the studio's latest signing, Hayley Mills. But he had the satisfaction of seeing his work reach the stage when, in 1988, the Czechoslovakian state theatre company performed a dramatisation in Brno.

Cyril Northcote Parkinson was the son of W. Edward Parkinson, principal of the York School of Arts. He was educated at St Peter's School, York, Emmanuel College, Cambridge, and King's College,

London. After obtaining his PhD, he became a fellow of Emmanuel College and director of studies in 1935, before taking a post as senior history master at Blundell's School, Tiverton, in 1938.

During the war he taught at the Officer Cadet Training Unit at Colchester, which was later moved to the Isle of Man "presumably on the grounds that in order to study war you need some peace". Further war service included stints with the RAF and as GS02 in the Military Operations Branch at the War Office. After the war he was made lecturer in Naval and Maritime History at the University of Liverpool, before moving to Singapore, where he stayed for ten years. He was rather too outspoken at faculty meetings to be a complete success with his colleagues at work, popular as he was at their dinner parties; but no one could question his dedication to his Asian students, whom he regularly took home to meet visiting academics.

After his metamorphosis into Parkinson, the globe-trotting guru, he was able to concentrate more fully on writing. Although he had published several well-received histories during his early academic career his scholarly reputation had not been helped by a parallel – and somewhat indiscriminate – stream of pamphlets, playlets and articles.

The more than sixty books which he did eventually produce together display an enormous breadth of learning and interest. As a specialist in naval history his publications included a well-received study of the East Indiamen, the aristocrats of the Merchant Navy in the India and China trade, *Trade in the Eastern Seas, 1793–1813* (1937). After the publication of *Parkinson's Law, the Pursuit of Progress* (illustrated by Osbert Lancaster), an expansion of his original article in 1958, he produced the detailed *British Invervention in Malaya, 1867 to 1877* (1960). His business books included *Big Business* (1974), while whimsical spin-offs such as *Mrs Parkinson's Law* (1968), which transferred the basic principle to the domestic level, never achieved the same popularity as the original. *Jeeves: a Gentleman's Personal Gentleman* (1979), a "biography" of the young Jeeves in pre-Wooster days, was written in homage to his beloved Wodehouse. Parkinson also published a number of novels and contributed regularly to *The Guardian, The Economist* and *The New York Times.*

In later years he was a doughty campaigner for other "laws" which he put forward in typically bull-doggish manner. A scourge of government overspending, and a self-appointed vigilante against the Inland Revenue ("We are being crushed under the burdens of tax, surtax and death duties"), he also had strong ideas about public monopolies, women "wearing the trousers" and travel ("There's only one way to cross the Atlantic, and that's drunk").

Besides his writing, Parkinson turned in later life to one of his first great enthusiasms, painting, and transformed his Guernsey home, to which he retired in the 1960s, with colourful murals: "I am by instinct an artist and a dreamer," he once characteristically boasted.

He was married three times, first in 1943, to Ethelwyn Edith Graves. This marriage was dissolved and, in 1952, he married Elizabeth Ann Fry who died in 1983. He is survived by his third wife, Iris (Ingrid) Hilda Waters, whom he married in 1985, a son and a daughter from his first marriage, and two sons and a daughter from his second.

b 30.7.09   d 9.3.93   aged 83

JO FRANCE

JO FRANCE came from very humble origins, for his mother was a washerwoman and his father a labourer. He went on to become one of the *rois de la nuit* in Paris where his club, Le Balajo, the revived Moulin Rouge and his huge café on the Boulevard St Michel attracted famous names of show business.

France's first job was as a layer of marble, but he always wanted to move into the entertainment world. He did so in his teens, opening a tiny cabaret called the Bastoche in the Rue de la Lappe just behind the Bastille Square in the east of the city. He then opened another, the Bal Vernet, in the same street and then came the Balajo in 1929. France was all of 18-years-old, the youngest dance-hall owner in Paris.

The Rue de la Lappe at the time was dangerous territory, the haunt of thieves who lurked in the doorways to rob the rich and famous who in the evenings liked to go "slumming", or *s'encanailler*, in the dark street.

The new club, or *bal musette*, was decorated in baroque style by the painter Henri Mahe who had previously decorated the celebrated Moulin Rouge music-hall in Montmartre.

The Balajo, where France sang and led the entertainment, was an immediate success. This was partly because the tall, handsome France had caught the eye of the most famous music-hall artiste of the epoch, Mistinguett, who incorporated the Balajo and a Bastille motif in the decor for her show at the Casino de Paris.

When she started going to the Rue de la Lappe, the success of the Balajo was assured.

The dance-hall, with its period atmosphere a mixture of theatre and circus, became a magnet for devotees of the tango and waltz. Among the regulars were the film star Arletty, later famous for her role in Marcel Carné's *Les Enfants du Paradis*, and another star, Jean Gabin and his mistress Marlene Dietrich.

France re-opened the Balajo after the war when he helped launch Edith Piaf. It was there that she celebrated her wedding to the boxer Marcel Cerdan, then world middleweight champion.

Piaf also appeared at the Moulin Rouge which France had rebuilt in 1951.

France continued the music-hall tradition dating back to the days when Henri Toulouse-Lautrec was the most famous customer. Piaf was a regular but other notable nights were those for the children's charity, Petits Lits Blancs, which attracted the French President René Coty, Bing Crosby and others.

When France sold the Moulin Rouge in the 1960s, the new owners changed the show to an American-style revue but kept the *cancan*.

France's other major interest was the large café, Le Capoulade on the Boulevard St Michel, when this famous thoroughfare in the Latin Quarter was lined with cafés, brasseries and clubs.

Today the Capoulade has disappeared to be replaced by a clothes-store.

France retired to the Riviera. He is survived by his wife and three sons.

b 25.12.11   d 12.7.93   aged 81

DIANA PYM

Diana Pym, political organiser and philhellene.

DIANA GOUGH − as she was born − was the descendant of attacking warriors. Her own life, however, was dedicated to mitigating the effects of warfare and injustice − in particular the rending effects of the Greek civil war (1946−49) which resulted in the imprisonment and, in many cases, the torture of thousands of anti-fascist Greek patriots.

She was orphaned at the age of six when her father, Brigadier-General J. E. Gough, VC, then serving as Douglas Haig's Chief of Staff, was fatally wounded while on a visit in February 1915 to his old regiment, the Rifle Brigade, at Fauquissart, northern France. He received the unusual honour of a posthumous KCB.

Both Diana Gough's grandfathers were generals in the Indian Army, one, Sir Charles Gough, being awarded the VC for four separate acts of gallantry during the Indian Mutiny of 1857−58. (Sir Charles's brother Hugh also won the VC.)

Her paternal uncle, General Sir Hubert Gough commanded the Fifth Army during the decisive spring of 1918; her maternal uncle, Admiral Sir Roger Keyes, was the hero of the Zeebrugge Raid on St George's Day, 1918; and her cousin, Lieutenant-Colonel Geoffrey Keyes, VC, died leading the commando assault on Rommel's headquarters in the Libyan Desert in 1941.

After taking her degree in history at Newnham College, Cambridge, in 1930, Diana Gough married the future architect John Pym. She was later elected a Labour borough councillor for St Pancras, north London, where she played an active part in housing policy and social welfare. Barbara Castle and Krishna Menon, India's future defence minister, were fellow-councillors.

In 1940 she joined the Communist Party of Great Britain, to whose aims she remained faithful throughout her life. During the war she served as an ARP officer in London (motorcycling through the blackout gave her considerable pleasure).

In 1945, through her contacts with the Greek Cypriot community in London, she became secretary of the Greek Maritime Unions. The agency issued the first eyewitness accounts of the prison camps in Eritrea and Sudan, where members of the Greek National Liberation Army (ELAS), taken in Athens while fighting the British in December 1944, were incarcerated. In October 1945 she was appointed honorary secretary of the newly-formed pressure group, the League for Democracy in Greece, under the presidency of Sir Compton Mackenzie and the chairmanship of D. N. Pritt, QC, MP, and for the next 26 years she was the league's unifying force.

The history of the LDG has been summarised in a paper for the *Journal of the Hellenic Diaspora* (summer, 1984), with characteristic modesty, by Diana Pym and the former Marion Pascoe, joint secretary of the league, until her marriage in 1952 to General Sarafis, ELAS's one-time Commander-in-Chief. The league's achievements, however, were singular; and its broad-based archive, given in 1977 to the Byzantine and Modern Greek Department at King's College, London, constitutes a unique historical resource.

The league's aims, in response to what it regarded as Churchill's and the Foreign Office's duplicitous treatment of the Greek wartime resistance movement, included the provision of relief to those Greeks, and their dependants, who suffered for their democratic beliefs and activities. It also worked tirelessly, from a series of small offices permeated with the aroma of ancient dust, newsprint, duplicating ink and sweet Greek cigarette smoke, for a general amnesty for all Greek democrats imprisoned for political reasons.

One early success was an emergency campaign in 1948 which roused the British and American governments to intervene to prevent the mass execution of nearly 3,000 members of the resistance jailed before the outbreak of the civil war. These executions (100 of which took place before they could be stopped) had been ordered by the Greek government as a reprisal for the assassination of the Justice Minister, Christos Ladas.

The LDG and its sister charity the Greek Relief Fund, which Diana Pym continued to organise after her retirement from the league in 1971, was responsible for a series of hard-hitting polemical pamphlets, for innumerable small acts of relief to the prisoners' often impoverished families, for translating thousands of letters from British supporters to their "adopted" Greek families, and for maintaining a ceaseless political pressure on members of Parliament.

The league will, however, be most widely remembered for its long campaign for the release from life imprisonment of the Greek seamen's leader Andonis (Tony) Ambatielos, whose Welsh wife Betty was for many years the league's organising officer. In 1963 Betty Ambatielos made front-page news with her scandalous "insult" to Queen Frederika while attempting to present a dignified petition for her husband's release during the Greek queen's state visit to London.

By January 1967, thanks in large part to the LDG's efforts in keeping their cause alive, all but 11 of Greece's political prisoners, including Tony Ambatielos, had been released and it seemed that the league's work might be done.

Then in April came the colonels' coup. Tanks appeared on the streets of Athens and the junta's left-wing opponents were arrested en masse. Diana Pym, who, despite disabling arthritis, relished nothing better than the prospect of meeting injustice head-on, the longer the odds the better, threw herself with renewed energy into the seven-year campaign for the restoration of democratic government in Greece.

The league, whose aims were now (for the first time) supported by politicians of all parties, found that its records and experience were considered invaluable by the many international organisations which formed to combat the junta. With the fall of the Colonels in 1974, the league called a halt to its activities and renamed itself "Friends of Democracy in Greece", under which title it still exists on a stand-by basis.

Diana Pym had a profound and instinctive love of all things Greek and was perhaps never happier than when talking (or arguing) politics with her many Greek friends. She bore long years of ill-health with soldierly fortitude and retained until the end an infectious delight in the exposure of political mischief.

She is survived by her husband, two daughters and one son.

b 18.10.08   d 9.9.93   aged 84

DAME FREYA STARK

Dame Freya Stark, DBE, writer and traveller.

IT IS not unusual for travellers to write well about their travels. Doughty, Burton, Kinglake, to mention only a few from Freya Stark's own territory, belong as much to literature as to geography. What was so rare about Freya Stark was that she was a woman who travelled the hard way in male lands, and that she would have been a writer if she had never got further than her front door. The movement and colour of words in many languages fascinated her; so did the nobility and absurdity of human beings; so did the world of ideas. Of course, travel provided her with the material for most of her books, but when she grew older and travelled less she wrote more, finding memory an even more productive vein than novelty.

For obvious reasons Freya Stark was often compared with that other intrepid female orientalist, Gertrude Bell; but the comparison is misleading. Gertrude Bell was a rich, masculine person, who "floored the pashas flat". Freya Stark was extremely feminine, without money or any worldly advantages and with a constitution which, though

fundamentally tough, was continually letting her down at critical moments, so that on more than one of her journeys she very nearly died. But a will of iron, infinite patience and powers of persuasion, an exact knowledge of her own aims and a sublime egoism, overcame all obstacles. Woe betide anyone − tribal sheikh, general officer, Italian greengrocer, Levantine merchant, guest sitting down at the scrabble board − if they thought they were going to be let off with anything less than total surrender.

With all this strength of character went a matching generosity. Freya Stark drew out the talents of others. She believed most men and some women capable of distinction, and they responded accordingly. Only the deliberately second-rate angered her. She regarded the world as a place thrown open for individual achievement, and she herself achieved much.

Freya Stark was born in Paris where her parents were briefly resident. Her mother and father were first cousins, both belonging to an old family with its roots in Devon. Here her father's branch had remained, but her maternal grandmother had settled in Italy. It was Italy that was to be Freya Stark's home (when eventually she had one) but her roots remained in Devon and, more particularly, in Dartmoor. No more fervent lover of everything connected with England has ever been a permanent and voluntary exile.

Both parents were artists of more than ordinary ability (some of her father's sculptures are to be seen at the Tate). Freya Stark's childhood was highly mobile. Houses were rented, bought, and built in London, Italy, France and on Dartmoor, but none occupied for long. "My parents were moderately well off people of good taste, with a liking for the arrangement of houses, and yet it is astonishing how much of our childhood was spent in dingy lodgings."

One place only came to rival Dartmoor in her childhood affections, and that was Asolo, the small fortress town which looks out under the lee of the Dolomites across the Venetian plain towards Padua. Before Robert Stark married he had taken the advice of Robert Browning's son, Pen Browning, and with an artist friend, Herbert Young, had escaped to Asolo from the summer heat of Venice.

Within a week Herbert Young had bought a house in the city walls with a wild garden enclosing the remains of a Roman theatre. Here he settled for the rest of his life, and when he died in 1941 house and garden passed by his will to Freya Stark.

For Robert and Flora Stark Asolo also became an early home, though a less permanent. In the first volume of her autobiography, *Traveller's Prelude*, Freya Stark described the growing incompatibility and eventual separation of two beings whom she loved with parallel but distinct devotion. With her sister Vera, a year younger than herself, the small Freya was a sorrowful spectator of a process which ended with her father's departure to Canada and her mother's settling in another hill town, Dronero in Piedmont.

Freya Stark had no regular schooling, but learnt to speak French and German almost as naturally as Italian. She read universally in the literature of all countries, including Greece and Rome. It was not until she was 19, and entered Bedford College, London, that her formal education began, and two years later the outbreak of war brought it to an end.

One great benefit of this brief academic interlude was that it brought her the friendship of W. P. Ker, who was quick to recognise the unusual qualities of this small, shy creature who spoke English (on the rare occasions when she opened her mouth) with an Italian accent. He directed her imagination and guided her literary taste, and in the vacations transformed her from a lover of mountains into an intrepid mountaineer.

When the first world war came, Freya Stark trained as a nurse and served with the Trevelyan hospital unit on the Italian front, finding herself caught up in the chaos of the Caporetto disaster of 1917, in which the Italians were utterly routed by the Austrians. Peace brought family complications and years of poverty and increasing ill-health – including three years as a bedridden and despaired-of invalid. It was partly for distraction, but always ultimately with the idea of travel, that she began taking lessons in Arabic from a white bearded Capuchin in San Remo. By 1927, a course at the London School of Oriental Studies behind her, improved health, plus a minuscule but assured income – and the traveller's prelude was completed.

Poor health and lack of funds remained troublesome, though successful authorship eventually counteracted the latter. In other respects Freya Stark was now, at the age of 34, well equipped for the hazards of the next 12 years. She had great curiosity and no narrow prejudices; she liked people, treating them as equals without condescension or diffidence; she was used to hardship; she knew languages, had acquired the elements of surveying and was a competent nurse. Two other things she quickly learnt – that journeys must be minutely planned, if they are to be successful, and how to take photographs. Armed with the cheapest instruments she became an artist in photography.

Freya Stark first set foot in Asia in November 1927. She settled for the winter at Brummana in Lebanon, spent some time in Damascus, and with a friend completed her first proper expedition, through the then disturbed Jebel Druze country, subsequently moving on to Jerusalem and Cairo. The literary product of this period was *Letters from Syria*, not published until 1942.

Two years later she was in Lebanon again, on her way to Baghdad. Here she established herself in the house of a shoemaker overlooking the Tigris, much to the disgust of the British community which considered such behaviour "a flouting of national prestige". Freya Stark never ceased to marvel at the blinkered views of expatriates. Upbringing and predilections made her in a sense "unconventional" though she cherished the traditional British virtues – courtesy, restraint, self-reliance – to an infinitely greater degree than most of her critics. She was, in fact, like her father, a High Tory anarchist as well as an artist.

There were, however, some British in Baghdad without blinkers who were quick to appreciate the newcomer. These included Sir Kinahan Cornwallis, then adviser to the Ministry of Interior and later ambassador, and Lionel Smith, adviser to the Ministry of Education. These two became lifelong friends, joining the ranks of the older men whose society always meant so much to Freya Stark. Such had been her father and W. P. Ker; such, too, were Sidney Cockerell and Lord Wavell.

Having absorbed oriental ways and languages in Baghdad, she used it as a base for invasions of Iran. Three tough but extremely rewarding solo journeys were carried out in 1929–31, two in Luristan and one in the mountains of Mazanderan, south of the Caspian sea. It was on this occasion that she "first stood consciously on the edge of death" as the result of severe malaria and dysentery combined. Out of these journeys came *The Valley of the*

Assassins (1934), the book which made her reputation as a writer, and which remains probably the most popular of all those she wrote. In it can be seen in all their freshness the qualities which combined to make Freya Stark so attractive a personality in print – strong sensitivity to places and people, humour, and a clear narrative style, free from the somewhat conscious adornment which sometimes accumulated later. (She herself said of her style: "There is nothing to it except a natural ear for cadence and the wish to get the meaning right." True enough.)

The first truly Arabian journey came in the winter of 1934–5. Her route was from Mukalla on the coast, northward into the Wadi Hadhramaut and to Shibam and Tarim. The episode ended with her rescue by the RAF, from Aden, after she contracted measles and carried on, not properly recovered, so that her heart was strained – and very nearly stopped altogether. Prolonged convalescence, and a return to Iraq, were followed by a second Arabian journey, again with Mukalla as a starting-point, in the winter of 1937–8, this time ending in dengue fever but no RAF rescue. These journeys were recorded in *The Southern Gates of Arabia* (1936), *Seen in the Hadhramaut* (1938), and *A Winter in Arabia* (1940).

The second world war engaged Freya Stark in political and publicity work, for the most part in Arab lands. She served in Aden, Yemen (showing propaganda films under the noses of Mussolini's ubiquitous agents), Cairo and Baghdad (where she was one of those besieged in the British embassy by Rashid Ali's revolt). She had, needless to say, her own ideas of how things should be run, and these ideas, more than directives from a remote ministry, governed her actions. Much of her time was devoted to an association she founded in Egypt – and later developed in Iraq – called the Brotherhood of Freedom. This consisted of groups of autonomous cells devoted to the cult of self-help, encouraged – and to a limited extent financed – from a centre which mainly consisted of Freya Stark herself. By a characteristic twist of fate, a lecture tour of the United States, arranged for her by the Ministry of Information in the autumn of 1943, involved her in what she was later to describe as much the worst of all her journeys – a burst appendix on the Halifax-bound liner *Aquitania*, then a troopship. Again, she cheated death by inches.

After the armistice of 1943 she went back to Italy where she worked for the British embassy. When, towards the end of the war, she was able to return to her house at Asolo she found it intact, in spite of its having been used as headquarters by both the retreating Germans and the Salò fascists. Its possessions had been hidden and preserved by loyal friends.

In 1947 Freya Stark married Stewart Perowne, diplomatist and orientalist, and accompanied him to his posts in Barbados and Cyrenaica, but five years later the marriage, which appears to have been based on a misunderstanding of his sexual orientation, ended in an amicable separation. She was now writing her autobiography, three volumes of which appeared in swift succession: *Traveller's Prelude* (1950) – the best of them, a graphic and at times most moving portrait – *Beyond the Euphrates* (1951) and *The Coast of Incense* (1953). A fourth volume, dealing with the war years, *Dust in the Lion's Paw* came out in 1961.

Now, at 60, she looked for new worlds to conquer, and found them in Anatolia and its history. She learnt Turkish (with the aid of a Turkish bible and Turkish detective stories). She made several arduous journeys, often on horseback, in the remoter parts of Turkey, acting as guide, interpreter and goad to younger friends whom she thus initiated into the joys of oriental travel. She brushed up her classics. Out of this came *Ionia: a Quest* (1954), *The Lycian Shore* (1956), *Alexander's Path* (1958), *Riding to the Tigris* (1959), and finally the product of three years' concentrated labour, *Rome on the Euphrates* (1966), a scholarly study of Rome's eastern *limes*, illuminated by

her own unique knowledge of the topography of the region about which she was writing.

Freya Stark had now all the resources for a graceful and comfortable old age – a beautiful house filled with beautiful things, troops of friends, a solid reputation, a contented mind.

But she had, besides, an unconquerable restlessness. In 1962, on the eve of her 70th birthday, she suddenly bought a hill near Asolo on which she proceeded to build an enormous house to her own design. The Balzacian complications of the sale of her old house and the financing of the new one at times strained even her composure. She sought relief in revisiting old haunts – Iran, Turkey, Greece – as well as discovering new ones, notably Afghanistan and Nepal.

After a few years the big house was abandoned for the final refuge of a flat in Asolo. There was more travelling, well on into her late eighties – on horseback in Nepal and the Pamirs, down the Euphrates on a raft for the BBC – continuing to outpace many of those half or even a quarter of her age. She enjoyed watching the publication in many volumes of her letters, the form in which her career as a writer had begun and in which she excelled.

Fortunately, since for the last five years the world had passed her by, she knew nothing of the publication of a shallow and hostile biography of her, produced to coincide with her 100th birthday earlier this year.

Freya Stark was appointed CBE in 1953 and created DBE in 1972. She received many geographical awards, including the Burton Medal from the Royal Asiatic Society in 1933, the Founder's Medal from the Royal Geographical Society in 1942, and the Percy Sykes Memorial Medal from the Royal Central Asian Society in 1951. She received an LLD from Glasgow University that same year and a DLitt from Durham in 1971. Her godson was her publisher, John (Jock) Murray.

b 31.1.93   d 9.5.93   aged 100

JOHN SYKES

John Sykes, translator, lexicographer, theoretical physicist and champion Times *crossword solver.*

THE son of a borough treasurer, John Sykes was one of the cleverest men of his generation. His life can be divided into three major segments and one spectacular hobby. Starting out as a theoretical physicist, he became an inspired translator and progressed from there to being an expert lexicographer – all the time maintaining his form as the most redoubtable competitor in *The Times* National Crossword Championship.

From St Lawrence College, Ramsgate, John Bradbury Sykes went up to Wadham College, Oxford, to read mathematics, and having taken his first degree, went on to write a DPhil thesis on aspects of theoretical solar physics. In 1953 he moved to the Atomic Energy Research Establishment at Harwell, where he did some work on neutron migration. The authorities soon discovered that his real interest lay in

another direction, namely translation. His phenomenal memory enabled him to acquire an outline knowledge of any language remarkably quickly (at the time of his death he had just added Welsh to his collection). The essence of his aptitude was speed: as an undergraduate he once went home for two weeks at Christmas and returned to Oxford able to translate Russian scientific papers.

In 1958 he was appointed head of the translations office at Harwell, a post which he held, to begin with, virtually single-handed. He was required to translate documents of many kinds from several languages, especially German and Russian, but also Spanish, Japanese, and so on. The secret, he quickly established, was to acquire a knowledge of the vocabulary of physics in the target language and an outline knowledge of the grammar, but to avoid the entanglements of the spoken forms of each language and also their literary works. The benefits to his colleagues were obvious. At a conference in 1967, for example, seven

Russians arrived with their papers written only in their own language. Overnight Sykes translated them into English and handed copies to his astonished colleagues the following morning before proceedings began.

He was a man who worked all his waking hours. He published translations of many Russian textbooks on physics and astronomy. In 1957, with Boris Davison, he translated *Neutron Transport Theory* from Russian, and in 1971 edited a *Technical Translator's Manual*. He was a fellow of the Institute of Linguists, serving on its council for six years and editing its journal. From 1986 he was also the first chairman of the Institute of Translation and Interpreting until forced to retire through ill-health. He was also a valued member of the Translators' Association, representing literary translation within the Society of Authors.

Around 1970 he discovered a new intellectual challenge. He noticed that the editor of the *Supplement to the OED* was appealing for earlier printed evidence for a large number of modern words, among which was the astronomical term "absolute magnitude". The hunt excited him and he was soon working in the *OED* department unpaid on Saturday mornings. It was not long before his obvious linguistic skills impressed the Oxford University Press to the extent that he left Harwell to become editor of the *Concise Oxford Dictionary* when the post fell vacant in 1971. This household dictionary had fallen somewhat behind the times, but its new navigator brought it back on course, preparing a new sixth edition (published in 1976) with all the inconsistencies removed, the etymologies successfully revised, and the new waves of scientific vocabulary (laser, neutron, and so on) inserted with conspicuous success. He went on to prepare a new edition of *The Pocket Oxford Dictionary* (1978) and a seventh edition of *The Concise Oxford* in 1982.

He then moved sideways within the OUP to become head of German dictionaries. Bilingual lexicography held no terrors for him and it was not long before he and his colleagues were at work mastering the complications of German modal verbs such as *sollen* and accepting the challenge of finding the German equivalents of terms such as *panic button* and *fundamental particle*. The completed bi-directional *Oxford-Duden German Dictionary*, the product of successful collaboration between Dudenverlag in Mannheim and the Oxford University Press, was duly published in 1990, with *Concise* and *Pocket* versions following soon after. He had been made an honorary DLitt of the City University in 1984.

His hobbies were of the kind that one would perhaps expect: chess, bridge, and, in a legendary manner, the solving of crossword puzzles. When he lived in Abingdon, for example, he used to take the bus to Harwell and had always completed *The Times* crossword before the bus reached Rowstock Corner, a journey of less than a quarter of an hour. He was the *The Times* National Crossword champion ten times, winning for the last time in 1990 when he solved the four puzzles in an average time of eight minutes each and won by a record margin of nine-and-a-half minutes. (Five years earlier he had resolved to compete only in alternate years in order to give others a chance: had he not made this self-denying ordinance, he would undoubtedly have won even more times.)

Throughout his working life he was renowned for his encyclopaedic grasp of detail, his immense capacity for work and his kindness to colleagues. But his extraordinary labours had taken their toll and his tall, impressive figure and imposing bearing began to show signs of frailty during his last years. Yet he was at work on a new dictionary of word origins the day before he died.

In 1955 he married Avril Barbara Hart, who also had an Oxford DPhil in astrophysics. There was one son of the marriage which was dissolved in 1988.

b 26.1.29   d 3.9.93   aged 64

DIGBY TATHAM-WARTER

On safari in Kenya's Aberdare Mountains (1980)

*Digby Tatham-Warter, DSO, former
company commander 2nd Battalion,
Parachute Regiment.*

DIGBY Tatham-Warter was famously
depicted in *A Bridge Too Far*, Richard
Attenborough's 1977 film of the Allied

defeat at Arnhem in 1944, as a crazed toff leading a bayonet charge sporting an old bowler hat and a tattered umbrella. But his character, personality and achievements were substantially greater than suggested by the film's rather trite cameo. He actually did wander around the ever-reducing perimeter at Arnhem Bridge urging his (and others') men on with the aid of a rolled umbrella, though there was neither bowler hat nor bayonet charge.

Educated at Wellington and Sandhurst (where he won The Saddle) Allison Digby Tatham-Warter was the second son of Henry de Grey Tatham-Warter, a country landowner with estates in the Midlands and the West Country. His father, having been badly gassed serving with the Artists' Rifles in the first world war, died prematurely when Tatham-Warter was 11. He had three sisters, one of whom, Kit, won the Croix de Guerre while serving with the Hatfield-Spears Unit in the Western Desert. Her heroism coincided with the action at El Alamein in which her brother John was killed serving with The Bays.

As in many families, the death of his elder brother was a further spur to Tatham-Warter's determined attempts to get in to the war and kill Germans (despite having been a regular officer since 1937 he had thus far seen no action). His family background had made him ideally suited to the Indian Army into which he was commissioned. However, on attachment to The Oxfordshire and Buckinghamshire Light Infantry he decided to stay with them, while still able to enjoy the rigours of tiger-shooting and pig-sticking. Determined to get into action, he transferred to the recently-formed Parachute Regiment where he soon found himself commanding A Company 2 PARA under the already famous Johnny Frost (another rifleman).

During the months of training for Arnhem the battalion was stationed near Grantham, and Tatham-Warter's well-known exploits in tiger-shooting and other entertainments in India with the Ox and Bucks were here enhanced by his ability to procure an American Dakota on at least one weekend to fly him and his company officers to London – where parties at the Ritz were in marked contrast to conditions in the sealed camp.

He is recalled as a particularly severe but inspirational commander of his men (few of whose names he apparently knew, or was interested in). The soldiers were there to follow and to fight and he, above all, to lead. His officers (mainly drawn from similar backgrounds as his) were expected to emulate his attitudes and standards.

This management technique, however bizarre today, can none the less be seen to have been effective in the desperate battles around the bridge at Arnhem, and the subsequent escape in which Tatham-Warter played a pivotal role.

The battle at Arnhem resulted from Montgomery's ill-fated orders to "Lay me an airborne carpet to the Rhine" (dashing over which he intended to beat Patton into the heart of Germany). The bridge at Arnhem was the most distant of three bridges in The Netherlands which the Allies needed to secure if they were going to outflank the Siegfried line and enable 30 Corps to cross the Rhine and advance into Germany. The operation was, of course, a complete and very bloody shambles and ended in what ought to have been a predictable disaster when a necessarily lightly-armed force of ten thousand airborne troops was ultimately surrounded by the 2nd SS Panzer Corps (two armoured divisions) – whose likely presence had been reported to the planners.

Tatham-Warter was subsequently never less than undiplomatic in his views on the politics of this forlorn hope – notwithstanding his pride in having played an important role in and after it.

It was after the battle, when he had escaped from a German-held hospital with his second-in-command, Tony Frank, that he helped to set up "Pegasus I". This was the successful escape across the Rhine by 133 airborne men and other assorted guests of the Dutch Resistance – assembled by Tatham-Warter in his travels in the occupied countryside on a bicycle lent to him by the Dutch family with which he was "billeted" (their *official* guests included SS Panzer troops who assumed Tatham-Warter to be a Dutch imbecile).

The escape party included airmen, the odd Russian, and even an Indonesian officer of the Royal Netherlands Navy whose unlikely presence was rather obvious in daylight. On his return, Tatham-Warter was awarded a well-deserved DSO (some thought a VC would have been more appropriate).

Postwar operations in Palestine — despite such entertaining diversions as teaching Arabs to shoot sand grouse and hunting desert fox — found little attraction for Tatham-Warter and he emigrated to Kenya in 1946.

There he was very nearly able to return to the time-warp in which he had conducted himself during his days of regular soldiering — and most certainly avoided the miseries of Attlee's great new socialist nirvana.

At Nanyuki, where he had purchased two very large estates, he set up a some-what desultory, though very successful, safari organisation (he would never have referred to it as a business) in partnership with Colonel Hilary Hook. Many of their wealthy clients were to remark on their culture shock on first meeting these two eccentric English gentlemen and the subsequent experiences through which they were led — which was, of course, precisely what they were paying for.

For all his seemingly ferocious manner and imperial background, Tatham-Warter was forty years ahead of his time in introducing the concept of safaris in which the game was shot by camera rather than gun (he perhaps considered his guests not up to the latter).

During the Mau Mau emergency Tatham-Warter, typically, raised, commanded and funded a mounted police unit from volunteer farmers and expatriates to some serious effect. This tied-in with his captaincy of the Kenyan Polo Team (6 handicap) and other equestrian activities both organisational and practical. He was able to combine a hefty social calendar with fishing, sailing and carpentry — which he undertook with typical enthusiasm — somewhat remarkably producing exquisite inlaid pieces.

He was quickly established in the higher reaches of expatriate existence (on which Kenyan independence had very little effect) to the extent that a series of British defence advisers would be told by the high commissioner to "look after Tatham-Warter". One such officer, late of his own regiment, was not entirely clear what this meant but soon found out when, after an introductory "I suppose you're another bloody mealy-mouthed diplomat", his charge took him off to a Beating of Retreat by a British infantry battalion. As Tatham-Warter, a VIP guest, stood for "Sunset" his trousers slowly, and in time with the lowering standards, dropped to his ankles. He later claimed "loss of weight" although the cognoscenti had their doubts.

Of course, the austere exterior belied a self-mocking humour and a fundamentally anti-establishment attitude (it never, after all, had been *his* establishment). Those picked, after rigorous selection, to join Tatham-Warter's very tight circle of friends were allowed a clear view of a complex character shaped by a background which today would simply not be understood. Within this exclusive circle, mostly though not entirely from his own world, he was a warm, lovable man who would do anything for his friends and a wonderful, even notorious, host. He left an indelible stamp on everything he did and had only one standard in all things — his own.

Gerald Lathbury, Tatham-Warter's brigade commander, once remarked (probably in Tatham-Warter's defence): "But every battalion needs a Digby!" Officers, and many of the men, serving today would almost certainly agree.

b 26.5.17 d 21.3.93 aged 75

ADINA SZWAJGER

Adina Blaldy Szwajger, a paediatrician in the Warsaw ghetto who performed euthanasia on suffering children.

IT WAS in her book *I Remember Nothing More: The Warsaw Children's Hospital and the Jewish Resistance,* published in Britain in 1988, that Adina Szwajger, first publicly described how, while working as a nurse in a children's hospital in the Jewish ghetto in Warsaw, she had administered fatal doses of morphine to children to give them a peaceful death, rather than have them endure further suffering and eventual death at the hands of the Nazis.

For more than 40 years she had resisted the idea of writing of what she had experienced and what she had done. "What had happened wasn't something to be written about, or read," she said. "I believed that I had the right to remain silent."

Adina Szwajger was a medical student when the war began. As a Jew she was condemned to live in the walled Warsaw ghetto and worked in a ghetto children's hospital. At her death she was one of the few remaining survivors of the ghetto where nearly half-a-million Jews died.

In March 1940 she had begun working at the hospital, eight months before it was sealed off from the rest of the city. Before long, she recalled in her book, the hospital had become little more than a hospice. Children were dying of tuberculosis, typhus and starvation. Bodies of babies lay in the gutter wrapped in newspaper. Hospital orderlies were slowly dying of hunger too. The doctors and nurses drank a glass of raw spirits each morning to keep their calorie intake just above the fatal minimum.

Adina Szwajger caught typhus but recovered. Then on July 22, 1942, the Germans began the first round-up of Jews for the trains waiting to take them to the gas chambers at Treblinka. At one point Szwajger took an overdose of pheno-barbitone with vodka but was found by friends and recovered.

After the hospital was moved to the Umschlagplatz, where the trains were loading, there were scores of children too sick to move, waiting to be thrown aboard the trucks or killed on the spot by Ukrainian guards.

It was at this stage, said Szwajger, that she first gave a lethal injection to one helpless but conscious old woman. Then she took a flagon of morphine, went to the infants' ward and – one by one – ensured that they would never wake up again.

After the destruction of the ghetto Adina Szwajger and other surviving members of the Jewish Fighting Organisation hid and supplied Jewish fugitives in "Aryan" Warsaw. During this period, she said, she performed abortions on some Jewish girls in hiding because their hiding places would have been given away by the cries of babies. She also admitted putting to death one Jewish girl who, she said, had gone mad and was thus endangering all the others hiding in the same house.

Szwajger went on to serve as a nurse in the 1944 Warsaw Rising. After the war she completed her medical studies in Lodz.

Adina Szwajger's first husband was killed by the Nazis and later, when she became pregnant while fighting in the resistance, she arranged an abortion for herself because she believed children should not be born into such a world. She married again after the war and had two daughters.

d 19.2.93   aged 75

GORDON WINTER

Presenting the Country Life Cup

Gordon Winter, horseman, journalist and writer.

GORDON WINTER died the way he always said he wanted to, riding a favourite horse and surrounded by his friends in the Honourable Artillery Company. Sitting comfortably in his saddle he merely closed his eyes. It was a mark of his energy that, despite his years, he still rode once a week at the Royal Mews. Life for him was an adventure which he lived with elegance and distinction.

He had two separate careers. In the Army he rose to the rank of lieutenant-colonel when he took over a Greek island at the end of the war. Later he became a first-class journalist and author.

Educated at University College School, Hampstead, he joined B Battery of the HAC in 1937. Being a countryman at heart he was delighted to be part of the last years of horse-drawn artillery. He would often say his happiest hours were those spent as an officer's horse-holder, having no responsibilities whatsoever. His more challenging times began on Salisbury Plain waiting for his first assignment of 140 unbroken horses, recently shipped from Australia, which it was his task to turn into a horse-drawn battery.

During the second world war he served in North Africa with the 1st Army and in Italy fighting at Anzio and ending his war in the Greek archipelago. After the war he returned to journalism working (as he had prewar) for *The Field* magazine and then *The Listener* before travelling to Canada as the BBC's representative. He joined *Country Life* in 1958 as assistant editor. This was the beginning of a long association with the magazine. He became deputy editor in 1966 and retired in 1977, but the connection was so strong he remained as consultant editor until last year. He was also editor of *Country Landowners* magazine until 1992. But he never left the HAC. He was a staunch supporter participating in all aspects of the organisation, especially the Saddle Club. He rode with the King's Troop in their St John's Wood barracks until last October.

Horses were his great love, so it was natural for him to work with the National Pony Society, becoming its president in 1991. He was an active judge and steward supporting shows up and down the country.

His one deep regret was that, because of family financial pressures, he never attended university. As a result he thirsted for knowledge and having a photographic memory devoured vast tracts of classics which he could and would quote verbatim.

He was a polymath and excelled in many fields, including languages and opera. He had a light, pleasant voice and it was said that he could sing the whole of *The Marriage of Figaro* without error. He was a natural teacher and coach,

taking under his wing young journalists. He wrote many books, two of which, *The Horseman's Weekend Book* and *Country Camera* became bestsellers.

He was a veteran conservation campaigner and long before the subject became popular took up the plight of the hedgerows. He promoted the Silver Lapwing award presented annually by *Country Life* for farming and wildlife achievements. He supported other forms of country sports by presenting the Mountain and Moorland Cup.

He was greatly admired by his colleagues for his professionalism, resourcefulness, and speed. He once dictated a letter to his secretary from Heathrow airport while waiting for a plane. He learnt the skill of writing fast at the BBC, where he had a secretary who worked much more slowly than he did (because, he suspected, she was paid by the hour). His two pieces of advice to writers were "Don't over-egg the pudding" and "Scrap your first line as it's only clearing your throat".

He was a member of the London Rowing Club, competing at Henley in 1947. Despite a hip replacement in the 1970s he regularly played squash rackets, enjoying his last game only a few days before he died.

He was a great raconteur revelling in telling stories about his life including his epic race in 1928 to Land's End and back from London overnight. He married twice and had three children. Living in Tonbridge on the Weald with his second wife Elspeth he became shepherd to a small flock of Clun ewes. The way he described himself was as a part-time peasant.

b 17.5.12   d 8.7.93   aged 81

DAME ELISABETH FRINK

Dame Elisabeth Frink, CH, DBE, sculptor.

ELISABETH Frink maintained an unusually independent career for a 20th-century sculptor. Avoiding the art world's promotional boosts of personality-cult and brand-image (the British Council, for instance, took little interest in her), she won a reputation in three quite distinct areas, each with its distinct audience. Her three essential themes were the nature of Man; the "horseness" of horses; and the divine in human form.

Elisabeth Jean Frink was born at Thurlow, Suffolk, the daughter of Brigadier Ralph Frink, DSO − as he was to become. The family was of Dutch and German descent, with Huguenots on both sides of the family (on her father's side, those who had sought refuge in Canada in the 17th century). Her father was a polo player, who at one point was attached to an Indian regiment as riding instructor. In Trieste in 1946 he had charge of the hundreds of horses "liberated" throughout Europe at the end of the war. Horses were around Frink most of her life, and she was riding from the age of four. An uncle was an accomplished carver of birds and figures and she drew regularly from the age of 12, when she took extra art lessons at her school, the Convent of the Holy Family, in Exmouth.

Growing up during the war left deep impressions on a nature like hers. Her father had served in the British Expeditionary Force and was evacuated at Dunkirk. The family lived near an airfield in Suffolk and she experienced some of the dramas of war. Sometimes she saw bomber aircraft burst into flames as they returned, badly damaged, from their raids. The twisted debris of crashes was a familiar sight to her. On one occasion she had to dive for shelter when a German fighter flew over, firing its cannon and machine guns. As for so many others, the end of hostilities, though welcome, brought further horrors with the revelations from Belsen and the other Nazi death camps.

The experience of growing up under these stresses shaped Frink's early work. She was a student at Guildford School of Art from 1947 to 1949, and Chelsea School of Art from 1949 to 1953. When she was encouraged to show her work to Bryan Robertson at Heffer's Gallery in Cambridge in 1949, two themes were already evident: naked men on powerful horses, and predatory, menacing birds — crows, hawks and eagles. She said that her birds were "vehicles for strong feelings of panic, tension, aggression and predatoriness"; but created to express "birdness" rather than as symbols. However, as a student at Chelsea, her work already matched that of the sculptors of "postwar Angst": Meadows, Butler, Chadwick, and the Henry Moore of the helmeted figures. Frink's prize entry for the "Unknown Political Prisoner" international competition in 1952 brought her to the attention of other sculptors such as McWilliams and Armitage; and the theme helped to set the direction for her future images of man.

The Tate Gallery had already bought in 1953 her *Bird* of 1952, which was exhibited at the Beaux Arts Gallery in London. Her first one-person show was at St George's Gallery in 1955. The birds led on to figures of "birdmen" commissioned by the LCC in 1958 and Sedgehill School, Lewisham, in 1961. These, in turn, led on to the aerial Christ figures of later religious commissions. (She carefully chose commissions which extended her imagery.)

Frink taught at Chelsea School of Art, 1954–61, and at St Martin's, 1956–62. It was during the period 1967–73, when she lived in France, in the Cevennes (discovered by chance to be only eight kilometres from her mother's ancestral Huguenot home), that the troubles in French North Africa, with the Algerian war and the Moroccan torture chambers, focused Frink's work on her most outstanding contribution to the imagery of the times. Her "goggle heads" are akin to the sun-visored motorcyclist messengers of death in Cocteau's film *Orphée*. They also relate to the sunglassed torturers of North Africa as seen in press photos. The power of these images lies in their ambivalence: bull-necked, hair cropped, thin-lipped, eyes shaded, hiding moral weakness under a show of physical strength.

After their first admiration critics tended to see a certain sameness and repetition in these figures. But this reaction overlooked the subtle variations of emphasis with which Frink imbued them. Some are merely unthinking thugs, but in others, a conscience seems to be stirring. There is a sense of brutalisation as a process not incapable of redemption. These studies provided a fruitful vehicle for Frink for some years, although they did not always gain from being shown together, as in the Royal Academy retrospective of her work in 1985. There was a curious resemblance to the head of the actor Alec Guinness as he appeared when playing his most ambivalent roles. It was a similarity which Frink found distinctly inconvenient when she was commissioned by the National Portrait Gallery to sculpt the actor's head in 1983.

She explained that the powerful effect of these sculptures came from her own twofold vision of man and mankind: she admired the male figure and maleness, but felt: "we are becoming brutalised". But she maintained an optimistic view of mankind which was supported by her Christian upbringing.

After 1975 Frink's view of stoical, passive resistance to violence found form in a transition of these thugs to equally brutalised, vulnerable victims and martyrs for their beliefs, in several sculptures arising from her interest in Amnesty International's work for prisoners of conscience. The busts developed into full male figures. (Frink seldom made female figures, the first exceptions being her *Walking Madonna* of 1981 for Salisbury Cathedral, and her self-portrait of 1987.) Critics commented on some facial similarities between the sculptress and her male figures, but she denied any androgynous feelings. Her male figures are often — again ambivalently — either running or running away. Totally relaxed figures were rare — *Man* of 1970 and *Seated Man* of 1983 being notable exceptions.

Around 1988 Frink, who had previously hated using colour, was inspired by the discovery of some early Greek sculptures of unusual appearance, the "Riace Warriors," to adopt a more stylised, wide-eyed face for her male figures, which she combined surprisingly with a roughened surface, more vigorous movement, and the use of colour, producing an "expressionist" effect which some commentators associated with German art.

Less well-known, but assured of continuous attention and a future audience, are Frink's religious commissions. These are strikingly original contributions to church and public art, beginning with the *Eagle Lectern* of 1962 for Coventry Cathedral, progressing through *Risen Christ* at Solihull and her *Crucifixion* in Belfast to her bronze *Christ* unveiled at Liverpool Cathedral only this month. She specialised memorably in presenting an airborne rather than an earthbound Christ.

Frink also made more than a score of portrait sculptures; and she illustrated Chaucer and Greek myth for books. Her favoured medium for sculpture was plaster — following Giacometti and Germaine Richier, two early artistic admirations of Frink, along with Rodin. She preferred it for its convenience in quick modelling which could then be finished off by carving. From the mid-1980s, however, she also tried some direct carving from stone.

Despite her creative work, she found time also for public service. She served as a trustee of the British Museum from 1975 to 1989, and was a valued member of the Royal Fine Art Commission from 1976 to 1981. In the 1980s there was a move to elect her as the first woman president of the Royal Academy. But she did not support this, on the ground that it would take too much time from her work as a sculptor.

Elisabeth Frink was appointed a CBE in 1969 and created DBE in 1982.

In 1992 she was appointed a Companion of Honour. She married Michel Jammet in 1955. They had a son, the painter Lin Jammet, who survives her. The marriage was dissolved in 1963 and in the following year she married Edward Pool, MC. This marriage was dissolved in 1974 and in the same year she married Alexander Csáky. He died earlier this year.

b 14.11.30   d 18.4.93   aged 62

SIR SIDNEY NOLAN

Sir Sidney Nolan, OM, AC, CBE, Australia's most celebrated painter of the 20th century.

SIDNEY Nolan was a born painter with magical gifts, who arrived on the scene at just the right time to make a major contribution to Australia's collective imagination and sense of national identity. Beginning as an abstract artist he turned to figurative painting and in a series of Australian landscapes – and the figures he placed in them – he was able to embody the essence and atmosphere of the island continent and to give it its own mythology. He made his name on the international stage with his pictures of the notorious outlaw Ned Kelly, whose fame actually preceded the artist to Europe in the postwar years. These and his desert scenes communicated Australia's sense of strangeness, which Nolan was able to describe in a pictorial idiom that was haunting and poetic.

Sidney Robert Nolan was a sixth-generation Australian of Irish descent on both sides of his family. His father was a tram-driver and his grandfather had been a police officer in Victoria at the time of the Ned Kelly gang; from him, Sidney heard many stories about the exploits of this legendary folk-hero, Australia's Robin Hood.

Nolan's first interests were cycle-racing and athletics. But he took art classes from the age of 12, received a training in craftsmanship at technical school and attended night school at the Melbourne Gallery school – where, however, he dodged the drawing classes to read Rimbaud and Ouspensky in the library upstairs. Employment from the age of 14 to 21 in the design and promotion department of Fayrfield Hats gave him an early ability in using spray paints and other mixed media not normally employed in fine art, which was to stand him in good stead later.

From 1937 to 1940 he was only interested in European art, imitating Klee, Picasso and the then little-known Kurt Schwitters in collage. However, in 1938 he came into the circle of the wealthy art patrons John and Sunday Reed, who were the sole support of the young Australian artists Arthur Boyd, Tucker,

Perceval, Vassilieff and subsequently Nolan himself. Nolan lived in their house at Heidelberg, near Melbourne, for several years, involved in both poetry and illustrations for the avant-garde magazine *Angry Penguins.*

Drafted into the Army in 1942 and isolated at a training-camp at Dimboola amid miles of wheatfields in the Wimmera district of Victoria, Nolan, bored with military life, began to paint the particular light of Australia on this landscape, the strangeness of the perspectives it produces, and the way that this strong sunlight, as he said, "isolates objects" – making the most dramatic events curiously static and timeless.

This observation of Australian light was an immediate contribution to national landscape painting, freeing it from romantic European models. To this Nolan soon added subject-matter from local stories and life, using the anti-stylism of child art, which Vassilieff had adopted. Putting this together with his understanding of European Surrealism and abstraction, and his fluent painting skills, Nolan arrived, in 1945, at the perfect amalgam of all this, his first Ned Kelly pictures.

The Ned Kelly story bites deep into the Australian subconscious – "a public shame and a private pride" it has been called. A wild young Irishman born in 1855 and hanged for murder and theft in 1880 after two years of battles against the police and raids on banks, wearing home-made armour, Kelly issued a series of crudely idealistic public calls for social justice and revenge; his last words as the noose was put around his neck were "Such is life". His courage, violence, rough justice and revolt against authority appealed to the imagination of this ex-penal colony; his last words typify the laconic, sardonic realism of Australian speech; and his career has been said to exemplify that Australian national existentialism which admires purposeful action without believing that this has any ultimate value: "Might as well give it a burl" (whirl).

Nolan intended the subject-matter as ironic commentary on the Australian psychology. For background, he had all the paradoxes of Australian landscape: three million square miles of ancient earth of which one-third is desert, with 10,000 species of flowers, weird animals and birds and a lingering aboriginal presence. This first Ned Kelly series, 1945–47, and the second series in 1954–5, brought world fame to Nolan – though the first showing in Australia was received with embarrassed indifference.

Sir Kenneth Clark discovered Nolan on a visit to Australia in 1949, noting "that truth of tone which is the surest sign of a natural painter"; but he also saw the potential dilemma for Nolan, of whether to leave the source of his inspiration and move to a Europe of wider response to his art. Nolan himself did not see this as a dilemma, believing he could move forward, and from 1953 made Europe his base, from where he visited Italy in 1954 (he was Australian Commissioner at the Venice Biennale of 1954, showing also twelve paintings) and Greece in 1955–6. Then a world tour sponsored by Qantas Airways took him on to Turkey, India and Cambodia; followed in 1957 – the year of his retrospective at the Whitechapel Gallery – by visits to Japan and Mexico. In 1957 he studied engraving and lithography at Hayter's *atelier* in Paris; from 1958 to 1960 he was in the USA.

Nolan's visit to the Dardanelles inspired a series of 105 paintings – subsequently given to the National Gallery in Melbourne in memory of his younger brother – on the theme of the Gallipoli campaign, that event etched deep in Australian memory, from which Nolan conjured up parallels with the Trojan wars. And in 1957 he provided the dust-jacket illustration for that other Australian cultural event on the world scene: Patrick White's novel *Voss.*

Nolan continued his huge output and bursts of creativity with such projects as *Paradise Garden* of 1970, 768 paintings of indigenous flowers shown as an immense group on a single wall; but despite increasing popularity and royal patronage, critics believed they detected a falling-away of his powers. His *Leda and the Swan* series in 1960 pleased only a few critics; his 1972 exhibition at the Marlborough Galleries was poorly received; and his *Notes for Oedipus* series in 1976 sold only one painting, and that to his dealer – subsequently returned to him.

He himself said that he needed to get "steamed up" over subject and form to produce good work; Bryan Robertson characterised him as "a magician who occasionally resorts to conjuring tricks in order to prove his magic". Nolan's weakness was that his love of painting was sometimes greater than his imagery. A deeper reason for his failure to follow up Australian mythology with universal mythology was his feeling, on coming to Europe, that the West was in decline. The underlying tragic thread of Nolan's work is that of a waste land – as God's glorious gift, spoilt by man. Lord Clark summed up in 1977: "When time has weeded out his colossal output and the didactic snobbery of abstract art has declined, he will be of even greater renown."

Neglect of Nolan's work in London over three decades was partially redeemed by a splendid retrospective at Folkestone Art Centre in 1979, and later in 1988 when his 1940s work was shown in the context of the *Angry Penguins* exhibition at the Hayward Gallery, which introduced his art to a new generation. The catalogue-book accompanying the Australian exhibition *Nolan: Landscapes and Legends* in 1987, which subsequently toured the world, and Nolan's biography, *Such is Life*, by Brian Adams, published in the same year, brought back to the public eye the greatest innovator in Australian art to date.

Nolan completed many theatre projects. His earliest was the commission by Serge Lifar for designs for *Icare* for the De Basil company in Australia in 1939; his most successful, for the opera *Samson et Dalila* by Saint-Saens at Covent Garden in 1981, with the Australian producer Elijah Moshinsky –

a setting in shades of rose, with drop curtains and painted gauzes and 200 costumes, which gained Nolan five curtain calls on the first night. For Covent Garden he had also designed the ballet *Rite of Spring* in 1962 (revived in 1987), and in 1987 provided the décor for *Il Seraglio*. Also, in 1970, Benjamin Britten – whom Kenneth Clark had linked with Nolan in their "reckless innocence" with regard to subjects and media – had toured Central Australia with Nolan; until Britten's death in 1976 they were planning a ballet based on the initiation rites of Australian aboriginal youths, to be set against a chorus of Oxford choirboys, and using the true story of an Oxford suicide on his wedding day.

Nolan's chief personal quality was self-possession. Quiet and abstemious, he had a gentle, diffident charm, with a sharp eye, a poetic quick wit, a toughness of intellect and an openness of imagination, which could be precise and sensible or extremeley fantastic. His irreverent humour and enjoyment of the irrational and absurd could lead him, with his gregarious nature, to playing the Australian larrikin on public occasions. He claimed that the misunderstanding of his work by the critics had given him a kind of freedom: "I can work as I did as a boy, knowing that nobody cares."

Sidney Nolan was appointed CBE in 1963 for services to art in Britain – a somewhat ironic honour in terms of Britain, Australia and the British Empire; he was created a Knight Bachelor in 1981 and appointed a member of the Order of Merit in 1983. Finally, he was made a Companion of the Order of Australia in 1988.

He married Elizabeth Patterson in 1938, by whom he had a daughter; they were divorced in 1942. In 1948 he married Cynthia Hansen (née Reed), who committed suicide in 1974. In 1977 he married Mary Elizabeth à Beckett Perceval, settling in 1983 on the Welsh border of Herefordshire.

b 22.4.17   d 28.11.92   aged 75

LOTTE LASERSTEIN

Lotte Laserstein, the last great survivor from the heyday of German realist painting.

THE return of Lotte Laserstein to public attention in 1987, with an extensive London exhibition, could not help but seem odd to her. From her own point of view, she had never been away from it. Though she had travelled and changed countries, she had never stopped painting, and had never lacked patrons.

But to most people outside Sweden, her adopted land, her work, when it was exhibited internationally again, came like a trumpet blast from the past. And yet it seemed amazingly of the present: a certain kinship might immediately be recognised, in colouring, style and general approach, between her large, dashingly painted nudes and the most recent work of Lucian Freud.

Where had she been for the previous half-century? The literal answer is Sweden. Harassed by the Nazis (she was a quarter-Jewish), she had been forced to close her Berlin studio in 1935, and a major success with her first show at a commercial gallery in Stockholm in 1937 seemed providential. She stayed on, then settled when the war came, and was still living largely in Stockholm at the time of her death.

In Sweden her reputation was almost entirely as a portrait painter. She never wanted for commissions and was still making portrait drawings regularly in her nineties, as well as exhibiting at the Konstnaremes Riks, the Swedish Academy of Art, of which she was a member for more than 50 years. She also continued to paint her favourite model from the 1920s, the tennis player Traute Rose, who had been instrumental in getting her paintings out of Germany in 1938 and, with her husband Ernst, also an old friend, visited Laserstein in Sweden annually after the war.

In the wider sense of the term, portraiture made up most of Laserstein's output throughout her working life, but few of the earlier paintings were formal portraits. Rather, she loved to paint the human figure, nude or clothed, male or female, and devoted herself entirely to it. Several of her most famous paintings, such as *Artist and Model in the Studio, Berlin, Wilmersdorf* (1929) and the splendid group around a table of approximately the same date, *The Roof Garden, Potsdam*, have finely rendered landscapes in the background, but she never seems to have been tempted to bring such background to the fore.

Only models of very special qualities would work with her (or for her), as she was quite merciless in her demands. Tireless and buoyantly healthy herself, she worked long hours without flagging and expected her models to do the same, holding difficult poses if required for hours at a stretch.

Traute Rose's husband, one of the figures in the Potsdam picture, endured valiantly one of the most tiresome poses. But on the whole, Laserstein had difficulties with men sitting for their portraits, since they tended to fidget.

The foundations of Laserstein's amazing technique were laid early. Sketchbooks of great accomplishment survive from her 11th year, and she determined at that age, she maintained, to become a professional artist and never to marry. When she was 18 she entered the Berlin Academy of Arts where she remained for six years, the last two as "Atelier Meisterschüler" which meant that she was regarded as the star pupil and had a right to her own studio at the academy. In 1925 she went on to win the gold medal, the academy's highest award.

She had to support herself with routine jobs in rug and toy design, china decoration (like her mother before her) and illustrating an anatomical textbook which required long periods spent in the company of bodies preserved in hydrochloroform. After leaving, she set up her own studio and rapidly achieved her mature style which was like a looser, more fluid version of the Neue Sachlichkeit, a very precise form of realism then dominant in German painting. She also taught, until the Nazis found her pupils' choice of subjects among the peasant poor suspicious, and travelled when she could afford to, making significant painting trips to Paris, Florence and Rome.

After the war she began to travel again, renting a house in Provence for several summers and making sketching trips to southern Spain and Greece with the Swedish painter Else Celsing. She never cared to return to Germany for any length of time – understandably, as her mother (who was not Jewish) had been persecuted for harbouring her sister Kate and had eventually died in Ravensbrück concentration camp.

When she last visited London in 1990, Laserstein was still inexhaustible, bright as a bird and slightly intimidating. When asked what she though of Lucian Freud (the comparison has frequently come up) she said briskly: "The technique is extraordinary but his nudes are . . . too nude."

As keeper of the flame of realism for some eighty years, she knew what she was talking about.

b 28.11.99 d 24.1.93 aged 94

ALADENA FRATIANNO

Aladena "Jimmy the Weasel" Fratianno, a former Mafia hitman turned informer.

DYING in his sleep was the most unlikely end to the life of Aladena Fratianno. He had admitted committing five murders and participating in six others and − ever since he became a government informer in 1977 after 30 years in the Mafia − his former associates had had a contract out on him.

The Mafia "Godfathers" had good reason for wanting him dead. Once the top Mafia enforcer in Los Angeles, Fratianno, helped send to jail 30 of his former partners in crime, including six gang bosses, among them: Carmine "The Snake" Persico, the New York boss; Fat

Tony Salerno, the New Jersey chief; Johnny "The Rope" Roselli of Los Angeles; and Johnny "Blackie" Licavori of Cleveland.

By testifying for the government, Fratianno broke the Mafia's oath of secrecy − "Omertà" − for which the penalty is death. "They tell you when you come in. You come in alive and you go out dead," he told a Los Angeles jury.

His account of Mafia life closely resembled scenes from the Hollywood film *The Godfather*. At his initiation in 1947 in Los Angeles, he said, there were 50 men in the room and a gun and sword on a table. The sword was used to draw blood and then he kissed each member on the cheek.

Fratianno was considered a skilled prosecution witness who would spend days preparing for trials. His graphic accounts of mob "hits," were delivered in matter-of-fact tones. Life in the mob was simple but deadly, he told an interviewer. "When the boss tells you to do something, you do it. You don't do it, they kill you."

He later said he became a government witness when he was confronted with murder charges in a Cleveland car-bombing and learnt at the same time that the Los Angeles mob had put a $100,000 contract on him.

Born in Naples, Fratianno moved to the US as a young boy and grew up in Cleveland's Little Italy district. He received his nickname as a boy for demonstrating to onlookers how he could outrun police officers "fast as a weasel" after stealing fruit from street vendors.

He was one of the first recipients of protection under a federal government witness programme. In return for regular testimony in organised crime cases, he received a new name, a new identity, a new address and $100,000 a year living expenses.

But in 1987, almost ten years after he first turned informer, the US Justice Department decided to curtail his living expenses, on the ground that even ex-Mafia informants were expected to try to earn an honest living eventually.

Fratianno was not pleased: "I am a dead man," he told a news agency. "They just threw me out on the [expletive deleted] street. I put 30 guys away, six of them bosses and now the whole world is looking for me. I'm 74 years old. Where am I going to work at my age?"

In fact, financially, Fratianno had put his underworld experiences to good use after leaving the mob, writing two books about his life and times as a mobster and appearing on television talk shows. His books, *The Mob: Vengeance is Mine* and *The Last Mafioso* were illustrated with pictures of him with celebrities including Frank Sinatra. He claimed that the Mafia had infiltrated politics right up to the White House and estimated its income from illegal activities at more than £50 billion. After losing his government income, Fratianno went on television to appeal to the authorities to let him leave the country.

"My life is in grave danger," he said, "The Mob have a contract out on me and they mean to carry it through."

Just how long he waited fearing that the next knock at his door might presage a violent death is not clear. His wife said he had been suffering for some time from Alzheimer's disease.

b 1914 d 1993   aged 79

JOHN POULSON

John Poulson, the disgraced architect who went to prison in the 1970s for the improper influencing of property contracts.

CORRUPTION has seldom been a major feature of British politics. For that reason alone, John Poulson's niche in political history is likely to remain assured. In the 1960s and the 1970s he was at the centre of a web of bribery and corruption that ended up by forcing the resignation of a Conservative Home Secretary, the fall and disgrace of the rising chairman of a regional planning authority – to say nothing of the conviction and imprisonment of Poulson himself, together with a senior Scottish Office civil servant, on seven separate criminal charges. In sentencing the Yorkshire architect to five years in jail (later increased to seven) the judge at the original trial at Leeds Crown Court called him an "incalculably evil man".

Poulson himself vigorously dissented from that judgment, claiming "I have been a fool, surrounded by a pack of leeches. I took on the world on its own terms, and no one can deny I once had it in my fist."

Though never a formally qualified architect "because I was too busy to complete my examinations," Poulson had become a member of the Royal Institute of British Architects by the now defunct method of admission through experience and commonly accepted ability. But, while some of his designs won awards of merit, his business sense always overruled his appreciation of the aesthetic.

The accepted architectural method of completing a design then handing it over for costing, planning and building was too slow, too cumbersome and not profitable enough for the ambitious Poulson. So he developed a combined architectural and design empire where all the separate disciplines could be housed under one roof and one ownership, his own. At its peak it employed some 750 people, making it one of the largest of its kind in Europe. Poulson was involved in the design of numerous council houses and flats; an international swimming pool for Leeds; The Cannon Street Station redevelopment in London; the £3 million Aviemore tourist centre in Scotland and the £1.5 million Victoria Hospital at Gozo, Malta.

In theory it was a fine idea and, for a period, was highly successful. At its apogee, the Poulson empire was averaging an annual turnover of £1m and Poulson himself admitted to being a personal millionaire. But such a vast and expensive array of specialised knowledge needed some feeding and was consuming contract work faster than it was becoming available.

He resorted, in the end, to solving his problems by the methods for which he became a household name in Britain; bribing and corrupting councillors, local authority officials, public servants at all levels. It proved expensive and, during the last few years in business, he "gave away" an estimated £½m.

Finally, in 1972 he filed his own petition in bankruptcy for £247,000 and opened the doors for the investigation during which Reginald Maudling, then Home Secretary, resigned his position and five public officials – and the wife of one of them – were arrested and charged with conspiracy. His public bankruptcy examination at Wakefield was the stuff that headlines are made of and Poulson's love of the lavish and ostentatious, his desire to rub shoulders with the Establishment and prove his financial superiority served only to show what a lonely, friendless and insecure man he really was.

John Poulson was the son of a Methodist lay preacher. Educationally he was "bright but not outstanding". He studied architecture at Leeds Polytechnic but failed to complete the course. Instead, at the age of 22,' he opened a small practice above a bank in Pontefract and soon began cultivating contacts in the local borough council and among officials of the larger, West Riding county authority. Within a short time, work began to arrive and John Poulson told his friends that he was "on his way".

The practice expanded "beyond my wildest dreams" and by the beginning of the 1950s was recognised as amongst the biggest in Britain. Within the next fifteen years Poulson had opened offices in London, Middlesbrough, Newcastle upon Tyne, Edinburgh, London and abroad in Beirut, Lagos and temporary offices in South America.

His "contacts" included peers, members of parliament, top civil servants in Whitehall and elsewhere and local officials and councillors at all levels. Most of them, at some time or other, received some token of John Poulson's regard, even if only a bottle of whisky or a turkey at Christmas. Even the late Anthony Crosland was to live to rue his wholly innocent acceptance of the gift of a silver-plated coffee pot. In fact, his generosity, sometimes motivated by sheer goodwill, more often by hopes of a future construction contract, brought the comment from Muir Hunter, QC, during the bankruptcy proceedings: "In fact, Mr Poulson, you were distributing largesse like Henry VIII!"

Poulson built himself a £60,000 mansion, "Manassah," just outside Pontefract which won a magazine's "House of the Year" award. But, as his money troubles began developing, he sold it to a young couple for just over half the cost price. One of the more curious aspects of his bankruptcy was that his biggest creditor was the Inland Revenue to which he owed around £200,000. But, while they were pressing for a settlement, he was still sitting in judgment on fellow defaulters as a Commissioner of Inland Revenue at Wakefield.

A man who had not enjoyed good health for some years, John Poulson's life was shattered when he was arrested on June 22, 1973, and charged with conspiracy and corruption over the awarding of building contracts. On February 11, 1974, after a 52-day trial at Leeds Crown Court which received the widest publicity, he and George Pottinger, a Scottish civil servant who had been arrested on the same day, were both found guilty on seven charges of corruption involving £30,000 worth of gifts from Poulson to Pottinger. They both received five-year sentences. Pottinger's was subsequently reduced to four years on appeal. Poulson's sentence, however, had been provisional on the outcome of the trials of others who had been charged with corruption. After a subsequent trial at which a hospital board secretary, George Braithwaite, was sentenced to three years, Poulson's own sentence was increased to seven. He had already told one friend at the time of his arrest: "I'll never survive this lot, you know. Prison will kill me."

It did not do so. On May 13, 1977, after periods in Wakefield and Oakham prisons, Poulson was discharged from Lincoln prison hospital, having been granted parole. Four years later he published his memoirs in a book entitled *The Price*. A self-righteous, self-justificatory work, it was almost immediately withdrawn under the threat of libel proceedings. It, nevertheless, summed up Poulson's own view of himself as a man more sinned against than sinning.

Poulson is survived by his wife, Cynthia, and by two daughters.

b 14.4.10   d 31.1.93   aged 82

T. DAN SMITH

T. Dan Smith, the former Newcastle upon Tyne Labour council leader who was jailed for six years after corruptly receiving money from the architect John Poulson.

KNOWN as "Mr Newcastle" at the height of his power in local government, T. Dan Smith was jailed for six years in 1974 after pleading guilty to receiving corruptly £156,000 over seven years from the architect John Poulson. He had been a controversial figure in the northeast of England throughout his public career which began in 1950.

By the mid-1960s he was being seen as a city boss along the lines of Chicago's Mayor Daley. He had cleared Newcastle's notorious Scotswood slums. He was the unveiler of a £200-million plan to make Newcastle the "Brasilia of the North". Some saw him as the Willy Brandt of British politics. He was not merely a show-figure for Labour but a favourite in Whitehall – the redoutable Dame Evelyn Sharp, permanent secretary at the Ministry of Housing and Local

Government, being a particular admirer.

Nor was it just a matter of his being the forward-looking leader of a major city. For in 1965 George Brown gave him regional power by making him chairman of the Northern Economic Planning Council. It turned out to be the apogee of his fame and influence.

His remarkable career finally crashed in ruins in one of the many shock waves which spread out from "The Poulson Affair" of the 1970s. John Poulson, a millionaire architect, had gone bankrupt in 1972. By bribing and corrupting councillors, local authority officials and other public servants he had built up a substantial practice. But his methods had cost him dear. Examination of his books revealed that he had given away £½ million over several years, including payments of over £150,000 to Smith-owned companies.

As the hearings rumbled on, a number of establishment names became involved. Among the casualties at the highest level was the then Conservative Home Secretary, Reginald Maudling, who, because of his responsibilities for the Metropolitan Police, felt compelled to resign. Smith had already survived one close shave when, in 1970, he had been acquitted on charges of giving bribes to a Wandsworth councillor. On this second occasion he was not so lucky. He was paroled after serving three years of a six-year sentence.

T. Dan Smith was the son of a miner. His father was frequently unemployed during his childhood and drank and gambled heavily. Smith often recalled the impression made on his mind by the spectacle of his mother rising at 5am each day to clean the Wallsend telephone exchange before moving on to wash floors at the Shell-Mex office. "She cracked up under the strain and died of a broken heart," he would say when explaining his allegiance to socialist principles long after he had entered the world of business tycoonery.

After attending the Weston Boys School at Wallsend, Smith became a printer's apprentice at 13. At 22 he started his first business, having acquired the capital for a set of ladders and brushes. In lean days on Tyneside, he made a success of painting cinema exteriors.

By the time he was first elected to public office in 1950, as a Labour city councillor for the Walker ward of Newcastle upon Tyne, he had become a businessman of some substance. But he had not forgotten the grim lessons of his childhood. On the council he represented a tough waterfront area where the fears of a return to conditions of 20 years earlier were rife.

He first achieved real power − which he always frankly admitted he enjoyed − when Labour took control of Newcastle council in 1958. This made him the leader of one of the country's most important local authorities and he also held the key chairmanships of the housing, finance and planning committees.

He had long dreamt of organising the total rebuilding of the city and his first act was to initiate the clearance of the Scotswood Road area which at that time had little to recommend its continued existence, beyond its place in the words of Blaydon Races.

Close on the heels of this project came his idea for a sweeping rebuilding of the city as a whole. With the help of a fellow councillor, who was a mathematician and a member of the city architect's staff, he drew up a £200-million plan for what he called a Brasilia of the north of England to replace "the dark and brooding" existing city. Wilfred Burns, the designer of Coventry city centre was appointed to execute the task. Smith was made "Man of the Year" by the *Architects' Journal* in 1960 for his contribution to town planning.

His appointment as the first chairman of the most significant of the Regional Economic Planning Councils set up by the Labour government in 1965 was surrounded by controversy. It was attacked by Conservatives as smacking of politics (university vice-chancellors had been appointed to the other two councils in the north of England) and Smith had already been under fire from his own side because of his unabashed use of such capitalist symbols as a large Jaguar with a DAN 68 registration, private schools for his three children, and a London *pied-à-terre* in St James's. By then he had added a public relations consultancy to his business interests and his original painting firm had grown to a labour force of 250.

He refused to give ground to any attacks on his mixture of avowals to socialist principles and capitalist practices. He said he saw nothing incompatible between making money, achieving power and being a socialist. He claimed that both gave him the opportunities to do something practical for the people of Tyneside and the northeast region as a whole.

His career had first stumbled early in 1970 when a summons was issued against him in connection with alleged corruption involving one of his public relations companies and Wandsworth borough council. Two days before he was named by Scotland Yard he resigned his first post, the joint chairmanship of the Northern Regional Committee of the United Europe Association.

The case hung over his head for 18 months and by the time he was acquitted in July 1971 he had either resigned from or lost all his political appointments. (It was characteristic that his role, even as the shadows drew in, should have been robustly defended by Richard Crossman, who devoted a whole front-page leading article in the *New Statesman* to championing him as the kind of man who got things done.)

Early in 1973 his name was mentioned in connection with the Poulson affair. By then he had slipped out of the public eye altogether and was working in a managerial post for an old friend in Northampton who owned an electrical contracting firm. Of the 20 companies Smith had been associated with, three had gone bankrupt and nine had been struck off the register for failing to keep adequate records.

In October 1973 he was arrested in Newcastle upon Tyne by police officers conducting the Poulson investigation and charged with conspiracy to corrupt. Jailed for six years in 1974 he served only half his sentence before being released in 1977 on parole from Leyhill open prison in Gloucestershire.

Over the past 16 years he had worked for the rehabilitation of offenders and campaigned for the rights of prisoners. Another of his campaigns was for a better deal for pensioners. As the years went by an odour, if not of sanctity, then at least of a sort of rugged decency began to hang about him again. There was an increasing tendency for people to remember what he had done for Newcastle rather than the methods by which he had achieved his aims.

His case continued to provoke interest and his life was the subject of a documentary film. He himself was a frequent guest on chat shows and phone-in programmes.

In 1987, after years out in the political cold, he was readmitted to the Labour party in the Newcastle Central constituency.

He leaves his widow Ada, one son and two daughters.

b 11.5.15   d 27.7.93   aged 78

ARTHUR ASHE

Arthur Ashe, the American tennis player who won the Wimbledon singles championship in 1975.

IF HE was not among the truly great lawn tennis champions of modern times, Arthur Ashe will nevertheless be remembered with respect for his civilising influence on the game. As the first black man to achieve the heights he did as a player, he used his celebrity status to fight racism and was a pioneering figure in the advancement of Afro-American sport. His personal demeanour on court — and off it — set an example to young players in a game which was becoming increasingly bad tempered.

Arthur Ashe had a number of firsts to his credit. In 1963 he was the first black player to be selected for a US Davis Cup team. In 1973 he defied South Africa's apartheid laws by becoming the first black man to play in the country's open championship. Finally — and his crowning achievement — he became the first black player to win the men's singles title at Wimbledon, in 1975. He had won

the Australian Open in 1970 and the US Open in 1968.

Ashe's victory at Wimbledon was the more piquant, even in a championship which thrives on surprise, for being so utterly unexpected. Jimmy Connors, who had brutally swept aside the aging Ken Rosewall the year before, was almost thought to have a natural right to the title. No one could stand against him. But through resourcefulness and guile, Ashe did just that, to record one of the most unexpected as well as most popular wins in the tournament's history.

In his early years on the international circuit, Ashe was often known as "The Shadow". Dark and skinny, he seldom packed more than 11 stone into his 6ft 1in. He was blessed with a droll sense of humour and did not mind the nickname, having learnt to live, from his childhood in Virginia, with far more wounding allusions to his skin colour. Moreover, the sobriquet was always affectionate because there have been few players who inspired — and gave — as much respect and personal warmth. All who knew him will remember the man just as vividly as the achievements.

Ashe had mixed blood but, essentially, was a descendant of West African slaves. He followed, and built on, the example of Althea Gibson. Like her, he was no newcomer to the challenge of a segregated community. He had been brought up in one, and had learnt to live with racial prejudice and injustice. Ultimately, he broke down all the barriers and, by his example, paved the way for those who followed. In his youth, local tennis clubs and tournaments had no room for black players. Ashe and his kind had to look elsewhere for opportunities. As a result, he acquired a disciplined outward serenity and a composure that concealed any stress he might be feeling. The family's regular fishing and deer-hunting expeditions helped to develop a sportsman's self-discipline and patience.

But Ashe also had an aptitude for study, which eventually steered him to the University of California at Los Angeles – and the intensity of collegiate coaching and competition. He emerged as a distinguished tennis player and a world citizen. He was a gentle, quiet, thoughtful man with a restless mind, intellectual leanings and an all-encompassing tolerance.

Ashe sprang to international prominence in 1968 when he won the inaugural US Open championship (the Open was the first competition to be opened to all categories of players, whether professionals, amateurs or shamateurs). That year, he won 30 consecutive singles matches in two months while supposedly serving as a lieutenant in the US Army. He also made news by changing his shirt alongside the court, with the referee's permission. Ashe was among the first players to wear coloured clothing, an example of his persistent knack of taking tradition by the scruff of the neck and shaking the nonsense out of it.

Ashe won the Australian singles title in 1970, Wimbledon in 1975. The Wimbledon final against Connors remains a striking testimony to his ability,

his intellect and his self-discipline. As a player, Connors was on song. Indeed he was reckoned so formidable at that stage of his career that hardly anyone gave Ashe a chance, because he habitually played at a pace on which Connors thrived.

But on that day Ashe played a very different match from normal. He varied pace and spin, angle and trajectory. He broke up Connors's rhythm and gave him no pattern to respond to. Connors was confused and finally beaten – by an opponent unrecognisable as the Ashe he thought he had come to know.

To the astonishment of the Centre Court, Ashe took the first two sets 6-1, 6-1. Connors fought back strongly to take the third, 7-5, but Ashe found new reserves of ingenuity to end it in the fourth, which he won 6-4. Connors can have had few greater surprises in his own long and distinguished tennis playing career.

Ashe was lithe, with fast wrists. He could be inconsistent, veering between the dazzling and the commonplace. His service and backhand were often lightning fast. But he was no great volleyer and was often teased, in particular, about the deficiency of his forehand volley. The paradox about Ashe was that he was a quiet, cerebral man who played a brutally violent game. But he always enjoyed the mental challenge of playing on slow clay, especially in Paris. Although this type of tennis did not complement his technique, it suited his nature.

Ashe was a modest man who never developed the superstar aura and its accompanying carapace of tantrums which have become de rigueur in the contemporary game. On one occasion in Bristol a young woman approached him with a request for his autograph. At the time Ashe was the only black player of front rank and one of the very few, in any rank, who wore glasses, so he was not difficult to recognise. "I don't know who you are", the young woman said, "but would you please give me your autograph?" Ashe did not mind. He smiled, murmured something self-effacing and took care with his signature for this perhaps not most tactful of fans.

In 1971, however, after a semi-final of the US championship had been affected by rain, Ashe tried contact lenses, took to them and thereafter his bespectacled visage was never again seen on court.

Ashe was one of the founders – later, president – of the Association of Tennis Professionals. He was always an innovator – as a black champion, as a pivotal figure in organising professionals as a corporate body, and as a driving force behind the game's administrative evolution and related revision of the rules of play. He was also involved in a variety of business ventures and social and charitable work.

In 1979 Ashe's playing career was suddenly curtailed when he had a heart attack. He underwent quadruple bypass heart surgery and later announced that he intended to return to the game. But in 1980 he suffered a setback in his come-back plans and announced his retirement later that year. In 1983 he had further surgery, this time a double bypass operation. He continued to be unwell and in 1988 he had an exploratory brain operation. Finally, last year he announced that he had contracted Aids, presumably from a blood transfusion which he had received as he recovered from the surgery. It was a condition he bore with dignity to the end.

He had used the intervening years well. One tangible legacy of Ashe and all he stood for is his three-volume work, *A Hard Road To Glory* (1988), a history of black American athletes. Most of all, "The Shadow" will be remembered as a gentle man who was also a gentleman.

Arthur Ashe leaves his widow, Jeanne Moutoussamy, a photographer, and their daughter, Camera.

b 10.7.43   d 6.2.93   aged 46

DANIE CRAVEN

Daniel Hartman Craven, joint president of the South African Rugby Football Union and one of the world's leading rugby administrators.

DANIE Craven was one of the few genuine innovators that rugby union has produced who carried his gifts from the playing field, through a career in coaching and selection and into the administrative arena while also maintaining a high profile academic career. His domination of the South African rugby scene lasted for over 30 years, from his election as president of the old-style South African Rugby Board in 1956 until the unified body which now governs the sport was agreed last year.

As president of the board he also represented his country's interests on the International Rugby Football Board from 1957 onwards, until ill-health reduced his ability to travel over the last four years. In that capacity he fought to keep South Africa involved in the world rugby calendar even when sporting isolation began to bite elsewhere. And when

apartheid began to weaken he was the first sporting administrator to make contact with the African National Congress to plan the way ahead.

It was a source of huge satisfaction to him that the centenary of the South African Rugby Board could be celebrated in 1989 by the appearance of an international XV in two games against the Springboks, and that he saw the return to genuine international fixtures last year of South Africa, when they played the touring New Zealanders and Australians.

Craven's family was from Yorkshire and his father, James, a first generation South African, named the family farm after the Yorkshire village of Steeton. One of eight children, Craven matriculated from Lindley High School and went on to the University of Stellenbosch where he established roots that lasted all his life.

Although he initially hoped to become a minister of religion he took a degree in anthropology and, after leaving university, taught at St Andrew's College, in Grahamstown. By that time he had won Springbok honours, touring Britain with the South Africans in 1931–2 as a scrum half though, remarkably, during his 16 internationals he played also at stand-off half and centre; on tour in New Zealand in 1937 he even played in the forwards, at No 8.

He captained his country four times, against New Zealand in 1937 and three times against the British Isles the following year.

On the outbreak of the second world war he served as a military attaché in London before becoming head of the physical training branch of the South African Military College in Pretoria; but in 1947 he became head of the PE department at Stellenbosch where he remained until 1975. Subsequently he was appointed director of sport and recreation at the university.

His own playing career, and his teaching career, convinced him that individual skills had to form the basic armoury of any ambitious rugby player. In his instructional *Rugby Handbook*, published in 1970, Craven suggested that, once the fundamental principles of the game had been established, all players should master positional skills.

He became a national selector between 1949 and 1956 and coached the touring teams to the British Isles in 1951–2 and to New Zealand in 1956, one of the most bitterly contested series in the often controversial rugby history of the two countries.

That same year he was proposed as president of the South African Rugby Board, a nomination he was uncertain whether to accept since it was made by men known to be members of the Broederbond, the Afrikaner secret community of which he was not, and did not become, a member.

His subsequent stands against government policy of the day frequently produced conflict; in 1965, en route to New Zealand to watch South Africa on tour, he travelled in the same aircraft as a diplomat who bore instructions to the team to decrease friendly relationships with the Maoris.

He clashed with John Vorster, the prime minister who followed the assassinated Hendrik Verwoerd, but won a concession by insisting on fielding a mixed race XV against the touring French in 1975.

But perhaps his finest hour was in 1988 when, aged 78, he flew secretly to Harare with Louis Luyt, the president of the Transvaal Rugby Union, to meet representatives of the banned African National Congress, then calling for a new governing body for rugby and total integration of rugby players in South Africa.

Craven had already helped institute, during the 1980s, coaching clinics which took rugby to youngsters of all colours. At the same time he was desperate to keep the national team on the world stage: 1981 marked the last South African tour for 11 years to one of the recognised rugby playing countries and that tour of New Zealand was marred by violent protests.

After England's visit in 1984 there were no incoming tours for eight years either, hence his encouragement of international tour parties, and, ultimately, the unauthorised New Zealand Cavaliers of 1986 which brought great criticism upon his head outside South Africa.

Following that tour his influence in world affairs declined but he remained a charismatic figure at home and the one focal point amid the political manoeuvring which has always complicated South African rugby.

He was dogged by ill-health during his declining years and had to have major heart surgery on two occasions. But his youthful enthusiasm never dimmed and he remained vigorous enough to be able to accept the joint presidency of the South African Rugby Football Union, the unified non-racial governing body established in February 1992.

Danie Craven was twice married and is survived by his second wife, Merle, three sons and a daughter.

b 11.10.10   d 5.1.93   aged 82

S. C. GRIFFITH

S. C. (Billy) Griffith, CBE, DFC, TD, secretary of MCC from 1962 to 1974.

DURING his 22 years with MCC, first as assistant secretary to Ronnie Aird and then, from 1962 to 1974, as secretary, Billy Griffith was at the centre of events at a time when cricket was having to reconcile itself to modern demands. It was a period, too, when, as an international game, cricket underwent unprecedented stresses. At home he was closely involved with the introduction of one-day cricket (1963), the demise of the amateur (1968–70) and the onset of "player power", of which, however, he was instinctively suspicious. Such was his anxiety to see that the spirit of the game was never compromised that he appeared at moments to be somewhat reactionary.

On the international front his period as secretary coincided with the acute crisis which faced the game over apartheid in South Africa. The "D'Oliveira affair" of 1968 – in which MCC was clearly seen to bow to a South African government

diktat in leaving out of its touring side a coloured player of such persuasive credentials – caused an explosion of public outrage against MCC which could, and should, have been foreseen. As MCC's spokesman, Griffiths, highly sensitive to the issue, offered his resignation. It was not accepted – to the relief even of those who were MCC's most persistent critics. Though he could not escape implication in MCC's errors of judgment, Griffith was generally regarded as having acted with total integrity throughout the affair.

The fact was that he personified an age when cricket was a more carefree business. He longed, unrealistically as he would have admitted, for the era before politics entered the game and worried fearfully about the rights and wrongs with which players were confronted as a result. As secretary throughout an exceptionally difficult period, he was widely respected for his conscientiousness and for his concern for players as human beings.

Stewart Cathie Griffith was known universally as Billy. According to his own version his father, who had wanted to christen him William — Cathie was an inescapable family name — had bridled at the font, realising that the initials "W. C." might expose his infant son to a lavatorial nickname in later life. He was educated at Dulwich College, where he excelled as a player of all sorts of games, and at Pembroke College, Cambridge, where he won a cricket blue. Soon afterwards he toured Australia and New Zealand with an MCC side, though not their strongest. The tour helped to calm the waters that had been so ruffled by the now notorious "bodyline" tour of 1932–33. For two years, 1937–39, he taught at his old school before war service claimed him.

His war was a distinguished one. He served as a pilot in the Glider Pilot Regiment, reached the rank of lieutenant-colonel and in 1944 won the DFC, piloting to the Normandy invasion the glider bearing the commander of the Airborne Division.

When the war was over Griffith went at once into cricket. From 1946 to 1950 he was secretary of Sussex, which he captained in the first of those years. He was a fine wicket-keeper, good enough, in fact, to tour the West Indies in 1947–48 (when he was also assistant manager of the MCC team, in charge of tour finances) and to be preferred to Godfrey Evans for the last two Test matches in South Africa in 1948–49.

He was also a tenacious batsman. Indeed, he made the first of his three first-class centuries in a Test match — against the West Indies at Port of Spain, Trinidad. With the England team beset by injuries he was called to open the batting on his debut for his country and performed magnificently on a day of such sweltering heat that by teatime, when he came in on 73 not out, his pads were completely soaked through with sweat. That evening, in spite of the salt pills he had taken, Griffith collapsed in the team's hotel, totally immobilised from cramp. He went on to score 140 in the second innings.

After giving up the secretaryship of Sussex, and before being appointed to Lord's in 1952, Griffith was for two years cricket correspondent of *The Sunday Times*. The burdens the secretaryship of MCC placed on him were much exacerbated by illness which forced him to curtail his own playing career and plagued him thereafter. In 1961 he had a lung removed and was subject to bad bouts of bronchial pneumonia for some years.

Public reaction to the D'Oliveira affair made it clear that the projected South African cricket tour of England in 1970 would inevitably be in jeopardy. With anti-apartheid groups making threats that they would disrupt the matches, turning cricket grounds into battlefields, Griffith and M. J. C. Allom, who as president of MCC was also chairman of the Cricket Council, were called to the Home Office on May 21. There they were asked by the home secretary, James Callaghan, to cancel the tour. It was the end of cricketing relations between England and South Africa for many a long day. This was a matter Griffith could not help regretting, even while he understood it. In this he flew in the face of mainstream opinion, but his reasons for feeling as he did were respected even by such authoritative leaders of the "anti" party as the Right Rev David Sheppard. Simply, he cherished the belief that it was better to keep playing than to sever links.

In 1974 Griffith was appointed CBE, and in 1979–80, he was president of MCC. He was also responsible for the 1980 recoding of the Laws of Cricket, an onerous undertaking which kept him much occupied during the early years of his retirement. He had maintained, too, his interest in soldiering part-time and in 1954 received the Territorial Decoration. His son, Mike, captained Sussex from 1969 to 1972.

S. C. Griffith, who had been in a nursing home for a number of years, is survived by his wife Barbara, his son and a daughter, Pauline.

b 16.6.14   d 7.4.93   aged 78

JEREMY TREE

Jeremy Tree, trainer and former master of the Beckhampton stable.

JEREMY TREE bore a much-remarked resemblance in generous rotundity to Orson Welles. He also shared with him a gift for astringent wit. His career on the Turf matured most notably at Royal Ascot, and in the Classics, although the Derby eluded him.

His most important winner was Rainbow Quest, who captured the richest race in Europe, the Prix de l'Arc de Triomphe, in 1985, for Khaled Abdulla. But Tree always preferred Only For Life who in 1963 won the Two Thousand Guineas for Miss Monica Sheriffe, the trainer's first Classic winner.

The Guineas victory in itself was not the sole source of Tree's affection for Only For Life. The colt's connection on his maternal side was with the man primarily responsible for setting Tree up as a trainer – his uncle, the Hon Peter Beatty, younger son of Admiral of the Fleet Lord Beatty. When Peter Beatty, who had owned the 1938 Derby winner, Bois Roussel, died in tragic circumstances

in 1949, he left to his nephew his broodmares and foals including a filly named Life Sentence, out of Borobella, a Bois Roussel mare. Life Sentence was trained by Tree, then sold, and eventually became the dam of Only For Life.

Andrew Jeremy Tree was a son of the pre-war Conservative MP and Master of the Pytchley, Ronald Tree, and Nancy Field, niece of Nancy, Lady Astor. He had no racing background as such and at prep school he was forbidden sight of the racing press lest it interfered with work. But he managed to place his first bet: on Colombo, the favourite for the 1934 Derby, who finished third behind Windsor Lad.

At Eton he made frequent visits to Cliveden and the Astor Stud. He served in the war in The Life Guards but, after demobilisation, he announced his intention of becoming a racehorse trainer. His father disagreed and Tree spent two years in a merchant bank before getting his way.

He went as assistant to Colonel Dick Warden at Newmarket and, on the death of his uncle, was able to race the produce of his stud. In 1950 he had his first winner, Rumpelstiltskin, in the Bessborough Stakes. In 1952 Tree took out a licence to train on his own account and bought Lansdowne House, Newmarket. The following year, Beckhampton became vacant, Noel Murless having moved out.

As Tree himself put it, when he arrived at Beckhampton (which many years later he bought) with 20 horses, they were "largely my own and those of a few brave friends". This all changed within two seasons with the advent of Double Bore, yet another of Borobella's foals, who grew into a first-class stayer.

In Tree's own colours, Double Bore won half-a-dozen races including the Goodwood Cup of 1955. This was a turning point in the young trainer's fortunes.

Double Bore's performance attracted patrons. Among the first was Miss Monica Sheriffe who was to remain with the stable throughout Tree's career. Only

For Life apart, her other first-class horses included Sharpo, the European sprint champion in the early 1980s, and Constans, another fast horse who won the Prix de Saint-George in France in three successive seasons.

Other owners included the American ambassador, the late "Jock" Whitney, a sporting *aficionado* of the English racing scene, and John Morrison, later Lord Margadale, who had bred a first-class filly called Spree at his Fonthill Stud. Spree won the 1963 Nassau Stakes and was runner-up in the One Thousand Guineas and Oaks of that year. Spree's failure to beat the French-trained Hula Dancer in the earlier Classic cost her trainer a considerable amount of money, but perhaps more important to him, it represented the very near-miss of a sporting and old-fashioned "tilt at the ring" on a somewhat larger scale than his youthful wager on Colombo.

Classic success came when he sent out the 1975 Oaks and Irish Oaks winner Juliette Marny, and the 1979 Oaks winner Scintillate, both fillies being bred and owned by Lord Margadale's heir, the Hon James Morrison. But, of all his earlier owners, it was "Jock" Whitney for whom Tree achieved the most consistent record. He sent out no fewer than eight of his considerable total of Royal Ascot winners in the Whitney colours.

Involvement, too, in the Whitney breeding interests, gave Tree as much, if not more, pleasure than racecourse performances *per se*. He was fascinated by getting to know an equine family over several generations and seeing how they turned out. A good example of this was the filly Peace, a promising two-year-old but nothing more on the racecourse. Yet her first three foals, Peaceful, Quiet Fling and Intermission all won important races which included the Coronation Cup and the Cambridgeshire.

By the time of Whitney's death and the dispersal of his racing interests in 1983, Tree's career had already taken a fresh turn. Through the choice of Khaled Abdulla's then racing manager, Humphrey Cottrill, he became principal trainer to the Saudi Arabian prince. In the United States in 1978 he was instrumental in buying a yearling later named Known Fact for $225,000 in preference to a more expensive animal eventually called Nureyev and trained in France for the Greek shipowner, Stavros Niarchos.

The irony which, as a result, crystalised in the Two Thousand Guineas of 1980, is now part of racing folklore: Nureyev won, but was controversially disqualified, and Known Fact, the original runner-up, was awarded the race; Tree thus had saddled the first-ever English Classic winner for an Arab owner.

After that, Tree achieved third place in both the Derby and Irish Derby for Khaled Abdulla with Damister in 1985, two thirds in 1981 and 1989 in the Two Thousand Guineas with Bel Bolide and Danehill respectively, and a string of other important successes including Rainbow Quest's "Arc" victory. Stavros Niarchos was another owner in this latter phase, for whom Tree performed a training feat in keeping Valuable Witness sound and saddling him to win top staying races.

Tree decided to retire at the end of the 1989 season. That year saw a fitting climax to his brilliance at Royal Ascot. He saddled three winners, all for Khaled Abdulla: Danehill took the Cork and Orrery Stakes; Two Timing won the Prince of Wales's Stakes, while True Panache captured the Royal Hunt Cup at last for the trainer thus realising one of his great ambitions.

Tree's special qualities were his excellent eye for a yearling and his not always conventional approach (he was, for example, wary of the merits of all-weather gallops). He was a realist, once saying: "You go out in the morning thinking you have a star and come back realising you have nothing – though it occasionally works the other way."

He never married, but this gregarious man with an Olympian frame and presence to match, will be hugely missed by the world of racing.

b 21.12.25 d 7.3.93 aged 67

Hunt at Brands Hatch 1976 when he became world champion

James Hunt, former world motor racing champion.

A HANDSOME, charismatic figure who took effortlessly to the lifestyle of a Grand Prix driver, James Hunt became world champion in 1976 driving for the McLaren team. He and glamour were indivisible. Besides fast cars, beautiful women were a feature of his life. When his first wife, a model, left him and later married the actor Richard Burton it seemed to be of a piece with an exotically turbulent existence.

James Hunt was educated at Wellington College, where he represented the school as both a cross-country runner and a squash player. Like so many of his contemporaries he began his motor racing career at the wheel of a Mini. In 1968 he graduated to Formula Ford and in the following year he moved up into the more demanding Formula Three category.

A series of successes in his privately-owned car in 1970 led to an invitation to drive a works-entered March Formula Three car for the 1971 season. But a series of accidents, which did little injury to his body (though some to his pride) earned him the nickname "Hunt the Shunt" which was to take a long time to live down.

In 1972 Hunt's link with March was terminated and he seemed destined for the motor racing wilderness. But a few weeks later he was invited to drive a car owned by Lord Hesketh, an association that was to have far-reaching consequences. Hesketh bought a Formula Two car and Hunt achieved some outstanding results with it. The aim was to enter for a full season of Formula Two races in 1973. But after watching Hunt drive a borrowed Surtees-Ford in a non-championship race at Brands Hatch Hesketh made arrangements to hire a March-Ford for him to drive in one or two world championship events. Their first outing was the Monaco Grand Prix, where, in spite of a late engine failure, Hunt's performance was beyond the team's most ambitious hopes. It led to the decision of

Hesketh Racing to become full-time participants in Grands Prix.

Successes came rapidly: Hunt was sixth in the French Grand Prix, fourth in the British and third in the Dutch. The Hesketh team's season ended on a high note when Hunt chased Ronnie Peterson all the way to lose the United States Grand Prix by less than a second.

For 1974 Lord Hesketh exchanged Hunt's borrowed car for a purpose-built Hesketh-Ford car and Hunt scored his and his team's first Formula One win in the non-championship International Trophy race at Silverstone. The breakthrough to Grand Prix success came in The Netherlands in 1975, when Hunt fought and won a wheel-to-wheel duel with Niki Lauda and his Ferrari. It was the highlight of a Formula One season during which he had already finished second in Argentina and sixth in Brazil.

Alas, the team now discovered that Lord Hesketh's personal fortune was insufficient to cover the costs of designing, building and running a Grand Prix car and team. When efforts to find a sponsor bore no fruit, it was disbanded and Hunt was out of a job.

Marlboro McLaren team secured Hunt's services for the 1976 season and he soon established himself as the chief threat to Lauda's continuing domination of the Grand Prix scene for Ferrari.

He set his standard in the opening race of the 1976 world championship by setting the fastest practice lap and running second to Lauda until stopped by a jammed throttle. In Britain he won the Race of Champions at Brands Hatch and this country's other non-championship Formula One race, the International Trophy, at Silverstone. In between had come the first United States Grand Prix West, in California. In the Spanish Grand Prix at Jarama he chased, then overtook a far from well Niki Lauda and went on to lead him across the finishing line – only to be robbed of the victory during a post-race examination of his car during which it was discovered that its rear track was five-eighths of an inch too wide.

Hunt failed to score in his next two

races; at this stage he had scored only eight world championship points to Lauda's 55.

Luck changed in France. While Lauda's Ferrari failed him Hunt took his McLaren to victory and the following day he learnt that he had been reinstated as winner of the Spanish race as well. Lauda then had a near-fatal accident in the German Grand Prix. Hunt won the race, was fourth in Austria and first again in Holland, while Lauda prepared for a comeback in Italy. There, Hunt's was one of three cars to be moved to the back of the grid because of a stated fuel infringement (the officials were subsequently found to be in error) and he came off the track in his efforts to move up through the field.

Hunt won in Canada, where Lauda failed to score, and in the United States, where his rival finished third. The final race, in Japan, would decide the title; Lauda now had 68 points and Hunt 65. But Lauda pulled out of the race, blinded by spray, and Hunt had only to finish third to become world champion. He led the race in impressive style, but rapid tyre wear on a drying track brought him into the pits shortly before the finish, with two punctures. His mechanics worked brilliantly and he was away again in 27 seconds, now in fifth place. Over the next two laps he passed two other cars to regain third place and the title was his.

Although there was universal admiration for the way in which Lauda had fought back from close to death, Hunt had also earned his title the hard way. Though he carried on racing, Hunt was not able to repeat his 1976 success and eventually announced his retirement in 1979.

He exploited to the full the stardom which his world championship gave him pursuing social and commercial engagements with the same vigour that he applied to his races. Being both photogenic and articulate, he was at ease in front of camera or microphone. From 1980 he worked for the BBC and his voice was a familiar one to viewers of Grands Prix on television where his insights backed up the main commentary from Murray Walker. He was also a provocative journalist and his most recent article, an assessment of the current Grand Prix season, appeared in *The Daily Telegraph* on the day of his death.

He had retired from motor racing a millionaire but the past few years had not been kind to Hunt. The James Hunt Racing Centre, which he had established at Milton Keynes in May 1990, collapsed with debts of £2 million.

His marriage to the model Susie Miller ended in divorce as did a second marriage to Sarah, the mother of his two sons. In a newspaper interview he gave earlier this year he claimed that his only wheeled assets were a bicycle and a 26-year-old van.

b 29.8.47   d 15.6.93   aged 45

DAN MASKELL

Dan Maskell, CBE, former British professional tennis champion and All England Club coach, who became the doyen of tennis commentators.

ALTHOUGH Dan Maskell was 16 times Britain's professional tennis champion, coached at the Queen's Club and the All England Club (Wimbledon) and guided Britain to success as coach of the Davis Cup team in the 1930s, it is as a BBC television commentator on tennis at Wimbledon from 1951 to 1991 that he will be pre-eminently remembered. Indeed, his reputation as "the voice of Wimbledon" and as a repository of tennis history overshadowed his earlier successes as player and coach − and his career as a squadron leader who became the RAF's first rehabilitation officer.

As the years went by the voice of Dan Maskell came to seem as much a part of Wimbledon as its strawberries-and-cream, its occasional scorching days or its perhaps more frequent torrential rain. True, his unique species of enthusiasm under restraint harked back to an English moral climate that had well and truly disappeared by the latter part of his commentating life. Yet even in the raucous Eighties, with dissent from umpiring decisions, foul language and unbridled tantrums on the court the norm rather than the exception, his calm, gentle tones did not seem inappropriate.

The seventh of eight children, Maskell had a happy childhood in modest circumstances. His father was an engineer and later managed a pub. Dan Maskell's aptitude for study could not be fully explored because of the family's limited means. But he was also a gifted and versatile games player and the proximity of Queen's Club attracted his interest. He earned pocket money by part-time work as a ball boy and, soon after his 15th birthday, that work became full-time. In 1924, a year marking his first visit to Wimbledon, he became a junior professional at Queen's, and he remained at the club until 1929, when he became the first permanent coach at the All England Club. Except for his wartime service he retained that position until 1955.

In Maskell's playing days there was a strict distinction between professionals and amateurs. He rose to the top (and remained there) of the comparatively small heap of British professionals. From 1928 to 1951 he was Britain's professional champion 16 times: 17 if one counts the 1927 "world professional tournament", which boiled down to a domestic championship. He was good enough to compete with some of the great players of his era and sometimes beat them. His victims included Bill Tilden, often regarded as the finest of all tennis players.

As a coach, Maskell acquired a treasured memory via his association with the 1933 Davis Cup team, led by Fred Perry, which went to Paris and defeated France to win the trophy for the first time since 1912. Britain retained the cup in the next three years before Perry turned professional.

During the war Maskell served in the RAF, reaching the rank of squadron leader in the rehabilitation unit. For him it was a richly rewarding period and − though it did not involve flying − one, nevertheless, potentially replete with danger. On one occasion in October 1942 Maskell had been given the day off duty to play golf with a colleague who, his commanding officer confided to him, was on the verge of a nervous breakdown. Maskell and the colleague were chipping and putting their way round the links in the sunshine at the beautiful seaside course at Saunton in North Devon that afternoon, when a lone German raider sneaked under the coastal radar defences and dropped three sticks of bombs on their Torquay base. One struck the hospital bowling green, another demolished the gymnasium and the third, and most lethal, destroyed the top floor of the rehabilitation unit killing 23 people − patients and duty staff, including the officer who was standing in for Maskell. For a long time afterwards Maskell felt keenly the providential nature of his deliverance. He put a great deal of himself into his pioneering work in rehabilitation for which he was appointed OBE in 1945. In after years he always said that nothing in his life gave him more satisfaction than that wartime period at Torquay and then at Loughborough, reinforcing the work

of medical staff who patched up the airmen by devising remedial exercises to restore their mobility and confidence, thus accelerating their recovery. Such an attitude to professional duties was of a piece with his life. He was a man who cared deeply and in his 1988 autobiography, *From Where I Sit*, he confessed that if he had his time over again he would like to have been a GP in a small country town. This care for civilised standards was much in evidence at Wimbledon as the years went by, and he deplored the exhibitionist behaviour of so many members of the new generation of rising stars.

In 1955 he became the Lawn Tennis Association's training manager. He kept that job until 1973, by which time his horizons had widened. In 1949 and 1950 he worked at Wimbledon as a summariser for BBC Radio and in 1951 he began the commentating career for which he became internationally renowned and for which he was promoted CBE in 1982.

Maskell's close association with the mannered, ordered world of the Queen's and All England clubs between the wars influenced his character and conduct for the rest of his life. As apprentice and established professional in turn, he soon felt at home in the company of celebrities. He practised and competed with the great names of international tennis. He coached the royal family, politicans, and others prominent in society. He fitted easily into the glamorous, now vanished era dominated by protocol and etiquette. In later years, his gentility remained relentless.

It was joked among his journalistic colleagues that if the camera caught a player making an obscene gesture, Maskell's comment (if any) would be something like "How perfectly timed!" or "How very fortunate". Such Maskellisms as "Oh, I say!" and "You'll never see a better forehand volley than that" became as familiar as old jokes, and provoked affectionate laughter among those accustomed to his commentating. This was sad in a way, because many viewers were laughing at Maskell rather than with him. He could, at times, be too bland, too deliberately inoffensive, too prone to put a mute on his critical faculties and exaggerate the quality of a match.

That weakness, if weakness it was, sprang from Maskell's insistence on seeing only the best of everything and everybody. The joy of the game and its players, in all their nuances and moods, dominated his thinking. He had an unquenchable zest for tennis and his role within it. He enjoyed the roses so much that he ignored the thorns. As a commentator he was probably at his best when working with Jack Kramer from 1960 to 1973, because of the marked contrasts in their manners, accents, and critical approach. They were complementary.

Maskell had two enviable gifts as a commentator. One was that rich, rumbling, reassuring voice, which emerged from subcutaneous caverns with oracular authority. The other was his infectious enthusiasm, which swept breezily past accumulating birthdays and, to the last, made his colleagues feel that if he was getting so much fun out of tennis and out of life, so should they. He was such a wise and genial broadcaster that he did much to popularise tennis in general and Wimbledon in particular. In this respect he had much in common with John Arlott in cricket and Peter Alliss in golf, though he could not match their sense of humour and gift for the graphic phrase. Maskell continued to be a keen recreational golfer, though he had even more pleasure from skiing.

Maskell's enthusiasm was such that, even when he was in his eighties, it could be difficult to get him off the microphone for a spell of rest and refreshment. He was meticulous, too. Often, he set an example to colleagues half his age by turning up first in the Press Room and poring over reference books, swotting up facts relevant to players and matches he would later have to discuss. He never took his experience and knowledge for granted. He was always highly critical of his own performance and on one rare occasion when, through what he felt was inadequate preparation, he made more mistakes – in an admittedly minor match – than he was prepared to tolerate, he actually asked the producer to take him off the air. Work discipline was part of his nature. An example of this was his awareness of when to keep quiet on television, a practice that could not have come easily to a garrulous raconteur with an astonishing grasp of distant detail.

Maskell was an Establishment figure immersed in the traditions and mores of Wimbledon and British tennis as a whole. But he mixed easily at all levels and enjoyed being included in the mocking banter of the Press Room. That made him feel younger. He was the kind of man who wakes up happy and seldom, if ever, turns crusty. If he had a single regret it was that his professional status had prevented him from playing tennis for his country. But he never harped on that. In general he could not believe that life had been so good to him. In truth, he had more cause than most for bitterness, but did not indulge in it.

Maskell and his first wife, Con, had a daughter, Robin, and a son, Jay. At the age of 25 Jay was killed in an air crash. In 1979 Con drowned while swimming off the coast of Antigua. Maskell's wartime work in physical and psychological rehabilitation, plus his basic nature, helped him to bear these personal tragedies far better than might have been expected.

In 1980 he married an old friend, Kay, and – Kipling-style – made a new beginning. (It became something of a tradition during the Wimbledon fortnight that at some point Maskell would comment on the quotation from Kipling's "If" which adorns the arch through which the players reach the Centre Court.) For Maskell, every day was a new beginning.

b 11.4.08   d 10.12.92   aged 84

BOBBY MOORE

Bobby Moore, OBE, England captain in the 1966 soccer World Cup victory and captain of West Ham.

FOOTBALLER of the year in 1964 when he led his club West Ham to FA Cup success, Bobby Moore was one of the greatest defenders, and finest captains, England has ever had, winning 108 caps for his country between 1962 and 1973, when he surpassed his predecessor Billy Wright's record of 105.

Tall, blond, cool and clean cut, Moore was the epitome of the England captain, a post he filled with distinction. But his team-mates and opponents were under no illusions that behind the perfect image was a fiercely ambitious competitor, with a touch of ruthlessness. "He had a great 'golden boy' image, Moore, but he was hard," testified his club and international partner, Geoff Hurst; and opponents who

tried to take liberties with Moore discovered the truth of that assessment to their cost.

Watching him at his peak, totally unflappable at the height of the battle, winning the ball with steely certainty and then dispatching it tellingly, a picture of unruffled assurance, it was hard to imagine that his path to the top had been anything but smooth. But after attracting little attention as a schoolboy, he made himself into a player by sheer hard work.

At 17 he captained England Youth, with whom he won 18 caps, and later the England Under-23 team, winning eight caps. His 108 appearances for England was a world record until 1978 and an English record until 1989. For 90 of them he was captain – equalling Billy Wright's record.

Bobby Moore had been a professional a matter of months when he made his debut for West Ham as a 17-year-old against Manchester United at Upton Park in 1958, but no one there doubted that they were watching the arrival of a major talent.

By the time Ron Greenwood arrived to replace Ted Fenton as West Ham's manager two years later, Moore had established himself permanently. He had already come under the influence of Greenwood, one of football's most progressive coaches and tacticians, in the England Youth and Under-23 teams, and Greenwood confessed that the appeal of having Moore to build a team around was an important factor in persuading him to leave Arsenal, where he had been assistant manager.

Initially the relationship was a rewarding one. Greenwood's open admiration for Moore, whom he later described as "for a time the best player in the world," persuaded Walter Winterbottom to take the young Londoner, still only 21, to Chile for the 1962 World Cup.

Moore had found his natural habitat. An untried candidate when they left London, he returned home as an established international after making his debut against Peru and playing in all four World Cup matches. In 1963-64 he was declared footballer of the year.

The game was changing rapidly, the old defensive wing-half, which he began as, soon becoming a second centre-half, a role for which Moore's talents were ideally suited.

However, he had to wait until Alf Ramsey replaced Walter Winterbottom as England manager half-way through the following season for England to adapt the formation. It did not take long. Ramsey started with a 5-2 defeat by France, and quickly decided that changes were necessary. Moore captained the side for the first time in a 4-2 victory over Czechoslovakia as Ramsey began preparing for the 1966 World Cup.

By the time it arrived, Moore had settled in as captain, and alongside Jack Charlton as second centre-half. It was undoubtedly his finest hour.

"Moore should play all his games at Wembley," Greenwood once said of his captain as their relationship soured. Moore always resisted the implication that he needed the big occasion to stir him, but England did play all their games at Wembley on their way to winning the World Cup for the only time, and Moore's outstanding contribution as player and team leader was recognised in his selection as the player of the tournament.

It was some compensation for Moore's growing discontent with his club football. With two other West Ham players, Hurst and Martin Peters, also making major contributions to the victory, the East London side were expected to be a force in the game, but after their FA Cup and European Cup Winners Cup wins in 1964 and 1965, they continually failed, earning something of a reputation for being soft touches.

The failures were a bitter disappointment for Moore, whose dream of a championship medal was never realised. West Ham refused to release him when Derby, under Brian Clough, and Tottenham — both clubs where he might have fulfilled his ambition — wanted him.

His international stature was unquestioned, however, as England enjoyed a spell of prosperity, coming third in the 1968 European Championships, and going to Mexico for the 1970 World Cup as one of the favourites. But before they reached Mexico Moore was faced with a personal crisis. He was accused of stealing a gold bracelet from a shop in Bogota, and was detained in Colombia for investiations while the team went ahead of him.

Fortunately he was cleared and released in time to take his place in the team as England began their defence of the World Cup. It was ultimately unsuccessful, England losing to West Germany in the quarter-final, but before that Moore, revelling in a personal duel with Pele, had played what he believed was the best game of his life against the eventual winners, Brazil.

Mexico was to prove a watershed for

England under Ramsey. A decline set in, and after losing to West Germany in the 1972 European Championships, England failed to reach the 1974 World Cup finals. Moore, who was criticised for the defeat in Poland which led to the failure, lost his place for the return in October 1973. He made his final appearance for England against Italy a month later.

Soon after that he left West Ham to enjoy an Indian summer at Fulham, captaining the club to the 1975 FA Cup Final, ironically against West Ham, before retiring. He had played 1,000 matches at senior level. Although financially secure, with clubs and pubs in the East End, he was expected to go into management, but the opportunities, surprisingly, were few and far between. His only attempts were with the non-league side Oxford City from 1979 to 1981 and with Southend United from 1983 to 1986, after which he spent three years as sports editor of *Sunday Sport* and had brief spells as a coach in Hong Kong and North Carolina. Since 1990 he had been a sports commentator for the Capital Gold radio station.

Bobby Moore, who was appointed OBE in 1967, was married twice, first in 1962 to Tina with whom he had a son, Dean, and daughter, Roberta; and, following a divorce in 1986, to Susan (Stephanie) in 1991. His wife and children survive him.

b 12.4.41   d 24.2.93   aged 51

E. P. THOMPSON

E. P. Thompson, social historian and author of The Making of the English Working Class.

THE life and work of E. P. Thompson exemplified the social and cultural struggles that were taking place in the Britain of the 1950s and 1960s, a period which gave the working class access to higher education in a way that had never happened before. His writings, polemical, astringent and tough-minded, had an imaginative sweep which questioned social complacencies and compelled institutions and individuals to look beyond their own narrow concerns and their conception of their past.

His *The Making of the English Working Class* (1963) appeared a little after the late Raymond Williams's *Culture and Society* (1958) and Richard Hoggart's *The Uses of Literacy* (1957). In a sense its concerns are cognate with theirs. While it takes the industrial past as its starting point, it extended their frontiers and amplified their scope.

When the work appeared, it astounded Thompson's contemporaries by the sense it communicated of recreating history in the flesh. In Thompson's own words — perhaps the most quoted words from his writings: "I am seeking to rescue the poor stockinger, the Luddite cropper, the obsolete hand-loom weaver, the Utopian artist, and even the deluded follower of Joanna Southcott, from the enormous condescension of posterity." In its passionate exposition of the living conditions and aspirations of the working-class in the period after 1709 it altered the parameters of historical writing. It offered the most compelling analysis of class yet presented by any British historian. It established Thompson as a major figure in the New Left movement in the Britain of the 1960s.

E. P. Thompson was much in the public eye for a range of activities: campaigns for freedom from persecution in Eastern Europe, for nuclear disarmament, for dialogue between East and West. His teaching years at the Centre for Social History at the University of Warwick were also influential ones. His well-publicised departure from the Communist party in the wake of the Soviet suppression of the Hungarian uprising of 1956 added another dimension to the reputation he had already garnered through his first book, *William Morris, romantic to revolutionary* (1955). But it is his writings that are his most enduring monument.

Edward Palmer Thompson was the son

of Edward John Thompson, a Methodist missionary who had worked in India. Thompson senior was a scholar and poet, a friend of Rabindranath Tagore and the Nehrus. When he returned from India he became a tutor in Bengali and Sanskrit at Oxford. Thompson's mother, Theodosia Jessop, had also been a missionary, in Lebanon.

Thompson went to school in Oxford, before going up to Corpus Christi College, Cambridge, where he eventually took his degree in 1946. During the second world war he spent some time serving in a tank regiment in Italy. His brother Frank, to whom he was very close, was dropped by the Special Operations Executive into Bulgaria. There he was captured by the Bulgarian authorities and shot. This had a profound effect on Thompson, and his brother ever afterwards remained something of a hero to him.

Thompson had joined the Communist party at the age of 18. After leaving Cambridge he went to Leeds University where he taught in the extra-mural department from 1948 to 1965. From 1965 to 1971 he was Reader in Social History at the University of Warwick.

In 1955 he published his first major work, a magisterial 900-page biography of William Morris. This was, as Thompson freely admitted, something widely different from a narrative biography. Indeed, he was content to say that Mackail's life of the subject, published more than fifty years previously, covered that aspect of Morris's career quite adequately. Thompson's aim in writing was to disinter what he saw as the essential Morris from beneath the neglect of "middle-class philistines". These, as he saw it, had reduced Morris's stature by stressing his achievements "merely" as a poet, textile and tapestry maker and typographer. Thompson's account exhumed the prose romances as being, in his opinion, central to Morris's work and emphasised Morris the socialist. It was a view of Morris – not widely shared by the reviewers of the day – that made Morris's politics central

to the man and his art. *William Morris, romantic to revolutionary* had a second edition in 1977.

In the year following the appearance of *William Morris* the Hungarian people rose against their Soviet overlords in a revolt that was bloodily suppressed. This denial of basic freedoms led to bitter debate within the communist movement outside the Soviet Union and Thompson occupied a central role in it in this country. Leaving the Communist party, he became the outstanding spokesman for socialist humanism in the English-speaking countries.

By the time of the appearance of *The Making of the English Working Class* it was noticeable that Thompson had abandoned the routine Marxist analysis which insists that all societies are class societies, for a view of the working-class which emphasised the power of shared experience and the articulation of identity of interest. In short, Thompson treated the working-class as an historical and not a dialectical phenomenon. This gave his study the humane dimension which was to make it such a permanently valuable document. *The Making of the English Working Class* went into a second edition in 1968.

Two years after its publication Thompson went to Warwick University. There he gathered around him a group of young scholars who, under his influence, gave a new impetus and direction to the historiography of the 18th century – the period to which he now turned his attention. *Whigs and Hunters*, which appeared in 1975, was just one of the outward manifestations of this new direction. It took as its subject the Black Act adopted by the Hanoverian Whig parliament in 1723, which, by bringing in the death penalty for almost every offence members of the underclass were likely to commit, provided landed proprietors with a catch-as-catch-can. In an account which let the unvarnished facts speak out eloquently against the enormity of the injustice Thompson provided a damning indictment of the attitude of the ruling class, the "great predators" of the day, to those they governed.

Nevertheless, Thompson was not all moral indignation. He could give vent to zany wit, as in the essay which gave its title to the collection *Writing by Candlelight* (1980). In a completely different vein the acerbic *The Poverty of Theory*, which had been published in 1978, renewed his apologia for his own brand of socialist humanism, and led naturally to his involvement in the peace movement, when that took on a new lease of life in the early 1980s. He remained one of its leading figures and was one of the main speakers at a large Trafalgar Square rally in 1980.

Even though struck down by illness four years ago he kept abreast of the complex issues addressed by the movement, almost to the end, and was seldom silent when conflicts broke out on the world stage. He was not afraid, for example, to condemn the Gulf War as a "bloody disaster" while accepting the fact that the Saddam Hussein regime in Iraq was "no way to conduct human affairs". His was not a mind to duck the equivocal facts that face most liberal intellectuals in a world of often violent politico-military action.

In retirement in Worcestershire, Thompson was working on a study of William Blake, with whose powerful radical intellect his own outlook had much in common.

E. P. Thompson married, in 1948, Dorothy Towers. She, too, was an historian and teacher. She and their two sons and a daughter survive him.

b 3.2.24   d 28.8.93   aged 69

Speaking at Hyde Park (1981)

OLIVER VAN OSS

Oliver Van Oss, former Eton master and headmaster of Charterhouse.

OLIVER Van Oss came of mixed Dutch and Scottish parentage. His father was a prominent newspaper proprietor in Holland, but Oliver's education was entirely in England: at the Dragon School, then Clifton College and finally Magdalen College, Oxford. And it was to English academia that he was to devote his working life.

While still an undergraduate Oliver Van Oss was appointed to a post at Eton, which he offered to resign when he achieved only a fourth in Modern Greats at Oxford. But the headmaster, Dr Alington, had the wisdom to see that this was no true indication of his abilities, and in 1930 he embarked on a career at Eton which spanned 35 years. His exuberant vitality, genial temper, and enthusiasm for every aspect of school life soon made him an outstanding figure, and he became successively head of the modern language department, house-master, Lower Master, and for one half, acting Head Master.

Headmasterships, though, eluded him until, in 1965, at the unusually advanced age of 56, he was appointed to Charterhouse. This was not too far away for him to be able to maintain old contacts and friendships with Eton, and his devotion to the college can be seen in the letterpress which he contributed to *Eton Days*, a book of photographs by his pupil Nicholas Barlow, published in 1976.

In his inevitably short reign of eight years at Charterhouse Van Oss exercised a markedly civilising and liberating influence. He caused some dismay in conservative circles by sweeping away a host of minor rules and petty privileges, and he actively encouraged musicians and artists, doing a good deal of teaching himself on the history of art, of which his knowledge was deep and extensive. He was an amateur painter of reasonable standard.

But the achievement of which he was proudest, perhaps because it was not what one would have expected from a man whose gifts were pastoral rather than administrative, was the transformation of the boarding houses. By selling off the sites of several houses which had become obsolete it was possible, without resorting to an appeal, to build seven new houses, in which every boy had a room of his own and none, to quote Van Oss's axiom, had to spend his school career looking out on a drainpipe.

On his retirement in 1973 he was appointed Master of the London Charterhouse, the first layman to hold that office and an inspired choice. His artistic taste and flair made him an ideal custodian of the ancient buildings, and he lavished on the elderly brethren of the Charterhouse, as well as on other aging friends, the same attention and kindness that had won him the affection of Etonians and Carthusians.

The position also provided him with time and opportunity for many other activities. He was a governor of a number of schools, was in great demand as a speaker and preacher and gave many lectures, particularly on ceramics. He greatly enjoyed club life, and devoted much time and trouble to the affairs of the Athenaeum, on whose committee he was prominent, and of the Beefsteak, of which he was chairman.

He was a widely cultured man with great stores of information and a remarkable memory. In early days an almost Falstaffian flamboyance sometimes raised a smile, and he was never one to speak depreciatingly of his own talents and achievements. But all this was part of an exceptionally warm and outgoing nature. His fun was irresistible, and no one left his company without feeling cheered and stimulated.

He was co-editor of the eighth edition of Cassell's French-English dictionary and a Chevalier of the Légion d'Honneur.

In 1945 he married Audrey Allsopp, whose first husband, also an Eton master, had been killed in the war, leaving her a widow with two young sons. To them Oliver was as perfect a stepfather as he was a father to his own two daughters. But his happy married life was cut short by his wife's death in 1960 after a long illness which both knew must be ultimately fatal. The shadow of this hung over him for several years, but he never allowed it to diminish his zest for life or to cloud the cheerful face which he showed to the world.

b 28.3.09   d 14.11.92   aged 83

Eton College exit from chapel

PROFESSOR W. W. ROBSON

Professor William Wallace Robson, scholar and critic.

WALLACE ROBSON was one of the finest critics of his generation. He founded no schools and did not encourage passionate discipleship but — through his strenuous intelligence, teaching and writing — stimulated students and colleagues for over half-a-century.

William Wallace Robson attended Leeds Modern School before going up as a scholar to New College, Oxford, in 1941. He read English under the guidance of Lord David Cecil, for whom he retained a continuing affection, editing a volume of essays and poems in his honour in 1970. On graduating in 1944 with first-class honours Robson was appointed to an assistant lectureship at King's College,

London. He returned to Oxford in 1946 as a lecturer and, from 1948, as tutorial fellow in English at Lincoln College.

Nowhere more at home than in Oxford, never happier than as a college tutor, Robson was a widely admired yet strongly independent figure within the English faculty. Recognising more swiftly than many of his colleagues the importance of new developments then overtaking the discipline in Cambridge and elsewhere, he negotiated the celebrated annual visits of F. R. Leavis to the Oxford Critical Society, of which he was president for many years. Through his personal contacts he also introduced undergraduates to a range of critical ideas not in wide currency in Oxford at that time.

In the early 1950s he helped F. W. Bateson to found the Oxford journal,

Essays in Criticism, which sought to combine the critical boldness of Leavis's *Scrutiny* with the rigour of traditional Oxford scholarship and the lucid, at times irreverent, style of the new writing of the day (John Wain, Kingsley Amis and Philip Larkin being all associated with the journal in its earliest period). Later he strenthened his links with Cambridge English via *The Cambridge Quarterly*, of which he was a founding editor, and continued to encourage good criticism nearer to home through his association with *The Oxford Revic v.*

Tipped in the late 1960s as successor to Lord David Cecil as Goldsmiths' Professor of English Literature in Oxford, Robson moved instead in 1970 to a Chair at the University of Sussex. Two years later he was appointed to the Masson Chair of English Literature at the University of Edinburgh, remaining there until his retirement in 1990.

Though scarcely designed by nature as an academic administrator, Robson won the loyalty and affection of his department throughout the period of his chairmanship, often using to superb advantage the laconic phrase and telling judgment that he had so perfected in his critical writing.

His health deteriorated sharply in the years preceding and following his retirement; but he retained to the last a keen interest in the work of friends and former colleagues both at home and abroad. Visiting appointments had taken him at different stages of his career to Southern California, to Adelaide, to Delaware, to Smith College and, in the early 1980s, back to New College, Oxford, and to All Souls. In his final weeks he was busy catching up with the work of Australian writers he had first encountered during his visit to the Antipodes nearly forty years earlier.

Wallace Robson's friends and former pupils will remember him seated placidly within the benign chaos of his study, books heaped tumultuously about his armchair and protruding at varous angles from the shelves. He read widely and voraciously, yet with sharp discrimination. He could map a big field – as in his *Modern English Literature* (1970) and *Prologue to English Literature* (1986) – and, with the same directness, ponder a local problem, as he did memorably and repeatedly throughout his *Critical Essays* (1966).

He could balance severity and generosity with an almost Johnsonian skill. "Empson is paying Milton the highest compliment he can, when he tries to make Milton as clever as himself," wrote Robson in a review of William Empson's study, *Milton's God* – adding "But Empson's own work, in verse and prose, is a more convincing demonstration that it is possible for a mind to be subtle and devious, yet kind and honest." The humane swerve of this judgment was characteristic.

Robson's powerful dissection of the failings of C. S. Lewis – whom he characterised as sharing with W. H. Auden "a wish to be reborn as Beatrix Potter in some other phase of the moon" – needs likewise to be read against his subsequent and more yielding account of Lewis's later work: "In both the old and modern senses of the word," wrote Robson, "he was a truly magnanimous man." It is not a bad phrase by which to remember Wallace Robson himself.

He worked hard in his final months, completing his volume of *Critical Enquiries* (published this year by Athlone Press), and finalising his *Oxford History of English Literature, 1890–1950*, and his edition of *The Oxford Book of Edwardian Verse*, as well as a number of Sherlock Holmes and Father Brown volumes which will appear in the World's Classics series.

He is survived by his wife Anne and two sons.

b 20.6.23   d 31.7.93   aged 70

DAME JANET VAUGHAN

Dame Janet Vaughan, DBE, FRS, Principal of Somerville College, Oxford, 1945–67, and pioneer of the wartime blood transfusion service.

JANET Vaughan was a towering influence on students at Somerville during the 22 years she was principal. She was a remarkable woman who in many ways seemed larger than life. She had a great sense of style and her strong presence and handsome features created a vivid and lasting image wherever she went. But it is for her tremendous optimism, her courage and determination, her warmth and humanity and sheer practicality that she will be best remembered.

For Somervillians there was, first and foremost, the example she set. She showed it was possible to combine a distinguished career in scientific research with the headship of an Oxford college (in itself a demanding role in a women's college). In addition, there was her service

to the university, to the NHS, and on various national and international committees. And unlike many of the early women achievers she had brought up a family of two daughters, too. (Her husband, David Gourlay, must have been a great support and she never quite recovered from his death in 1963.)

She achieved all this through her amazing energy and powers of organisation. Her day started hours before breakfast and she would complete her college work by around 9.30am so that she could spend the rest of the day in the laboratory or on other business. Yet she kept in touch with everything going on in the college and would keep dropping in on people to check what were the problems.

She followed the progress of all her students and made a point of interviewing every undergraduate at the beginning and end of every term. Small talk did not come naturally to her and she was not easily impressed – recalling even the young Margaret Roberts (later to become Lady Thatcher) as "a perfectly good second-class chemist, a beta chemist". But whenever there was a problem she showed real concern and gave practical help. Each new intake of undergraduates was lectured on the importance of getting about in vacations and seeing the world. "Whatever you do don't stay at home in the kitchen sink."

Janet Vaughan was the daughter of William Wyamar Vaughan, Headmaster of Wellington and Rugby, and of Margaret Symonds. She read medicine at Somerville, whence she proceeded to University College Hospital. Her early career in medicine was, however, shaped by her determination to help her father after her mother's death: although she would have chosen to become a physician she decided that clinical pathology would allow her more scope to run her father's home. Successive awards of fellowships (Rockefeller 1929, Beit Memorial 1930, Leverhulme 1933) marked her achievement in this field of study. She specialised in diseases of the blood and of the bone-marrow, and worked loyally and enthusiastically under some of the great physicians of the era following the first world war – among them, Sir Thomas Lewis, Dr C. Price-Jones, Dr George Minot – all celebrated for their contributions to the scientific development of clinical medicine. To their influence can be traced her own conviction that the future growth of medicine should be linked with a wide and rapid expansion of the clinical sciences.

In the time of crisis preceding the second world war, Janet Vaughan's energies were engaged in the planning of an emergency blood transfusion service for London. By July 1939 the Medical Research Council had appointed her director of the north-west London Blood Supply Depot. Her friendliness and accessibility and her gift for taking decisive action made her a good administrator – a capacity quickly recognised by government authorities and other bodies. She was appointed a Nuffield trustee in 1945, a member of the Commission on Equal Pay in 1944, chairman of Oxford Regional Board 1950–51, and a member of the Phillips Committee on the Economic and Financial Problems of the Provision for Old Age in 1953.

Meanwhile, in 1945, she had been elected Principal of Somerville College. From the beginning her aim was expansion: she advocated, and worked indefatigably for, additional buildings, additional staff, more undergraduates in science, more overseas graduates. She had the capacity to think big and was the first to plan a special college block for graduate students.

It was in recognition of an exceptional career that Oxford University gave her the exceptional distinction for a former head of a house of an honorary degree in 1967.

b 18.10.99   d 9.1.93   aged 93

LORD ZUCKERMAN

Lord Zuckerman, OM, KCB, FRS, chief scientific adviser to the Secretary of State for Defence, 1960–66, and chief scientific adviser to the government, 1964–71.

FROM HIS career beginnings as an academic anatomist Solly Zuckerman branched out to become one of the most influential British scientific brains in the second world war. Thereafter he was, successively, chief scientific adviser to both Conservative and Labour defence ministers in the first half of the 1960s, and was (for the first two years, in tandem with his defence job) chief scientific adviser to the Cabinet Office in the first two administrations of Harold Wilson. In such a post, given the Labour prime minister's attachment to the idea of exploiting the "white heat of the technological revolution" in what was to be a thoroughly modern socialist government, much was expected, if not actually delivered. But by that time Zuckerman's most valuable work — notably that on the effects of wartime bombing — had been done.

Becoming an expert on the use of air power was not a forseeable progression for a man whose early work had been on such subjects as *The Social Life of Monkeys and Apes*. But by the end of his career the same man was writing books like *Star Wars in a Nuclear World*. Yet the wider recognition of Zuckerman's remarkable talents began from his anatomical work. While a lecturer in anatomy at Oxford he had been asked to research on the effects of bomb blast on mammalian tissue. From that relatively limited task he became an authority on the effectiveness of bombing in general. His success in this owed much to his personality. He was able to make himself trusted by the army and air force commanders in the field — men of a type often not given to taking "boffins" on trust.

Thus he was able to make his ideas effective in practice. The invasion of Italy and, later, the Normandy landings greatly benefited from his insights. Had he been listened to at the very top of Bomber Command, the continuing and wasteful area bombing campaign might have been exchanged for something much more precise and effective in terms of paralysing supplies to the German armies. Zuckerman himself remained convinced to the end that such a redeployment of air forces to a tactical role would undoubtedly have shortened a war which, in spite of the awesome weight of the strategic air offensive, only ended with the surrender of the enemy on the battlefield.

Zuckerman was educated at the South African Collegiate School and the University of Cape Town where he was Libermann Scholar. His first inclination had been to study chemistry but other counsels directed him to the Medical School of the University of Cape Town, where he completed his pre-clinical studies in 1923. Cape Town had no clinical school; Zuckerman accordingly came to London with letters of introduction to Arthur Keith and Grafton Elliot Smith, and the manuscript of a paper on the growth of the skulls of baboons that was soon accepted for publication in the *Proceedings of the Zoological Society*. Elliot Smith persuaded Zuckerman to enrol at University College as a medical student. But clinical work had no appeal to him, and after qualifying he was appointed Research Anatomist to the Zoological Society. To the zoo, in one capacity or another, he remained faithful all his life.

Zuckerman's student work on the growth of skulls laid the foundations of one of the most insistent of his later interests: his determination to compare bones and skulls by measurement rather than by mere description, and so to put speculation upon the ancestry of man upon new and firmer foundations.

Zuckerman owed his scientific success to great intelligence and intellectual thrust; to speed of apprehension, grasp and energy. It is a mixture that will serve many other purposes, and Zuckerman was the kind of scientist who could have been a great many other things instead, and with equally great success.

It was his first book, *The Social Life of Apes and Monkeys* (1931) which brought him an invitation to run a new ape research centre being set up in Florida by Yale University; though he decided that the centre was too isolated, he remained for a time at Yale as a research associate and Rockefeller research fellow. He returned to Britain in 1934 as a lecturer and demonstrator in human atanomy at Oxford and became immersed in the study of hormones and reproductive rhythms; the idea of developing an oral contraceptive was not ignored. Since it was difficult to draw up a programmed series of experiments on human beings he acquired a collection of apes. These greatly enlivened the environs of the university museum, excelling themselves on the night they got loose and sported among the skeletons.

Early in the second world war it became urgently necessary to decide what blast damage the human frame could withstand. A variety of experiments was conducted, in some of which Zuckerman's unfortunate apes played

their part. It was his grisly task to analyse the results obtained.

From the middle years of the war he became closely associated with Sir Arthur Tedder, successively AOC-in-C RAF Middle East, Air C-in-C Mediterranean Air Command, and deputy supreme commander under General Eisenhower. An early instance of this association was in the reduction of Pantelleria, a preliminary to the invasion of Sicily. It was the first defended place to be reduced to surrender (in the second world war) as a result of air and naval bombardment alone. The campaign began on May 15 and was ended by the island's surrender on June 11.

Throughout the planning and execution Zuckerman, with Tedder's encouragement and support, studied operations and directed research. He made a thorough analysis of the nature and construction of the defences, the types of bombs and fusing needed and the accuracy of the different types of squadron. Zuckerman's report after the surrender and his later analyses of the bombing in Sicily and Italy markedly influenced Tedder's thinking when the use of air power in the support of the Normandy landings came to be discussed and formulated.

Referring to the earlier stages of the Italian campaign Tedder wrote in *With Prejudice* (1966): "One lesson of real importance, however, we began to learn. It was this: that concentrated, precise attack on railway targets scientifically selected would produce a degree of disruption and immobility which might make all the difference to the success or failure of the long-awaited invasion of France. The clear and detailed reports submitted by Professor Zuckerman convinced me that this was the right method of attack."

Zuckerman had become involved at an early stage in some aspects of the British nuclear weapons programme, but in the postwar period he returned actively to the broader field of defence when he accepted an invitation from the Air Ministry in 1958 to act as an independent adviser on their current operational problems and future policy. It was soon clear that he was bringing to bear on the problems of that period the methods which he had developed during the second world war. He conducted an objective and at the same time ruthless enquiry into established operational aims and doctrines. He demanded objective analyses and called into question any element of subjective judgment. In this respect he provided a timely though (understandably) not always popular stimulus to the Royal Air Force; he demanded that they redo their homework.

In May 1958 the Lord President had set up a committee to report on the management and control of research and development by government departments, under the chairmanship of Sir Claude Gibb. Zuckerman was one of its members and became chairman after Gibb's death in January 1959. Although the enquiry covered the whole field of research and development much of the committee's work was centred on defence, since this accounted for over three-quarters of the total expenditure. The committee reported in July 1961, and among its most important recommendations were the "Zuckerman Procedures" for the control of defence projects and a strengthening of the role of the defence research policy committee. As Zuckerman had succeeded Sir Frederick Brundrett as chief scientific adviser to the Ministry of Defence in 1960 it fell to him to chair the defence research policy committee and implement his own proposals.

He remained chief scientific adviser until 1966. Throughout he maintained his aim that decisions should be taken on the basis of objective analyses and supported wherever possible by studies in depth as opposed to subjective judgments. It soon became obvious that the old DRPC was a cumbersome instrument for digesting the studies which were generated. In 1963 Zuckerman effected a considerable improvement in the machinery, including the formation of an operational requirements committee designed to do

the detailed devilling at a more appropriate level than that of the deputy chiefs; in parallel, he started to create a centralised operational analysis organisation. Had this organisation existed in the 1950s some of the major errors made in project selection during that period might well have been avoided.

As chairman of the DRPC his exceptionally quick brain tended at times to be a liability. His colleagues were often unable to match his nimbleness and this led to inevitable misunderstandings and, in some respects, a failure on Zuckerman's part to express clearly the guidance which he wished to give. His methods were regarded as opportunist by some senior officers. But, paradoxically, they were understood and even appreciated at lower levels in the staffs. His greatest contribution during this period was undoubtedly the codification of procedures and the creation of the staff structure which allowed the Ministry of Defence to conduct a step-by-step appraisal of each new project, with limited commitment of funds at each stage.

As chief scientific adviser to the government from 1964 Zuckerman wielded less political influence than he had at the defence ministry. The work was inevitably more diffuse, and his functions more of an advisory nature. With a staff working to him, he tackled surveys such as the assessment and deployment of the nation's scientific resources and advised the prime minister when a conflict of interest in the allocation of scientific resources arose; he maintained contact with users of scientific resources in government service, and was responsible for tasks such as population projections. He also chaired the Central Advisory Council on Science and Technology.

Retiring from public service in 1971, when he was created a life peer (he had been made OM three years earlier), he remained active, particularly in the Zoological Society of London of which he was president from 1977 to 1984. He continued to write and speak about defence matters and in his book of 1980, *Nuclear Illusion and Reality*, came out strongly against the notion of using tactical nuclear weapons to check any Soviet invasion of Western Europe. He was likewise against Trident, believing that in Britain's case the money could be better spent on two more armoured divisions. To the end he was wont to remind scientists – and those who placed unreserved faith in their powers – that they were not visionaries and had no power over the consequences of their discoveries. It was essentially a humane message, for all his scientific eminence, he remained at heart a man of the humanities – even if his three volumes of memoirs, published in the last 15 years of his life, lacked literary distinction and displayed a certain vanity.

In politics, too, he was always slightly innocent – witness the notorious visit he paid, with Lord Mountbatten, to Cecil Harmsworth King when, admittedly to his horror, he found the subject of a military take-over of the government being actively proposed. To his credit, he beat a hasty retreat – forcing Mountbatten to follow in his wake – but a more politically sophisticated chief scientific adviser to the government would never have put himself in such a position in the first place.

Zuckerman married in 1939 Lady Joan Isaacs, elder daughter of the second Marquess of Reading. They had a son and a daughter; his wife and son survive him.

b 30.5.04   d 1.4.93   aged 88

With (from left) Lord Hailsham, Admiral Ricketts, Mr Thorneycroft, Lord Mountbatten (1963)

INDEX

LIVES REMEMBERED 1991

Foreword by LORD ANNAN
Edited by David Heaton and John Higgins

ISBN 0 9518282 0 7   368 pages   181 pictures

The first in the *LIVES REMEMBERED* series contains 180 lives from *THE TIMES* obituary pages in 1991. These include:

John Arlott	Dame Peggy Ashcroft	Coral Browne
Oona Chaplin	Eric Heffer	Dame Margot Fonteyn
Sir Angus Wilson	Sir Kenneth Cork	Sir Isaac Wolfson
Rajiv Gandhi	Graham Greene	Freddie Mercury
Stan Getz	Bud Freeman	Lord Penney
Lord Miles	Soichiro Honda	Sir Y K Pao
Robert Maxwell	King Olav	Sir Alec Rose
Lee Remick	Jean Rook	Wilfrid Hyde White

Available in hardback, price £19.95

THE TIMES OBITUARIES OF 1992

Foreword by ALISTAIR COOKE
Edited by David Heaton and John Higgins

320 pages   160 pictures
Hardback ISBN 0 9518282 1 5   Paperback ISBN 0 9518282 2 3

This second edition in the *LIVES REMEMBERED* series contains some 140 entries including:

Alex Haley	"Teasy Weasy" Raymond	Viscountess "Bubbles"
Duke of Montrose	Anthony Perkins	Rothermere
Admiral Lord Fieldhouse	Pat Taaffe	Sir Robert Muldoon
Benny Hill	Peter Jenkins	Lord Devlin
Francis Bacon	John Piper	Sir Geraint Evans
Lord Rootes	Menachem Begin	Lord Cheshire VC
Frankie Howerd	Robert Beatty	Isaac Asimov
Marlene Dietrich	Lord Havers	Wily Brandt
Denholm Elliott	Robert Morley	Denny Hulme
Marquess of Bath	Earl Spencer	Elizabeth David

Available in hardback, price £12.95 and paperback, price £5.95

Previous editions available from: The Blewbury Press, Pound House, Church Road, Blewbury, Oxon OX11 9PY.
Telephone 0235 850110   Fax 0420 478664